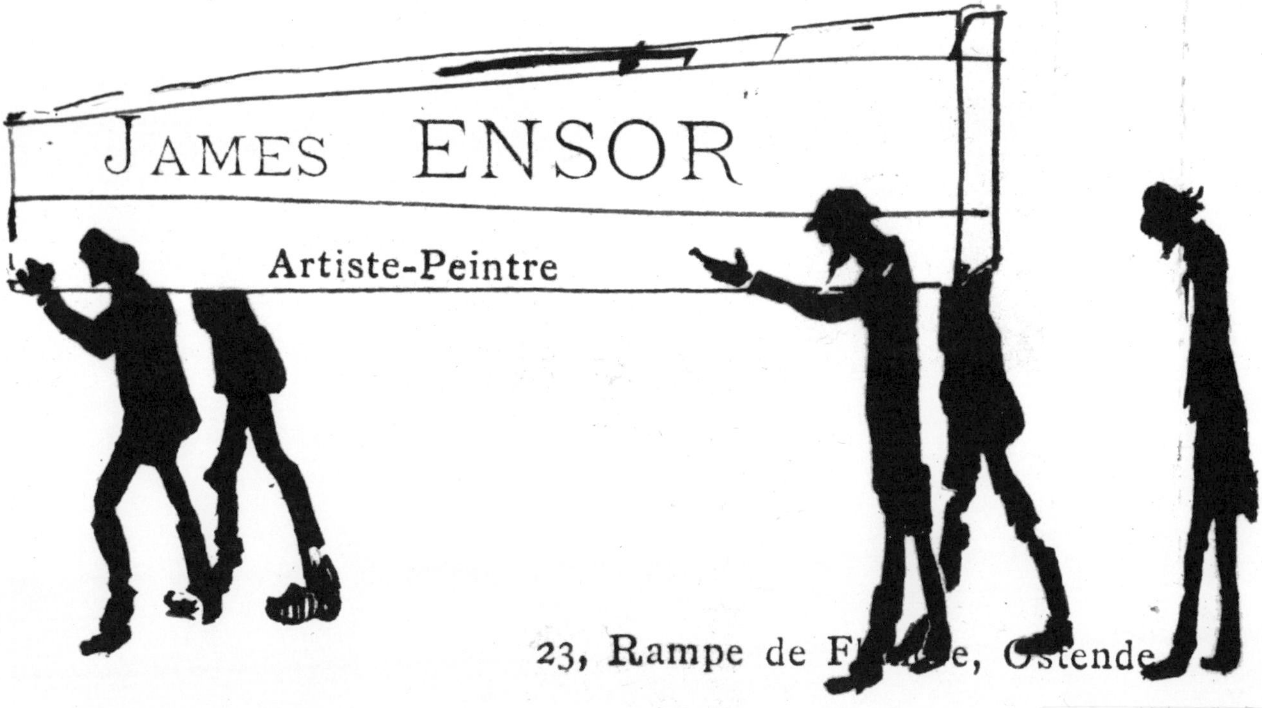
JAMES ENSOR
Artiste-Peintre

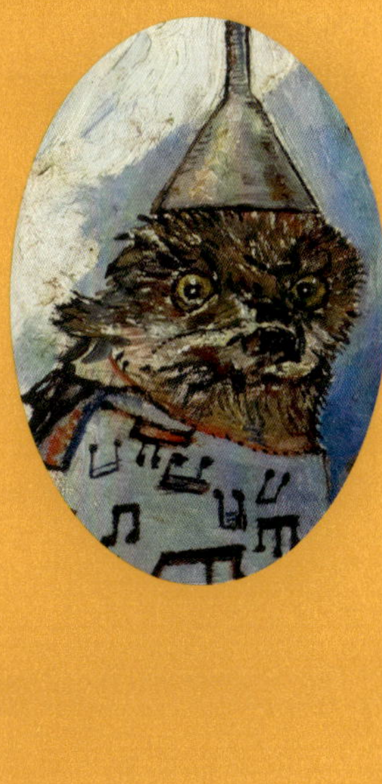

The Museum of Modern Art, New York

James ENSOR

ANNA SWINBOURNE

with essays by:

SUSAN M. CANNING

JANE PANETTA

MICHEL DRAGUET

ROBERT HOOZEE

LAURENCE MADELINE

HERWIG TODTS

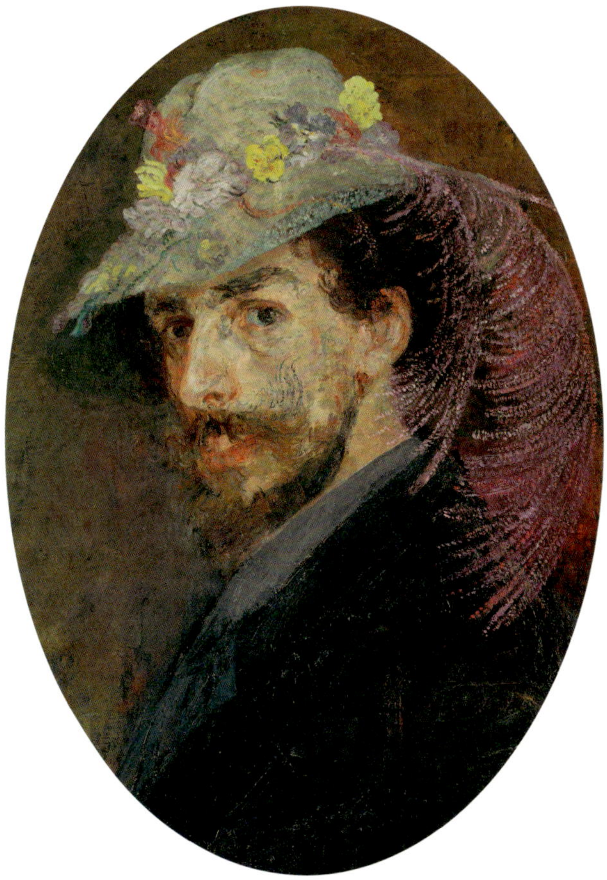

Published in conjunction with the exhibition *James Ensor*, June 28–September 21, 2009, at The Museum of Modern Art, New York, organized by Anna Swinbourne, Assistant Curator, Department of Painting and Sculpture

FLANDERS FITS YOU

MoMA wishes to sincerely thank our lead exhibition sponsor, Flanders House, the new cultural forum for Flanders (Belgium) in the United States.

The Museum gratefully acknowledges the important support and assistance of the Kingdom of Belgium, Ministry of Foreign Affairs, Foreign Trade and Development Cooperation.

Additional funding is provided by the Society of Friends of Belgium in America and by Maja Oeri and Hans Bodenmann.

Major support is provided by an indemnity from the Federal Council on the Arts and the Humanities.

Special thanks to American Airlines for assistance with air transportation.

Produced by the Department of Publications
The Museum of Modern Art, New York
Edited by David Frankel, Libby Hruska, and Diana Stoll
Designed by Gina Rossi
Production by Marc Sapir
Printed and bound by Cantz Druckerei, Kemnat, Germany
This book is typeset in Adobe Caslon Pro and Romana
The paper is 135 gsm GardapatKiara

Library of Congress Control Number: 2009926553
ISBN: 978-0-87070-752-0

Published by The Museum of Modern Art
11 West 53 Street, New York, NY 10019-5497
www.moma.org

Distributed in the United States and Canada by D.A.P./Distributed Art Publishers,
155 Sixth Avenue, 2nd floor, New York, NY 10013,
www.artbook.com

Distributed outside the United States and Canada by Thames & Hudson, Ltd, 181 High Holborn, London WC1V 7QX, www.thamesandhudson.com

Printed in Germany

Endpapers: James Ensor's visiting card from *Sketchbook* (detail). 1883–96. India ink, pen, Conté crayon, graphite, and black chalk on paper, 11 5/16 × 16 3/16" (28.7 × 41.1 cm). Fifty-three bound drawings, seven additional loose drawings, and one visiting card. See plate 16

P. 1: *The Frightful Musicians* (detail). 1891. Oil on panel, 6 5/16 × 8 1/4" (16 × 21 cm). See plate 74

P. 3: *Self-Portrait with a Flowered Hat* (detail). 1883/1888. Oil on canvas, 30 1/8 × 24 3/16" (76.5 × 61.5 cm). See plate 17

Pp. 11, 12: *Skeletons Trying to Warm Themselves* (detail). 1889. Oil on canvas, 29 1/2 × 23 5/8" (74.8 × 60 cm). See plate 54

P. 45: *The Astonishment of the Mask Wouse* (detail). 1889. Oil on canvas, 42 5/16 × 51 9/16" (109 × 131 cm). See plate 56

P. 79: *The Lively and Radiant: The Entry of Christ into Jerusalem* (detail). 1885. Black and brown crayon, with collaged paper, mounted on canvas, 6' 9 1/8" × 59 3/16" (206 × 150.3 cm). See plate 27

P. 81: *The Intrigue* (detail). 1890. Oil on canvas, 35 7/16 × 59 1/16" (90 × 150 cm). See plate 66

P. 82: *The Lamp-Lighter* (detail). 1880. Oil on canvas, 59 7/16 × 35 13/16" (151.5 × 91 cm). See plate 3

P. 131: *The Grotesque Singers* (detail). 1891. Oil on panel, 6 5/16 × 8 11/16" (16 × 22 cm). See plate 73

P. 190: *Demons Tormenting Me* (detail). 1888. Graphite and black chalk on wove paper, 8 9/16 × 11 3/4" (21.8 × 29.8 cm). See plate 49

CONTENTS

FOREWORD

The Museum of Modern Art has long been a pioneering supporter of James Ensor. In 1940, when it acquired the artist's hallucinatory take on an age-old art-historical theme, *Tribulations of Saint Anthony* (1887), the Museum became the first American institution to own one of his paintings. In 1951, only two years after Ensor's death, MoMA hosted the first retrospective in this country, and published the first volume on the artist in English. The present exhibition—the first of Ensor's paintings, drawings, and prints to be held at an American institution in a generation—is the latest expression of a long-standing commitment. Comprised largely of works from the artist's most creative period, 1880 to the mid-1890s, this exhibition demonstrates a prodigious diversity of subject, size, style, and technique. Together, these works create a complete picture of Ensor's daring and experimental nature and highlight key aspects of his art, including his innovative use of light, his interest in satire and theatricality, and his active engagement with the issues of his times, particularly debates on the nature of modernism.

Presenting Ensor's work in close proximity to the nineteenth-century works in the Museum's permanent collection, in particular those by Vincent van Gogh, Paul Gauguin, Georges Seurat, and Paul Cézanne, offers a unique opportunity to study the Belgian's singular (and often overlooked) contribution to early modern art, a contribution that can be felt over subsequent generations of artists and that continues to resonate in our world today. It is our hope that this presentation of his work and vision will be a source of inspiration for many.

Anna Swinbourne, Assistant Curator of Painting and Sculpture, conceived and organized this exhibition and the accompanying publication with keen intelligence and imagination. She was advised by Susan M. Canning, who has dedicated her professional life to the study of Ensor and the nineteenth-century Belgian avant-garde. Anna joins me in thanking the lenders as well as the many individuals at the Museum and elsewhere who have offered their time, talent, and resources to this endeavor. We are especially grateful to those among them who have their own long-standing commitments to the artist and his legacy, such as Sabine Bown-Taevernier, whose grandfather Auguste Taevernier advised the Museum in its preparation for the 1951 retrospective; these supporters have indelibly enriched the present exhibition and catalogue.

Lastly, a project of this magnitude could not have been realized without significant financial support. The Museum sincerely thanks our lead sponsor, Flanders House, the new cultural forum of Flanders in the United States, whose primary function is to foster, promote, and support the initiatives that reflect the rich and diverse Flemish cultural heritage. MoMA gratefully acknowledges the support and assistance of The Kingdom of Belgium, Ministry of Foreign Affairs, Foreign Trade and Development Cooperation. Additional generous funding was provided by the Society of Friends of Belgium in America; Maja Oeri and Hans Bodenmann; American Airlines; and the Federal Council on the Arts and the Humanities, which granted an indemnity for the exhibition. To each we owe an expression of deep gratitude.

Glenn D. Lowry
Director, The Museum of Modern Art

ACKNOWLEDGMENTS

I must begin by acknowledging three individuals who have been with me in this endeavor from the first proposal: John Elderfield, Chief Curator Emeritus of Painting and Sculpture, who entrusted me with organizing this show, offered guidance and wisdom, and also taught me excellence; Glenn D. Lowry, Director, who supported the project unfailingly with sustained energy and enthusiasm; and Susan M. Canning, Professor of Art History at the College of New Rochelle, who served as a consultant, giving of her time, knowledge, insight, and intellect with exceeding generosity. It has been a privilege and pleasure to work with all three.

The Trustees of the Museum of Modern Art, led by Jerry I. Speyer, Chairman, and Marie-Josée Kravis, President, have faithfully supported the project; I am especially grateful to them.

Worldwide financial realities changed dramatically as this exhibition and publication unfolded, placing additional strain on the Museum's staff and resources. Many responded to the unforeseen challenges with grace and ingenuity; to them I am humbly indebted.

Gratitude is due to my colleagues in the Department of Painting and Sculpture. Ann Temkin, The Marie-Josée and Henry Kravis Chief Curator, offered valuable advice and collegially lent works from the collection. Joining her in helping are Anne Umland, Curator; Cora Rosevear, Associate Curator; Rosa Berland, Assistant Curator; Carla Bianchi, Lauren Mahoney, and Veronica Roberts, Curatorial Assistants; Mattias Herold, Department Manager; Lida Sunderland, Administrative Assistant; and interns Merel Driessen, Laura Prins, and Laura Rugarber. I am particularly indebted to Fereshteh Daftari, Assistant Curator, for her thorough research on the works exhibited and to Delphine Huisinga, Research Assistant, for her insight and encouragement. Additionally, I thank former members of the Department, Carolyn Lanchner and Kynaston McShine, Chief Curator at Large Emeritus, whose past projects inspired this one, and the late J. Kirk T. Varnedoe, whose voice was in my head throughout, ever demanding and cheering.

The curatorial departments of Drawings and of Prints and Illustrated Books also granted reciprocal loans of works from their collections. For this I owe thanks to Deborah Wye, The Abby Aldrich Rockefeller Chief Curator of Prints and Illustrated Books, and Emily Talbot, Curatorial Assistant, Prints and Illustrated Books; as well as to Connie Butler, The Robert Lehman Foundation Chief Curator of Drawings, and in particular, Kathy Curry, Assistant Curator of Research and Collections, Department of Drawings. I also thank Whitney Snyder and Stefanii Ruta-Atkins in the Department of the Registrar for their assistance with the administrative details of such loans. In addition, Starr Figura, The Phyllis Ann and Walter Borten Associate Curator of Prints, was helpful in indentifying prints for this exhibition.

With characteristic skillfulness, Jennifer Russell, Senior Deputy Director for Exhibitions, Collections, and Programs, has kept the project on administrative course and done everything possible to accommodate my seemingly endless requests. I owe her, her assistant, Emily Scaros, and her Exhibitions staff members, Maria DeMarco Beardsley and Carlos Yepes, most sincere thanks.

In similar fashion, Michael Margitich, Senior Deputy Director for External Affairs, along with Todd Bishop and Mary Hannah, Exhibition Funding, secured important financial support for the project, while James Gara, Chief Operating Officer, and Jan Postma, Chief Financial Officer, oversaw fiscal planning.

I also wish to thank a number of Museum colleagues from a variety of departments who helped realize this project: Diana Pulling, Chief of Staff; Rebecca Stokes, Development; Daniela Stigh and Meg Blackburn, Communications; members of the Library staff, particularly Jennifer Tobias, Alexa Goldstein, Ian Goulston, David Senior, and Jen Bandini; Laura Beiles and Sara Bodinson, Education; Nicholas Apps and Bic Leu, Special Programming and Events; Patty Lipshutz and Nancy Adelson, General Counsel; Ramona Bannayan and the Collection and Exhibition Technologies staff; and, finally, Erik Landsberg, Robert Kastler, and Roberto Rivera, Imaging Services.

Certain Museum colleagues diligently undertook the care, handling, and installation of the artworks themselves; I owe them special gratitude. Members of the Department of Collection Management and Exhibition Registration, specifically Allison Needle and Susan Palamara, arranged for the safe transportation of loaned works to the Museum, while James Coddington, The Agnes Gund Chief Conservator, ensured their physical welfare while here. Jerry Neuner, Director of Exhibition Design and Production, helped me work and rework the installation space with great imagination and creativity, with Michele Arms providing the miniature replicas, and Peter Perez the framing.

Led by Christopher Hudson, Publisher, and Kara Kirk, Associate Publisher, the Department of Publications worked tirelessly to prepare this publication. David Frankel, Editorial Director, expertly shepherded the volume along a winding path, joined in the last stages by Libby Hruska, Editor. I stand in awe of David's generosity and talent—he is a maestro—and wish to echo here the words of a famous sculptor who once advised, Those of you who do not know David Frankel, should. The beautiful images in this book were supervised by Production Director Marc Sapir, who, assisted by Christina Grillo, Associate Production Manager, has singularly contributed to Ensor studies by ensuring what are arguably the best reproductions in existence of the artist's work. Intern Jennifer Zimmer aided with fact-checking. A number of outside professionals contributed as well: Gina Rossi furnished the volume's sensitive design; Diana Stoll admirably edited several essays; Beth O'Brien and Elise Nussbaum translated texts from Dutch and French, respectively; Elizabeth Smith diligently proofread; and Patricia Berman carefully read and critiqued most of the manuscript. Lastly, the authors shared their extensive knowledge of the artist and his work by contributing exemplary essays. I am very grateful to them all.

I wholeheartedly thank the lenders to this exhibition, who entrusted their works to the Museum and its audience. Several of them, upon whom we placed many demands and who responded with exceptional generosity, deserve special recognition. From European public institutions: in Brussels, Michel Draguet, Anne Adriaens-Pannier, Dominique Marechal, and Patricia Robeets; in Antwerp, Paul Huvenne and Herwig

Todts; in Ghent, Robert Hoozee and Cathérine Verleysen; in Ostend, Philip Van den Bossche and Norbert Hostyn; and in Paris, Guy Cogeval and Laurence Madeline. Among the people who assisted with private loans are Patrick Derom, Willy d'Huysser, and Ronny and Jessy Van de Velde and Jan Ceuleers, and lastly, to whom I owe more than I can express, Sabine Bown-Taevernier and Tom Firman.

Other individuals outside the Museum who deserve thanks for their enthusiasm and assistance include Alexander Apsis, Guy Bennett, Jaclyn Carr, Rachel Churner, Patrick Florizoone, Evelyn Franck and her children Eric and Martine, Peter Freeman, Sarah Ganz, David C. Georgiades, Eric Gillis, Diana Kunkel, Roger Netzer, Theresa Papanikolas, and Xavier Tricot. Thanks are also due to Alice Whelihan, Indemnity Administrator, National Endowment for the Arts.

I conclude by recognizing those who worked most closely with me on this project, intimately sharing its rewards and challenges. First and very foremost is Jane Panetta, Curatorial Assistant, an ideal colleague and valuable asset to this institution. In inimitable fashion, she contributed to every aspect of the exhibition and this publication with acumen and professionalism. For her assistance, reason, and devotion, I have thanked my stars daily. Blair Hartzell, Research Assistant, who joined the project midway through and brought a delightful combination of intelligence and poetry, contributed exemplary work to this volume. Lastly, on a personal note, I wish to express my deepest gratitude to C. John and Nancy Swinbourne and Benjamin and Susan Minard, who cared for my loves when this project took me away from them, and to those loves—Willis, Lukie, and Leilee—without whom this endeavor simply would not be.

Anna Swinbourne
Assistant Curator
Department of Painting and Sculpture

ESSAYS

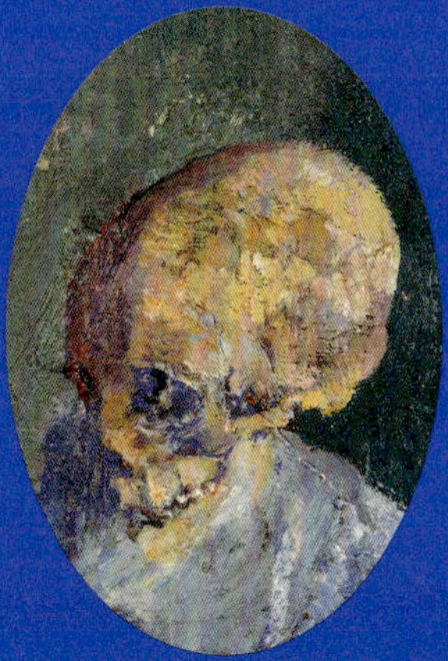

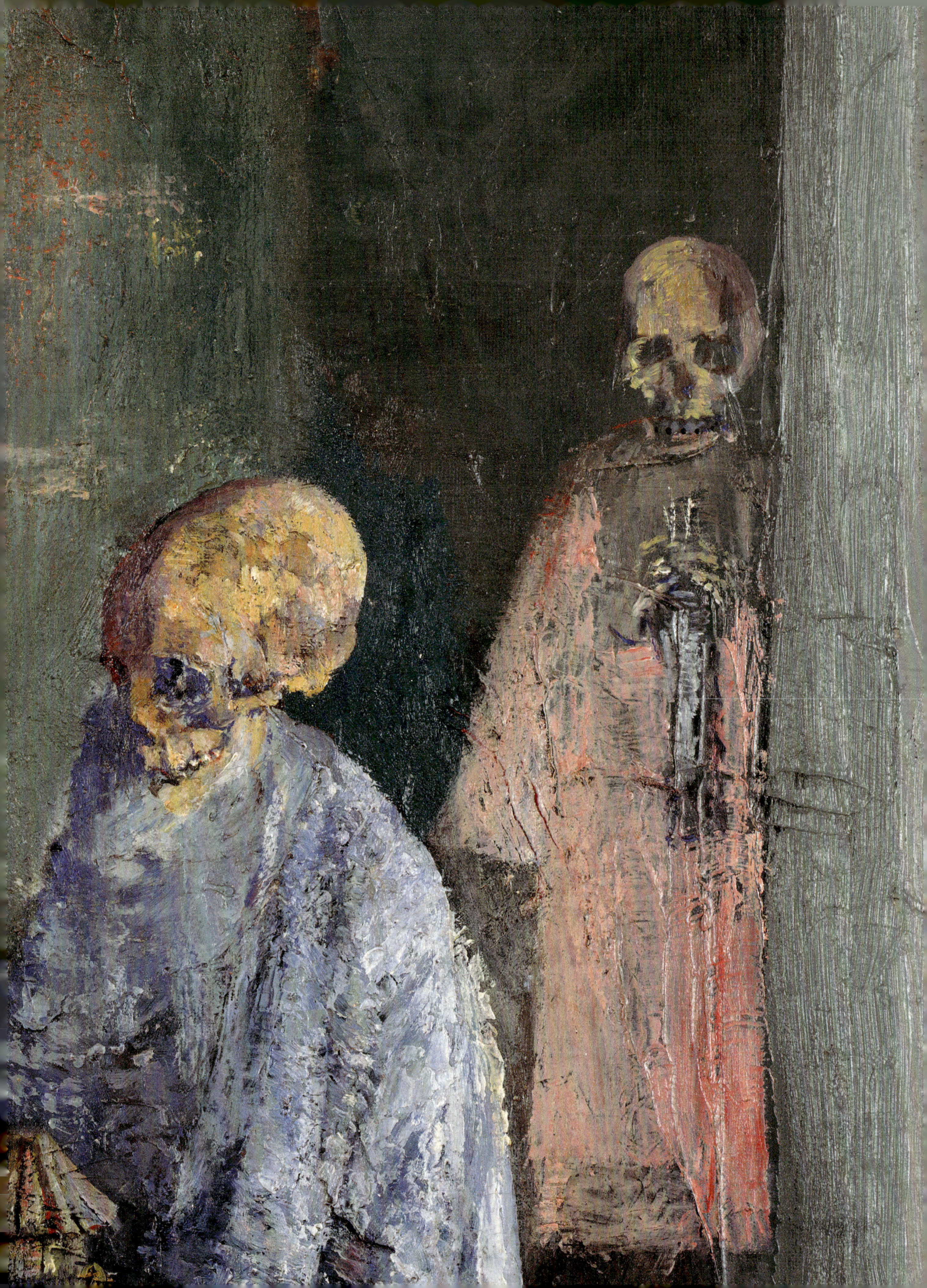

Meeting James Ensor

ANNA SWINBOURNE

The mobility, the anxiety, and the wavering of his nature explain at once the feverish searches, the steps forward, the steps backward, the brusque advances and the sudden retreats, in a word all the changes and also all the unevenness of his art. After a light picture, he reverses to a dark picture; after a character sketch he begins an atmosphere drawing, after a completely delicate etching he engraves a copper plate as if with nails. He is turbulent and abrupt in many a composition; the continuous or symmetrical development of lines hardly worries him; he proceeds by blows; he astonishes more often than he charms. He shows clumsiness and he is far from banishing unruliness and chaos from his art. He is never able to stay still and is often even unable to stay in his seat.

—*Émile Verhaeren, 1908*[1]

It was the writer and poet Émile Verhaeren who first named James Ensor "the painter of masks," in his 1908 monograph on the artist. Ensor has since become widely known as such, but Verhaeren's description above of the artist's nature, from the same essay, touches upon a voracity of character and a diversity of work that are less well-known. In the first two decades of his career, generally considered his most creative years, Ensor tackled both traditional subjects, including religious allegory and satire, and invented ones—fantastical scenes and the visionary rendition of light. He made paintings, drawings, and prints, in a wide range of styles and dimensions, from tiny prints of only a few inches to his monumental magnum opus *Christ's Entry into Brussels in 1889* (*L'Entrée du Christ à Bruxelles en 1889*, 1888; p. 29, fig. 1), which measures over eight feet high and fourteen feet wide. A restless and incessant experimenter with a variety of mediums and techniques including collage and hand-printed etching, he even revisited works completed years earlier, adding colors and images that often radically transformed them.

Then and now, the diversity of Ensor's work has enabled him to slip cunningly out of the grasp of anyone seeking to seize and place him, whether in an artistic movement or a historical continuum. This is part of the magic that has seduced us for over a century. Artists in particular—the most sensitive among us to originality and innovation—have come to revere him as an "artist's artist," a title bestowed only on the most deserving. Given its daring and heterogeneity, Ensor's art should be considered in a manner in keeping with the spirit of its creation—as Verhaeren writes, by blows.

James Sidney Édouard Ensor was born in 1860 in the Belgian seaside town of Ostend. Once a small fishing village, Ostend had been distinguished in 1834 when the first king of Belgium, Leopold I, had chosen it for his summer residence. In the ensuing decades, burgeoning growth as well as the economic and cultural initiatives of the king's successor, Leopold II, who came to the throne in 1865, dramatically transformed the quiet town.[2] A bustling, fashionable resort renowned for its beaches, spas, and casino, the Ostend of Ensor's youth attracted English and European visitors from all social levels. It was there that Ensor's father, James Frederic Ensor, a wealthy educated Englishman, met his mother, Marie Catherina Haegheman, a local woman whose petit bourgeois family owned a souvenir and curiosity shop catering primarily to leisure-class visitors. Centrally located for the tourism traffic, the shop did its best business during the busy summer season and, immediately preceding Lent, the annual carnival, which the town celebrated with infamously raucous parades and festivities. This eccentric familial setting was to have a defining and lasting impact on Ensor and his art, as he would later acknowledge:

> *My grandparents had in Ostend . . . a shop selling sea shells, lace, rare stuffed fish, old books, prints, jams, china, an inextricable jumble of assorted objects constantly being knocked over by a number of cats, deafening parrots, and a monkey. . . . My childhood was filled with marvelous dreams and frequent visits to my grandmother's shop, with its iridescent glow from the reflections of the shells, sumptuous lace, strange stuffed animals and terrible savage weapons that terrified me. . . . This exceptional milieu without doubt developed my artistic faculties and my grandmother was my great inspiration.*[3]

At some point after November 1860, James Frederic Ensor went alone to the United States to find work as a civil engineer, as an alternative to the merchant career offered by his wife's family. This effort, however, was thwarted by the outbreak of the Civil War, in 1861, and James Frederic returned to Belgium to run his in-laws' shop. He was ill-suited for business and unable to develop much interest in it, and by 1875 the family had declared bankruptcy, at which point the Haeghemans, and principally his sister-in-law, Marie Louise, assumed control of the finances. This failure was devastating for James Frederic, both diminishing him within the family and cementing its matriarchal hierarchy. But the embarrassment did not lessen his son's affection for him; in fact the young Ensor felt a special kinship with this man, whom he would later describe as a superior being.[4] His adoration is evident in a portrait he would paint in 1881 (plate 7): alone in a corner, caressed by soft light, his distinguished father sits absorbed in a dog-eared manuscript, at once cultivating his mind and oblivious to the world around him.

Ensor's father, sensitive, intellectual, and cultured, surely encouraged him to pursue his interest in art from its first appearance. James began his formal training in his teenage years with two elderly artists in Ostend, Michel Van Cuyck and Édouard Dubar. Their work and methods in the naturalist tradition helped the young James to establish a foundation for his own artistic discipline and attentiveness,[5] which he then applied to his captivating surroundings: in Ostend, sandwiched between marshes and lowlands and the North Sea, Ensor saw beauty and drama, and began making drawings and paintings of the setting, rendering the port and its fishermen, the dunes, the countryside, local landmarks, the beach, and the ever changing sea. The subtle tonalities and brushy application of paint in these small-scale works reveal a keen sensitivity to light and its effects—some of the works are even inscribed on the reverse with the time of day they were made—and evoke a feeling of genuine tenderness for the subjects depicted. *The Bathing Hut* (*Cabine de bain*; fig. 1), for instance, painted in pale, sun-baked hues, depicts a solitary cabin warmly ensconced in a desolate yet tranquil landscape of sand, sea, and sky.

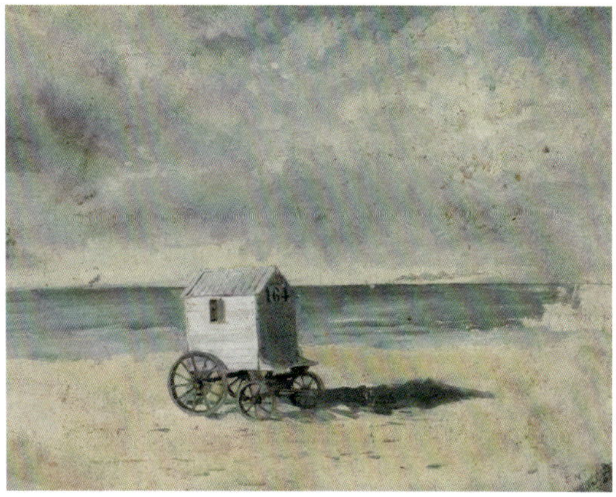

FIG. 1: JAMES ENSOR. *The Bathing Hut*. Afternoon, July 29, 1876. Oil and pencil on board, 9 1/16 × 7 1/16" (23 × 18 cm), Koninklijk Museum voor Schone Kunsten, Antwerp

In 1877, seeking further instruction, Ensor left Ostend for Brussels and enrolled in the Académie royale des beaux-arts, a prestigious training ground for young artists aspiring to show in the national Salon. Under the tutelage of director Jean Portaels and professors Joseph Stallaert, Alexandre Robert, and Joseph Van Severdonck, he took classes in painting after nature and drew antique heads, busts, and figures. His professors' critiques of his work were harsh, his marks were mediocre, and this discouraging reception planted in him a biting disdain for academicism in all its forms.[6] The works from these years that survive in their original states are an unremarkable group of studies and biblical or mythological scenes. Ensor's self-portraiture from this period, however, stands in sharp contrast. One painting from 1879 presents a young man in three-quarter view (p. 95, fig. 4), his gaze and brooding countenance speaking volumes. Another from the same year[7] demonstrates in every aspect—the composition's jagged forms and angles; the unruly application of paint, especially on the artist's centrally positioned palette; and the more carefully articulated features of his eyes and face—the energetic turmoil raging within its sitter/subject.

Equally but differently influential were Ensor's fellow students, particularly Darío de Regoyos, Willy Finch (also from Ostend, also of English parentage, and Ensor's future studio-mate), Fernand Khnopff (who would quickly become a competitor), and, perhaps most important, the aspiring painter-poet-playwright Théo Hannon. It was Hannon who greatly enriched Ensor's world by introducing him to his sister, Mariette, and her husband, Ernest Rousseau. The couple, she a scientist and he a professor, hosted a regular salon in their home in Brussels, where Ensor met Guillaume Vogels and other avant-garde artists as well as members of the city's intellectual elite who gravitated to the city's Université Libre, where Rousseau served briefly as rector. In this exciting, stimulating environment, Ensor flourished.

The Rousseaus soon came to embrace Ensor as a family member, making their house his home away from home and exposing him to the most progressive intellectual, cultural, and political circles of the day. Ensor's gratitude, respect, and fondness would evidence themselves in many flattering depictions of Rousseau family members for years to come. The couple's son, Ernest Jr., who shared Ensor's delight in mischief and pranks, played the leading role as a thoughtful, forlorn Pierrot (plate 85), while Ernest Sr. was depicted either playfully or reverently in several works. Mariette, however, received the best treatment, for she was the object of Ensor's profound admiration and private fantasy. She is the studious mycologist at her microscope (p. 29, fig. 2), the benevolent overseer and arbiter (plate 71), and, perhaps most endearingly, a dainty dragonfly gazing upon the artist's own beetle-self in a whimsical double portrait (plate 41).

Disaffected from the Académie and officialdom yet nourished by the exuberant Rousseaus and their friends, Ensor returned to Ostend in 1880. But for the occasional trip to London, Holland, or Paris, and frequent journeys back to Brussels, he would stay there for the rest of his life. In the attic of the building that housed the family shop on the ground floor and living quarters above, he built a private universe. This studio was bathed in light from a large window in the mansard and a pair of smaller windows on either side, providing ideal working conditions for his art-making as well as a refuge from the disinterest of many family members and the mercantile affairs below. Upstairs, he was free to complement the lessons he was learning from fellow artists such as Hannon and Vogels by pursuing the solitary practice of copying reproductions from art books and periodicals. In this way he acquainted himself with the work of dozens of past and contemporary masters, including Rembrandt, Joseph Mallord William Turner, Eugène Delacroix, Jacques Callot, Honoré Daumier, and Édouard Manet.[8] Filled with inspiration, he would venture out of the studio in search of subjects in his immediate surroundings, finding many in the domestic interiors downstairs and more outside in the town.

It is at once apparent how much the young artist had grown in his three years away. He makes bolder landscapes, often on a much larger scale than the *cartons roses*[9] of his youth and no longer exclusively en plein air in front of the motif. From the elevated, interior position of his studio, he paints receding vistas of the hushed, empty street in a variety of weather conditions (plates 4 and 5).[10] Paint application is heavy and sketchy, with visible strokes from the brush and palette knife, and the tonalities are rich, dark, and earthy, creating an overall effect of vivid atmosphere. This style of painting, called "tachist" from the French verb "*tacher*," to mark or stain, had been developed by the previous generation of Belgian Realists and by this time, 1880, had become the preeminent modernist mode for Ensor and his like-minded contemporaries.[11]

Ensor turned equally careful attention and the same tachist brush to the world indoors. The Ostend of the time led a distinctly double life; during the Lenten carnival and the summer season, the shops and streets were hectically busy, but during the rest of the year, days were quiet, as if the town and its citizens were hibernating. Though Ensor's family members were subjects close at hand, he often complained about how much they slept. These often dozing women—his most frequent sitters during this period were his mother; his aunt, Marie Louise, called "Mimi"; and his sister, Marie, known as "Mitche"—people his darkened interior scenes; when they are not asleep, they are engaged in quiet domestic pursuits such as reading, knitting, or taking tea. The cloistered, often stuffy, even airless interiors reveal the artist's interest not only in the material objects that decorate people and rooms—rugs, fabrics, furniture, ornaments, bibelots—but also in the interaction of matter and light, which usually streams into the composition from a heavily draped window (fig. 2).

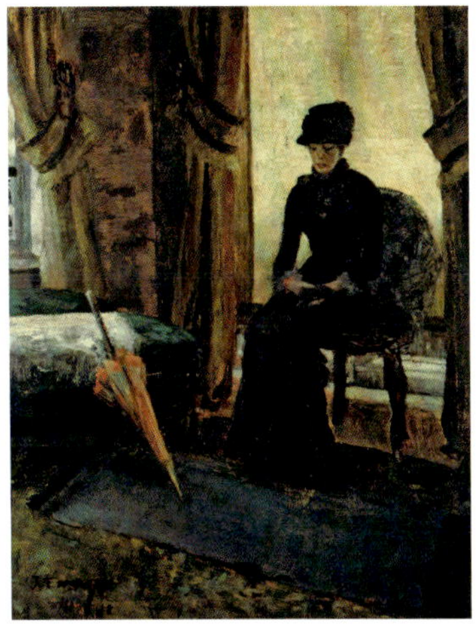

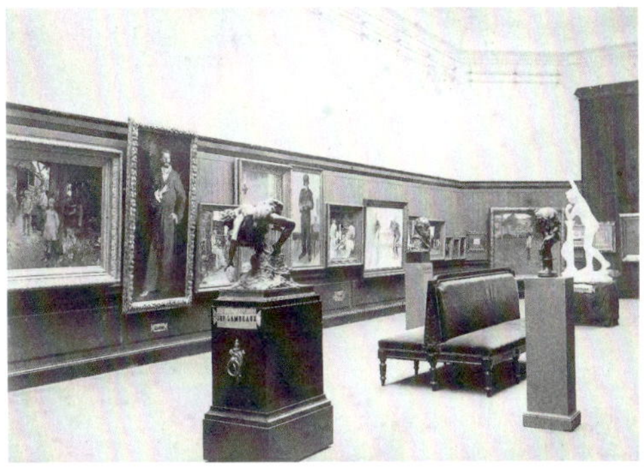

FIG. 2: JAMES ENSOR. *The Somber Lady*. 1881. Oil on canvas, 39 3/8 × 31 1/2" (100 × 80 cm). Musées royaux des Beaux-Arts de Belgique, Brussels

FIG. 3: Installation view of the first exhibition of Les Vingt, Palais des Beaux-Arts, Brussels. 1884. Visible on the wall from left to right are *A Colorist* (1880; plate 6); *The Scandalized Masks* (1883; plate 15); *The Lamp-Lighter* (1880; plate 3); *Chinoiseries with Fans* (1881; plate 2); and *The Drunkards* (1883; plate 14)

The still life gave Ensor another way to explore his fascination with light and its play off textures and surfaces. Clustered compositions on bare or draped tables initially contained objects traditional to the genre, such as dishes, fruits, and vegetables, which were soon joined by more personal items, like fans and chinoiseries (plate 2), or more indigenous pieces such as seafood or shells. Ensor masterfully combined the two genres of still life and interior scene in a painting considered among his best of the period, *The Oyster Eater* (*La Mangeuse d'huîtres*, 1882; plate 13). This life-size image shows his sister Mitche absorbed in a meal of oysters at a table conspicuously set for two. An array of flowers, dishes, and linens spreads out in front of her. Every element, from the liquids shimmering in glasses and bottles to the reflections in the background mirror, betrays Ensor's overarching interest in the power and qualities of light, and particularly in its ability to enliven both objects and place. The overall tonality and brightness create a feeling of warmth, while the sitter's calm, despite her absent dinner companion, evokes a mysterious, poetic mood. As Ensor likely knew it would, the painting, with its unfinished character, proved too much for the conservative art establishment; the triennial salon held that year in Antwerp refused to exhibit it.[12]

While some of the establishment reception of Ensor had been negative, he was not completely without success in traditional circles. He exhibited one painting at the Brussels Salon in 1881 and two at the Paris Salon in 1882. Yet he was beginning to explore the Belgian art societies established as alternatives to the official academic Salon. He exhibited *A Colorist* (*Une Coloriste*, 1880; plate 6) and *The Bourgeois Salon* (*A Salon* [*Impression*]) (*Le Salon bourgeois*, 1881; p. 31, fig. 3) with La Chrysalide in Brussels in 1881, for example, and in 1882 he joined L'Essor, a group of academy students with some progressive elements. When L'Essor too refused to exhibit *The Oyster Eater*, however, in 1883, Ensor joined the more progressive members dissatisfied with the society's exhibiting policies and cofounded a new society, Les Vingt, or Les XX.[13] These Vingtists included many artists Ensor knew from his academy years in Brussels—his friends Finch and de Regoyos as well as Vogels and Khnopff. With the writer and lawyer Octave Maus stewarding as secretary, Les Vingt hosted an annual exhibition in Brussels's Palais des beaux-arts (now the Musée d'art ancien; fig. 3), strategically timed to occur one month before the official Brussels Salon. They also presented a program of lectures and concerts in conjunction with the show. In theory, the members advocated freedom of artistic expression over any one style, and in that pluralistic vein they invited leading artists from Belgium and abroad to exhibit with the founding members, deciding installation placement within the galleries by lot. Foreign participants who strongly influenced the group were James McNeill Whistler in 1884, the French Impressionists Claude Monet and Pierre-Auguste Renoir in 1886, and the Neo-Impressionists Georges Seurat and Camille Pissarro in 1887. Flush with talent and resources, Les Vingt quickly rose to avant-garde prominence, with Ensor as one of its leading lights. In 1884, he was described as "the star . . . chief of the clan . . . in the spotlight" and by 1886 as "God . . . [the] mold . . . which they are trying to make all artists fit."[14]

I don't have children, but light is my daughter, light one and indivisible, light bread of the painter, light soft part of the loaf of the painter, light queen of our senses, light, light, illuminate us! Animate us, show us the new routes leading to joy and bliss.

—James Ensor, 1932[15]

In his early work, Ensor used light and luminosity to add nuance to imagery and a dramatic emotional component to his relatively dark canvases, but by 1885 he had elevated them to a far more important role: he saw light as the radiant source of color and, in its relation to line, the promising source in the search for an original style that he deemed essential for any true artist. As he would later write in a letter to author, critic, and curator Pol de Mont, "A correct line cannot inspire lofty sentiments; it demands neither sacrifice nor profound admixture. It is the enemy of genius, incapable of expressing passion, disquiet, struggle, pain, enthusiasm or poetry—any of those fine and grand feelings—nor any firmly held principle. . . . In the distortion that light inflicts upon the line, I saw the immensity waiting to be explored and a new vision to be established."[16]

In pursuit of this new vision, Ensor devoted himself to drawing. He was trying to create a vibrating line, to dissolve the material contours of objects so that they would seem suffused by light. Discovering that this formal innovation had expressive potential, he soon made light a subject in itself, an agent of symbolic intention, conveying ideas and evoking mood. In 1885, Ensor began to use this approach to transform drawings he had executed earlier. *The Mystic Death of a Theologian* (*Elated Monks Claim the Body of Theologian Sus Ovis, in Spite of the Resisting Bishop Friton or Friston*) (*La Mort mystique d'un théologien* [*Moines exaltés réclamant le corps du Théologien Sus-Ovis malgré l'opposition de l'évêque Friton ou Friston*], 1880 / 1885–86[?]; plate 22), for example, he had made while still at the Académie. Now he added motifs and reworked large portions of the sheet, which he had enlarged with additional paper. He perfected these techniques in a series of six drawings begun in 1885, Visions: The Aureoles of Christ or the Sensibilities of Light (Visions: Les Auréoles du Christ ou les sensibilités de la lumière; plates 26 and 27), which also strikingly demonstrates his shift away from the representation of material reality toward the more intangible worlds of imagination and the spiritual. Each drawing depicts an episode from the life of Christ and has a two-part title both naming that moment and attaching a state of mind to it.[17] The first two in the series, *The Rising: Christ Shown to the People* (*La Crue: Jésus montré au peuple*, 1885; plate 26) and *The Lively and Radiant: The Entry of Christ into Jerusalem* (*La Vive et rayonnante: L'Entrée à Jérusalem*, 1885; plate 27) (hereafter referred to as *The Entry of Christ into Jerusalem*), present a biblical event in a contemporary urban setting. The site of Christ's entry in *The Entry of Christ into Jerusalem*, for example, is not ancient Jerusalem but the Brussels of Ensor's day, revealed by banners with slogans such as "Les XX" and by the teeming street scene, a reference to the massive processions and social-protest demonstrations taking place in Brussels and the southern part of Belgium in the 1880s. Simultaneously emerging and receding, the figures in Ensor's crowd create an effect of palpable motion, as though the sheet itself were teeming too. The effect is directly attributed to his new drawing style, in which line varies from densely woven to nearly transparent, from thick and strong to fine and whisperlike. The drawing's contours dissolve, melding objects one into another, and the light is otherworldly.

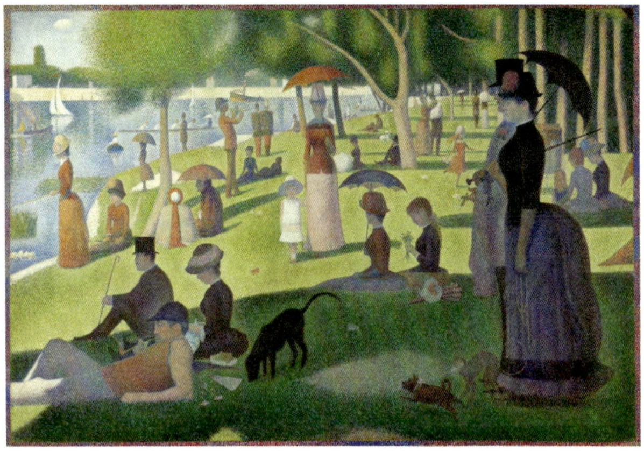

FIG. 4: Georges Seurat. *A Sunday on La Grande Jatte–1884*. 1884–86. Oil on canvas, 6' 9 3/4" × 10' 1 1/4" (207.5 × 308.1 cm). The Art Institute of Chicago. Helen Birch Bartlett Memorial Collection

When Ensor exhibited the series for the first time, at the annual Brussels exhibition of Les Vingt in 1887, the reception was mixed. Some admired his technical prowess and innovation, as well as his daring in drawing on a scale usually reserved for painting (*The Entry of Christ into Jerusalem* is just shy of seven feet [just over two meters] high). But more found his religious subject matter fatally retrograde. The works by Seurat and Pissarro on view in the same exhibition, especially Seurat's stupendous *A Sunday on La Grande Jatte–1884* (fig. 4), were thought more thoroughly modern, and Maus and many of the group's artists embraced the Neo-Impressionist method of rendering light through optical division and mixture. Ensor, however, remained unconvinced, seeing his own methods as the way forward. This competitive rift, while typical of the internal strife, clashing egos, and disagreements about mission and direction occurring in many avant-garde groups, was a source of anguish for Ensor, who was sensitive to criticism, resented being overshadowed by his French counterparts, and feared losing the recognition he had enjoyed as one of the group's leaders.

While Ensor's new drawing style helped to precipitate his demise as a leader of Les Vingt, it also served as a creative watershed. In focusing on drawing, he looked anew at his earlier graphic work and saw potential there: a drawing in its original state could serve as both material support and catalyst for something new. Working directly on existing drawings, which in some cases he enlarged by adhering new sheets to them, Ensor let his hand and mind spin associatively. In the fertile details of his older naturalistic imagery, such as the pattern on a vase or curtain, he found inspiration for imaginary forms that he could layer on top, building the new work gradually. Using two distinct styles—fine, densely packed lines to render light, and continuous arabesques to render form—he transformed these more conventionally representational works into their hallucinatory brethren: new drawings, hard to read yet seductive in this very ambiguity (plates 32, 33, and 34; p. 38, fig. 6; and p. 87, fig. 5).[18]

In 1886, in a similarly experimental mode, Ensor began to make prints. With possible exposure to printmaking from his early teacher Dubar, his friend Hannon, and the

FIG. 5: JAMES ENSOR. *The Stars in the Cemetery*. 1888. Etching with drypoint, plate: 5 1/2 × 7 1/16" (13.2 × 17.3 cm). Museum Plantin-Moretus, Antwerp

Vingtist Félicien Rops, he charged ahead intuitively, quickly learning drypoint and copperplate etching. Two of his most accomplished prints come from that first year: *Christ Calming the Storm* (*Le Christ apaisant la tempête*) and *The Cathedral* (*La Cathédrale*; plate 31). In the latter, a massive imagined edifice—woven together from images of three different cathedrals[19]—looms above an equally massive crowd. The print draws its power from the tension and opposition between uniformed regiments and plebeian chaos, present day and medieval past, vertical and horizontal line, colossal and human scale. Ensor went on to make 133 prints over the course of his career, 86 of them between 1886 and 1891. The nature and breadth of their subjects resemble those of his paintings and drawings: in addition to portraiture and landscapes, there are religious allegories and fantastical scenes (often inspired by the etchings of past masters such as Rembrandt and Callot); illustrations of the works of Edgar Allan Poe, a literary favorite; and social commentary on political issues of the day, as in the scatological *Doctrinaire Nourishment* (*Alimentation doctrinaire*, 1889; plate 51). Other prints reproduce his own paintings and drawings. Working with a variety of professional printers,[20] Ensor could indulge his craftsman tendencies, choosing papers and inks carefully and experimenting with a variety of combinatory effects. A celebrated example is *The Stars in the Cemetery* (*Les Étoiles au cimetière*; fig. 5), which originally depicted caricatural figures. When the plate was bitten too hard by the acid, accidentally creating a starry sky, Ensor added a field of tombstones in drypoint, transforming the burlesque original into a peaceful nocturnal scene. Once the printing was done, he also explored the transformative effects of color by hand-applying accents and flourishes to the black-and-white sheets. Some works are covered so thoroughly and thickly with color that the result seems more drawing than print.[21]

The little bits of collage that Ensor had done up to this point—pasting a portrait of positivist philosopher Émile Littré, copied from a photograph by Nadar, into the lower-right corner of *The Entry of Christ into Jerusalem* (fig. 6 and p. 79) and adding sheets or panels to older drawings before reworking them—surely sparked his ambition to forge a collage practice on a grander scale, which he accomplished in *The Temptation of Saint Anthony* (*La Tentation de Saint-Antoine*; fig. 7). The old art-historical theme of a saint battling spiritual and material evils was receiving renewed attention from the Belgian avant-garde, as a topic discussed in the influential art periodical *L'Art moderne* and as a subject treated by contemporaries such as Khnopff, Rops, and Odilon Redon. To make his version, which included supernatural evils as well, Ensor joined sixty-eight individual sheets of paper, drawing across the seams to integrate each mushrooming motif into a dizzying sea, and obliterating traditional pictorial space and perspective. Again he worked on a monumental scale—the drawing is nearly six feet high—and again set a story from the history of Christianity in a situation replete with references to the contemporary world. Where Anthony is conventionally depicted in a solitary wilderness, Ensor's saint kneels amid a grotesque, caricatural crowd. The details

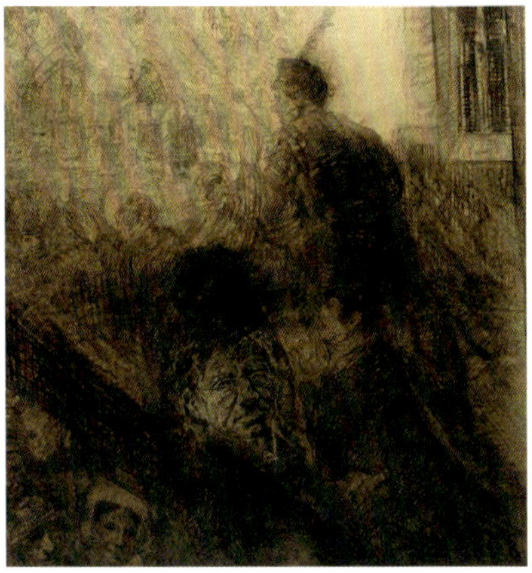

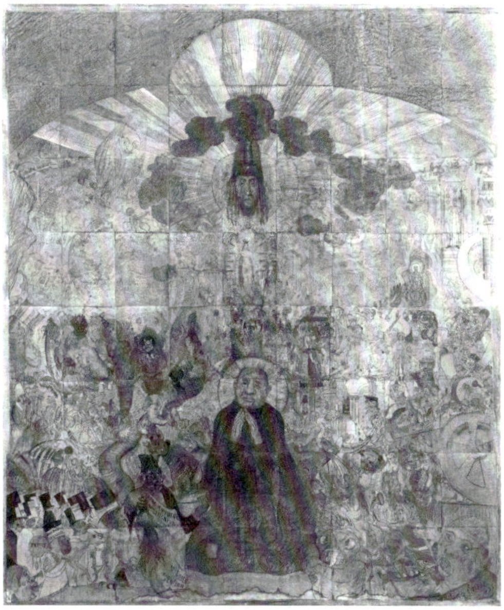

FIG. 6: JAMES ENSOR. *The Lively and Radiant: The Entry of Christ into Jerusalem* (detail). 1885 (see plate 27)

FIG. 7: JAMES ENSOR. *The Temptation of Saint Anthony*. 1887. Charcoal, graphite, colored pencil, pastel, and watercolor, possibly fixed, with cut-and-pasted elements, on sixty-eight sheets of paper mounted on canvas, 70 1/16 × 61 13/16" (178 × 157.5 cm). The Art Institute of Chicago. Regenstein Endowment and The Louise B. and Frank H. Woods Purchase Fund

with which the scene overflows include battle scenes, saints, men in top hats, banners and slogans advertising Belgian treats such as french fries, and countless demons and monsters—an enthralling visual cacophony and an imaginary tour de force.[22]

The theme of Saint Anthony and his struggles would be one of the first Ensor tackled when he returned his focus to painting later in 1886. In *Tribulations of Saint Anthony* (*Terribles Tribulations de Saint-Antoine*, 1887; plate 37) the temptations are reduced to tribulations momentarily interrupting the saint's reading, but the spirit of the work is clearly in keeping with that of its collage predecessor. Rendered in thick strokes of paint, Anthony sits at the water's edge in a visionary landscape of chaotic action. Around him bizarre creatures engage in mischievous and obscene play. This and other works from around the same time (plates 36 and 38) make it clear that Ensor's investigations into rendering light in drawing had a dramatic impact on his painting: he abandoned the earlier work's darker palette (both intentionally darker and growing darker with age, an effect he believed was the result of mixing pigments) and made his color purer and brighter. Furthermore, his use of color was no longer descriptive but expressive. Rather than painting the environment around Anthony in naturalistic, earthy tones, he chose red, crimson, pink, and ocher, giving heat to the throbbing scene. As these stylistic and expressive developments emerged, references to contemporary life simultaneously receded, signaling a new mode of working that Ensor was adding to his repertory: pure imagination.

Ensor's gradual embrace of the illusory in his art is often linked to his difficulties in dealing with those around him—besieging critics, fellow avant-gardists who rejected his innovations, a practical-minded family with little use for his talent and ambition. He needed their support and approval and, when denied it, became adversarial in turn. He did in fact have the support of influential critics such as Verhaeren and Eugène Demolder, and the lifelong companionship of Augusta Boogaerts, an Ostendaise whom he met in 1888, yet he felt himself an alienated army of one and carried on as such, fighting for the art whose genius he was certain assured victory. It was Ensor himself who perpetuated the idea that he was antagonized and isolated; "Hounded by followers," he would later write, "I joyfully took refuge in the solitary land of fools."[23] But reasons and rhetoric aside, the move into fantasy was an advance of quantum proportions. Freed from the constraints of convention—modern and academic alike—Ensor redirected his energy, jumping from such revelatory real-world experiences as discovering the phantasmal art of Odilon Redon,[24] or looking into Mariette Rousseau's microscope, to a fantastical place of his own making.

To this illusory realm belongs his single most celebrated work, *Christ's Entry into Brussels in 1889* (1888; p. 29, fig. 1).[25] Amid a dizzying screen of garish color, impasto, and grand scale, Ensor appears as Christ riding a donkey in a procession through the streets of Brussels. Simultaneity is a key element of the painting. In subject, it is at once self-portrait, religious scene, and social and political critique. Similarly, its motifs operate on numerous levels: the parade is religious procession, political demonstration, and Mardi Gras celebration all at once. And through this plurality the painting speaks manifold messages, including both fascination and disgust with humanity, and a sense of self as both persecuted and superior relative to the art world and indeed other people generally.[26]

Front and center, literally and figuratively, in the surging crowd that so fascinated the artist are masks. Ensor had known masks for as long as he could remember, seeing them on sale in his family's shop and worn by revelers in the socially topsy-turvy Ostend Carnival. For Ensor these objects were ideal in their visual forcefulness; he would later write, "The mask means to me: freshness of color, sumptuous decoration, wild unexpected gestures, very shrill expressions, exquisite turbulence."[27] He also clearly understood the mask's role in both disguising individuals and revealing inner truths about them, both extending or enlarging a person's character and serving as psychological Other. This race of constructed faces, as endlessly individual as the human one, imposed no limit on the pictorial permutations Ensor's imagination could devise. He used them in self-portraits, for instance *The Man of Sorrows* (*L'Homme de douleurs*, 1891; plate 76), in which a grimacing Japanese Noh mask becomes an agonizing likeness of himself as Christ;[28] they are characters in fictive dramas, such as *The Assassination* (*L'Assassinat*, 1890; plate 65) and *The Intrigue* (*L'Intrigue*, 1890; plate 66);[29] and they appear with their more human counterparts, sometimes obviously, as in *The Despair of Pierrot* (*Pierrot jaloux*, 1892; plate 85), sometimes more stealthily, as in *Monsieur and Madame Rousseau Speaking with Sophie Yoteko* (*Monsieur et Madame Rousseau parlant avec Sophie Yoteko*, 1892; plate 75), in which a cross-dressed likeness of the artist hides an upside-down, hook-nosed mask, outlined in black, in the shapes of his or her bonnet.

Mask and face in Ensor's work may be separated by a line so thin that it dissolves. *Old Lady with Masks* (*Theater of Masks*) (*Bouquet d'artifice*; fig. 8), for example, originally a commission, was reworked after the client rejected it; the final pockmarked visage,

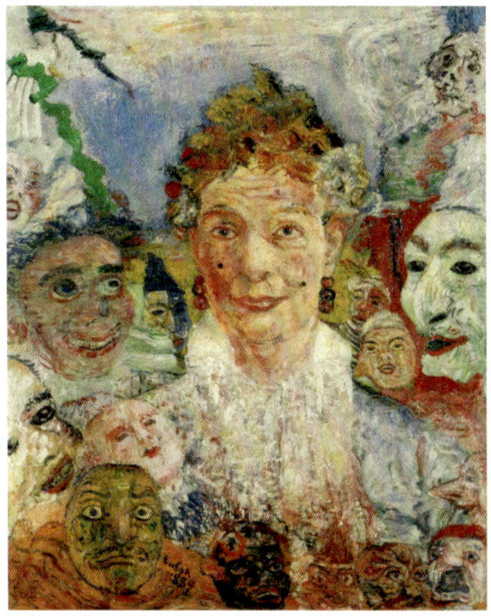

FIG. 8: JAMES ENSOR. *Old Lady with Masks* (*Theater of Masks*). 1889. Oil on canvas, 21 1/4 × 18 1/16" (54 × 47.5 cm). Museum voor Schone Kunsten, Ghent

with pronounced, masklike edges along hairline, chin, and left side, is surrounded by masks to which it bears a striking resemblance, both in the frozen aspect of the woman's expression and the garish coloring of her cosmetics. Ensor often operates by making the distance between mask and face indefinable, as in *Series of Small Masks* (*Série de masques réunis en théâtre d'expression*, c. 1890[?]; plate 60). In *The Wise Judges* (*Les Bons Juges*, 1891; plate 78), for example, some of the faces of the red-robed judges and black-clad lawyers may be read as either distorted individual countenances or donned disguises.

The mask has a counterpart in Ensor's art: the skeleton. Their symbiotic relationship is evident in works like *Skeleton in the Mirror* (*Le Miroir au squelette*, 1890; plate 62), where a reflected skeleton bust hovers in a vertical wash of floating masks. Ensor had a number of lifelong obsessions—the sea, light, himself—but chief among them was death. It is surely more than coincidence that the subject came to the fore in his work in 1887, when both his father and his maternal grandmother passed away. Their deaths must have been traumatic: in his grandmother Ensor lost an eccentric inspiration, in his father a sympathetic supporter at home. The obsession with death entered his vocabulary of images as skull or full-body skeleton, appearing repeatedly and in a variety of ways. Death may be subject, as in *Death Pursuing the Human Flock* (*Triumph of Death*) (*La Triomphe de la mort*, 1887; plate 45), where a flying web-footed skeleton brandishes a long-bladed scythe above a panicked crowd, or actor, as in *Skeletons Trying to Warm Themselves* (*Squelettes voulant se chauffer*, 1889; plate 54), whose group of skulls, whether disembodied or atop draped figures, absurdly and vainly seek heat from a dead stove. As model, death stands in for people Ensor despised—for example the two critics ripping apart the witty metaphorical version of the artist in *Skeletons Fighting over a Pickled Herring* (*Squelettes se disputant un hareng saur*, 1891; plate 72).[30] And death stands in for those Ensor adores, principally himself. A skeleton version of the artist abounds in his work, playing different notes: comic, in, for example, his imagined likeness in 1960 (plate 39); earnest, in the print of paired self-portraits (plates 57 and 58) in which he reworked the copper plate to transform the head of one image into the hirsute skull of the second; haunting, with the artist at his easel in front of a visual autobiography, an account of his career (plate 89).

Two of Ensor's self-portraits, *My Skeletonized Portrait* (*Mon Portrait squelettisé*, 1889; plate 58) and *The Skeleton Painter* (*Squelette peintre*, 1895 or 1896[?]; plate 89), were based on photographs. Ensor's use of photography as pictorial source material, like his *avant la lettre* practice of collage, was consistent with his experimental nature. Again, his methods varied. While remaining relatively faithful to the original image (fig. 9), he might retain some details while omitting others in transcribing the image to the plate, which he used for one single impression before the subsequent skeletonizing reworking. Or he might change parts of the imagery completely; *The Skeleton Painter* stands rather timidly at his easel, having risen from the chair in which the artist is pictured in

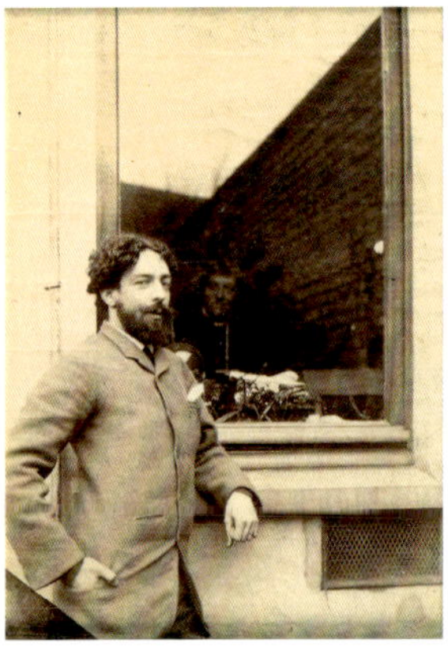

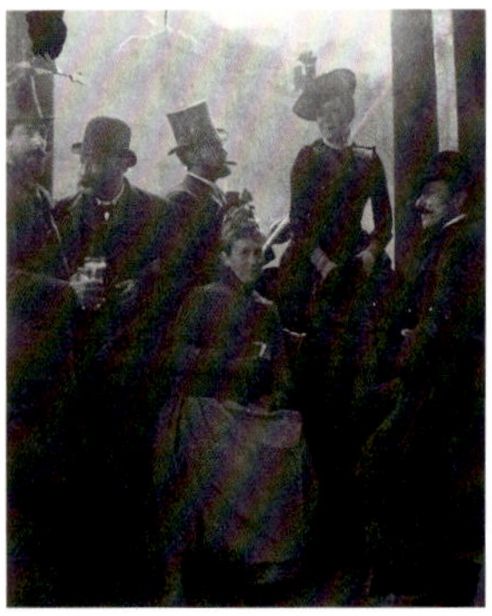

FIG. 9: James Ensor in front of the Rousseau residence in rue Vautier, Brussels. c. 1888

FIG. 10: James Ensor, Ernest Rousseau, Willy Finch, Mariette Rousseau, Mitche Ensor, and Antonio Roiti on a trip to Bruges. 1888

the photograph (p. 39, fig. 9). He might also boldly cull images from photographs and rearrange them, Photoshop-style, as in *Plague Above, Plague Below, Plague All Around!* (*Peste dessous, peste dessus, peste partout!*, 1888; plate 44). For this scathing comment on the clash of social classes, Ensor lifted his bourgeois models—Mitche, Willy Finch, Ernest and Mariette Rousseau—from a photograph of the group on a trip to Bruges (fig. 10). Extracting them from the tiered arrangement of the photograph, he set them in a horizontal line, disjointedly filling in feet and legs and whatever anatomical parts were not visible in the original.

Photographs were only one type of object in the brimming group of models for Ensor's art. We know from contemporary accounts how his studio was filled:

> *Anyone who surprised Ensor at work upstairs saw him emerge from a clutter of disparate objects: masks, rags, withered branches, shells, cups, pots, worn-out rugs, books littering the floor, prints piled up on chairs, empty frames leaning against the furniture, and the inevitable skull surveying the scene with two vacant sockets and missing eyes. A friendly layer of dust covers these innumerable strange objects, protecting them from the sudden movements of visitors. They are there waiting for the painter to breathe life into them, to make them speak, and, thanks to his devotion to them and the hushed eloquence he sees in their silence, to introduce them into his art.*[31]

That introduction involved Ensor's arrangement and rearrangement of his studio props, like the composing with objects that any still life painter must master. In fact many of Ensor's fantastic compositions are not wholly removed from the still lifes he had made years earlier (plate 12). *Masks Mocking Death* (*Masks Confronting Death*) (*Masques raillant la mort*, 1888; plate 53), for example, at first seems to show masqueraders flanking a skeletal being, but closer inspection reveals masks, hats, a skeleton, and bits of drapery cunningly arrayed on a table. Ensor crafted the elements of his imagined dramas—actors, costumes, props, scenery—from these disparate objects, and, like an ingenious theater director, positioned them against the backdrop of his studio. In this way he conflated imagination and reality, in the form of constructed mise-en-scènes. A broomstick draped with swatches of fabric and topped by a mask or skull could become an actor; many in the artist's cast of characters were made up of variations on devices like this. Again as in the theater, this cast played comedy (plate 50) and tragedy (plate 83), and the scenarios they enacted were often laced with absurdity or gruesomeness, blatant in some works (fig. 11), veiled in others (plate 92).

Some of the actors on Ensor's stage, rather than being constructed of studio props, were modeled after real or stereotyped individuals from the social institutions he so disliked in Belgium. With fervid energy and sardonic wit, he caricatured members of the monarchy, the clergy, the military, the medical profession, and society at large, as in the humorous and absurd beach scene *The Baths at Ostend* (*Les Bains à Ostende*, 1890; plate 64). These pointed satirical critiques treat both specific issues—universal suffrage, say, or compulsory military service—and the general hypocrisy and ineptitude that Ensor thought rampant in the world. No one was spared his bite, including his artist colleagues: in *The Dangerous Cooks* (*Les Cuisiniers dangereux*, 1896; plate 88), a dining table of gross and eager art critics — some of whom had championed Ensor's work — are served the severed heads of Ensor and other young upstarts (Georges Lemmen, Anna Boch, and others) by Maus and Vingtist supporter Edmond Picard.

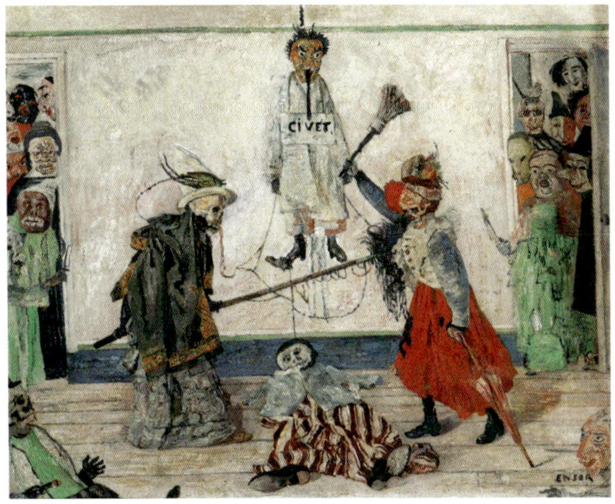

FIG. 11: JAMES ENSOR. *Skeletons Fighting over a Hanged Man.* 1891. Oil on canvas mounted on panel, 23 1/4 × 29 1/8" (59 × 74 cm). Koninklijk Museum voor Schone Kunsten, Antwerp

Over Ensor's adamant objections, Maus and other members of Les Vingt dissolved the group in 1893 to establish its successor, La Libre Esthétique. This proved just one of many disappointments in a very difficult year. Most disruptive of all was a crisis Ensor later claimed to have had, the nature and details of which are now unclear; it may have been financial, despite the sale of a large number of etchings to the Cabinet des estampes in Brussels that same year. Whatever the exact circumstances, the despairing artist put the entire contents of his studio on sale. No one bought, and a period of decreased artmaking ensued. In fact Ensor virtually abandoned painting in 1895, and would not return to it in earnest until the following year. And though he continued to work until a few years before his death, in 1949, many of his images from this point on were remarkably different in tone: a lyricism and lightheartedness appear, a new note of humor. While Ensor continued to produce prolifically in painting, drawing, and printmaking, he repeatedly turned to his own works from the 1880s and early 1890s as models for reinterpretation, in terms either of new palettes or techniques. The works from the twentieth century are generally brighter, often acidic, with freer application of color and paint.

Many scholars have seen Ensor's later habits of recycling as evidence of his artistic decline, for which they offer a variety of reasons. One of the most charitable, Libby Tannenbaum, suggests that after communicating so eloquently during the tumultuous and adversarial years of his youth, the artist consciously decided to develop another voice.[32] He did in fact explore other art forms: taking an almost childlike delight in words and phonetic sounds, he did a great deal of writing, in the form of correspondence, speeches, or essays. He also used the black keys of his harmonium — he was superstitiously afraid of the white ones — to compose a ballet, *La Gamme d'amour*, for which he also created costumes and scenery.[33]

The raging young artist-warrior mellowed somewhat as the twentieth century progressed, bringing with it the recognition Ensor so needed: major museums acquired and exhibited his work, young artists made reverent pilgrimages to his home and studio, and in 1929 the king of Belgium even made him a baron and a major retrospective of his work was held at the Palais des beaux-arts in Brussels. In the end, Ensor's art ensured his importance, as he had been confident it would. We can only truly appreciate its magnitude when we tear ourselves away from his bedazzling masks to see the forces and powers they hide.

NOTES

I am greatly indebted to James Ensor's long list of scholars, critics, and enthusiasts, beginning with Eugène Demolder, who published a pioneering monograph in 1892. The contributions of these authors are detailed in the Selected Bibliography in the present volume. The title of my essay was inspired by They Might Be Giants, whose song "Meet James Ensor" is an ode to "Belgium's famous painter."

1. Émile Verhaeren, *James Ensor* (Brussels: G. Van Oest & Cie, 1908), p. 93. Trans. from the French by Blair Hartzell. Unless otherwise noted, the translations in this essay are by the author, who wishes to thank Delphine Huisinga for her generous assistance.
2. See Patrick Florizoone, *James Ensor: Les Bains à Ostende* (Brussels: Snoek-Ducaju & Zoon and Pandora, 1996), pp. 29–31, and Floorizone, "The Baths of Ostend," in Ingrid Pfeiffer and Max Hollein, eds., *James Ensor* (Frankfurt: Schirn Kunsthalle Frankfurt, and Ostfildern-Ruit: Hatje Cantz, 2005), pp. 108–13.
3. James Ensor, letter to Louis Delattre, August 4, 1898. In *James Ensor: Lettres*, ed. Xavier Tricot (Brussels: Éditions Labor, 1999), pp. 105–06.
4. Ensor, letter to Jules Du Jardin, October 28, 1899. In ibid., p. 275.
5. Ensor later denounced his early teachers: "I got a taste for painting when I was around thirteen; then two old Ostend painters, Van Cuyck and Dubar, brined and oiled, introduced me professorially to the disappointing commonplaces of their sad, narrow, still-born trade." Ensor, "Ma Vie en abrégé," 1934, in *Mes Écrits ou les suffisances matamoresques*, ed. Hugo Martin (rev. and enl. 6th ed. Brussels: Éditions Labor, 1999), p. 13. Translated from the French by David Frankel.
6. Ensor parodied his art-school experience in a short text published in *L'Art moderne* 4, no. 35 (August 31, 1884): pp. 285–86. Eng. trans. as "Three Weeks at the Academy" in Paul Haesaerts, *James Ensor*, trans. Norbert Guterman (New York: Harry N. Abrams, 1959), pp. 355–56. On Ensor's poor grades, see Norbert Hostyn, *Ensor: La Collection du Musée des Beaux-Arts d'Ostende* (Ghent and Amsterdam: Ludion, 1999), p. 32.
7. James Ensor, *Portrait of the Artist at His Easel* (*Portrait de l'artiste au chevalet*, 1879; private collection).
8. On Ensor's copying, see Herwig Todts, " 'Make Way for the Old Ones! Respect Defunct Schools!' Ensor and the Art-Historical Canon," in the present volume.
9. *Carton rose* is the term often used to refer to the small nature studies that Ensor painted on pink cardboard in the 1870s.
10. See Stephen C. McGough's insightful commentary on the deserted state of these streets in his *James Ensor's "The Entry of Christ into Brussels in 1889"*, 1981, Outstanding Dissertations in the Fine Arts (New York and London: Garland Publishing, 1985), pp. 99–110.
11. On tachism, see Robert Hoozee, "James Ensor's Visions of Nature," in the present volume, as well as his "Ensor and His Environment: Landscape, Interiors, Still Lifes, 1880–1887," in Carol Brown, ed., *James Ensor: 1860–1949. Theatre of Masks* (London: Barbican Art Gallery and Lund Humphries, 1997), pp. 18–26.
12. Ensor submitted the painting, originally titled *Au pays des couleurs*, to the Antwerp Salon (Société Royale pour l'Encouragement des Beaux-Arts, Salon d'Anvers) in 1882, then to L'Essor in Brussels in 1883; both rejected it. The work finally made its public debut at the annual exhibition of Les Vingt in 1886. See Verhaeren, *James Ensor*, pp. 37–38. For more on Ensor's refused canvases, see his letter to André de Ridder, September 30, 1928, in *James Ensor: Lettres*, pp. 194–99.
13. On Les Vingt, see Madeline Octave Maus, *Trente années de lutte pour l'art, 1884–1914* (Brussels: Librarie l'oiseau bleu, 1926), Susan M. Canning, "A History and Critical Review of the Salons of Les Vingt, 1884–1893" (PhD diss., Pennsylvania State University, 1980), and Jane Block, "Les XX and Belgian Avant-Gardism, 1868–1894" (PhD diss., University of Michigan, 1980).
14. Octave Maus, "Le Salon de Bruxelles, sixième article, la jeune école," *L'Art moderne* 41 (October 12, 1884): 330, and an unknown author writing in *L'Impartial de Gand*, 1886, quoted and trans. in Sabine Bown-Taevernier, "Self-Portrait with Flowered Hat," in Pfeiffer and Hollein, eds., *James Ensor*, p. 48.
15. Ensor, "Lumière une et indivisible," 1932, in Ensor, *Mes Écrits*, p. 252.
16. Ensor, letter to Pol de Mont, n.d. (late 1894–early 1895). In *James Ensor: Lettres*, p. 124.
17. The six works are *The Lively and Radiant: The Entry of Christ into Jerusalem* (*La Vive et rayonnante: L'Entrée à Jerusalem*, 1885; plate 27); *The Rising: Christ Shown to the People* (*La Crue: Jésus montré au peuple*, 1885; plate 26); *The Gay: The Adoration of the Shepherds* (*La Gaie: L'Adoration des bergers,* 1886; Musées royaux des Beaux-Arts de Belgique, Brussels); *The Intense: Christ Rising to the Sky* (*L'Intense: Le Christ montant au ciel*, 1886; private collection); *The Sad and Broken: Satan and His Fantastic Legions Torment the Crucified* (*La Triste et brisée: Satan et les légions fantastiques tourmentant le crucifié*, 1886; Musées royaux des Beaux-Arts

de Belgique, Brussels); and *The Tranquil and Serene: The Descent from the Cross* (*La Tranquille et sereine: La Descente de croix*, 1886; private collection, Belgium). On this series, see Gisèle Ollinger-Zinque, "Les Auréoles du Christ ou les sensibilités de la lumière de James Ensor," in *Bulletin des Musées royaux des Beaux-Arts de Belgique* 17, nos. 3–4 (1968): 191–202, and Auguste Taevernier, *Le Drame Ensorien: Les Auréoles du Christ ou les sensibilités de la lumière* (Ghent: Erasmus, 1976).

18. See Marcel De Maeyer's pioneering studies, "De mystieke dood van een godgeleerde van James Ensor," *Jaarboek van het Koninklijk Museum voor Schone Kunsten Antwerpen*, (1962–63): 131–58, and "De genese van masker-, travestie- en skeletmotieven in het oeuvre van James Ensor," *Bulletin des Musées royaux des Beaux-Arts de Belgique* 10 (1963): 69–88. See also Robert Hoozee, Sabine Bown-Taevernier, and Jan Frederik Heijbroek, *Ik James Ensor: Tekeningen en prenten* (Brussels: Ludion, 1987), pp. 40–41.
19. See Eric Gillis with the collaboration of Florizoone, *James Ensor: A Collection of Prints* (New York: C. G. Boerner, 2002), p. 29.
20. Florizoone, "James Ensor's Printers," in ibid., pp. 197–214.
21. See "James Ensor Graficus," in Hoozee, Bown-Taevernier, and Heijbroek, pp. 99–101, and Bown-Taevernier, "Les Eaux-fortes," in Lydia M. A. Schoonbaert et al., *James Ensor* (Paris: Musée du Petit Palais, 1990), pp. 61–66. The several catalogues raisonnés of Ensor's prints are listed in the bibliography in the present volume.
22. On *The Temptation of Saint Anthony*, see Canning, "The Devil's Mirror: Private Fantasy and Public Vision," in Catherine de Zegher, ed., *Between Street and Mirror: The Drawings of James Ensor* (New York: The Drawing Center, and Minneapolis: University of Minnesota Press, 2001), pp. 63–66.
23. Ensor, "Discours au Kursaal d'Ostende," 1931, *Mes Écrits*, p. 180.
24. Ensor exhibited alongside Odilon Redon in Les Vingt's exhibition of 1886. See Canning, "A History and Critical Review of the Salons of *Les Vingt*, 1884–1893," pp. 121–23.
25. For thorough examinations of this work, see Patricia G. Berman, *James Ensor: Christ's Entry into Brussels in 1889* (Los Angeles: J. Paul Getty Museum, 2002), McGough, *James Ensor's "The Entry of Christ into Brussels in 1889"*, and Walther Vanbeselaere, *L'Entrée du Christ à Bruxelles* (Brussels: Weissenbruch, 1957).
26. It should not be forgotten that Ensor began *Christ's Entry* shortly after his position in the avant-garde was dramatically changed by the reception of Seurat's manifesto painting *A Sunday Afternoon on La Grande Jatte–1884*. On the painting's reception, see Berman, *James Ensor*, pp. 45–48.
27. Ensor, "Discours au Kursaal d'Ostende," p. 180.
28. Todts, "Le Grotesque dans l'œuvre d'Ensor," in Schoonbaert et al., *James Ensor*, pp. 47–48.
29. *The Intrigue* has been interpreted as a disparaging comment on the short-lived relationship between Ensor's sister, Mitche, and a Chinese art dealer. This interpretation was first put forth in Libby Tannenbaum, *James Ensor* (New York: The Museum of Modern Art, 1951), p. 83. It is problematic, however, because the date of the painting, 1890, and its first exhibition with Les Vingt in February 1892 predate Mitche's marriage, in August 1892. The discrepancy is addressed in Diane Lesko, *James Ensor: The Creative Years* (Princeton: Princeton University Press, 1985), p. 16, Todts, "L'Intrigue," in Schoonbaert et al., *James Ensor*, pp. 196–97, and Michel Draguet, *James Ensor ou la fantasmagorie* (Paris: Gallimard, 1999), p. 159.
30. The French for "pickled herring" is *hareng saur*, which in pronunciation is very close to "art Ensor." The phrase "art Ensor" in turn appears in *The Dangerous Cooks* (*Les Cuisiniers dangereux*, 1896; plate 88), in which Ensor's head, a fish's tail applied to it, is served at a grotesque dinner attended by critics.
31. Verhaeren, *James Ensor*, pp. 6–7.
32. Tannenbaum, *James Ensor*, p. 115.
33. The manuscript for *La Gamme d'amour* describes it as a one-act "Ballet-pantomime" in two tableaux. Set during Carnival in a shop filled with masks and puppets, the first scenes deal with the lovers Fifrelin and Miama, who are kept apart by their quarreling families. By the end of the first tableau a happy resolution is found and marriage is promised between the two, so that the entirety of the second tableau may be devoted to a festive wedding march in the town square. Ensor wrote the work between 1906 and 1911. An early part of it, featuring a waltz, was performed publicly on August 3, 1907, at the Kursaal in Ostend. The first full performance of the musical score took place on January 17, 1920, in celebration of Ensor's exhibition at the Galerie Georges Giroux, Brussels, and the full ballet premiered at the Antwerp Opera on March 27, 1924. On Ensor's interest in music, see Robert Wangermée, "*La Gamme d'amour* et la musique d'Ensor," in Pierre Alechinsky et al., *Ensor* (Brussels: Musées royaux des Beaux-Arts de Belgique, and Tournai: La Renaissance du livre, 1999), pp. 54–62.

James Ensor: Carnival of the Modern

SUSAN M. CANNING

James Ensor created the painting for which he is best known, *Christ's Entry into Brussels in 1889* (*L'Entrée du Christ à Bruxelles en 1889*; fig. 1),[1] when he was only twenty-eight years old. Portraying himself as Christ on a donkey parading down a broad boulevard in the midst of Carnival, Ensor announces in this work his own grand entry into Brussels. Intended for exhibition at the 1889 salon of Les Vingt (Les XX), the avant-garde Brussels exhibition society he had cofounded in 1883, this painting would serve as an ample demonstration of Ensor's role as a painter of modern life with both a social consciousness and a sizable ambition. Startlingly personal yet expressively direct in technique and color application, this satirical indictment of contemporary Belgian society immerses its viewing public in the spectacle and artifice of modern experience.

Modern life coexists with carnival travesty in this work. Allusions to theater and the sideshow abound, from the proscenium arch that frames this panorama to the burlesque of costumed and grotesquely masked figures—some caricatures of social types—that enter from the wings, competing for attention and space. Unmixed colors and strong contrasts suggestive of makeup and harsh stage lighting transform Ensor's observation of a contemporary event associated with socialist demonstrations, joyous entries of kings, and carnival parades into a performative farce intent upon provoking reaction and applause.

Along the top of the painting, a banner proclaims "Vive la sociale" (Long live the social [one]), boldly stating Ensor's resolutely contemporary agenda. Although the painting is situated in downtown Brussels, the immense urban space Ensor describes, with its cacophonous clutter of flags, signs, and banners, could pass for any large modern city. The spectator is thrust into a vast urban milieu and seemingly endless gathering of humanity. Marching bands and masked revelers fill the pictorial space, their movement and density embodying both the enticing energy of the crowd celebrated by Charles Baudelaire and the claustrophobia and foreboding fear of the lower classes articulated by sociologist Gustave Le Bon.[2] This spectacular experience is so immediate and overwhelming that the artifice of its representation seems almost natural. Melding street and stage, reality and imagination, social activism and visionary spectacle, Ensor constructs in *Christ's Entry into Brussels in 1889* (hereafter referred to as *Christ's Entry*) a theater of artifice where he performs his personal, witty, satiric, and critical appraisal of contemporary life. With its fluid dialogue between observation and subjectivity, grotesque exaggeration and parodic inversion, theatrical staging and performative self-fashioning, the painting serves up a carnival of the modern for all to see.

A Manet of Belgium

It was natural for Ensor to choose Brussels as the location for his and Christ's triumphal entry: it was in this capital city that he discovered modernist theory, then allied with Realist painting and naturalist writing, and came in contact with a lively community

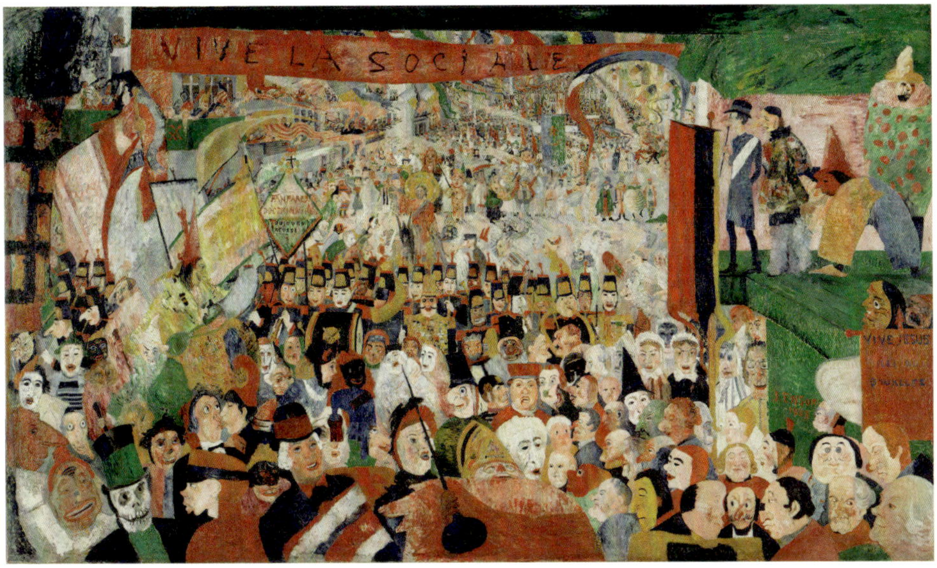

FIG. 1: JAMES ENSOR. *Christ's Entry into Brussels in 1889*. 1888. Oil on canvas, 8' 3 7/16 × 14' 1 1/2" (252.5 × 430.5 cm). The J. Paul Getty Museum, Los Angeles

FIG. 2: JAMES ENSOR. *Mariette Rousseau at the Microscope*. 1889. Black chalk on paper, mounted on panel, 9 5/8 × 7 7/16" (24.5 × 18.8 cm). Private collection

of artists, writers, scientists, and political thinkers involved with understanding how art, nationalism, science, and identity define modern experience. Responding to this stimulating environment, with its eclectic mix of influences and relationships, Ensor fashioned an artistic identity and manner of working that proclaimed his ambition to be in his country what Édouard Manet was in France: a painter of modern life. Ensor's atmospheric views of the North Sea and of the sky over the rooftops of Brussels and Ostend; images of bustling city streets, laborers, middle-class salons; intimate portraits of his family and friends; and expressively direct self-portraits, all mingling observation with subjective interpretation, left little doubt as to the painter's commitment to representing both the timely and the transcendent in his contemporary milieu.

Although associated in nineteenth-century Belgium with anti-authoritarianism, leftist politics, and social critique, by 1878—the year of Gustave Courbet's death—Realist practice had made its way into the curriculum at the Académie royale des beaux-arts in Brussels, where Ensor was in his second year.[3] As a young art student, Ensor was drawn to Realism, with its emphasis on direct observation and loose, gestural technique, and to the paintings of Courbet and Manet, whose work and portraits he copied into his sketchbook.[4] Ensor's friends and artistic contacts in Brussels encouraged his interest in Realism. The artist, critic, poet, and playwright Théo Hannon[5] shared essays written by Camille Lemonnier for the critical journal *L'Artiste*[6] and invited Ensor to exhibit at the artists' collective La Chrysalide.[7] Ensor's own evocative views of Ostend, Brussels, and the North Sea, painted in the late 1870s and early 1880s, reflect his exploration of Belgian Realism, especially his use of local imagery and atmospheric effects developed through both brush and palette knife.

Hannon also introduced Ensor to his brother Edouard;[8] his sister, Mariette, an amateur mycologist (whom Ensor later drew sitting at her microscope; fig. 2); her husband, scientist and academician Ernest Rousseau, and their son Ernest Jr. The Rousseaus, part of a progressive circle of scientists and politicians centered in Brussels around the Université Libre, were known for their weekly salons filled with lively discussion and debate, a heady atmosphere that Ensor poked fun of in a painting in which he pictured himself challenging General Gérard Leman to a mock duel, with Mariette Rousseau as referee (plate 71). Other frequent guests included the future leftist parliamentarian Hector Denis, the anarchist/geographer Élisée Reclus and his brother Élie (their sister, Louise Reclus-Dumesnil, was Mariette's best friend), as well as the writers Lemonnier and Eugène Demolder (plate 86) and the socialist lawyer and playwright Edmond Picard. The Rousseau-Hannon clan became Ensor's second family, providing him personal support and patronage and a place to stay whenever he visited Brussels. Through their salons he encountered a stimulating alliance of positivism, science, socialism, and politics that would radicalize his art practice throughout the 1880s.

Ensor's association with Les Vingt also reinforced his ties with Belgian modernism.[9] From the time of their first salon in 1884, Les Vingt promoted themselves as a revolutionary artists' society, "carriers of the new" who joined modernist theory with social activism. For many, Ensor epitomized the group's radical anarchist orientation. He was, as one critic sarcastically noted, "the giant of Les Vingt, the Rubens of Modernity, the chief of our Neo-Painters, the Atlas,"[10] an identification that Ensor embraced in his self-depictions *Self-Portrait with a Flowered Hat* (*Mon Portrait déguisé*, 1883/1888; plate 17) and *My Portrait* (*Mon Portrait*, 1884; plate 18).

The group's avant-garde posture was due in no small part to the promotional efforts of *L'Art moderne* and its editors, Octave Maus (also Les Vingt's secretary) and Picard, and of the writer and critic Émile Verhaeren, who joined the journal's staff in 1885.[11] Yet as Les Vingt grew in importance and gained international prestige with its salons, Ensor's influence within the group diminished, especially after 1887, when a number of its members (including Ensor's close friend Willy Finch [plate 13]) began to turn toward Neo-Impressionist techniques. Ensor signaled his disaffection for Les Vingt by slyly incorporating the group's emblem into a number of works; in *Christ's Entry*, for example, on a balcony not far from his self-portrait as Christ, two masked revelers defecate and vomit on Les Vingt's double-X insignia. *The Dangerous Cooks* (*Les Cuisiniers dangereux*, 1896; plate 88) also satirizes this power struggle within Les Vingt; here, Ensor portrays Picard and Maus—who viewed themselves as impresarios of modern Belgian art—as cooks serving up Ensor (his head on a platter like that of John the Baptist) and his colleagues as culinary delicacies that will surely fail to satisfy the hungry critics in the background.

Despite this ill will, Les Vingt proved an important association for Ensor, allying him with Belgian modernism and providing a highly visible venue through which to exhibit and sell work. Les Vingt also taught Ensor about self-promotion and the power of subversion, lessons that he assimilated into his art practice. In 1888, the year of the group's fifth anniversary, for example, Les Vingt showed its solidarity with anarcho-socialism by hanging a red banner at the entrance to its salon and printing its catalogue with a red cover; in the same year, Ensor included a red banner across the top of *Christ's Entry*.[12]

Whether it was directed at Maus, other Vingtists, or Belgian society, Ensor's antagonism toward his contemporary milieu only bolstered his emerging identity as a modern Belgian painter with an individualistic and increasingly anarchistic vision. Indeed, from the very beginning of his career, Ensor seemed intent upon engaging the Belgian public in a direct and often contrary conversation about their lives, values, and mores, even as he demonstrated his precocious talents. Drawn initially from the Realist notion of temperament and fortified by the anarchist espousal of individual action, Ensor's peculiar perspective on his contemporary Belgian life would eventually become the basis for his unique staging of modernist experience in *Christ's Entry*.

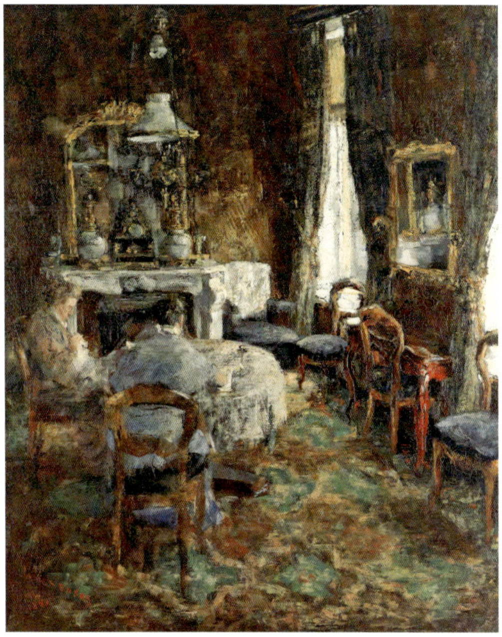

FIG. 3: JAMES ENSOR. *The Bourgeois Salon* (*A Salon* [*Impression*]). 1881. Oil on canvas, 52 3/8 × 42 5/16" (133 × 109 cm). Koninklijk Museum voor Schone Kunsten, Antwerp

The Drunkards (*Les Pochards*, 1883; plate 14), an early Realist-oriented work, focuses on a pressing social issue of the time: alcoholism among the lower classes. For many physicians of the day, alcoholism was a "social disease"—like syphilis or tuberculosis—associated with degeneracy and a progressive morbid pathology. Passed from generation to generation, alcoholism led, it was believed, to criminality, perverse behavior, insanity, and more broadly to the moral decline of the nation.[13] Ensor's painting, however, presents an objective report of working-class men in the throes of alcohol abuse and social alienation—a view that the artist tempered with a certain ambivalence drawn from his own background among the petite bourgeoisie (a group that had only recently reached middle-class status and were often fearful of slipping back). Made only a few years after the Ensor family's bankruptcy and four years before his father's death (probably of alcohol-related causes), *The Drunkards* contains a private reference—the bankruptcy notices in the background—that subtly melds Ensor's own experience of class and alcoholism into a perspective quite different from the moralistic views of his contemporaries.[14]

If at times Ensor's treatment of working-class subjects in his paintings and drawings seems awkward and distanced, his interior views, made in the same period, convey a sense of intimacy and familiarity. These scenes, made in the homes of the artist's family members and friends, explore the bourgeois salon, a setting that was relatively rarely depicted, but one that mirrored the private life experiences of Ensor's mainly middle-class audience. Interiors such as *Chez Miss* (*Russian Music*) (*La Musique russe*, 1881; p. 98, fig. 6), *The Bourgeois Salon* (*A Salon* [*Impression*]) (*Le Salon bourgeois*; fig. 3), *Afternoon in Ostend* (*L'Après-dînée à Ostende*, 1881; plate 9), and *The Oyster Eater* (*La Mangeuese d'huîtres*, 1882; plate 13), with their filtered light, thick drapes, and patterned carpets, provide a graceful inventory of all the material possessions, refined taste, and calm ambiance that bourgeois life could offer.

Many of these interiors investigate the rituals and everyday activities that demarcated the experience and social space of middle-class women of the day. Focusing upon a table as the site for daily activities (sewing, afternoon tea, a meal) and a specific time of day (the afternoon, perhaps), in these bourgeois salons, ambivalence mixes with artifice to suggest the tension, boredom, and disappointment that hover just below the surface materialism of middle-class life. Probing the psychological reality of these women's lives in a way seldom seen at this time, Ensor depicts the protocol and constraints that circumscribe their quotidian reality. Accommodating both a private world of apparent comfort and security and the more public display of propriety and social decorum, these quiet interiors inquire as to the nature of modern experience amid the intersecting discourses of class and gender.

The Soul of Things

The material things that accumulated in these bourgeois salons fill page upon page of Ensor's sketchbooks. Recycling older drawings, around 1886 he began adding new images or odd juxtapositions that mingle careful observation with imaginative fantasy, forming a generative process of free association and play that reveals the subjective, expressive meaning—"the soul of things"[15]—within everyday life. At the same time, this inventory of the familiar—lamps, armoires, vases, umbrellas, clocks, pitchers, candleholders, curtain tassels, mirrors, fireplaces—ties Ensor to this particular place, delineating his social identity.

As if to affirm this symbiotic relationship, Ensor at times inserts into the scene his own distinct, often comfortable, and sometimes contrary presence, in the form of a self-portrait among the furniture and bibelots of the family salon. Such is the case in *My Sad and Splendid Portrait* (*Mon Portrait* [*Le Peintre triste et somptueux*], 1886; p. 115, fig. 1), in which Ensor's head materializes from within a carefully rendered cabinet, or in *The Haunted Fireplace* (*La Cheminée hantée*, 1888; plate 48), in which his face emerges from the mirror above the family hearth. In the latter, his mother and sister, seated below, seem unaware of the artist's spectral presence, and Ensor does not look down at them but rather outward, his gaze engaging the spectator and the world beyond the frame. These drawings give form to the observed social spaces that exist simultaneously as the artist's subjectivity, thereby investing the fractured moments of Ensor's experience with both social and personal significance. In the course of this invention, Ensor fashions a self-representation and practice based upon process and performance—a continuum of looking and making that acknowledges the particular and relative experience of time while dismantling all notions of what constitutes observable reality.

Circumscribing his identity within the quotidian milieu, Ensor affirms his participation in the sphere of Belgium's capitalist society, even as the insistent note of his individualism interrupts the flow of daily middle-class life. The bonds between Ensor and his social space also suggest his engagement with current discussions on the complex nature of personal vision and subjectivity. Both Realist theory and the emerging disciplines of psychology and Freudian psychoanalysis were advancing the idea of modern experience as increasingly neurotic and in need of expressive representation. As the concept of "selfhood" and subjectivity began to take hold of the bourgeois imagination in the later part of the century, the realization that the personal space of "interiority" was just as real as the "observable" exterior world of everyday life inspired novelists, playwrights, architects, and artists such as Ensor.[16] Underscoring the new subjectivity, artists explored this contested space of the personal in "expressive interiors," where the limits and nature of identity merge with public life.[17]

Whereas the Realists and the Impressionists discovered their subjects in the social environment and in the external world of phenomena, the emerging Symbolist aesthetic drew more from internal experience, striving to make visible what the Symbolists termed "the inner Ideal." Even though, like the Impressionists, the Symbolists based their practice on rendering an interior state material and visible, they viewed the Impressionists' objectives as overly materialistic in comparison to their own more deeply emotional and internalized goals. With the shift of interpretation from Impressionist "descriptiveness" to Symbolist idealism, the social responsibility of the artist, implicit in the everyday commerce of the self within the world, became even more subsumed within individual expression. Following his own path through modernist theory from Impressionism to Symbolism, Ensor discovered in the material world of things and the private spaces of the interior both an expressive agency and a social role for his subjectivity.

The Social Allegory of Light

Ensor's sensitive observations of bourgeois life were one vehicle with which he could articulate his emerging social vision; allegory was another. Following a process of subjective intervention similar to that in his drawings, in 1885 Ensor began revising a work originally made some five years earlier at the Académie, *The Mystic Death of a Theologian* (*Elated Monks Claim the Body of Theologian Sus Ovis, in Spite of the Resisting Bishop Friton or Friston*) (*La Mort mystique d'un théologien* [*Moines exaltés réclamant le corps du Théologien Sus-Ovis malgré l'opposition de l'évêque Friton ou Friston*], 1880/1885–86[?]; plate 22).[18] Adding figures, architectural detail, and another drawing, Ensor created a scene of feverish devotion derived neither from the Bible nor from any other religious text. Yet even with its mysterious ambiance and intricate, hard-to-decipher detail, *The Mystic Death of a Theologian* leaves little doubt as to Ensor's mastery of academic quotation, skill at organizing complex composition, and ability to fill this invented world with an almost palpable sense of atmospheric light. Shimmering, flickering, forming into diaphanous shafts, or melting into a dramatic, smoky chiaroscuro, light consolidates the narrative into an evocative, visceral whole, lending a materiality to this esoteric scene that aligns it with current research on perception and discussions of the role of religion and spirituality in modern experience.

Distinguished by their subtle tonalities and sensitive evocations of the sky and the North Sea, Ensor's early marine landscapes and rooftop views of Brussels and Ostend, along with the ecstatic color harmonies of his large-format landscapes, all testify to his interest in light. For Ensor, light signified modernity in all its aspects.[19] As Eugène Demolder noted in the first published monograph on the artist, light was a language that allowed Ensor's work to be representational and allegorical: "It is this light that lends *signification* and life to things."[20] Eventually light becomes the means for Ensor to describe both the physical world as the embodiment of feeling and emotion, and the inner world of private experience, paralleling what contemporary scientists were discovering in their investigations into perception and vision.[21]

Drawing was a particularly fertile and experimental arena in which Ensor could explore the perceptual, evocative, and symbolic potential of light. When he began working on a series of modern religious allegories based on the story of Christ but intended for contemporary audiences, he decided to create large-scale drawings. He assigned these the collective title Visions: The Aureoles of Christ or the Sensibilities of Light (Visions: Les Auréoles du Christ ou les sensibilités de la lumière; plates 26 and 27).[22]

By the late nineteenth century, religious-themed allegories were regularly on view at official salons, as artists gave voice to current battles between Liberal and Catholic ideology. Belgium, a constitutional monarchy and predominantly Catholic in population, had struggled throughout the last quarter of the century to find a balance between religion and secularism. The right-leaning conservatives and clerics of the Catholic party, who controlled the government throughout the 1880s, the period during which Ensor was creating both religious allegories and his most politically engaged work, promoted obeisance to the pope and jurisdiction over education. The Liberal party, based in Enlightenment principles of individualism and rationalism, included left-leaning Progressives (who supported free, non-religious education and universal suffrage) and more reactionary Doctrinaires. The Socialist-oriented België Werkliedenpartij/Parti Ouvrier Belge (Belgian workers party [BWP]), formed in 1885, joined with the Progressives to advocate for voting rights and better working conditions. Through mass demonstrations and strikes, culminating in a general strike in 1893, they succeeded in extending the right to vote with the first Socialists elected to the Belgian parliament in 1894. By the late 1880s King Leopold II, whose colonialist exploits in the Congo had been supported by the Catholics, also emerged as a dominant political figure.[23]

The struggles of the workers and the resonance of religion in contemporary Belgium were certainly evident in the first drawing from Ensor's Aureoles series, *The Lively and Radiant: The Entry of Christ into Jerusalem* (*La Vive et rayonnante: L'Entrée à Jérusalem*, 1885; plate 27) (hereafter referred to as *The Entry of Christ into Jerusalem*). On the scale of a history painting, the drawing presents the New Testament story of Christ entering Jerusalem as a modern event taking place in a teeming commercial metropolis not unlike Brussels. A massive street demonstration presses forward, led by the positivist theorist Émile Littré, whose portrait head Ensor has collaged in the foreground (p. 21, fig. 6). Littré had pointedly associated Christ with a progressive Socialist discourse, adding his own contribution to current arguments over Christ's human nature and role as a social reformer.[24] The marchers, mostly workers, some with "Jesus" written on their foreheads or hats and others who wave placards with Socialist slogans, reaffirm the modern meaning of this biblical narrative.[25] Simulating the claustrophobic crush of the crowd and evoking the urban street with its tangle of colloquialism, commercialism, and Socialist invective, Ensor dramatically confronted the Belgian public who saw *The Entry of Christ into Jerusalem* at Les Vingt in 1887 with the contemporary significance of religion, Christ, and social activism to Belgian life and politics.

Drawing upon these progressive ideas, with their emphasis on Christ's social purpose, Ensor presents in *The Entry of Christ into Jerusalem*, and the other works in the Aureoles series, his distinctly personal interpretation of Christ's very public life, death, and resurrection. While these drawings explore the relevance of Christ's life to modern experience, they also continue Ensor's investigation of perception and light as aspects of sight and subjectivity. The spiritual narrative of Christ's life is affiliated here with both the "sensibilities" of natural light and a range of emotional states. *The Entry of Christ into Jerusalem* is thus "alive and radiant" with feeling while in other drawings (as likewise articulated in their individual titles) the ambiance is "gay," "raw," "sad and broken," "tranquil and serene," and "intense."[26] Serving as both a metaphor for Christ's spiritual and social mission and the embodiment of Ensor's own range of emotive possibilities, light operates in these drawings as a duality of sacred and profane, individual and collective, interpretive and observational, representational and symbolic. Light and vision coalesce in the Aureoles series into a mode in which Ensor reveals the engaged and increasingly performative role of his subjectivity.

Pierrot in the Theater of Artifice

Performance and theatricality are certainly evident in *Calvary* (*Calvaire*, 1886; plate 29). Drawn around the same time as the Aureoles series, *Calvary* is Ensor's first self-portrait as Christ. Replacing the traditional inscription, INRI ("Iesus Nazarenus Rex Iudaeorum": the mocking "Hail Jesus, King of the Jews"), with his own name, Ensor here "publicizes" his performance as Christ. With a halo around his thorn-crowned head, and the sky swirling with exuberant and colorful arabesque lines, Ensor stands on the cross with arms raised—a motif that links this self-portrait with leftist associations of Christ's crucifixion with martyrdom, unjust persecution, and resistance.[27] Lines that suggest rays of light further emphasize the artist's bright essence while plunging the foreground figures, including a man with the emblem of Les Vingt on his back, into darkness.

This alliance of Christ and Ensor with light, modernism, and social activism continues in *Christ's Entry*, in which the halo behind Ensor/Christ on the donkey is now a yellow sun and contemporary experience has been transformed into a grand theatrical procession of parody and grotesque inversion. Immersing his audience in this spectacle produced by his imaginative subjectivity, Ensor presents/performs his subversive critique of modern life and values.

Similar connections among presentation, masquerade, and performance are found in the improvisatory roles and comedic theater scenarios of the commedia dell'arte tradition that inspired Ensor. Thus in *Christ's Entry*, Ensor casts himself as Pierrot: wearing a yellow costume and tall red hat, he can be seen in profile facing Christ (fig. 4).[28] Now Ensor becomes part of the spectacle, linked with the crowd around him as well as with the parade, with its mixture of public performance and burlesque sideshow.

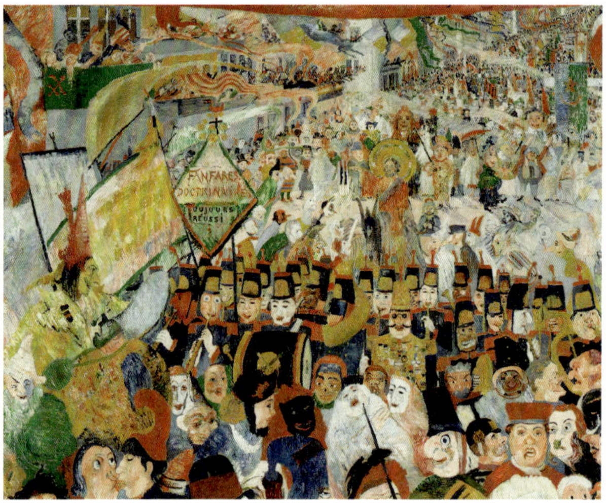

FIG. 4: JAMES ENSOR. *Christ's Entry into Brussels in 1889* (detail). 1888 (see fig. 1)

Ensor's self-fashioning performances as Christ and Pierrot reflect an enthusiasm for theater that began early in the artist's life. The annual Carnival celebration, with its parodic inversion of social codes and accent on excess, the bawdry puns and silly pratfalls of traveling vaudeville acts, and even his grandmother's eccentric penchant for dressing up in strange costumes[29] all nourished Ensor's appreciation for farce and disguise. Drawings of clowns, burlesque performers, and caricatures of African dancers animate a sketchbook owned by Ensor's friend Mariette Rousseau (plate 16), and numerous sketches of stage sets, costumes, and actors allude to regular attendance at theater performances—including no doubt the topical plays and revues for cabaret theater written by Ensor's friend Théo Hannon and presented at such popular venues as the Alcazar and Alhambra.[30]

Several years later Ensor would produce his own theater piece—a "flirt" for marionettes titled *La Gamme d'amour*; but even in this initial period, many of his paintings contain theatrical elements, including dramatic lighting and boxy, stagelike compositions. Through the years he included increasing numbers of costumes, props, masks, and puppet figures that move his work away from naturalist description as the pictorial space becomes an arena for subjective conjuring and performance. One of the earliest of these staged farces, *The Scandalized Masks* (*Les Masques scandalisés*, 1883; plate 15), replaces the family parlor and tavern setting with a dramatically lit but generic interior (most likely a corner of his own attic studio). Around a table, a clearly confrontational meeting is taking place between two lower-class types: a man with a top hat and woman holding a flute like a club. The disruptive combination of carnivalesque[31] masquerade, stark theatrical lighting, and strong shadows undermines any pretext that this might be a description of a real event. Focusing the audience's attention on this frozen moment—potent with interpretive possibilities and intimating travesty, social alienation, alcoholism, even violence—Ensor supplants anecdotal description with a broader, more psychological drama, staged for maximum pictorial effect.

Although the masks clearly added drama and mystery to the narrative of *The Scandalized Masks*, it was not until 1888, as he was working on *The Astonishment of the Mask Wouse* (*Étonnement du masque Wouse*, 1889; plate 56) and *Christ's Entry*, that Ensor began appending masks, skeletons, and other fantastic elements to earlier paintings.[32] In a period when phrenologists were interpreting the descriptive details of appearance as indicative of temperament, illness, and even moral decay, the mask, with its potential to conceal, its ties to popular entertainment and satire, and its capacity to unite naturalist description with symbolic form, proved the perfect vehicle for Ensor's expressive intent. Masks, along with skeletons, Pierrots, clowns, and puppets, were also prominently utilized in satirical journals of both conservative and liberal persuasion as figurative tools to ridicule Belgium's ruling order. An illustration from the anarchist journal *La Bombe* (fig. 5), for example, uses grotesque masks associated with Carnival to mock the legitimacy of religious and political figures, linking pretension and hypocrisy to contemporary politics in a manner similar to the masked paraders in the foreground of *Christ's Entry*.[33]

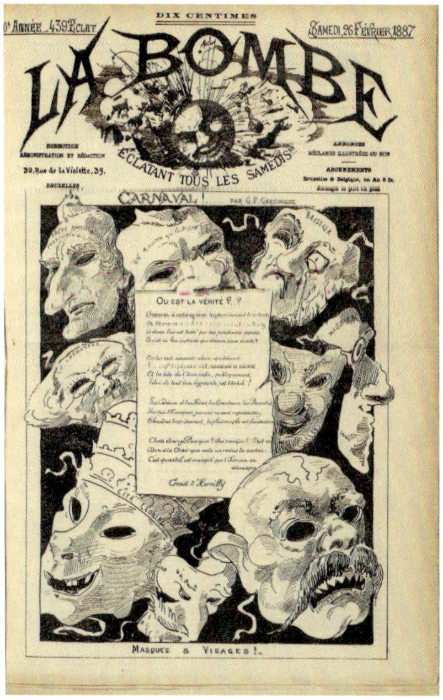

FIG. 5: G. P. GARGOUSSE. "Carnaval! Masques et Visages!" Cover illustration for *La Bombe,* February 26, 1887. Bibliothèque royale de Belgique, Brussels

The Scandalized Masks and Ensor's other works with stagelike spaces also call to mind the theatrical tableaux (sometimes with live models) of historical and current events in wax museums, and the panoramas and dioramas commonly found at fairs and expositions (such as the 1878 Exposition universelle in Paris, which Ensor may have attended), and museums such as the Institut royal des Sciences naturelles near the Rousseau home in Brussels. Playing to the prurience of the masses, these popular displays transformed history into an easily digestible commodity, one that naturalized and democratized modern experience while turning it into a spectacle of the continuously present.[34] In a similar fashion, Ensor's staged compositions authenticated the spectator's perspective, providing what seemed like an intimate view into what was in fact arranged artifice. Divesting realism of its mimetic, descriptive edge and constructing instead a personal scenario out of still-life materials, skulls, and masks, and making use of mordant humor and grotesque or absurd exaggeration, Ensor invests this simulated world with personal, expressive, and symbolic meaning even as he comments on social issues and contemporary life.

While Ensor had recruited working folk and members of his own family to pose for his Realist depictions of contemporary Belgian life, in *The Astonishment of the Mask Wouse* and *Skeletons Trying to Warm Themselves* (*Squelettes voulant se chauffer*, 1889; plate 54) the models are propped-up, puppetlike figures with masked or skeleton heads. Although it is not known when Ensor first saw puppet theater, he undoubtedly witnessed *guignols* in Ostend and visited the popular Théâtre royale de Toone marionette playhouse in Brussels. By the 1880s puppet shows had become a popular form of entertainment, especially among the working classes.[35] Filled with puns and wordplay, these improvisational plays mixed historical or religious narratives with contemporary references, much to the delight of their (often mostly illiterate) audiences. Ensor would certainly have been drawn to these plays, with their base scatological humor, hearty and subversive patter delivered in dialect and slang, and potential for political and social satire that frequently made fun of middle-class pretentiousness.

Puppet theater also appealed to Belgian playwrights Edmond Picard, Charles Van Lerberghe, and Maurice Maeterlinck, each of whom wrote a drama for puppets. They discovered in these plays a hybrid form, between a reading and a theatrical presentation, that moved beyond naturalism to a more universal and symbolic representation of ideas. The marionettes' essential and hieratic gestures gave voice to both subjectivity and expressive form. As Paul Margueritte, a playwright and author of the time, remarked: "Impersonal puppets, beings of wood and cardboard, possess a pure and

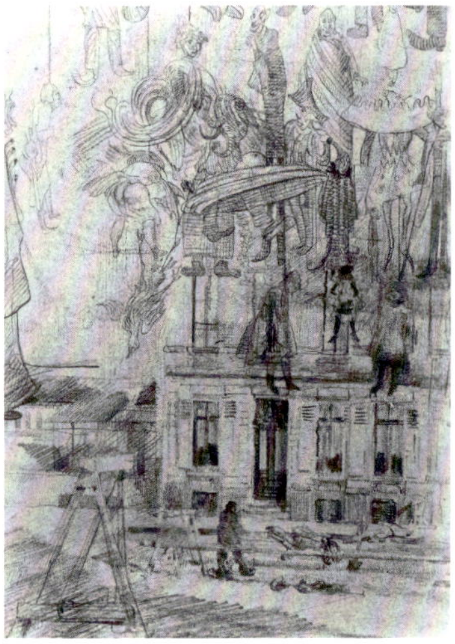

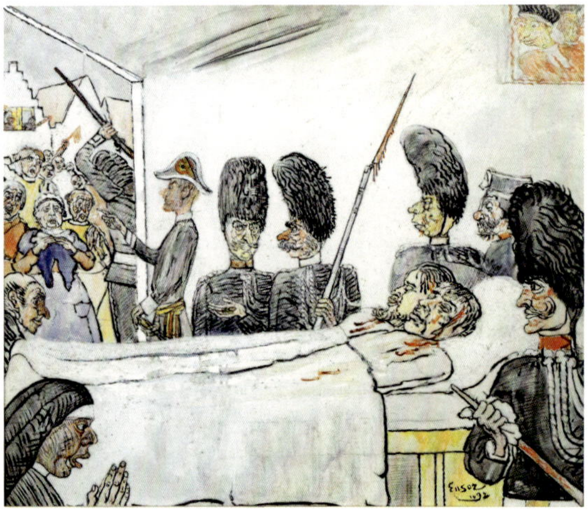

FIG. 6: JAMES ENSOR. *House with Puppets*. c. 1880–85/1886–88. Black crayon on paper, mounted on board, 8 7/8 × 6 1/2" (22.5 × 16.5 cm). Location unknown

FIG. 7: JAMES ENSOR. *The Gendarmes*. 1892. Oil on panel, 17 11/16 × 21 5/8" (45 × 55 cm). Kunstmuseum aan zee, Ostend. Collection City of Ostend

mysterious life. Their aspect of truth catches us unawares, disquiets. Their elemental gestures contain the complete expression of human feelings."[36] Ensor's *House with Puppets* (*Maison et marionettes*; fig. 6), a drawing of a street and building façades, evokes a familiar scene from puppet theater: a dangling array of rod puppets awaiting the puppeteer's hand and voice. Set apart from the street scene below, the stiff rods allude to the puppet's crude and bumbling movements and the contrived nature of the show. Indeed, posing and manipulating puppetlike figures in the theatrical artifice of his paintings, Ensor became a kind of puppet master in his own right, presenting to the public his particular and often satirical perspective on modern experience.

Masks, puppets, and skeletons, as well as silhouettes and Pierrot figures all link Ensor to *fumisme*[37] (called *zwanze* in Belgium), a popular, performance-based satire found in street puppet-theater, artistic cafés, and burlesque reviews.[38] Characterized by skepticism, critique, and black humor, intent on undercutting social pretense and pomposity, and at times associated with anarchism, the *zwanze* spirit intended to "cut open the smug sky under which we live."[39] *Zwanzism* appealed to Ensor's own sense of subversive play and its spirit finds its way into much of his art practice, especially in self-portraits and satirical works focusing on contemporary political and social issues. Indeed, his most politicized images were infused with *zwanzist* spirit—among them *Belgium in the Nineteenth Century* (*La Belgique au XIXe siècle*, 1889; plate 52); *The Strike* (*The Slaughter of the Ostend Fisherman [August 1887]*) (*Massacre des pêcheurs ostendais [août 1887]*), 1888; plate 43); the etching *Doctrinaire Nourishment* (*Alimentation doctrinaire*, 1889; plate 51); *The Wise Judges* (*Les Bons Juges*, 1891; plate 78); and *The Gendarmes* (fig. 7); as well as his broader social satires such as *Plague Above, Plague Below, Plague All Around!* (*Peste dessous, peste dessus, peste partout!*, 1888; plate 44); *The Bad Doctors* (*Les Mauvais Médecins*, 1892; plate 79); and *The Baths at Ostend* (*Les Bains à Ostende*, 1890; plate 64). All these works deploy grotesque exaggeration, base humor, and carnivalesque inversion to make their point. With themes drawn from folk tradition, satirical journals, *actualités*, and burlesque theater, these pieces make Ensor's radical individualism and political perspective patently clear. How could his audience fail to see the double entendres of image and text in *Doctrinaire Nourishment* or in *Belgium in the Nineteenth Century*? In both works scatology, caricature, and argot mingle with contemporary social debates to comment scathingly upon both the adulation and public humiliation inherent in the Belgian status quo, as held in place by King Leopold II.[40] Coaxing the verbal into collusion with the visual, Ensor thus undermines

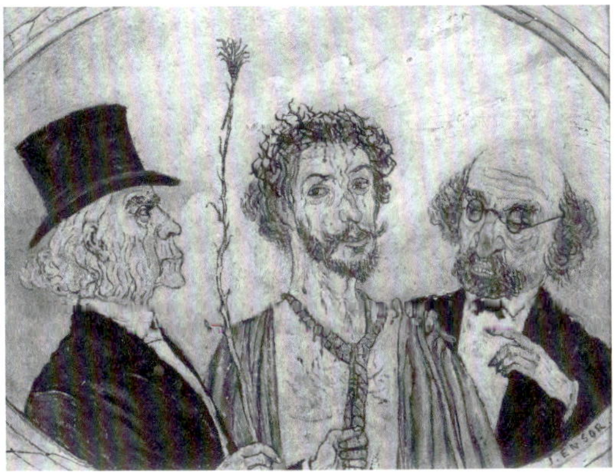

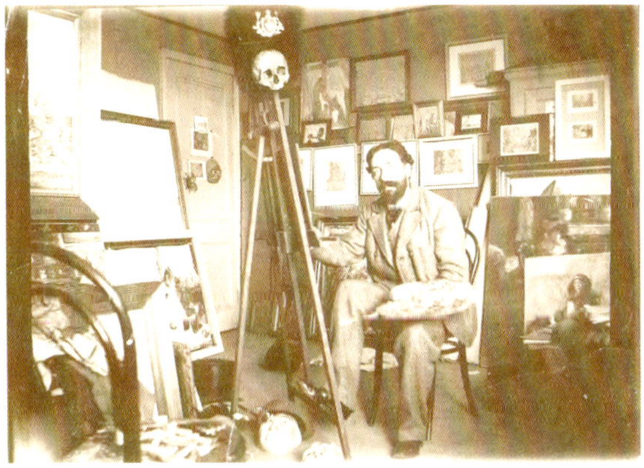

FIG. 8: JAMES ENSOR. *Ecce Homo* (*Christ and the Critics*). 1891. Oil on panel, 4 3/4 × 6 5/16" (12 × 16 cm). Succession — Estate Mme. Marteaux, Brussels

FIG. 9: James Ensor in his attic studio. Ostend, c. 1896

one discourse — that of the ruling political and artistic order — by juxtaposing it with a viable alternative drawn from the rhetoric of the street and popular culture, as well as with his own radicalized subjectivity.

But it was in his self-portraits that Ensor most directly voiced his irreverent and satiric spirit while divulging the influence of theater and popular culture on his work. Like an actor on his own artistic stage, Ensor assigns himself a variety of identities — some overt and some more disguised — each of which empowers him and his subjectivity while simultaneously reflecting back upon his contentious relationship with his contemporary world. As Christ, he is tormented by critics, crucified, or prayed over by angels. In other works, Ensor deploys surrogates: he is Pierrot or a skeleton, an insect or a fish (specifically a pickled herring, or *hareng saur*, a wordplay on "art Ensor"), or even — as in *The Pisser* (*Le Pisseur*, 1887; plate 42) — a fool. He cross-dresses as a woman and is surrounded by demons. Each masquerade speaks publicly to the artist's belief in his own importance as well as his desire to be respected by his contemporaries (see fig. 8 and plates 28, 29, 39, 41, 58, 75, 76, 80, and 88).

The Skeleton Painter (*Squelette peintre*, 1895 or 1896[?]; plate 89), serves as an apt summary of this self-fashioning strategy. Wearing a blue suit and with a skull for a head, Ensor stands at his easel, surrounded by his own paintings. Although he based this work on an undated photograph (fig. 9), Ensor changed his pose from sitting to standing to emphasize his presence. Leaning forward, the leering skeleton painter thrusts himself toward the viewer. The paintbrush also figures prominently: protruding like a bouquet from both a jacket pocket and his groin, the brush is associated with Ensor's artistic productivity and sexual prowess. Armed with brush, easel, and palette, and surrounded by an inventory of his own creations and social critiques, Ensor as the skeleton painter stands ready for his performance on this studio-stage of modern life.

In *Self-Portrait with Masks* (*Ensor aux masques*, 1899; plate 91) Ensor completely surrenders to travesty. With red-lipstick mouths parted and vacuous, doll-like eyes, a burlesque crowd presses toward the viewer. Some in the crowd wear masks; others have such exaggerated features and heavy makeup that their faces can hardly be distinguished from those of their masked neighbors. Even with careful modeling and scintillating color and light, an oppressive air spreads over this accumulation of grotesque visages as they cram themselves into the foreground plane. The somber and suffocating mood is reinforced by the presence of several skulls in the background. Immersed in the multitude, the likeness of Ensor himself is but one more participant in this parade of artifice. Intermingling his own image with the masked figures that nearly engulf him, the artist questions the very notion of portraiture as an act of self-conscious revelation. Portraying himself as a young artist—indeed, in the same pose as *Self-Portrait with a Flowered Hat* (plate 17), painted some fifteen years earlier—Ensor, with this frozen facial expression, projects a wariness reinforced by critical, inquiring eyes. His steady regard, outsize dimensions, and red hat set him apart from the masked crowd, to which he turns his back. Reprising his role as the intermediary between observable reality and subjective representation, Ensor provocatively invites his audience to compare his disguise with those that surround him. Proclaiming his allegiance with masquerade and performance, and rejecting intimacy, Ensor opts for a public image that is overtly and completely contrived. This painting serves then as a form of *publicité*, not for a current play or vaudeville act, but for Ensor, star of this carnivalesque parody of modern life.

Announcing his place within the social space of travesty, Ensor affirms here his strategies of subterfuge and performance, which first emerged in the mid-1880s with the artist's growing social engagement and public art career; by the late 1880s these tactics were integral to his art practice and by the end of the century found their most confrontational and brazen manifestation in *Self-Portrait with Masks*. Articulated as a strong and expressive individualism, this carefully fashioned identity supports the stance of critical dissent that Ensor so proudly declaimed in *Christ's Entry*. Through his self-portraits, landscapes, and expressive interiors, his religious allegories and his critical and satirical representations of contemporary social subjects and political issues, Ensor presents the Belgian public with his own creative comment on the nature of modern experience. In so doing, he proclaims his own starring role as producer and participant in this theater of artifice, this carnival of the modern.

NOTES

Research for this essay was generously supported by the Belgian Ministerie van de Vlaamse Gemeenshap, and a National Endowment for the Humanities Fellowship. I thank Jan Verlinden, head of the Department of the Arts of the Vlaamse Gemeenshap, and also Patricia Berman and Sura Levine for their comments on this essay.

1. Patricia G. Berman has written an excellent monograph of this painting, *James Ensor: Christ's Entry into Brussels in 1889* (Los Angeles: J. Paul Getty Museum, 2002). See also Walther Vanbeselaere, *L'Entrée du Christ à Bruxelles* (Brussels: Éditions Weissenbruch, 1957), and Stephen C. McGough, *James Ensor's "The Entry of Christ into Brussels in 1889"*, 1981, Outstanding Dissertations in the Fine Arts (New York and London: Garland Publishing, 1985).
2. Charles Baudelaire, "The Painter of Modern Life" (1859–60; pub. 1863), in *Baudelaire: Selected Writings on Art and Literature*, P. E. Charvet, trans. (New York: Viking, 1972), pp. 395–422; Gustave Le Bon, *La Psychologie des foules* (Paris: Alcan, 1895); English trans.: *The Crowd: A Study of the Popular Mind* (Mineola, N.Y.: Dover), 2002.
3. The Realist movement was not officially recognized in Belgium until 1875, when Charles Hermans's *At Dawn* (*À l'aube*; 1875), a realistic yet moralizing painting (later copied by Ensor) representing a confrontation between an inebriated bourgeois man accompanied by prostitutes and a humble working-class family, was accepted by the Brussels Salon.
4. On Manet's exhibitions and connections with Belgium, see Monique Nonne, "Impressionnismes," in Anne Pingeot and Robert Hoozee, eds., *Paris-Bruxelles, Bruxelles-Paris: Réalisme, impressionisme, symbolisme, art nouveau* (Antwerp and Paris: Fonds Mercator and Réunion des musées nationaux, 1997), pp. 174–79 and 529. On Courbet's influence, see Robert Hoozee, "Courbet en Belgique," in idem., pp. 152–56.
5. On Théo Hannon, see Paul Delsemme, "Hannon, Théo," in *Nouvelle Biographie nationale* 5 (Brussels: Académie royale des Sciences, 1999), pp. 189–94; and Lucien Solvay, "Hannon, Théo," in *Biographie nationale* 29, suppl. 1, pp. 644–47.
6. Lemonnier's essay "Gustave Courbet et son œuvre" was published in the January 27 and February 24, 1878, issues of *L'Artiste*.
7. La Chrysalide, an artist-run exhibition society formed in 1875, was made up of some of the former members of the Société libre des beaux arts, the first group in Belgium to show Realist paintings. On La Chrysalide, see Jane Block, "Les XX and Belgian Avant-Gardism, 1868–1894" (PhD diss., University of Michigan, 1980), p. 4.
8. Edouard Hannon, an engineer by training, may have been instrumental in introducing Ensor to photography. In 1874 Hannon was a founding member, along with Félicien Rops, of the Association Belge de Photographie, and he later became a leading proponent of Pictorialism in Belgium. See Cécile Dulière and Françoise Dierkens, *Edouard Hannon (1853–1931)*, exh. cat. (Brussels: Musée Horta, 1977); Jean-Louis Godefroid, *Retrospective Edouard Hannon*, exh. cat. (Brussels: Éditions Contretype, 1986).
9. On Les Vingt, see Madeleine Octave Maus, *Trente années de lutte pour l'art: 1884–1914* (Brussels: Librarie l'oiseau bleu, 1926); Susan M. Canning, "A History and Critical Review of the Salons of Les Vingt, 1884–1893" (PhD diss., Pennsylvania State University, 1980); and Block, "Les XX and Belgian Avant-Gardism."
10. Gustave Lagye, "L'Art jeune," *La Fédération artistique* (March 1, 1884): 156. Translated from the French by the author.
11. With *L'Art moderne* as a rhetorical platform, Maus, Picard, and Verhaeren, along with invited writers (including Ensor, who here published his first satirical essay, "Trois semaines à l'Académie," on August 31, 1884), advanced their interests in modernist aesthetics, progressive politics, and Belgian nationalism. For more on Picard and Verhaeren's social and political agenda, see Paul Aron, *Les Écrivains belges et le socialisme, 1880–1913* (Brussels: Labor, 1985).
12. For more on Ensor's relationship with Les Vingt, see Susan M. Canning, "Vervreemding en expressionistische visie: Ensor, Les Vingt en de Kritiek," in *James Ensor* (Antwerp: Koninklijk Museum voor Schone Kunsten, 1983), pp. 30–56.
13. See Dr. Bénédict-Augustin Morel, *Traité des maladies mentales* (Paris: Librarie V. Masson, 1860); and *De la formation du type dans les variétés degénérées ou nouveaux éléments d'anthropologie morbide* (Paris: J. B. Baillière, 1864).
14. As early as the 1860s, Société libre artists, in particular Charles Degroux, had sought to raise public consciousness about working-class concerns including alcoholism and poverty but the fatalistic spirit of their canvases was often associated with a conservative Catholic perspective. See David Stark, "Charles Degroux et le réalisme social dans la peinture belge," in *Charles Degroux et le réalisme en Belgique* (Brussels: Crédit Communal, 1995), pp. 41–56.

15. The "soul of things" ("l'âme des choses") alludes to the collective title of a series of charcoal drawings focused on common objects and quiet, contemplative interior spaces by Xavier Mellery, first exhibited in 1889 and 1890 (at Les Vingt) as "La Vie des choses," and then in 1895 as "Emotions d'art: L'Âme des choses." Reflective of the emerging Symbolist aesthetic in Belgium, these drawings sought to make visible the hidden meanings and intense expression beneath surface appearances, an aspect shared by Ensor in his drawings of the family salon.
16. On nineteenth-century concepts of the self, see Michael Foucault, *The Care of the Self: The History of Sexuality*, vol. 3, trans. Robert Hurley (New York: Vintage Books, 1984, 1988). Charles Taylor also discusses the modern self in *Sources of the Self: The Making of Modern Identity* (Cambridge, Mass.: Harvard University Press, 1989). Carolyn Steedman defines "interiority," as a "visceral sense of insideness," in her book *Strange Dislocations: Childhood and the Idea of Human Interiority, 1780–1930* (Cambridge, Mass.: Harvard University Press, 1995), pp. 4–5.
17. The term "expressive interiors" was coined by Susan Sidlauskas, *Body, Place, and Self in Nineteenth-Century Painting* (New York and Cambridge, U.K.: Cambridge University Press, 2000), p. x.
18. On this drawing, see Marcel De Maeyer, "Mystic Death of a Theologian," reprinted in Catherine de Zegher, ed., *Between Street and Mirror: The Drawings of James Ensor* (New York: The Drawing Center; Minneapolis: University of Minnesota Press, 2001), pp. 187–201; and Julius Kaplan, "The Religious Subjects of James Ensor, 1877–1900," *Revue belge d'archéologie et d'histoire de l'art* 35, nos. 3–4 (1966): 182–88.
19. Ensor wrote about light in his 1882 essay "Réflexions sur l'art." See the passage by Ensor in Michel Draguet, "James Ensor: A Theater of Matter," in the present volume; see also Herwig Todts, " 'Make Way for the Old Ones! Respect Defunct Schools!' Ensor and the Art-Historical Canon," in the present volume.
20. Eugène Demolder, *James Ensor* (Brussels: Paul Lacomblez, 1892). Translated from the French by the author.
21. In his *Techniques of the Observer* (Cambridge, Mass. and London: MIT Press, 1990), Jonathan Crary shows that early nineteenth-century philosophical inquiries into the relationships between the exterior world and subjective experience intersected with scientific research on the retina and optic nerves. The new physiological understanding of vision resulted in a shift in the understanding of perception that increased emphasis on temporality and subjectivity.
22. On this series, see Kaplan, "The Religious Subjects of James Ensor"; and Susan M. Canning, "Visionary Politics: The Social Subtext of James Ensor's Religious Imagery," in Carol Brown, ed., *James Ensor, 1860–1949, Theatre of Masks* (London: Barbican Art Gallery, 1997), pp. 58–69.
23. In exchange for trading rights, European colonial powers recognized the Congo State as Leopold II's personal possession in 1885. He maintained sovereignty over the region, which he ruthlessly exploited, until 1908, when the Belgian Parliament approved the law that turned the Congo into a Belgian colony. For a detailed discussion of Belgian political parties during this period, see Els Witte, Jan Craeybeckx, and Alain Meynen, *Political History of Belgium from 1830 Onwards*, trans. Raf Casert (Antwerp: Standaard Uitgeverij / VUB University Press, 2000).
24. See Émile Littré, *Conservation, révolution, et positivisme* (Paris: Librairie Philosophique de Lafrange, 1852).
25. Some of the clearly legible popular anticlerical and Socialist slogans in the painting include: "À bas la calutte" ("Down with the clergy") and "Ça ira" ("It will go [or work]") and "Liberté, égalité, fraternité." Other banners are dedicated to art groups, such as Les Vingt, the Impressionists, and the emerging "Flemish movement."
26. For further discussion of the Aureoles series, see Anna Swinbourne, "Meeting James Ensor," in the present volume.
27. Ensor's sources for this drawing are Rembrandt's 1653 *Christ Crucified between Two Thieves* (*The Three Crosses*) and Jean Portaels's 1885 painting for the Koudenberg Cathedral in Brussels. Christ's pose also calls to mind Léon Bonnat's 1874 *Crucifixion* (Paris, Musée du Petit Palais), another painting of Christ with "bras étroits" (raised arms). In the mid-nineteenth century, popular myth held that representation of Christ with raised arms was a reference to Jansenist doctrine: it was claimed that the Jansenist Christ exhibited a high degree of naturalism, intended to stress his human rather than divine nature. See Michael Paul Driskel, *Representing Belief: Religion, Art and Society in Nineteenth-Century France* (University Park, Penn.: Penn State University Press, 1992), pp. 88–95.
28. Both Walther Vanbeselaere (in *L'Entrée du Christ à Bruxelles*, p. 33) and Stephen McGough (in *James Ensor's "The Entry of Christ,"* pp. 174–75) view this figure as a self-portrait. In her monograph on this painting,

Patricia Berman sees in the right foreground another Pierrot figure whose fine features, whiteface, blackened eyebrows, rouged lips, and black cap she associates with the noted nineteenth-century mime Jean-Baptiste Gaspard Deburau. Berman links this figure to the other Pierrot in the yellow costume but does not see there a portrait of Ensor (Berman, *James Ensor: Christ's Entry*, p. 88).

29. Writing to a colleague in 1898, Ensor recalled his childhood and the influence of his grandmother's playful transgressions: "My grandmother sometimes dressed me up in strange costumes. . . . She loved masquerades. I can still see her standing at the foot of my little bed one evening during carnival. She was dressed as a coquettish peasant with a terrifying mask. I must have been about five years old, which means she was well over 60." Letter from Ensor to Louis Delattre, August 4, 1898, as quoted by Gisèle Ollinger-Zinque in "Me and My Circle," in *Ensor*, trans. Ted Alkins, exh. cat. (Brussels: Musées royaux des Beaux-Arts de Belgique, 1999), pp. 14–15.
30. For a discussion of Brussels's theaters and nightlife, see *L'Heure bleue: La Vie nocturne à Bruxelles de 1830 à 1940* (Brussels: Crédit communal, 1987).
31. Mikhail Bakhtin uses the term "carnivalesque" to describe the anarchic subversion and subterfuge based in the transgressive inversion that occurred during Carnival celebrations, seen by Bakhtin as providing the conditions for new ideas to enter the public sphere. For Bakhtin, this carnivalesque spirit is best exemplified in the writings of François Rabelais. See Mikhail Bakhtin, *Rabelais and His World*, trans. Hélène Iswolsky (Bloomington: Indiana University Press, 1984); Peter Stallybrass and Allon White, *The Politics and Poetics of Transgression* (Ithaca, N.Y.: Cornell University Press, 1986).
32. On Ensor's embellishment of his works with masks and skeletal figures, see Marcel De Maeyer, "De genese van masker-, travestie- en skeletmotieven in het oeuvre van James Ensor," *Bulletin des Musées royaux des Beaux-Arts de Belgique* 10 (1963): 69–88.
33. For more on the influence of caricature on Ensor's drawings, see Susan M. Canning, "The Devil's Mirror: Private Fantasy and Public Vision," in de Zegher, ed., *Between Street and Mirror*, pp. 56–63.
34. In her study *Spectacular Realities* (Berkeley: University of California Press, 1998), Vanessa R. Schwartz presents a fascinating analysis of this late nineteenth-century cultural phenomenon.
35. Antoinette Botsford, in *The Toone Marionette Theater of Brussels* (PhD diss., University of California at Los Angeles, 1980), cites documentation on twenty-two puppet theaters in Brussels by 1892, and notes that there were numerous other unofficial puppet stages in the city, often set up in lower-class homes.
36. Paul Margueritte, *Le Petit Théâtre* (Paris, 1889), pp. 7–8, as quoted (in English) in Christopher Innes, *Avant-Garde Theatre, 1892–1992* (London and New York: Routledge, 1993), p. 21. By the late 1880s, Belgian puppet theater had became linked with the idea of a nationalist "soul" and invested with hidden symbols and meaning.
37. *Fumisme* was an attitude, an art form, and a way of life that used skepticism, satire, and practical jokes to mock official cultural and social norms. At the turn of the century, the Fumistes (literally, "chimney sweeps") were a group of French artists and writers variously called the Hydropathes, Decadents, and Incoherents who met and performed regularly at Parisian cafés, including the Chat Noir cabaret in Montmartre.
38. In the 1880s there were several *zwanze* shows that lampooned artists, including Georges Seurat, Odilon Redon, and Ensor. See Jacques Van Lennep, "Les Expositions burlesques à Bruxelles de 1870 à 1914: L'Art zwanze—une manifestation pré-dadiste?," *Bulletin des Musées royaux des Beaux-Arts de Belgique* 19, nos. 2–4 (1970): 127–48. On Ensor, burlesque, and *zwanze* humor, see Patrick Floorizone, *James Ensor: Les Bains à Ostende* (Brussels: Snoek-Ducaju & Zoon and Pandora, 1996), pp. 123–30.
39. Georges Fragerolle, "Le Fumisme," *L'Hydropathe* (May 12, 1880), as quoted in Phillip Dennis Cate and Mary Shaw, eds., *The Spirit of Montmartre: Cabarets, Humor, and the Avant-Garde, 1875–1905* (Piscataway, N.J.: Rutgers University Press, 1996), p. 23.
40. Leopold II receives the full brunt of Ensor's indictment in these two highly irreverent works, in which banners and signs refer to military service, secular education, and universal suffrage. These current issues were being summarily ignored by the king, who is portrayed as a patronizing fool (in *Belgium in the Nineteenth Century*) or as seated on a balcony, excreting feces onto a group of eager followers assembled below (in *Doctrinaire Nourishment*). On Ensor's use of scatology as social commentary, see Susan M. Canning, "The Ordure of Anarchy: Scatological Signs of Self and Society in the Art of James Ensor," *Art Journal* 52, no. 3 (Fall 1992): 47–53.

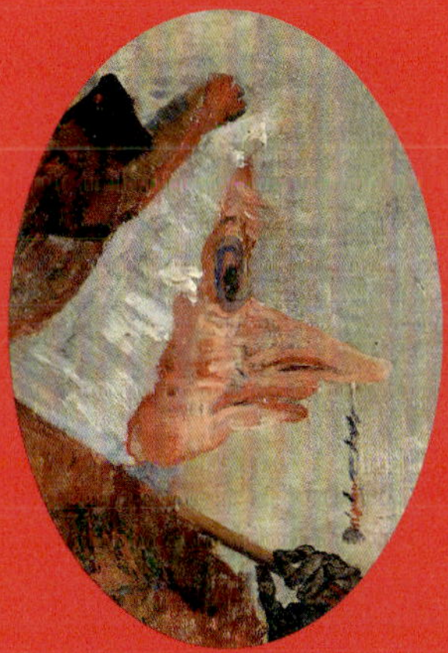

PLATES

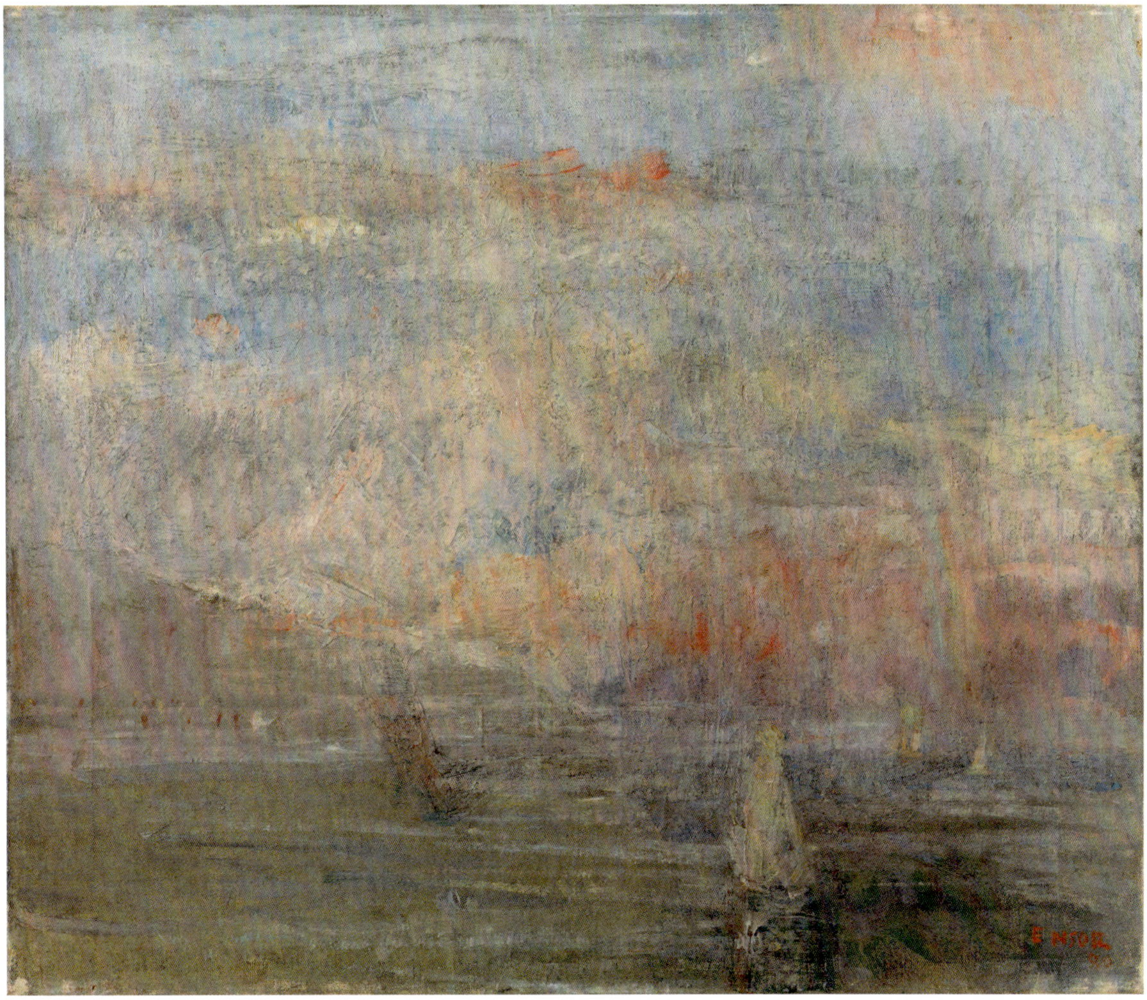

1. *The Rainbow* (*After the Storm*). 1880
Oil on canvas, 20 11/16 × 24 5/8" (52.5 × 62.5 cm)

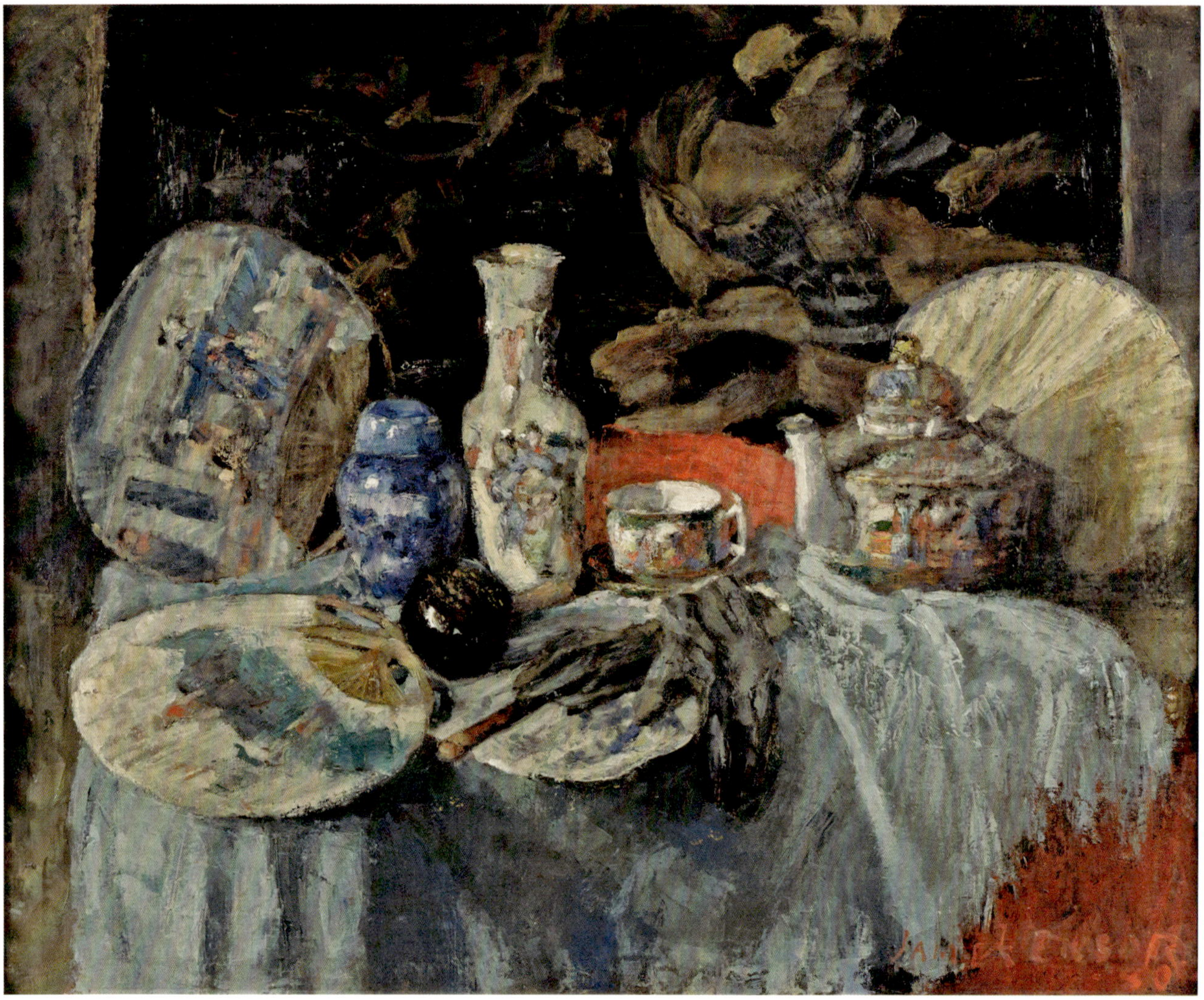

2. *Chinoiseries with Fans.* 1880
Oil on canvas, 31 1/2 × 39 3/8" (80 × 100 cm)

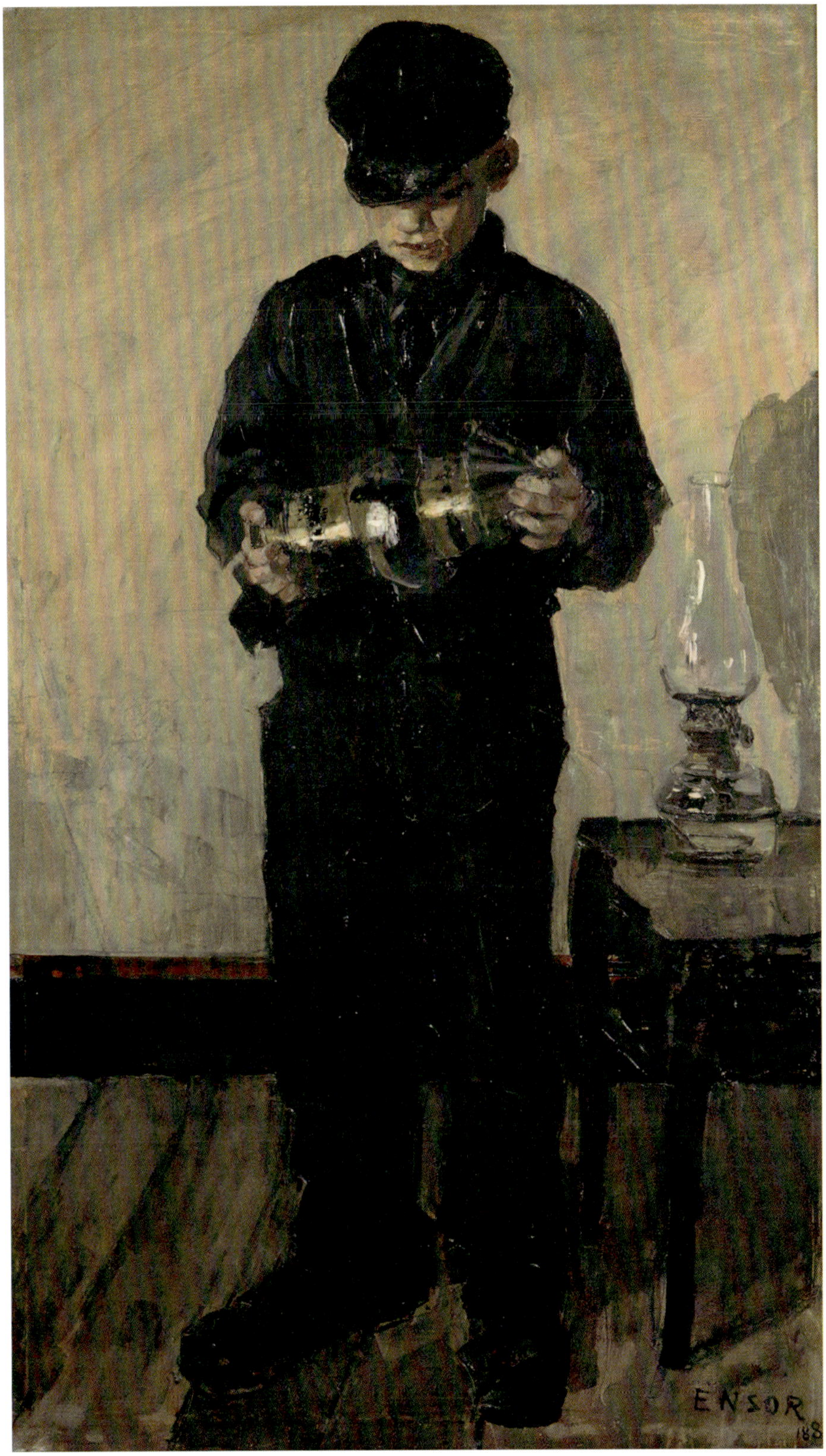

3. *The Lamp-Lighter.* 1880
Oil on canvas, 59 7/16 × 35 13/16" (151.5 × 91 cm)

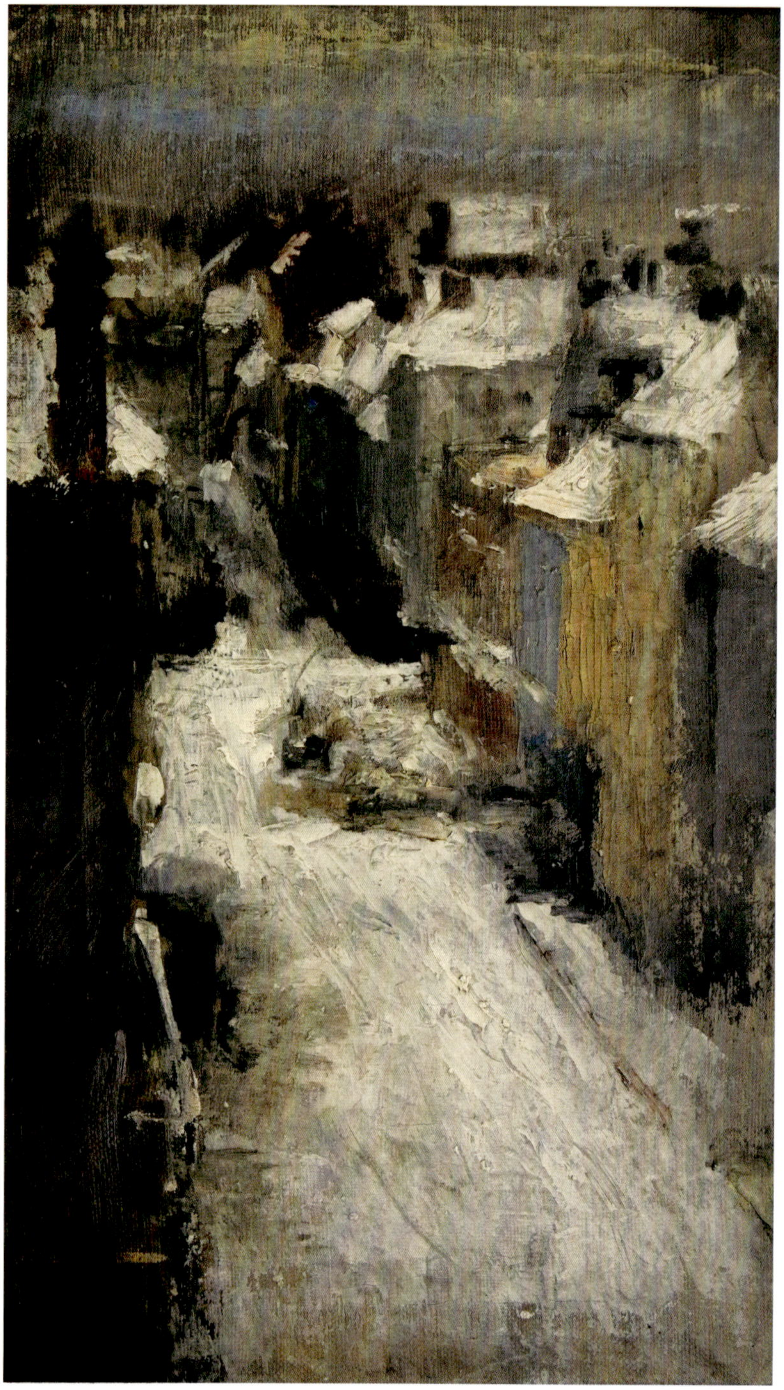

4. *Rue de Flandre in the Snow.* 1880
Oil on canvas, 18 1/8 × 10 1/16" (46 × 25.5 cm)

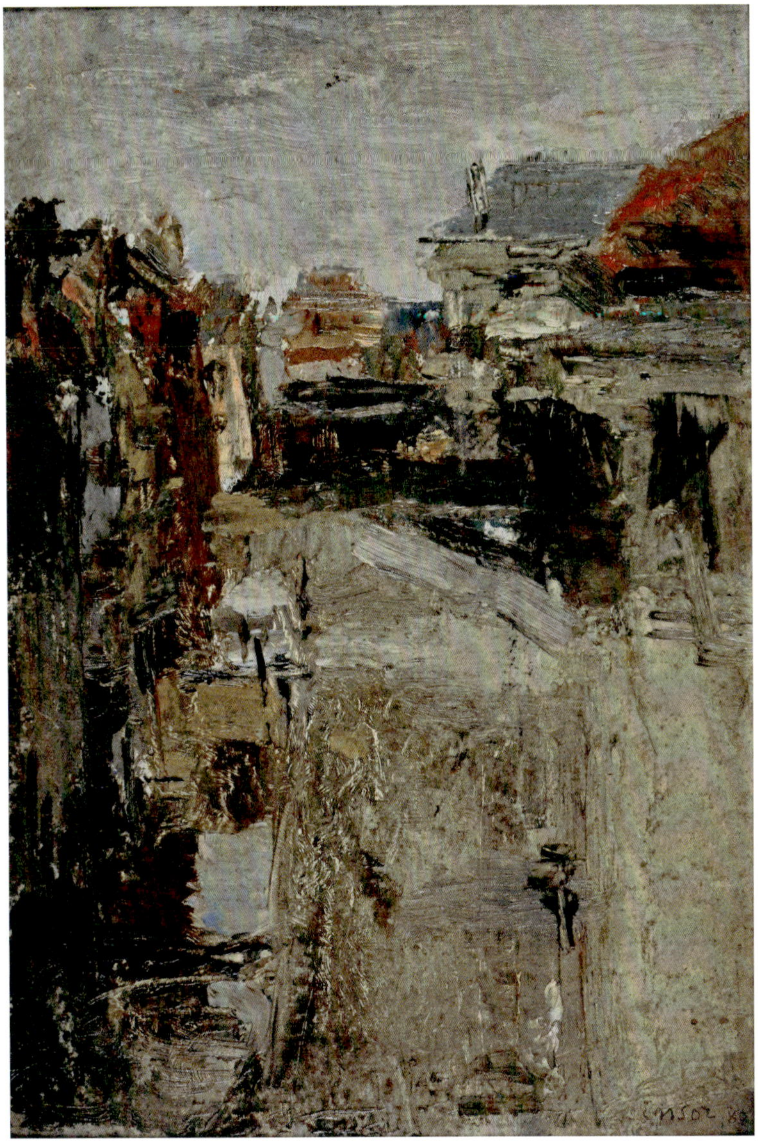

5. *Boulevard Van Iseghem in the Rain.* 1880
Oil on cardboard, 9 1/4 × 6 1/2" (23.5 × 16.5 cm)

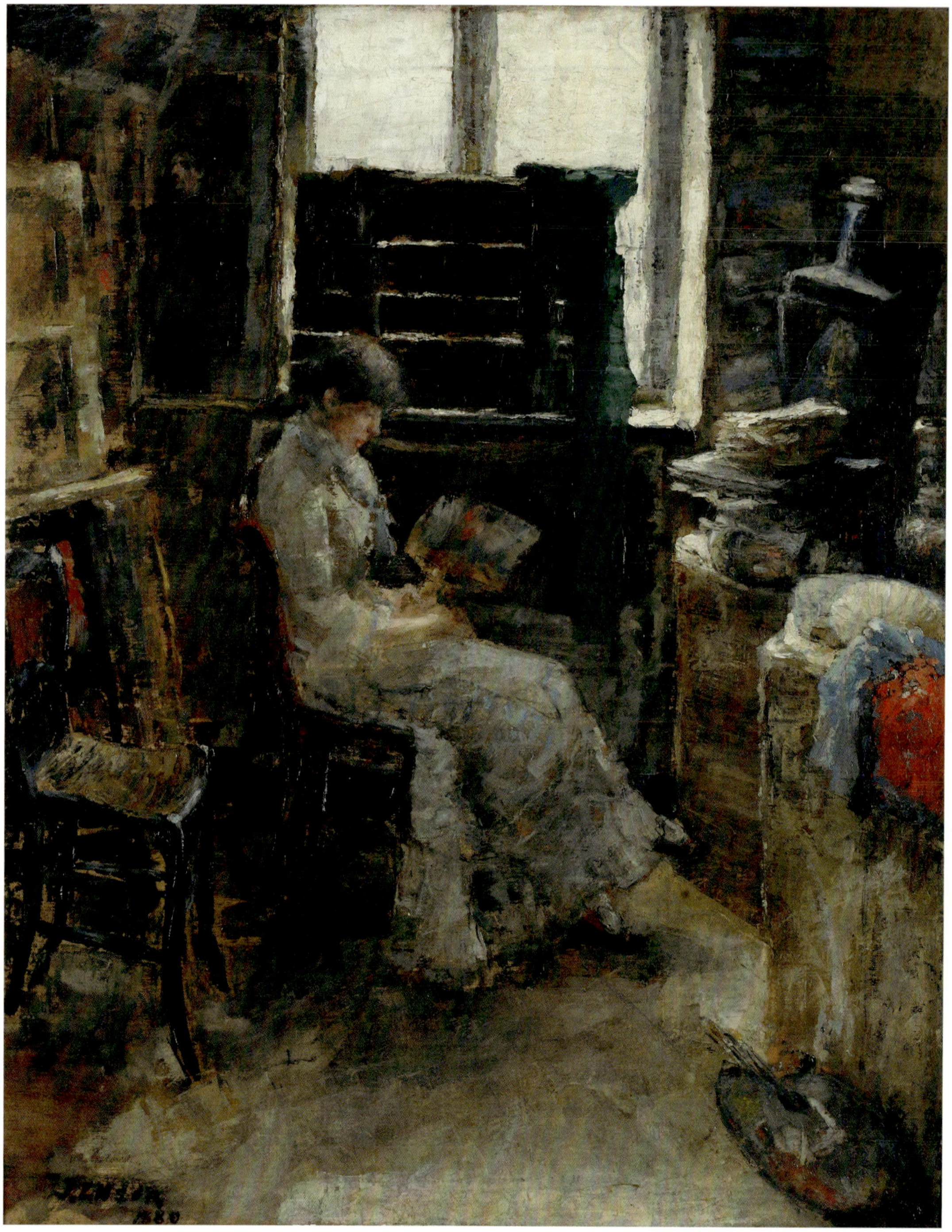

6. *A Colorist.* 1880
Oil on canvas, 40 3/16 × 32 5/16" (102 × 82 cm)

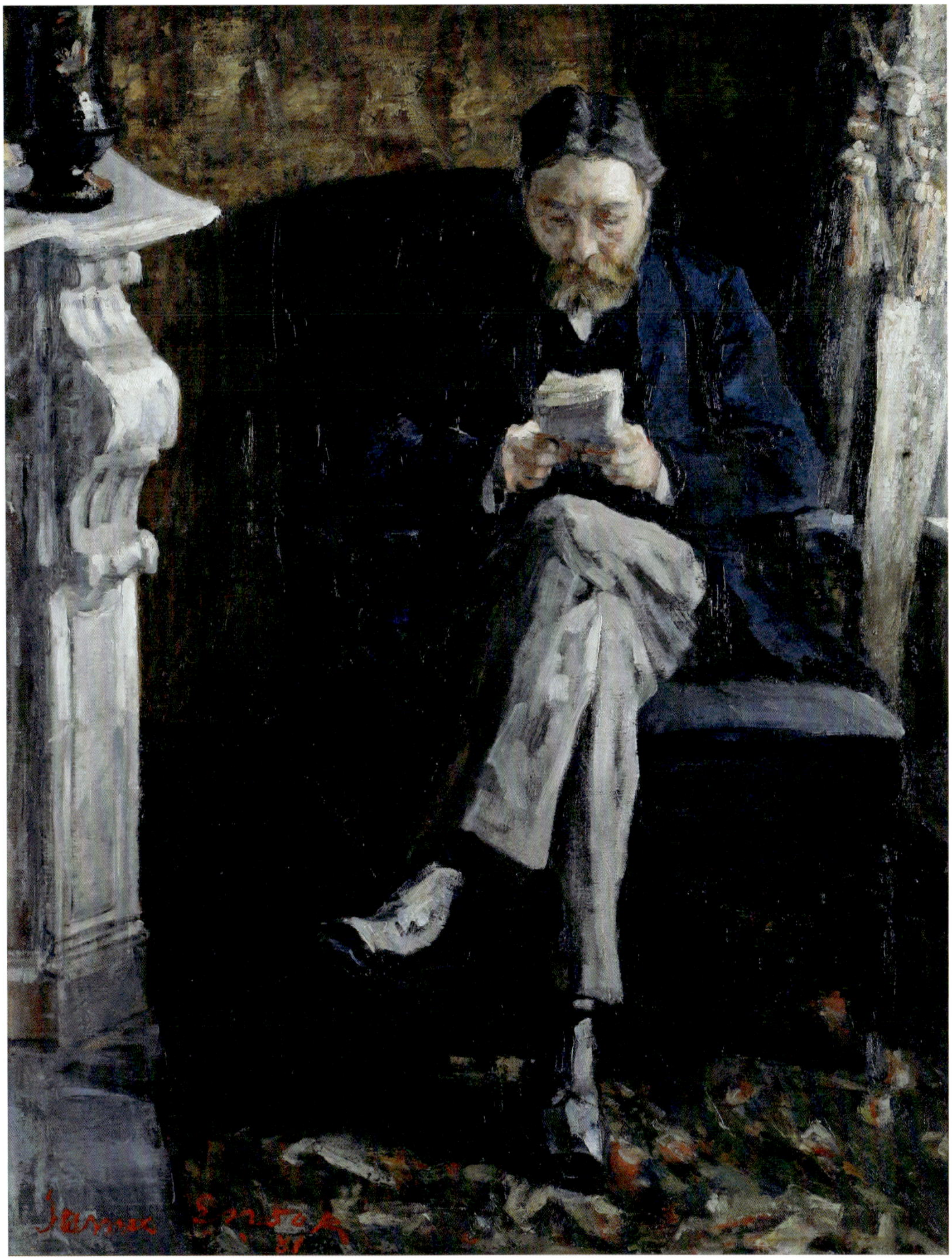

7. *Portrait of the Artist's Father.* 1881
Oil on canvas, 39 3/8 × 31 1/2" (100 × 80 cm)

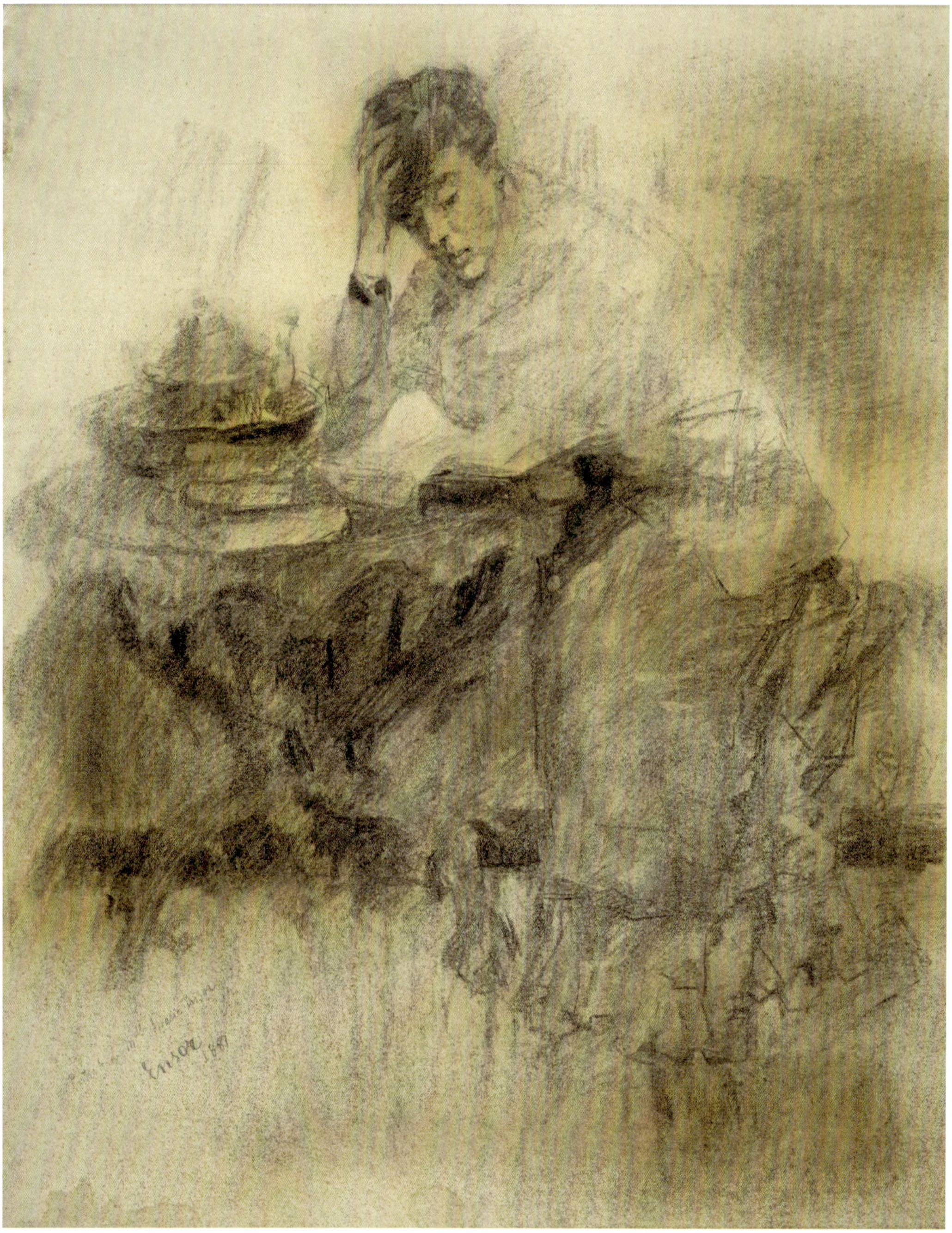

8. *Portrait of the Artist's Sister, Marie.* 1881
Charcoal on wove paper, mounted on board, on stretcher, 29 3/4 × 23 7/16" (75.5 × 59.5 cm)

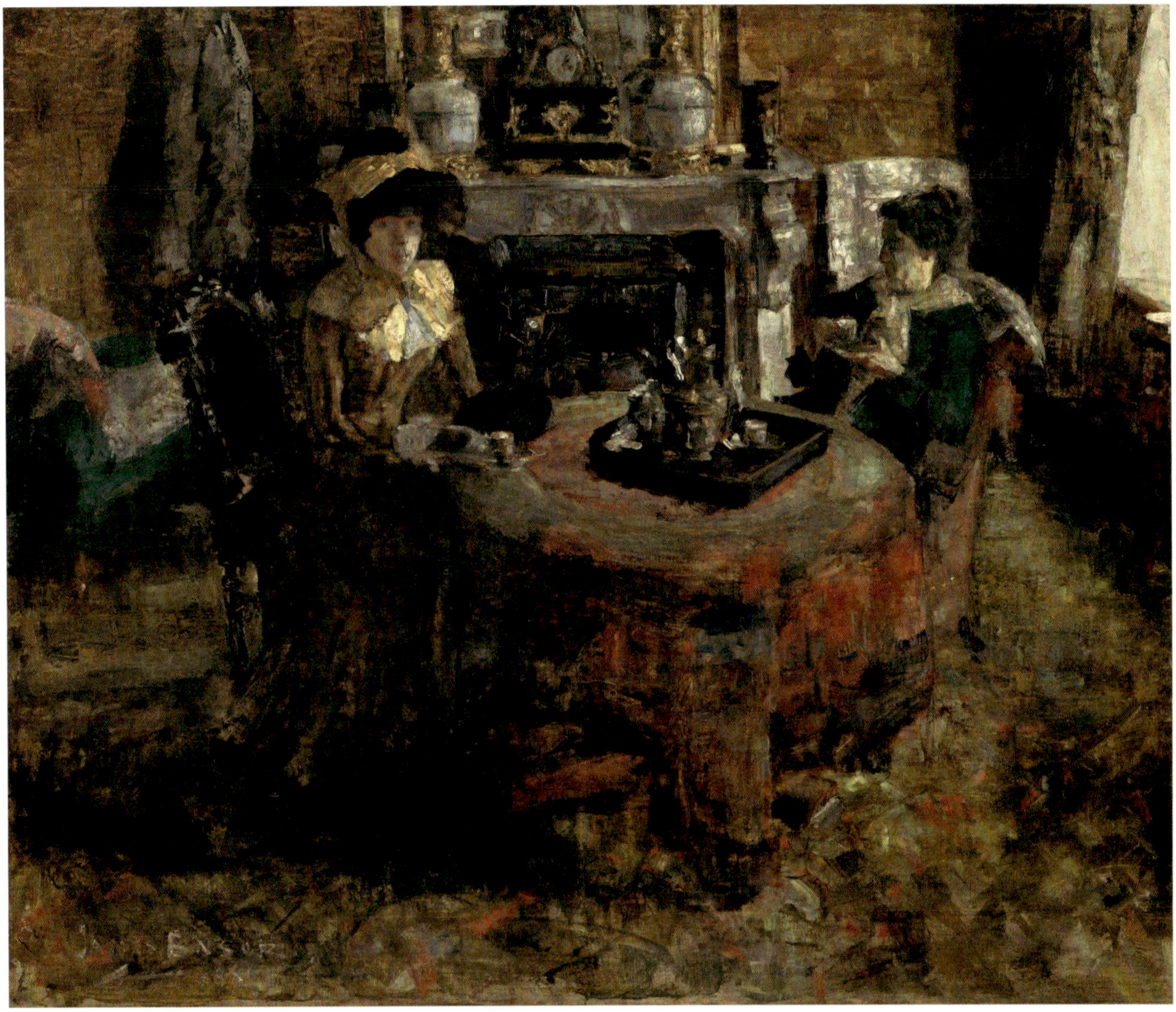

9. *Afternoon in Ostend*. 1881
Oil on canvas, 43 9/16 × 52 15/16" (110.7 × 134.5 cm)

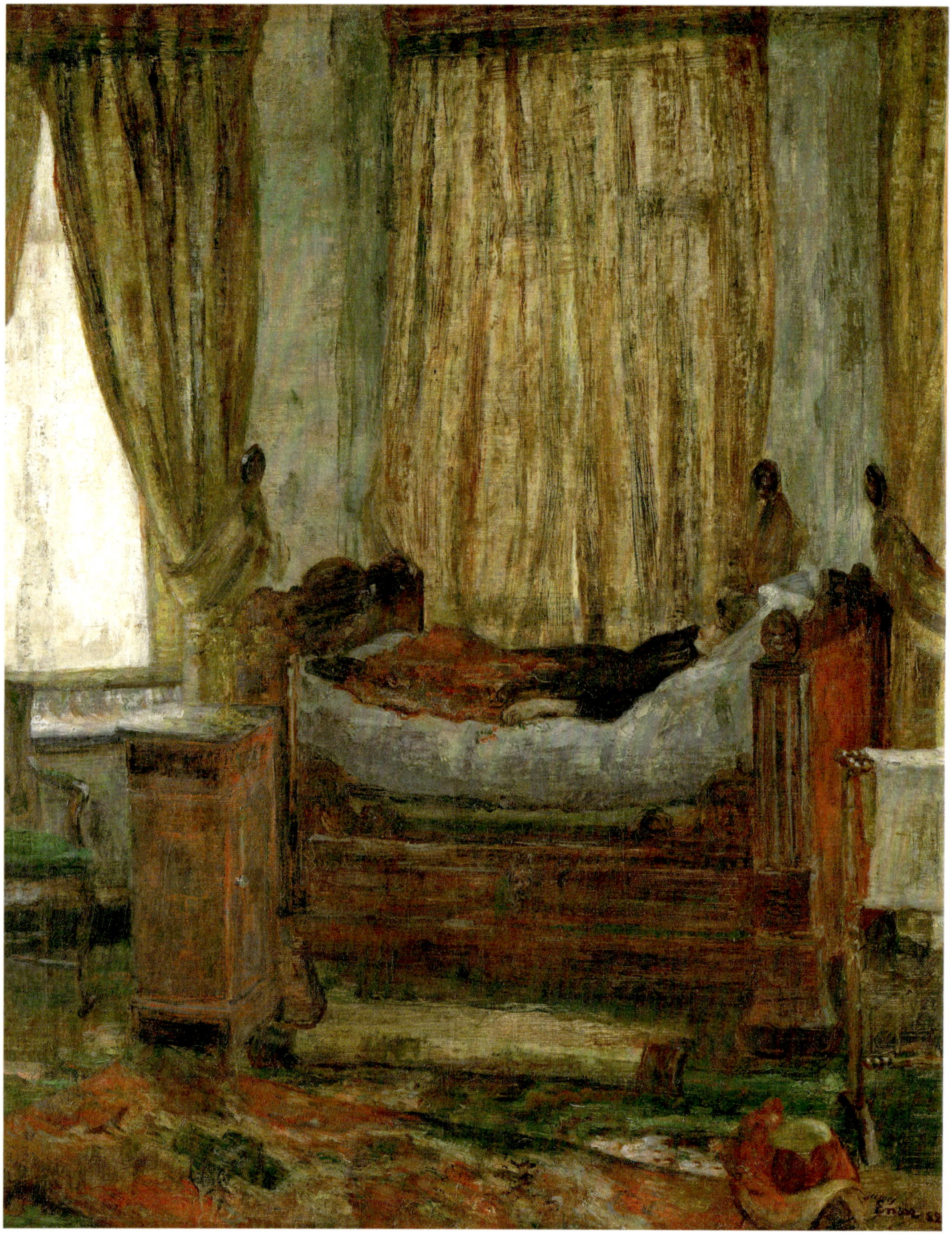

10. *The Lady in Distress.* 1882
Oil on canvas, 39 9/16 × 31 1/2" (100.5 × 80 cm)

11. *Portrait of Willy Finch.* 1882
Oil on canvas, 43 5/16 × 37 3/8" (110 × 95 cm)

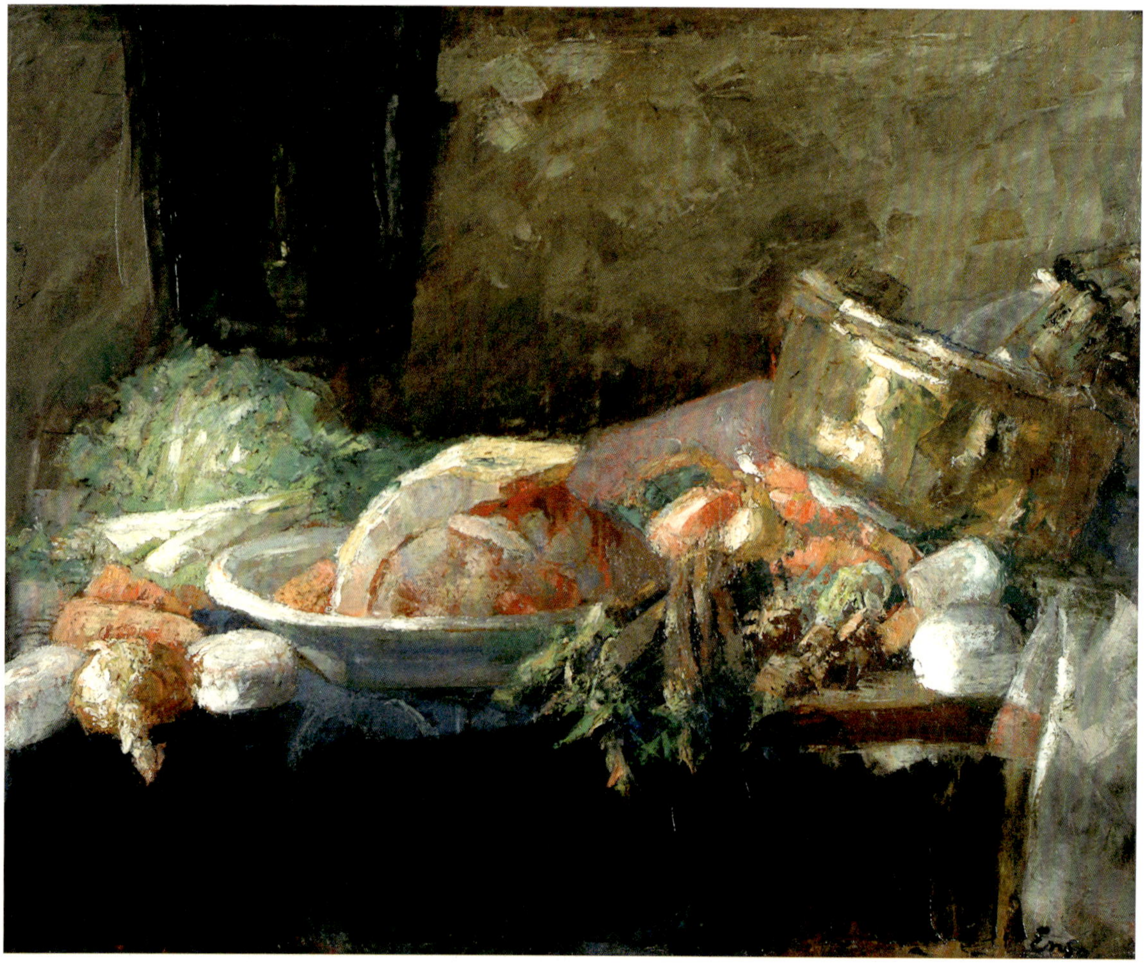

12. *Still Life with Vegetables.* 1882
Oil on canvas, 31 1/2 × 39 3/8" (80 × 100 cm)

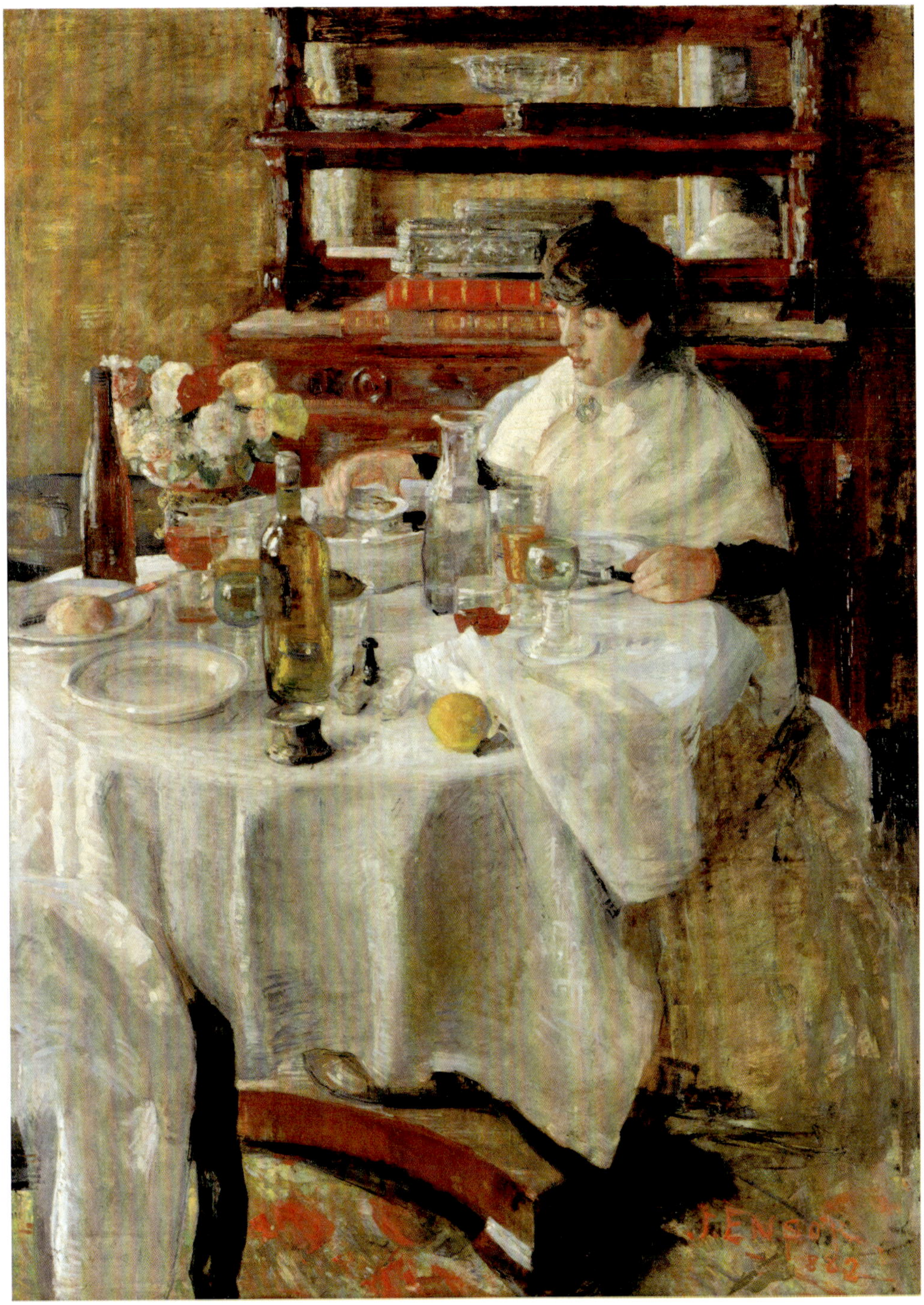

13. *The Oyster Eater.* 1882
Oil on canvas, 81 1/2 × 59 1/16" (207 × 150 cm)

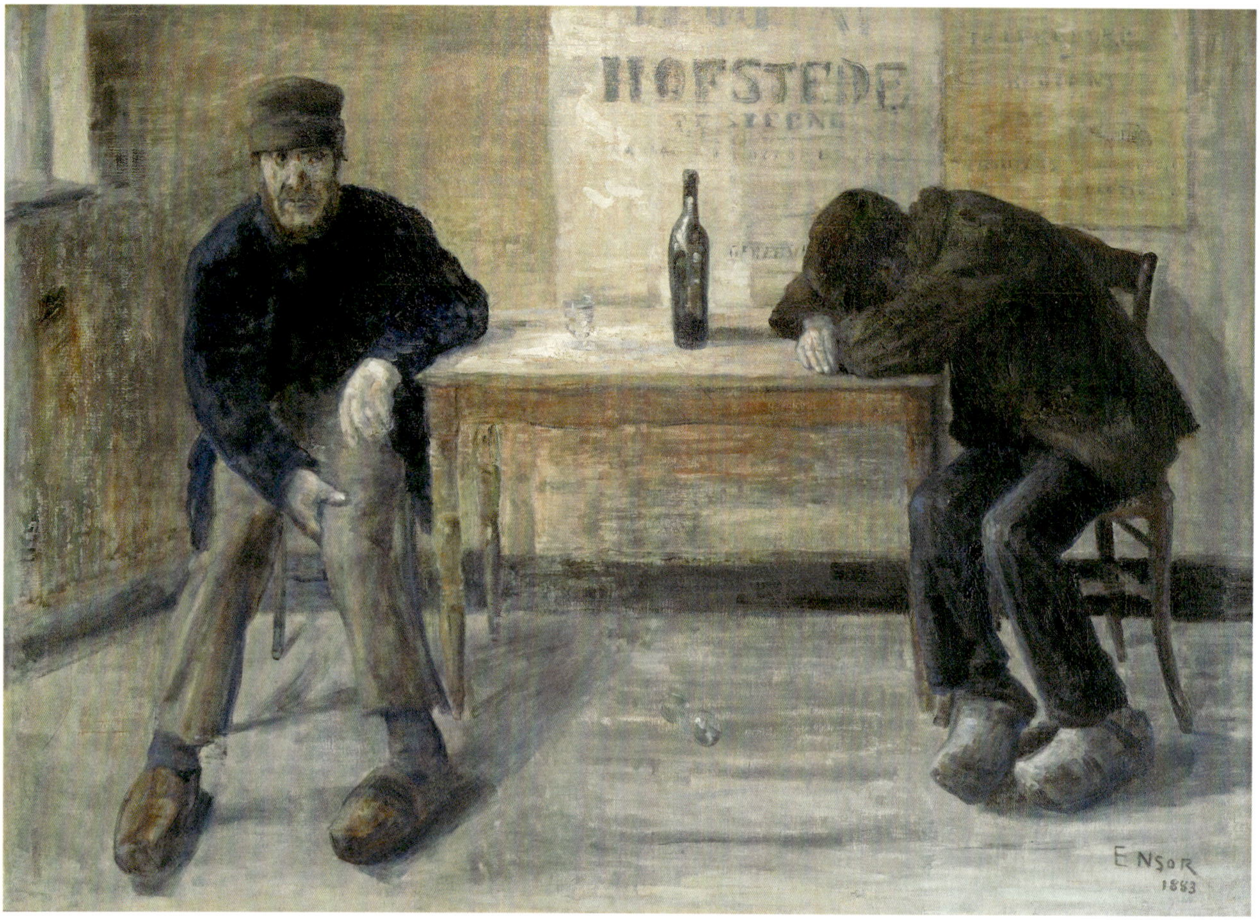

14. *The Drunkards.* 1883
Oil on canvas, 45 ¼ × 64 15/16" (115 × 165 cm)

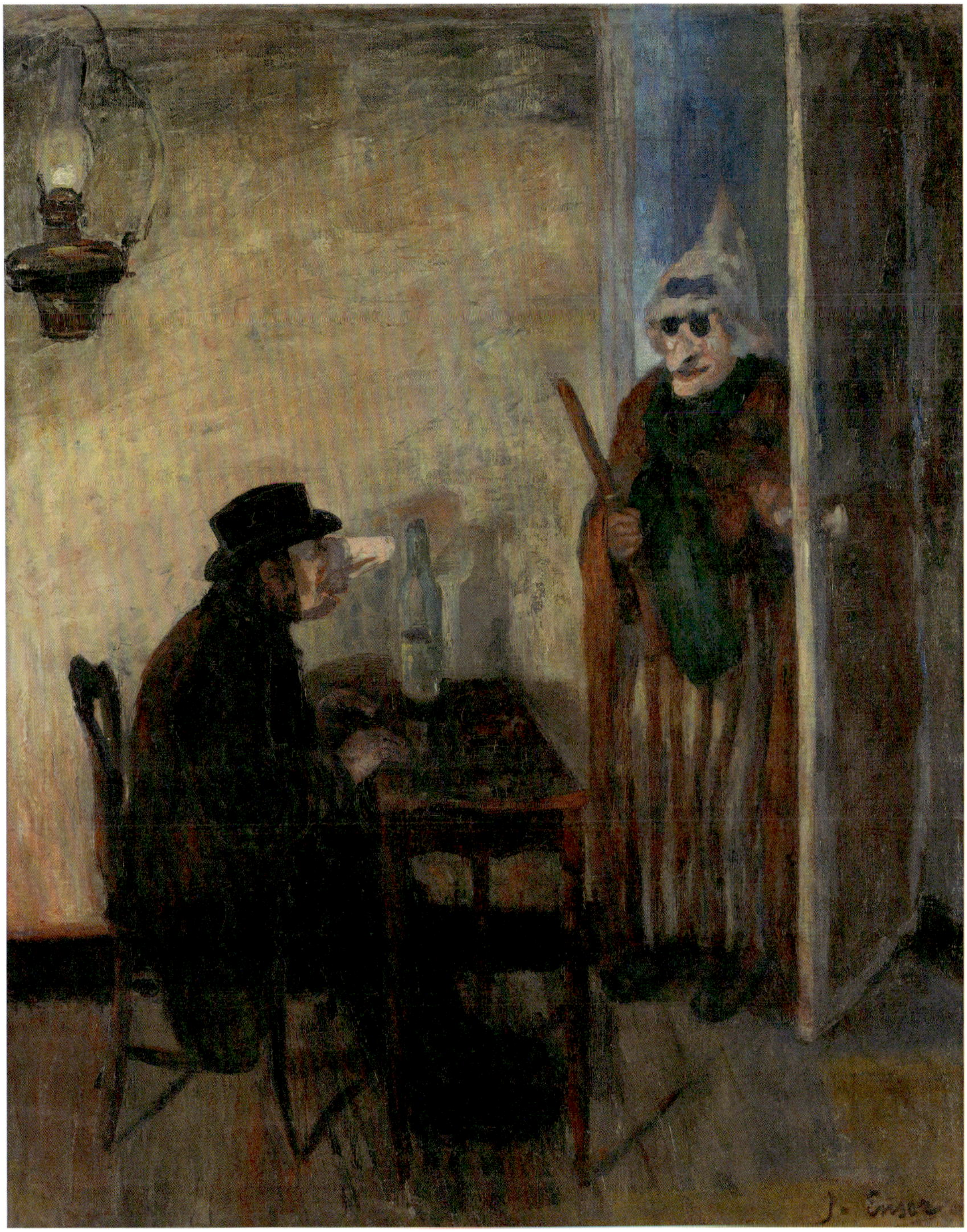

15. *The Scandalized Masks.* 1883
Oil on canvas, 53 1/8 × 44 1/8" (135 × 112 cm)

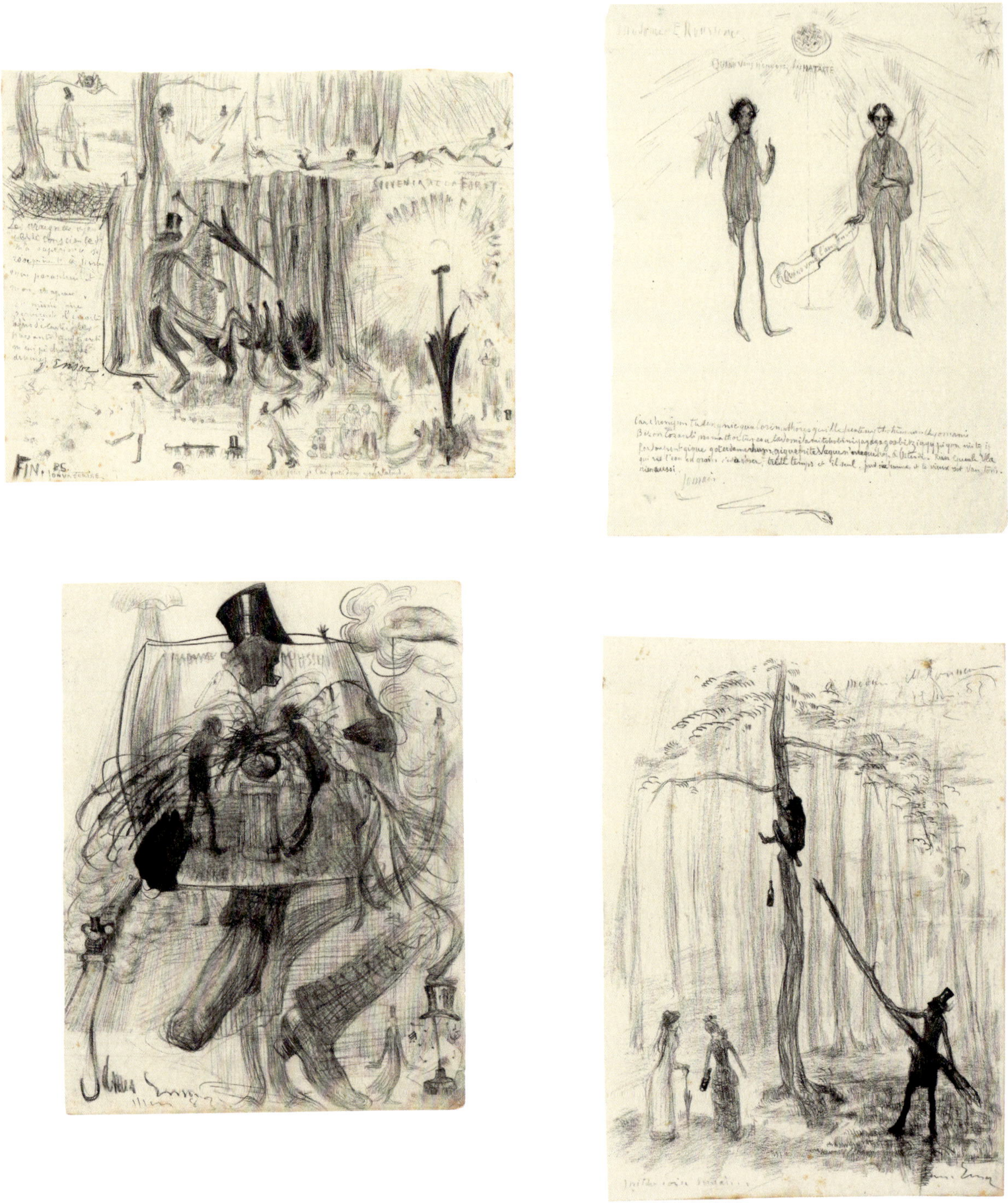

16. *Sketchbook.* 1883–96
India ink, pen, Conté crayon, graphite, and black chalk on paper, 11 5/16 × 16 3/16" (28.7 × 41.1 cm)

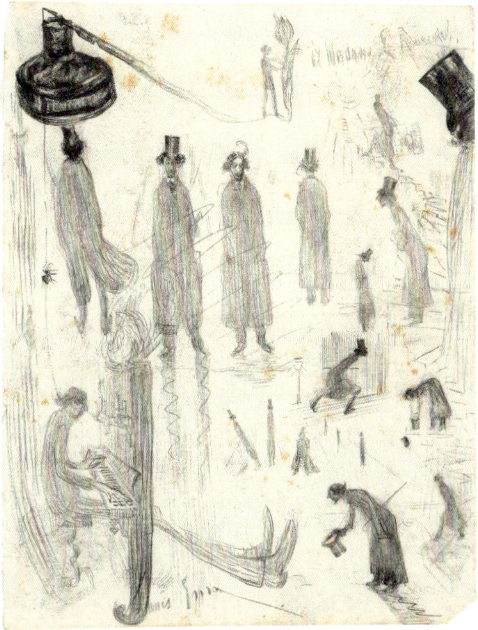
James Ensor

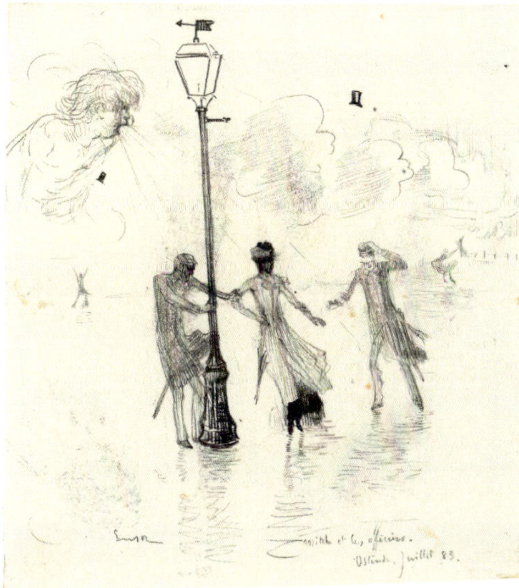
Ensor
Ostende, Juillet 83.

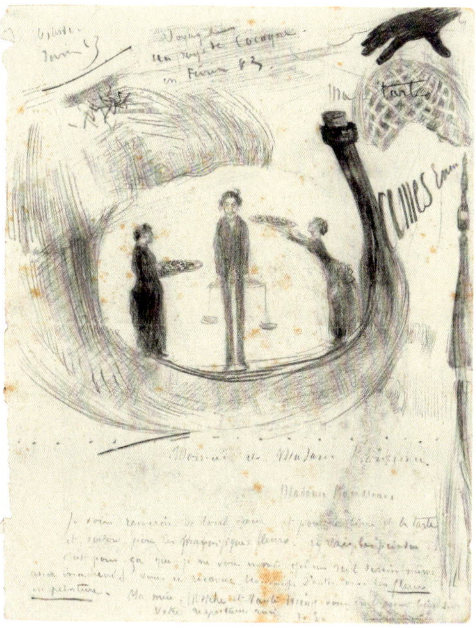

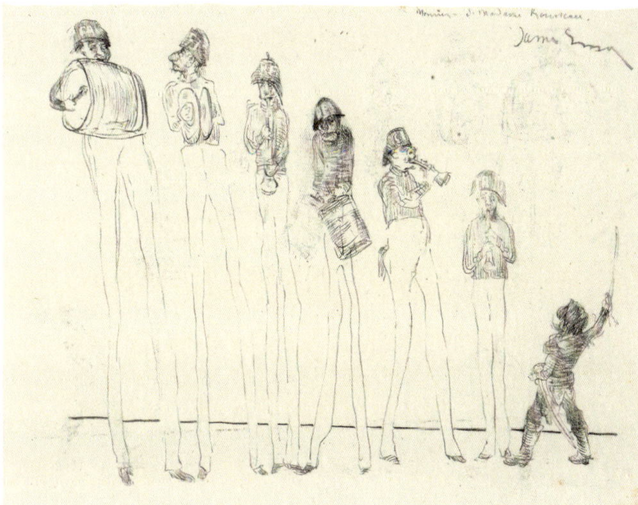
James Ensor

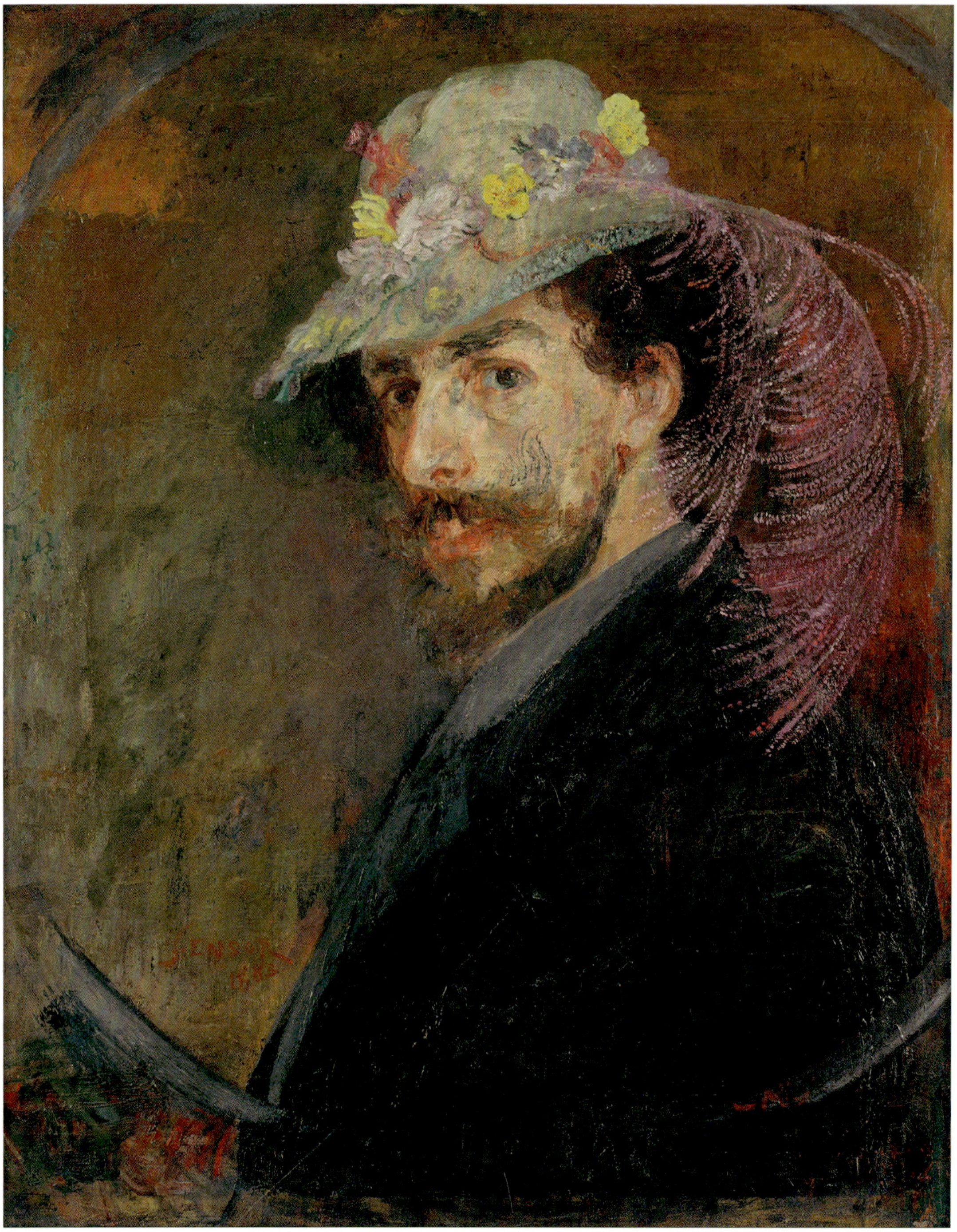

17. *Self-Portrait with a Flowered Hat.* 1883/88
Oil on canvas, 30 1/8 × 24 3/16" (76.5 × 61.5 cm)

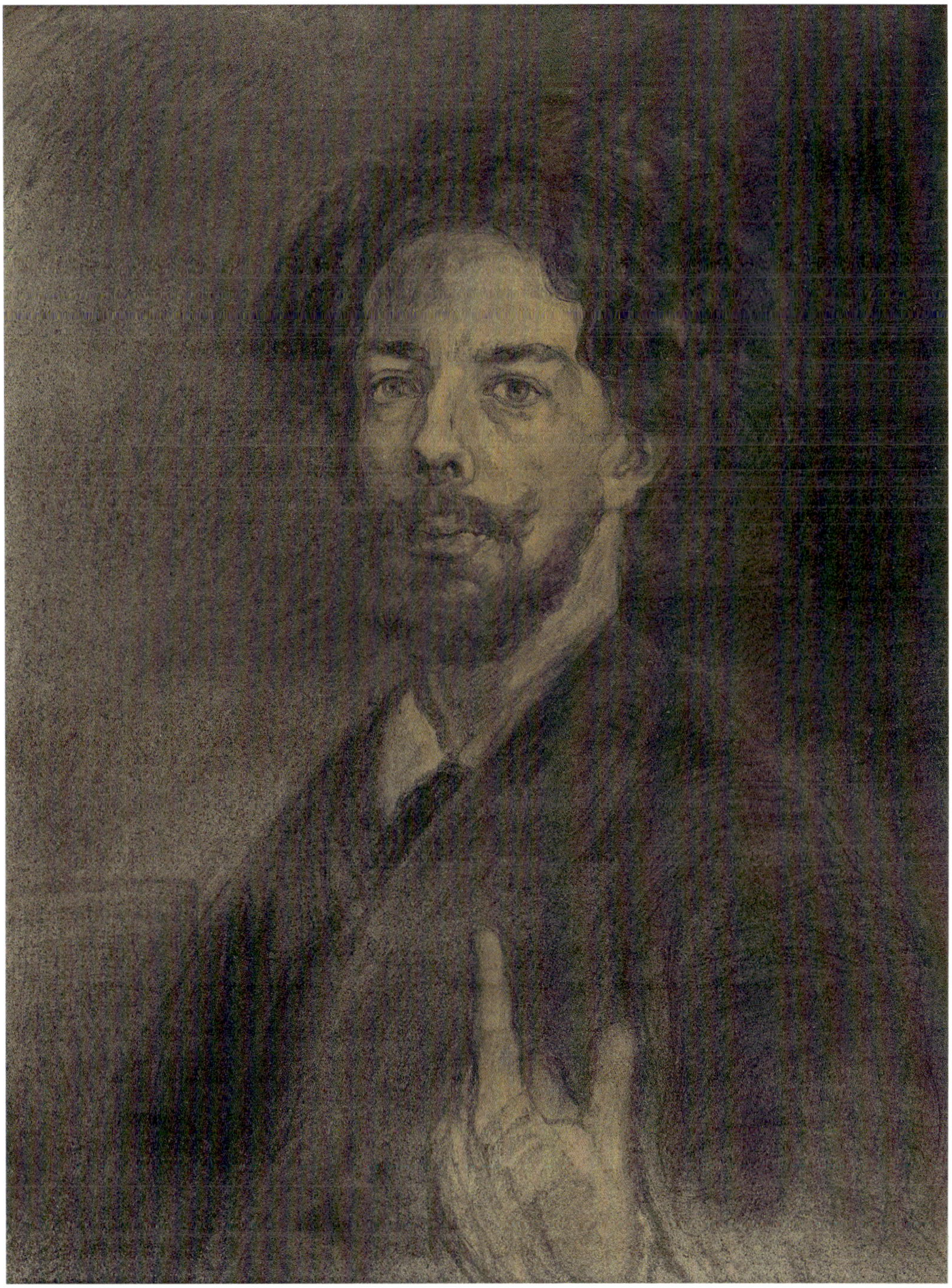

18. *My Portrait.* 1884
Charcoal and white chalk on paper, 29 ¾ × 22 ¾"
(75.5 × 57.8 cm)

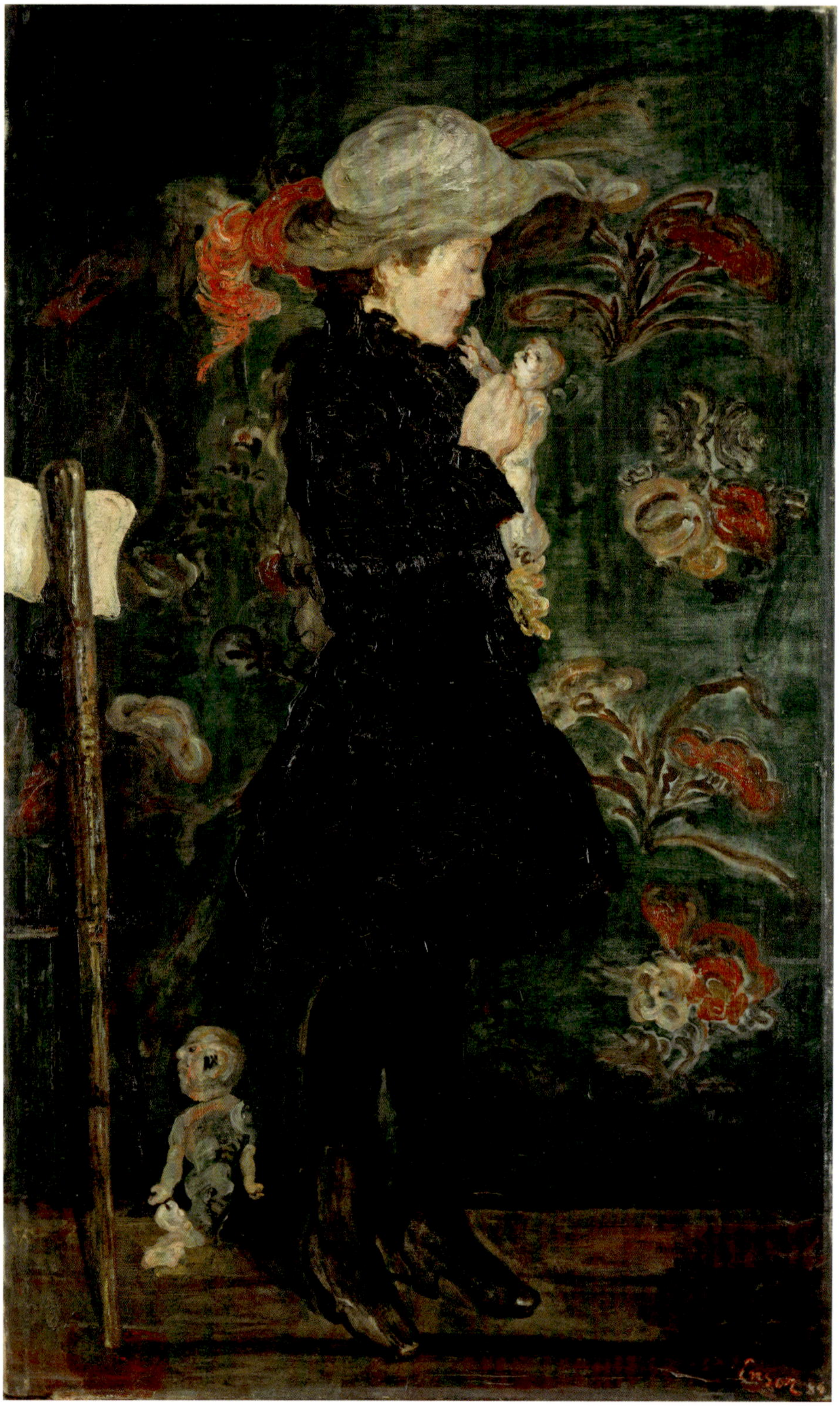

19. *Child with Doll.* 1884 / 1886–89(?)
Oil on canvas, 58 11/16 × 35 13/16" (149 × 91 cm)

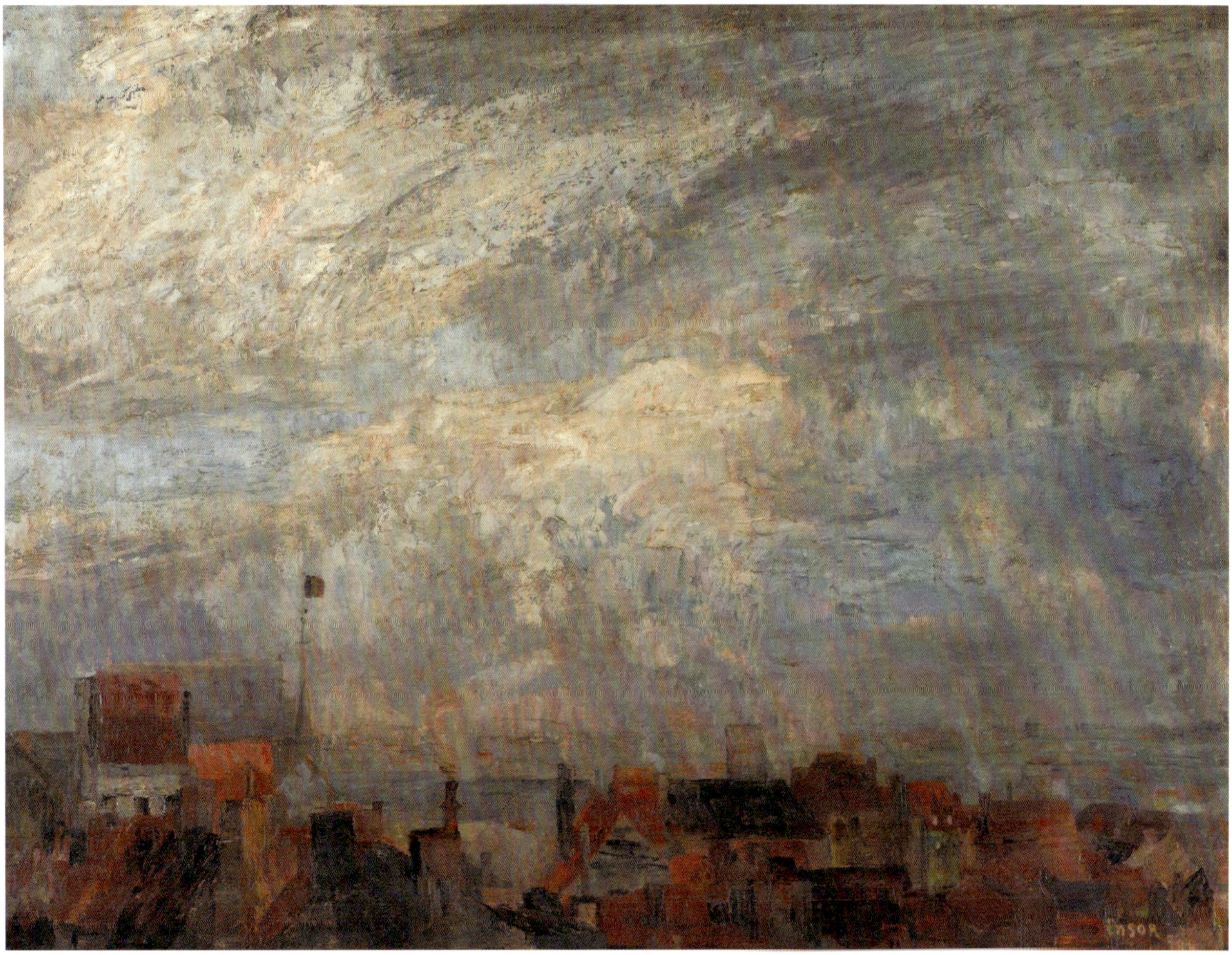

20. *Rooftops of Ostend* (*Grand View of Ostend*). 1884
Oil on canvas, 58 11/16 × 81 1/8" (149 × 206 cm)

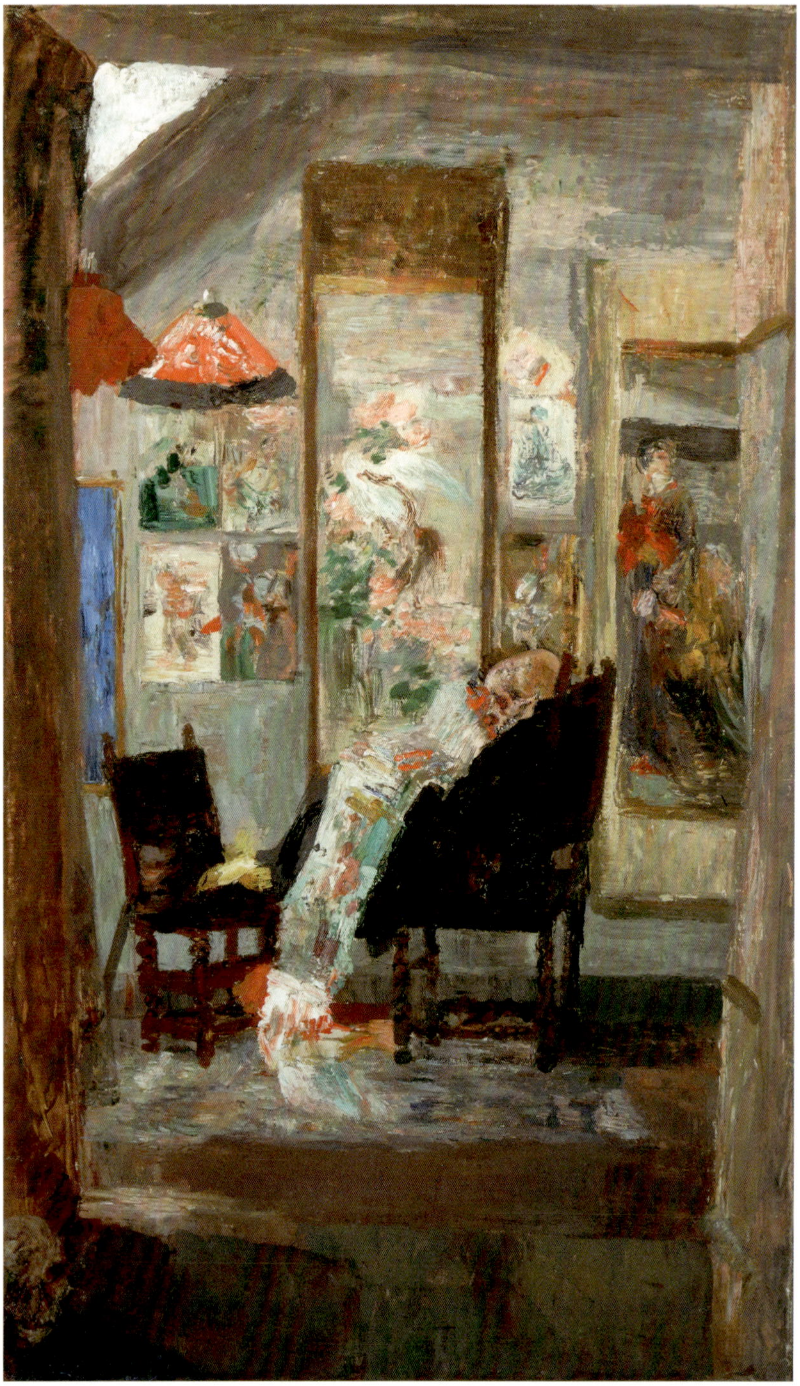

21. *Skeleton Looking at Chinoiseries.* 1885/1888
Oil on canvas, 39 3/8 × 23 5/8" (100 × 60 cm)

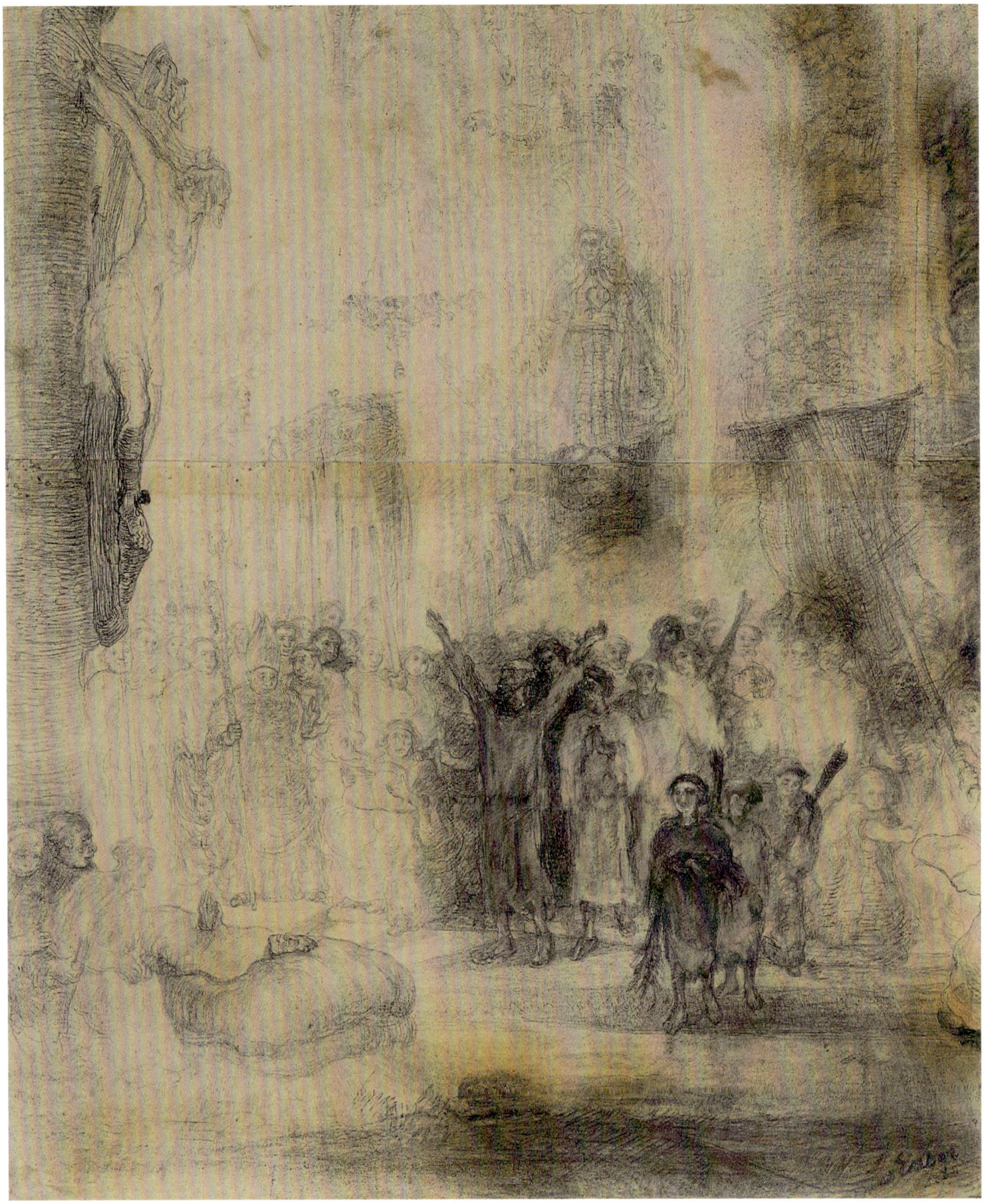

22. *The Mystic Death of a Theologian* (*Elated Monks Claim the Body of the Theologian Sus Ovis, in Spite of the Resisting Bishop Friton or Friston*). 1880 / 1885 – 86(?)
Pencil, charcoal, and black crayon on paper, mounted on canvas, 38 3⁄16 × 32 11⁄16" (97 × 83 cm)

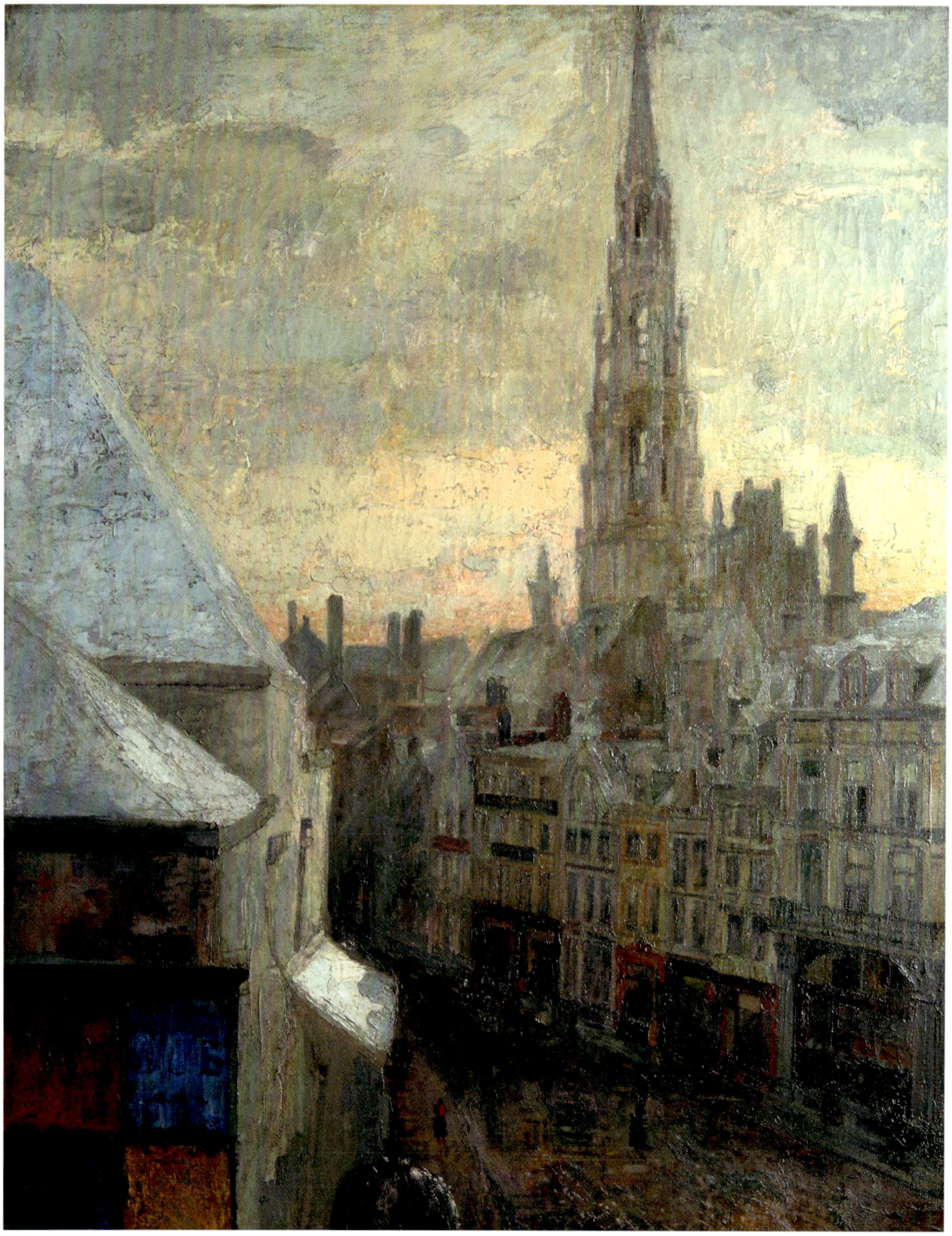

23. *Brussels Town Hall.* 1885
Oil on canvas, 39 3/8 × 31 7/8" (100 × 81 cm)

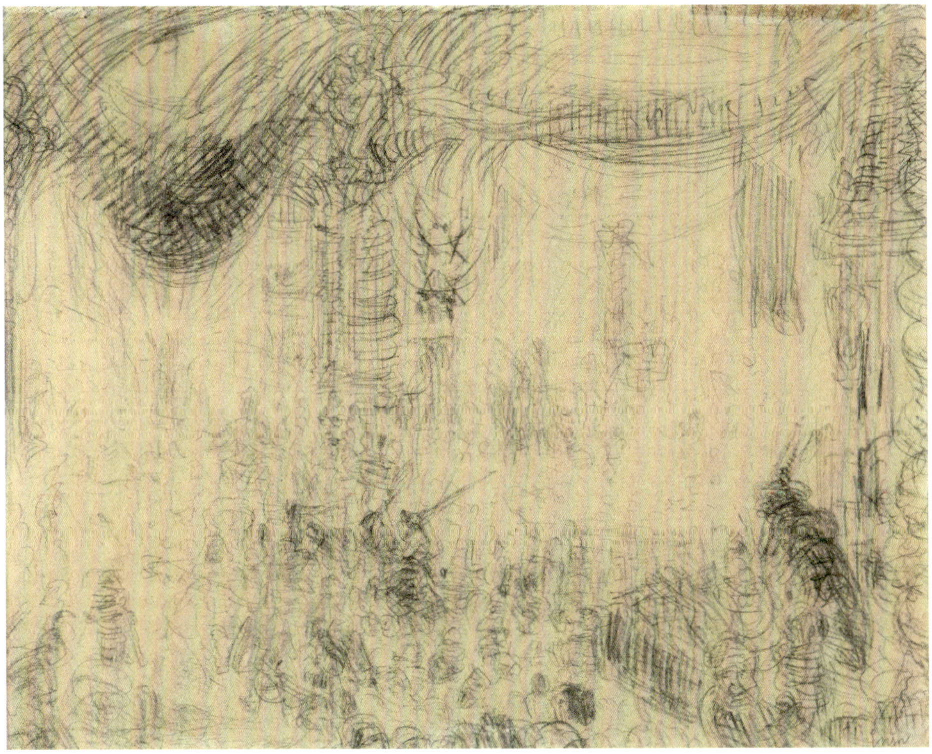

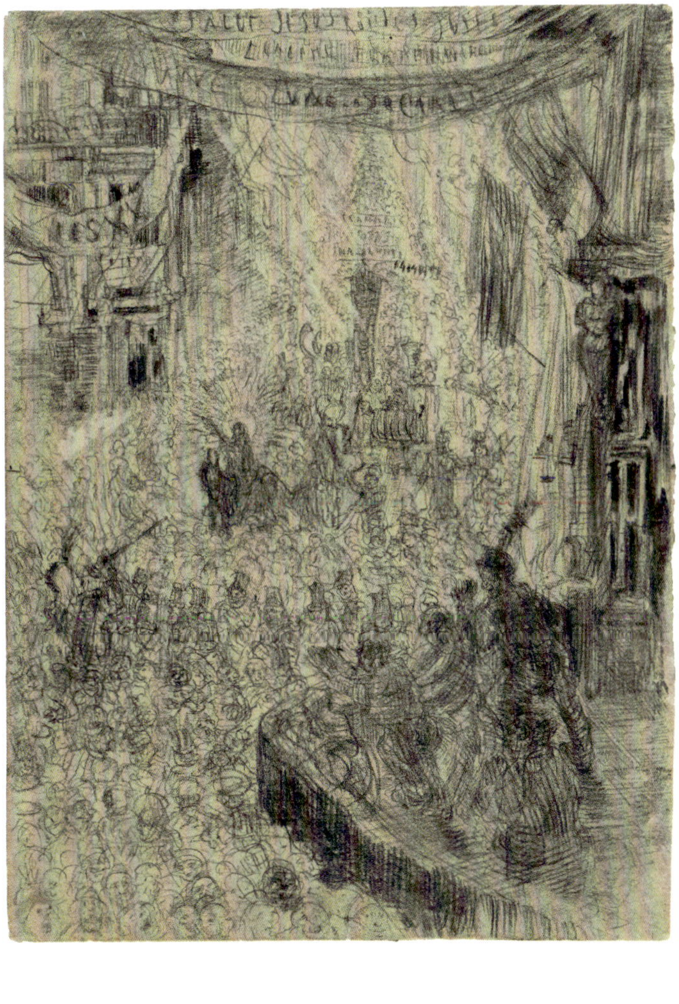

24. *Christ Shown to the People and the Entry of Christ into Jerusalem.* 1887
Black chalk on paper, 6 13/16 × 8 11/16" (17.3 × 22.1 cm)

25. *Christ's Entry into Jerusalem* (recto). 1885
Graphite and Conté crayon on wove paper, 8 7/8 × 6 1/2" (22.5 × 16.5 cm)

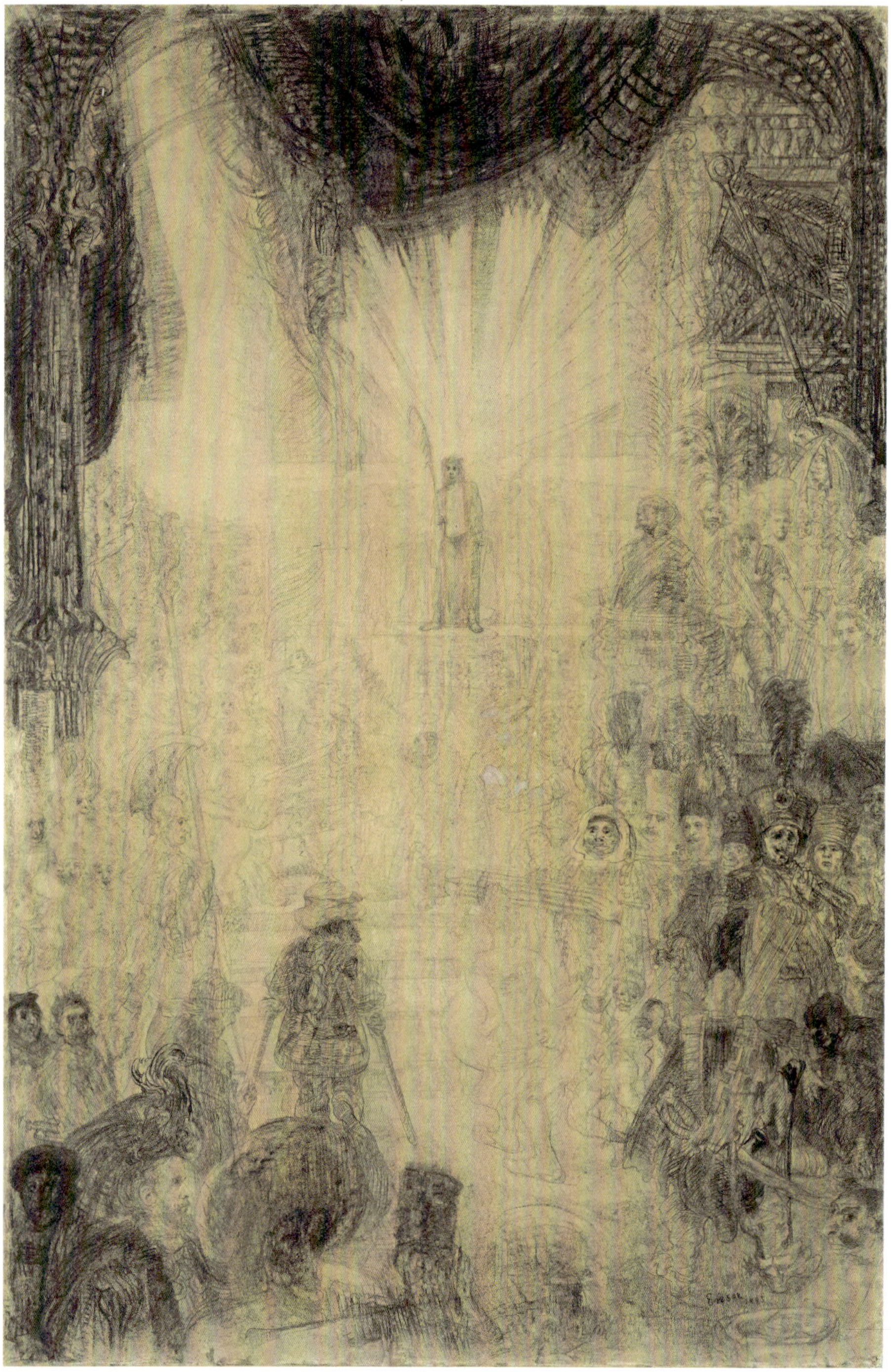

26. *The Rising: Christ Shown to the People.* 1885
Black crayon and watercolor on paper, mounted on canvas, 61 × 40 3/16" (155 × 102 cm)

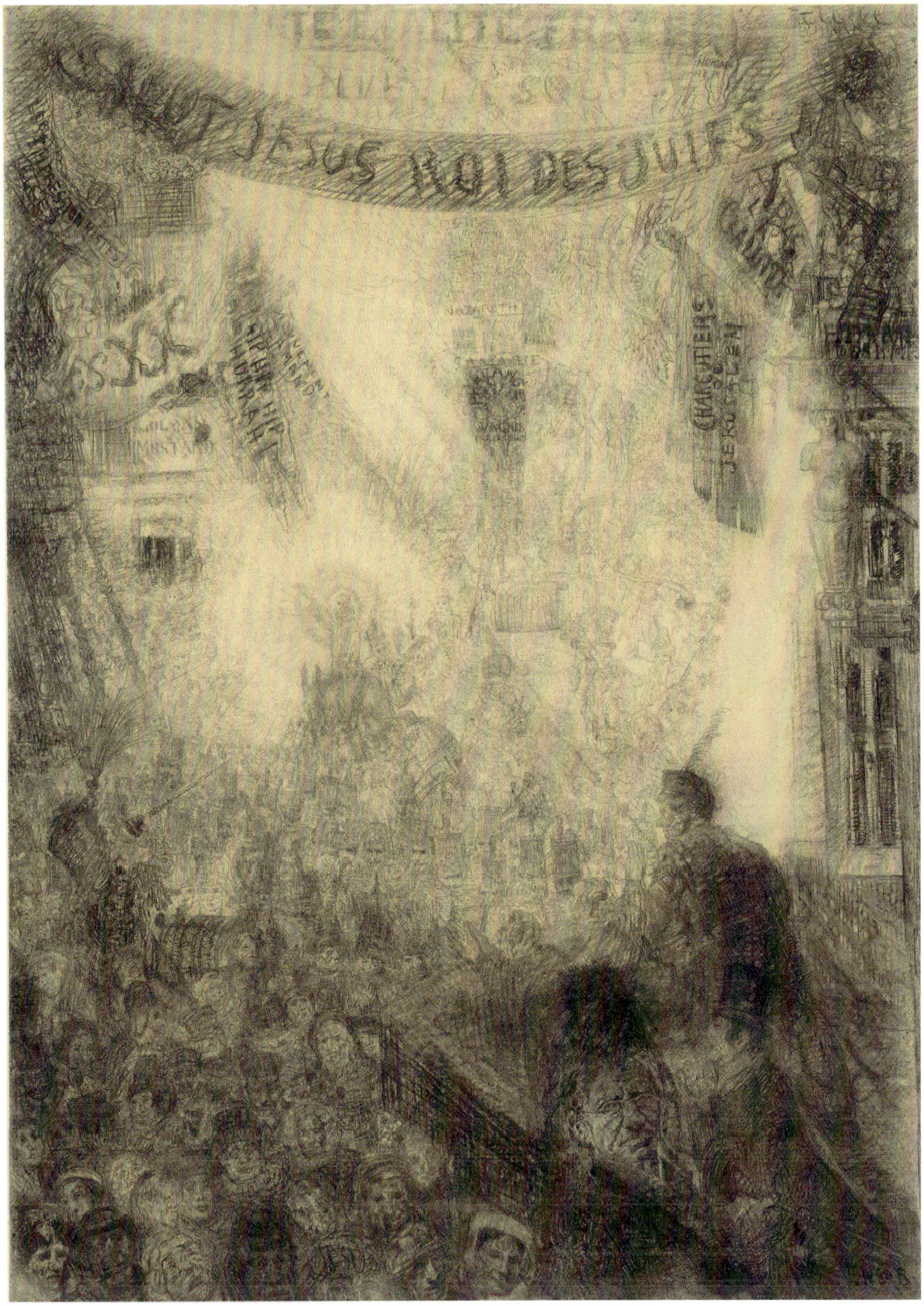

27. *The Lively and Radiant: The Entry of Christ into Jerusalem.* 1885
Black and brown crayon, with collaged paper, mounted on canvas, 6' 9 1/8" × 59 3/16" (206 × 150.3 cm)

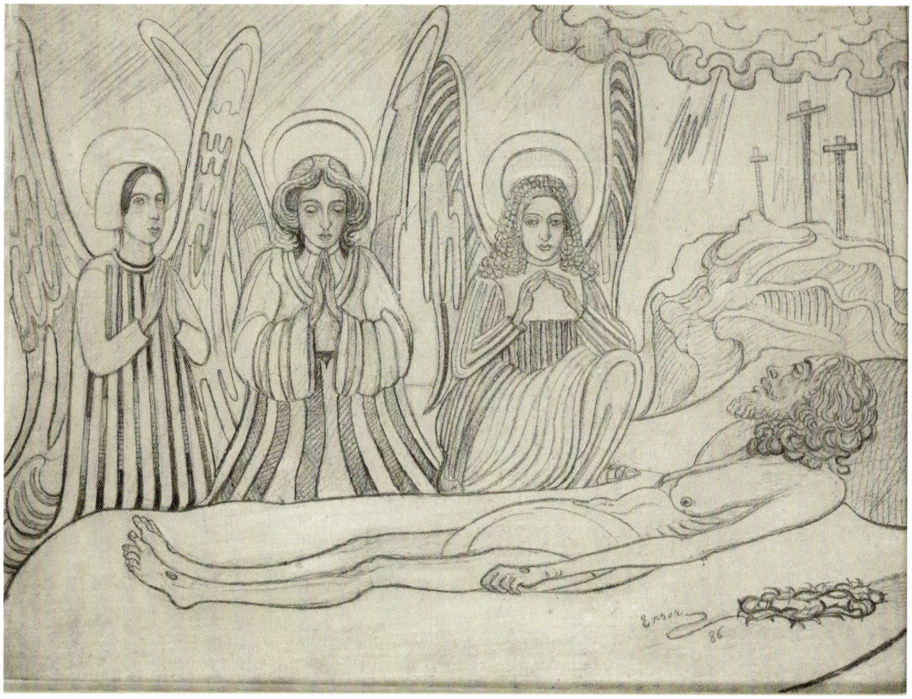

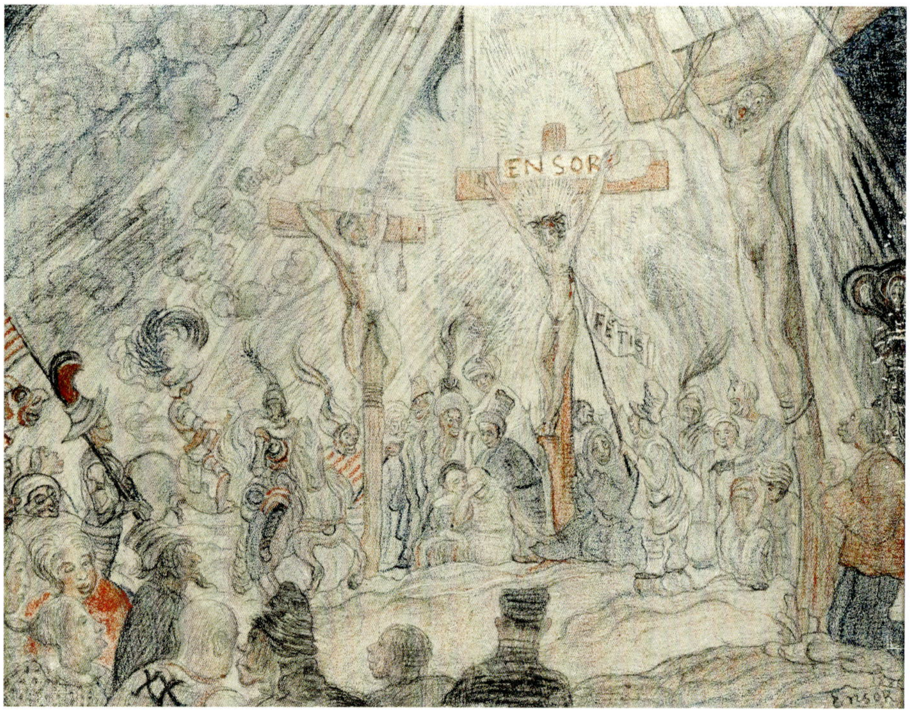

28. *Christ Watched Over by Angels.* 1886
Black chalk on panel, 6 1/2 × 8 7/16" (16.5 × 21.4 cm)

29. *Calvary.* 1886
Pencil, crayon, and oil on paper, 6 3/4 × 8 3/4"
(17.2 × 22.2 cm)

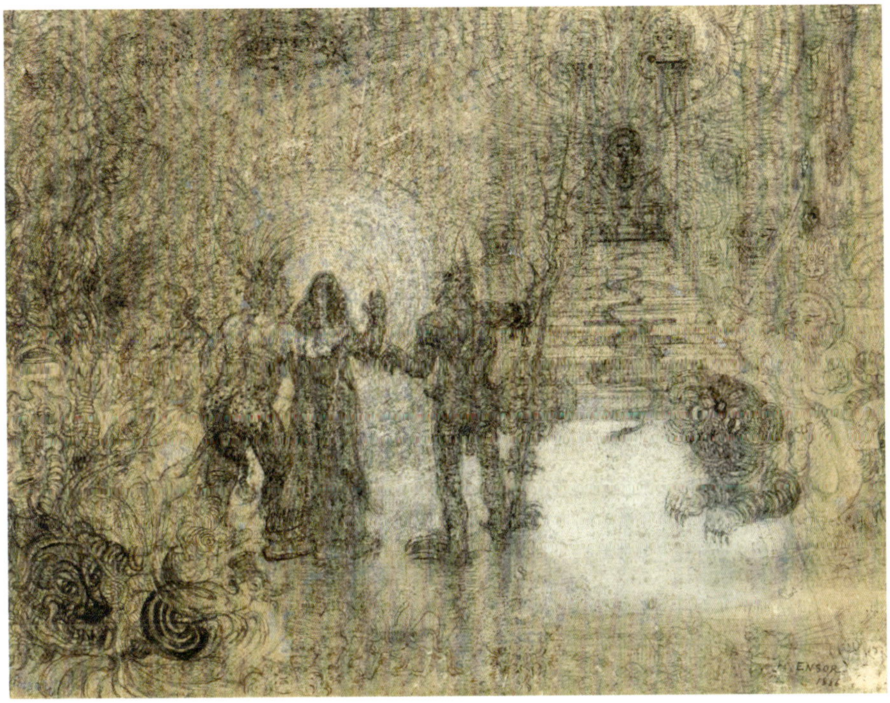

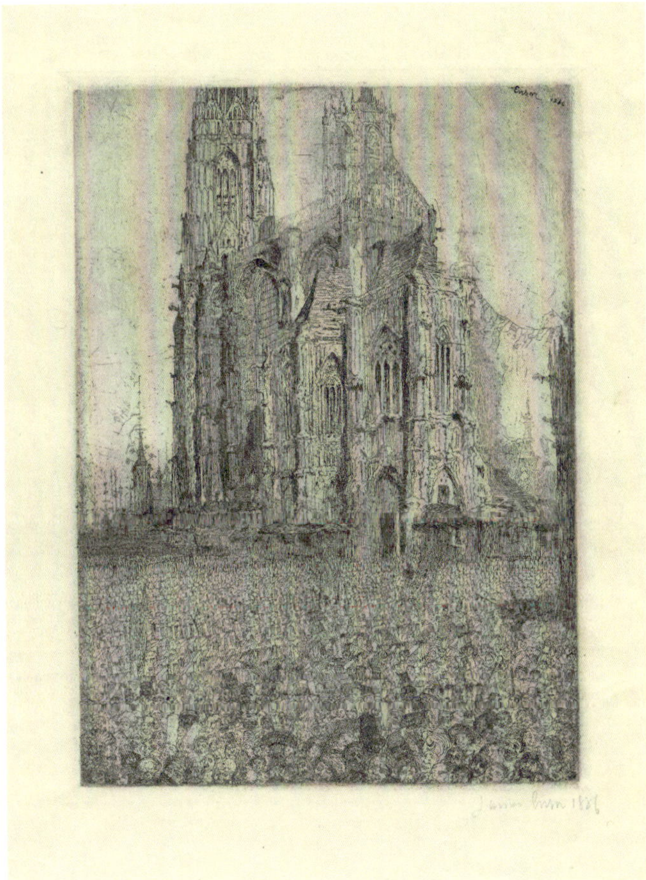

30. *The Devils Dzitts and Hihahox, Led by Crazon, Riding a Wild Cat, Leading Christ into Hell.* 1886
Pencil, Conté crayon, black chalk, brown India ink, pen, and white gouache on Japan paper, mounted on panel, 6 13/16 × 8 15/16" (17.3 × 22.7 cm)

31. *The Cathedral.* Plate I, state III. 1886
Etching on Japan paper, plate: 9 5/16 × 7" (23.6 × 17.7 cm)

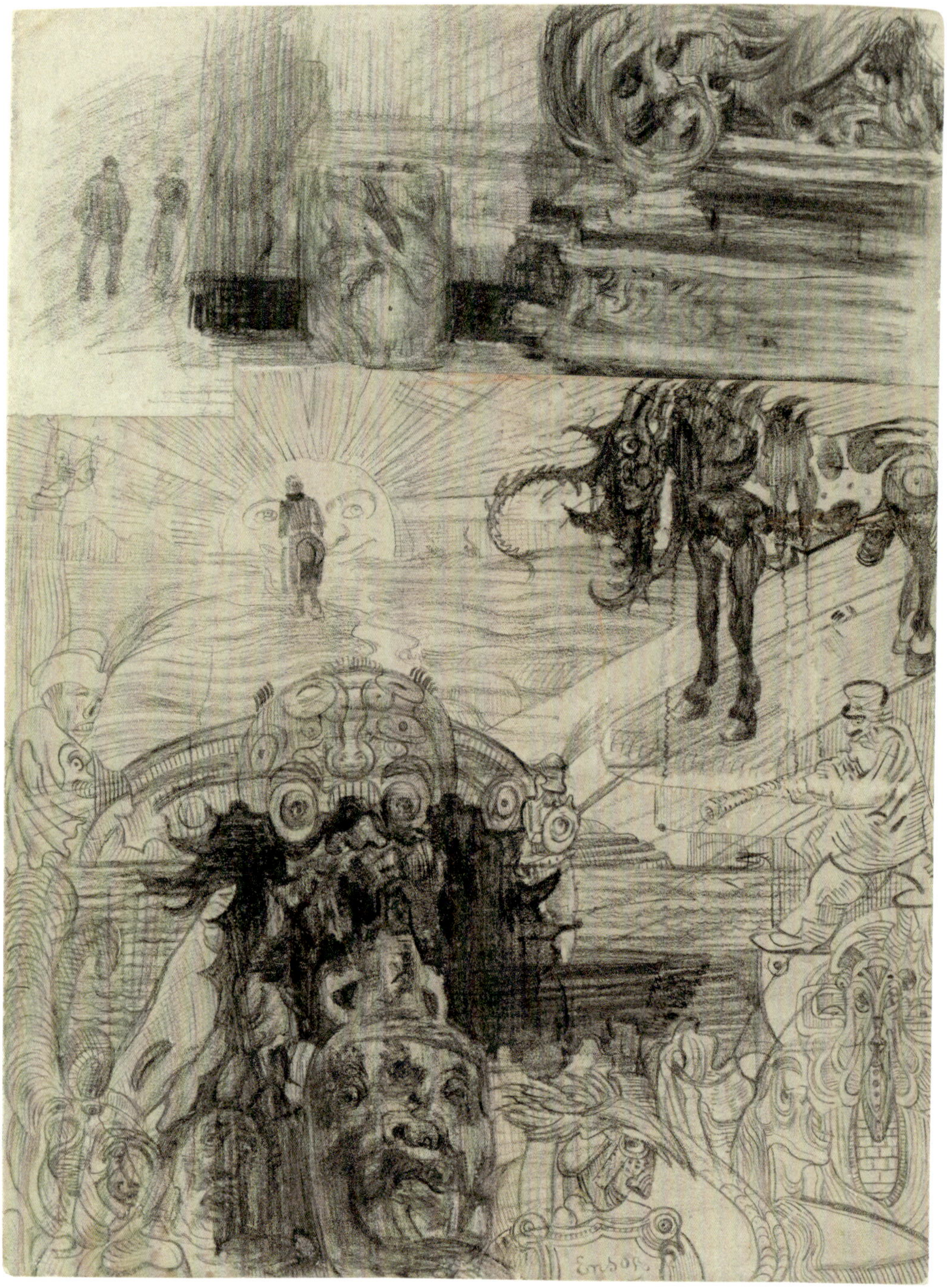

32. *Hippogriff*. 1880–83/1886–88
Black chalk on two sheets of paper, mounted on board, 8 7/8 × 6 11/16" (22.5 × 17 cm)

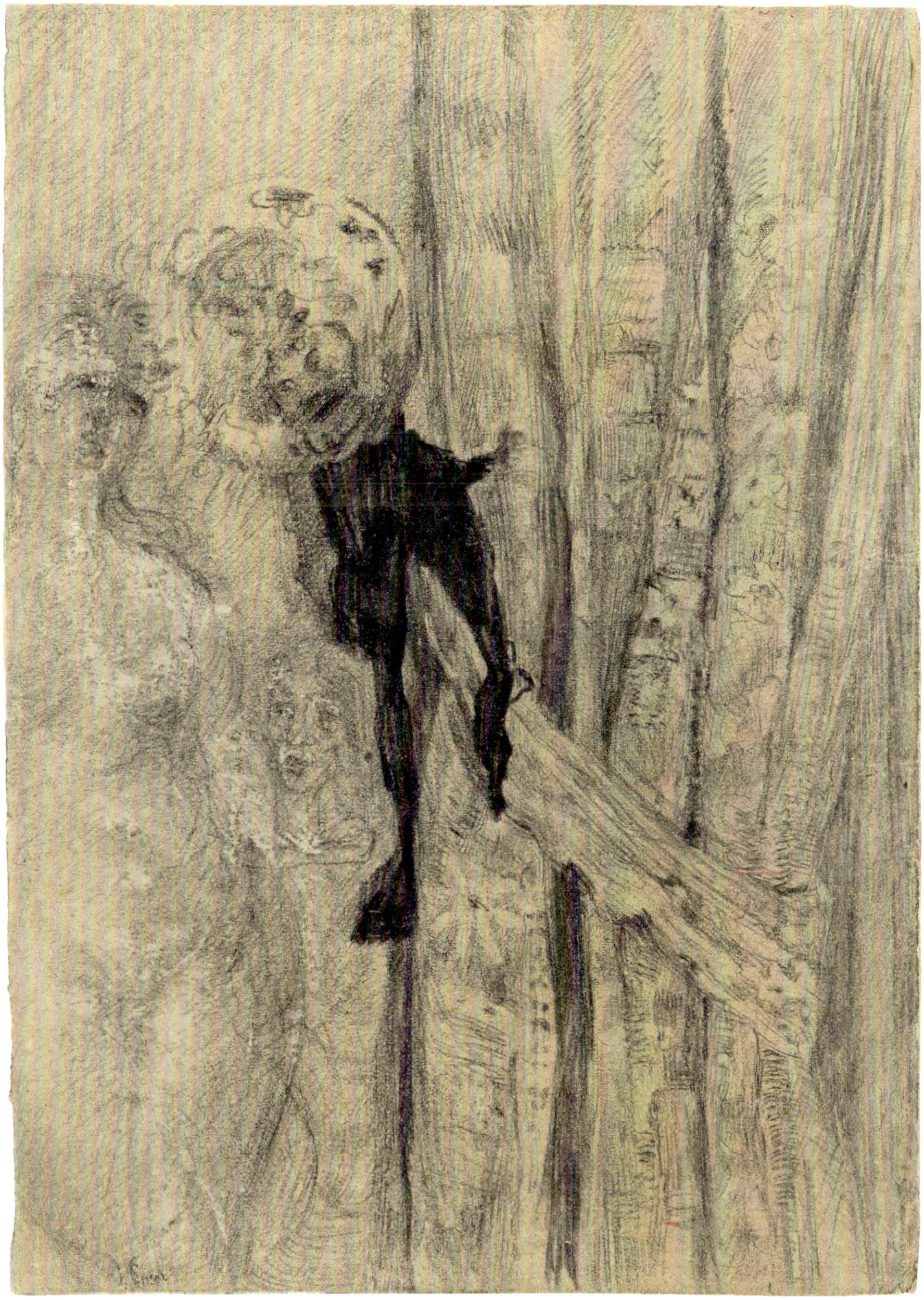

33. *Nude with Curtain.* 1880–85/1886–88
Pencil and black chalk on paper, mounted on board, 8 7/8 × 6 7/16" (22.5 × 16.4 cm)

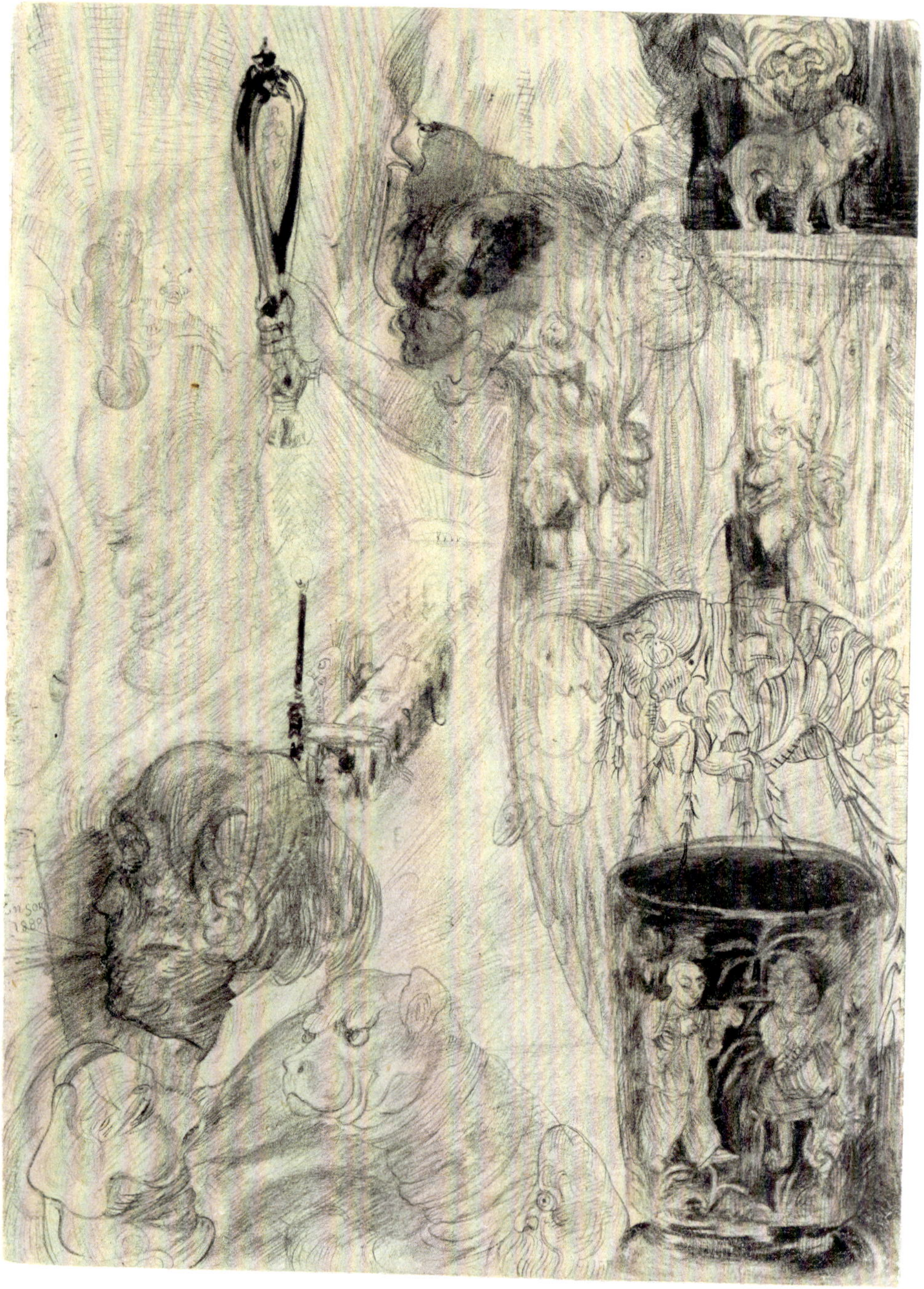

34. *The Flea.* 1880–83/1888
Black crayon on paper, mounted
on board, 8 7/8 × 6 5/8" (22.6 × 16.8 cm)

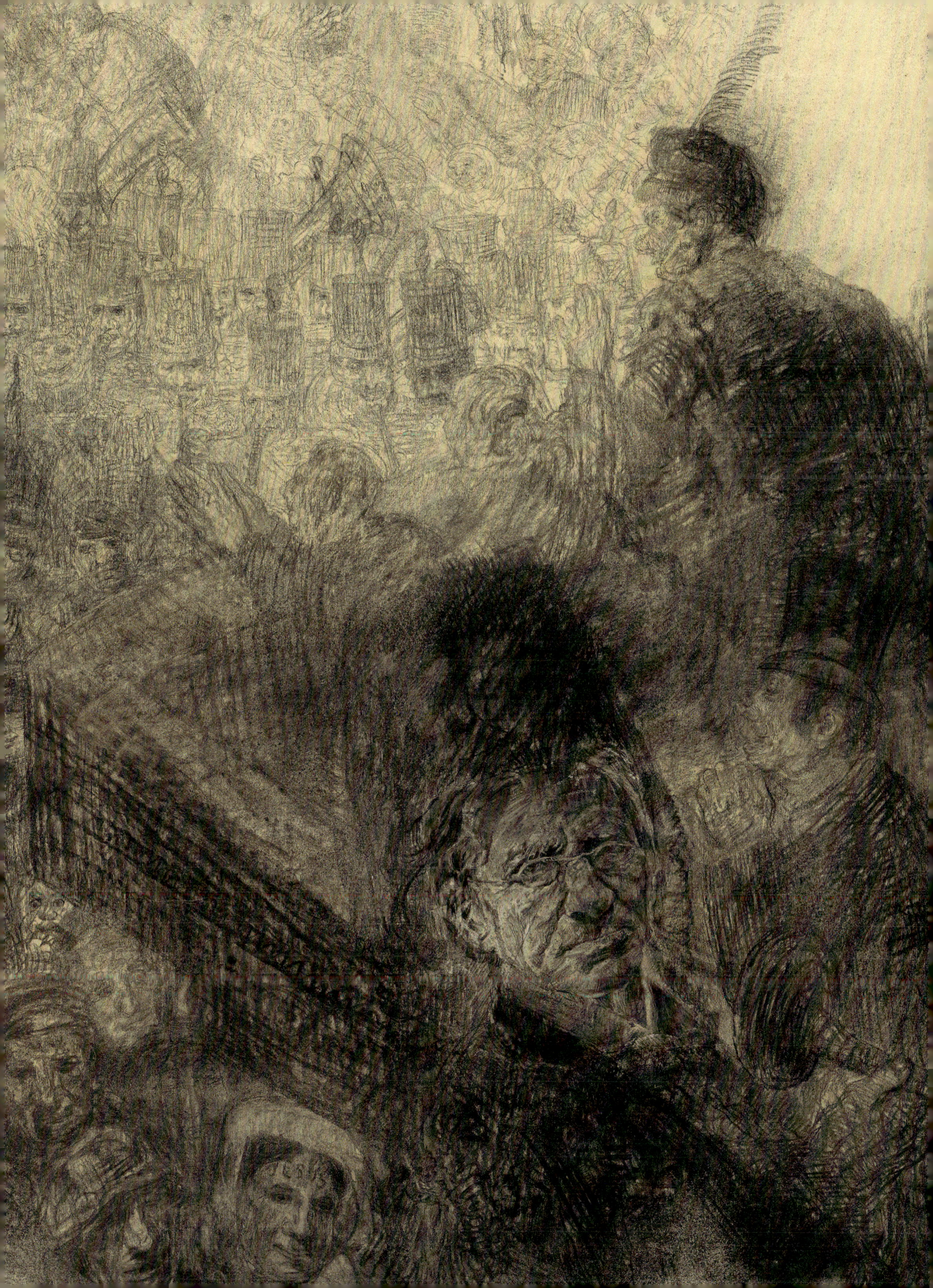

ESSAYS

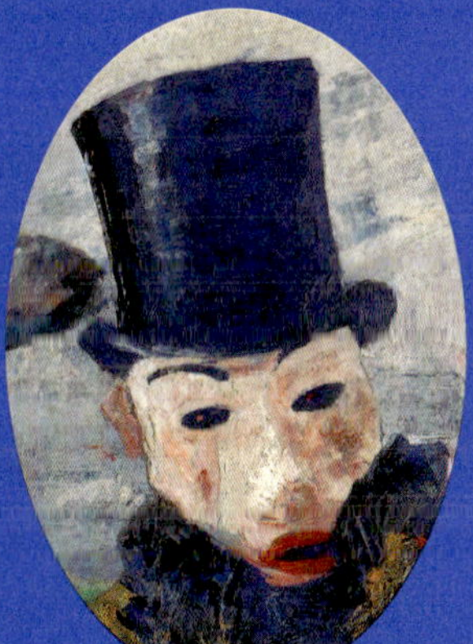

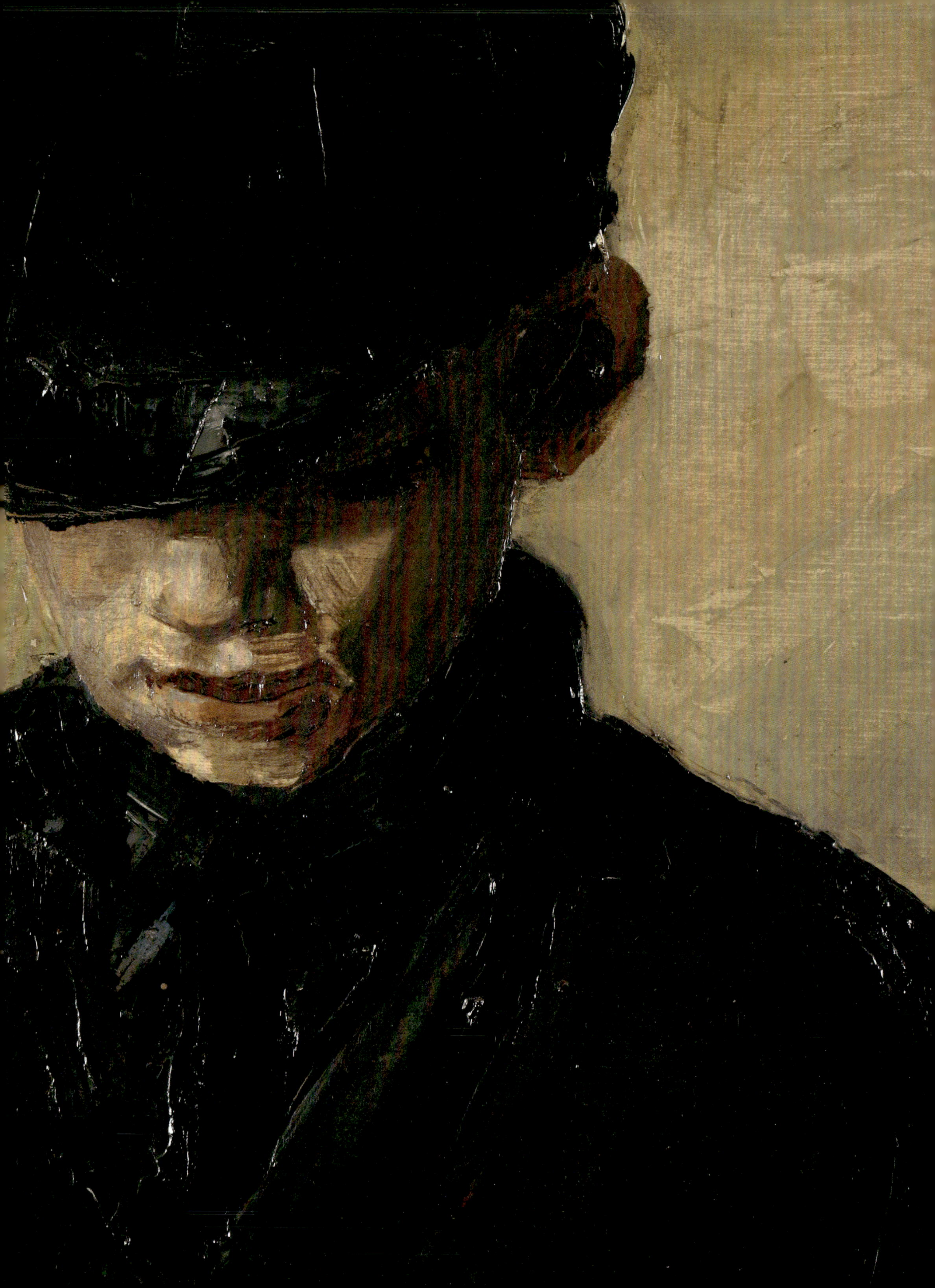

A View from Ostend

JANE PANETTA

To some extent, the future of modern painting was determined in that attic.
— *Paul Haesaerts*[1]

In a now iconic photograph of Ensor's Ostend studio, from 1921, a decorative metal globe hangs from the ceiling above the artist's worktable (fig. 1). The reflection on the globe records the room and its inhabitants, its papers, objects, and works of art, but does so in a distorting, even disturbing way. This reflection, grounded in the room's reality while simultaneously changing it, recalls much of the artist's work from the 1880s—work in which Ensor began with the world around him but viewed it through a subjective and highly personalized lens to arrive at a surreal, fantastical, less recognizable realm. This essay will examine Ensor's art from around 1880 to 1888, and the significance of the immediate reality available to him in Ostend, with a focus on his progressive, experimental works from the decade's first five years.

Ensor began his career as an interpreter, a transcriber of modern Belgian life. In the early 1880s he filled his sketchbooks with crayon drawings, usually made indoors, observing the streets outside his window and the objects and figures in his immediate sphere. He had grown up in Ostend, leaving it only to attend the Académie royale des beaux-arts, in Brussels. Ostend, a resort town on the Belgian coast, had come to prominence after the coronation of King Leopold II, in 1865, when it experienced a boom in the number of summer tourists visiting the port. Through its popular casino, its cultural activities, and the perceived health benefits of the sea, Ostend attracted more and more high-end tourists during the second half of the nineteenth century. Each summer Ensor witnessed the town and family shop come wildly alive for a few months, in stark contrast to the sleepy off-season.

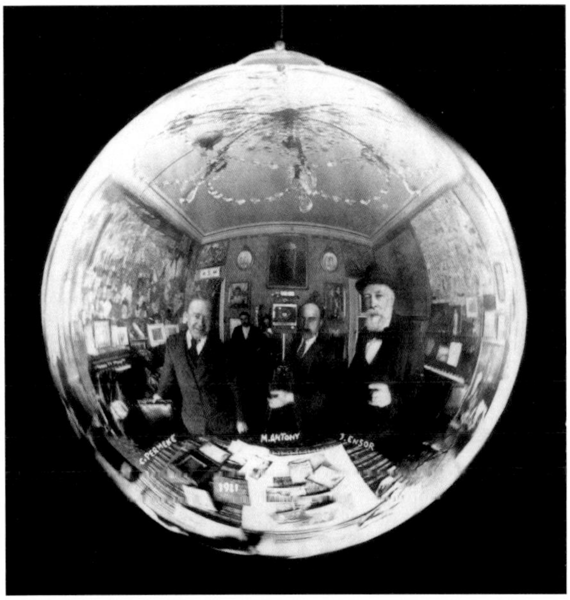

FIG. 1: Portrait by Maurice Antony showing, left to right, Constant Permeke, August Van Yper, Antony, and James Ensor in Ensor's drawing room, reflected in mirrored ball. Ostend, April 18, 1921

Returning from Brussels in 1880, Ensor ensconced himself in his parents' house at 23 Vlaanderenstraat, above the ground-floor family business, a curiosity shop. Throughout the 1880s he spent much of his time in his attic studio, working directly from local models—fishermen, servants, the ordinary people of Ostend—to paint portraits such as *The Lamp-Lighter* (*Le Lampiste*, 1880; plate 3 and detail opposite). Works like this, many agree, show the influence of Édouard Manet, whom Ensor admired and even copied.[2] While for the most part a realistic, basically traditional composition closely imitating the world in front of him, the work hints at the audacious future of the artist's work through subtle choices: the boy is darkly outlined against a stark bright background, "a wall that serves as a screen."[3] His frontal position dominates our view, encroaching on us almost aggressively, while his feet are dramatically lengthened, in an acknowledgment of what Ensor would later call "the distortion" implicit in this particular painting.[4]

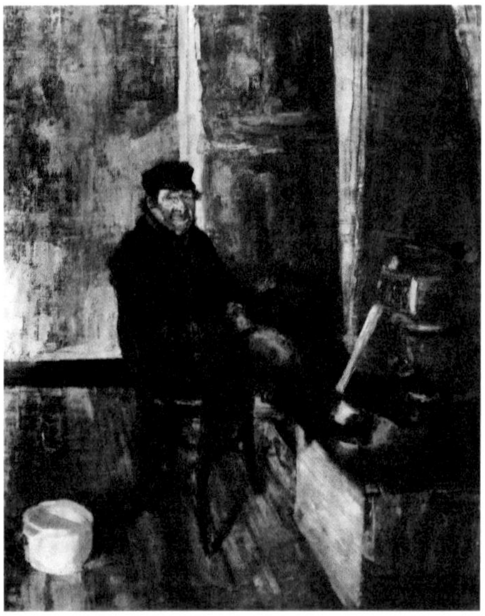

FIG. 2: JAMES ENSOR. *Sick Tramp Trying to Warm Himself.* 1882. Oil on canvas, 38 9/16 × 34 5/8" (98 × 88 cm) (destroyed)

Coarse, flattened color disrupts the realism and overall harmony of the composition in a quietly rebellious way—Ensor was determined to present a degree of his own subjectivity.[5] Here, in 1880, at the early age of twenty, he was already showing himself restless with existing academic practices.

Like *The Lamp-Lighter*, *Sick Tramp Trying to Warm Himself* (*Le Pouilleux indisposé se chauffant*; fig. 2) is essentially constructed as a mimetic portrait of a local model, but it suggests an approach similar to that of the more subjective works still to come.[6] In hat and coat, sitting on a wooden chair, the tramp with his masklike face looks pinned or caught. Ensor would reuse the figure the following year in *The Scandalized Masks* (*Les Masques scandalisés*, 1883; plate 15), an elusive and even more symbolic painting that fuses observation with invention more than either of the earlier works:[7] the male figure from *Sick Tramp Trying to Warm Himself* reappears, in the same nondescript room, but now the figure perhaps represents Ensor's father, who fought an ongoing battle with alcoholism; the woman carrying a carnival horn in the doorway may suggest his grandmother, both comic and disapproving; and the icy blue light beyond her may be intended to suggest death coming for his derelict father.[8] *The Scandalized Masks*, significant as one of Ensor's first uses of the mask motif, heralds a new phase in his work, in which, in his words, "reality and imagination walk entwined together toward the horizon line."[9] Much more than a genre scene, it announces Ensor's decision to engage with the symbolic and strange, and to explain to the viewer just how he will do it: using a realistic vocabulary—images of his immediate family, his native Ostend, the moody, expressive palette of the North Sea sky, and even borrowings from earlier works of his own—he creates an invented, ambiguous world.[10]

Objects such as the two masks worn in *The Scandalized Masks* reappear often in Ensor's paintings, suggesting that they were his own possessions and that he rearranged them repeatedly when painting in his studio. His use of these objects seems to have been less a Symbolist practice, in which the mask could be taken as a sign for the individual's social façade, than a subjective reflection of his own experience and surroundings. John David Farmer has identified some of his masks as specifically Flemish, probably carnival masks of a kind sold in his family's shop; indeed some of those shown in his work are actually known to have been available there.[11] Others, however, including the mask resembling an old, bonneted woman with blue glasses in *The Scandalized Masks*, seem not to have been based on any existing object but to have been his invention.[12] Even within the domain of the mask, by definition pushing toward the fictional, Ensor gave himself the freedom both to draw from objects in his studio and to combine these sources freely with personal invention.

In addition to documenting models in his studio and the street scenes he observed from his attic window, Ensor would venture downstairs to examine the quiet world of his family: his mother, father, aunt, grandmother, and younger sister, Mariette (or

"Mitche," as he liked to call her). This immediate subject matter became a rich terrain for portraits and domestic interiors, a representation of his life that Robert Hoozee has described as almost filmic.[13] In the most straightforward cases, this hermetic focus led to traditional portraits of female family members (Ensor rarely depicted his father) such as *Portrait of the Artist's Sister, Marie* (*La Soeur de l'artiste*, 1881; plate 8), an atmospheric drawing alluding to the many long days that the family spent indoors in Ostend in winter, waiting for the bustling tourist activity of the summer months. *Afternoon in Ostend* (*L'Après-dînée à Ostende*, 1881; plate 9) moves beyond the mundane to a murkier representation of domestic life, again during the bleak winter months. Here Ensor's sister and mother are seen seated in their living room, realistically detailed in its furniture, rugs, even curtains. As Herwig Todts has pointed out, though, the painting is less a double portrait of the two women—who essentially become objects in a still life—than a means to a something broader.[14] In setting, this seems a typical bourgeois scene, a predictable focus for a late-nineteenth-century painter. But the foreground is dramatic, perhaps even menacing, as figures and objects are engulfed by the aggressive patterning of the tablecloth and rug, seeming to move toward disintegration. In this suffocating interior space Ensor has deliberately fused the figures of the two women with their furniture and surroundings, as if to suggest that in their immobility through the long winter, they have eventually merged with the very environment they inhabit.

Only two years later, Ensor apparently tired of chronicling his family; after around 1882, he no longer created works overtly documenting this intimate group and moved to paintings on a more dramatic scale.[15] The monumental interior *The Oyster Eater* (*La Mangeuse d'huîtres*, 1882; plate 13) is an unorthodox rendition of a robust woman (while still based on his sister Mitche) purposefully eating a plate of oysters, a typical Flemish delicacy, at a table crowded with colorful glasses, bottles, and plates. Given the scale of this combined portrait and still life (the latter being Ensor's single most common genre over the course of his long career), the female figure is oversized and dominating, overpowering the canvas yet at the same time seeming to meld, through her white dress, into the white linen at the work's center. The menacing way the figure attacks her meal, and the fusion of her body with the dining room environment around her, reflect Ensor's determination to move beyond the parameters of his earlier work.

Submitted to the Antwerp Salon of 1882, *The Oyster Eater* was rejected. Critics thought it inappropriate, almost grotesque in its "lack of form";[16] for the most part they failed to recognize Ensor's ability to make the mundane unexpected through his use of color and light. (The critics Eugène Demolder and Émile Verhaeren celebrated this skill in their early monographs on the artist, published in 1892 and 1908 respectively, but in 1882 it went relatively unappreciated.) Ensor acknowledges the world around him in *The Oyster Eater*, but through a distorting style. The bottom right-hand part of the painting, for example, nearly disappears into sketchlike abstraction as figure and environment combine. If judged only by works like *The Lamp-Lighter*, Ensor might be called the Belgian Manet, but instead he abandons his more conventional representations in

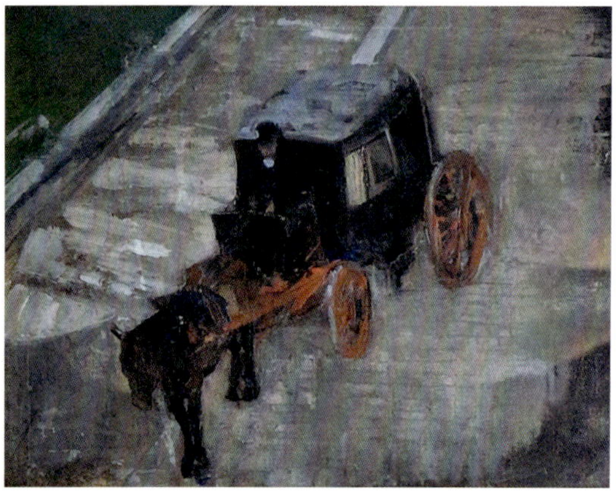

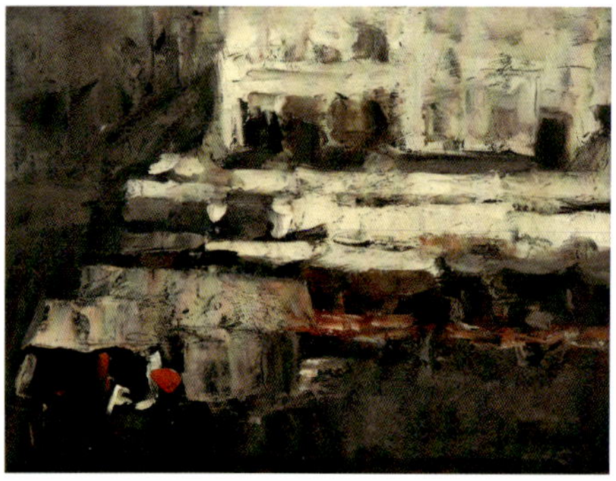

FIG. 3: JAMES ENSOR. *The Cab.* 1880/1882. Oil on canvas, 16 5/16 × 21 1/4" (41.5 × 54 cm). Private collection

FIG. 4: JAMES ENSOR. *The Market at Ostend.* 1881. Oil on panel, 9 5/8 × 12 5/8" (24.5 × 32 cm). KBC Belgium

favor of murkier interior compositions like *The Bourgeois Salon* (*A Salon* [*Impression*]) (*Le Salon bourgeois*, 1881; p. 31, fig. 3) and *Afternoon in Ostend*, engaging something haunted and disconcertingly alive, blending color and form into a patterned and colorful sea that seems to swallow its inhabitants. Discussing Ensor's drawings, Verhaeren wrote, "If for Ensor some furniture is haunted, then all the objects shudder, stir and feel. . . . Nothing is dead, completely."[17]

In the early 1880s the rendering of light became an increasingly important tool for Ensor, both a formal and visual device and a way to impart a symbolic vision, a vision that was often specifically Belgian, as he used light to recall the familiar Flemish landscape and sky. Often beginning from a realistic starting point, Ensor would use light and perspective to reenvision the world, whether a street scene, a religious or historical setting, or a still life. The most obvious basis for his formal exploration of light was his environment in Ostend; the sea and the unique light were important to him visually and made a lasting impact on him, present in his muted palettes and coarse brushstrokes, which generate translucent atmospheric results. This regional influence informed early landscape paintings like *The Rainbow* (*After the Storm*) (*L'Arc en ciel*, 1880; plate 1) and *Rooftops of Ostend* (*Grand View of Ostend*) (*La Grande Vue d'Ostende*, 1884; plate 20), which are ethereal and abstract in color and texture, directly acknowledging the light of the misty North Sea sky with which Ensor was so familiar in Ostend and able to witness daily, as it dominated the view from the south-facing windows of his attic studio.[18] A reviewer in an issue of *L'Art moderne* from 1883 understood the particular significance of place for Ensor: "Living in Ostend, in winter as in summer, his eye seems to have grown quite accustomed to seeing things only with the ill-defined edges bestowed on them by the maritime fogs."[19] Despite their traditional, indeed arguably academic choice of subject, these landscapes combine raw, near abstract renderings with a unique, expressive palette.

In *Boulevard Van Iseghem in the Rain* (*Boulevard Van Iseghem sous la pluie*, 1880; plate 5) Ensor described a familiar, uninhabited Ostend street, visible from his studio, but again showed himself unwilling to appease conventional expectations. Through frenetic brushstrokes and aggressive, angular lines that almost seem to anticipate the work of Willem de Kooning, the architectural landscape loses its points of reference; street and buildings become nearly indistinguishable, just as Ensor blended the disparate parts of a domestic interior. Similarly, paintings such as *The Cab* (*Le Fiacre*; fig. 3) and, still more forcefully, *The Market at Ostend* (*Marché à Ostende*; fig. 4) obscure naturalistic imagery in a sea of dark hues (characteristic of these early works), abstract brushstrokes, and unusual perspectives — *The Cab* seems to have been painted from above, perhaps from Ensor's attic window. Although these works are without the visionary details that would appear in Ensor's later paintings, they seem to anticipate his imminent abandonment of mimetic realism in exchange for his own imagination. We are already confronted with a reality only precariously tethered to recognizable form.

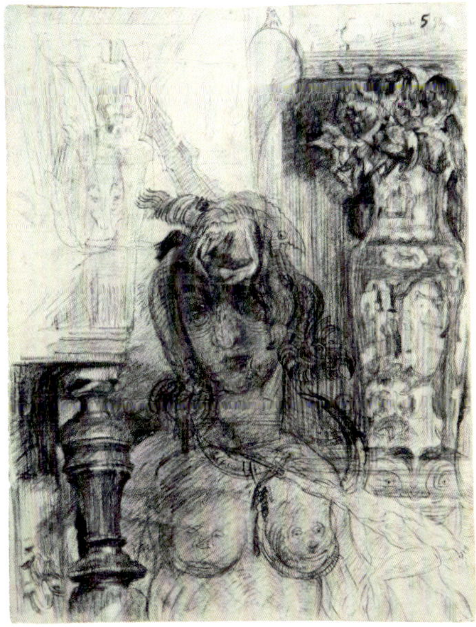

FIG. 5: JAMES ENSOR. *Nude with Balustrade*. 1880–85/1886–88. Charcoal on paper, mounted on board, 8 ⅞ × 6 11/16" (22.5 × 17 cm). museum kunst palast, Düsseldorf. Graphische Sammlung

In 1880 Ensor began a series of thirty-one drawings, primarily based on domestic objects and interiors, that he would later revise, returning to them by 1885. In his revision he experimented by embellishing his relatively traditional compositions of a few years earlier, dramatically augmenting his original observations of the everyday world—figures walking in the street, architectural details—by adding fantastical imagined objects undoubtedly informed by the curiosities in the family shop, where Ensor sometimes worked.[20] The shop was filled with carnival masks, fans, shells, stuffed animals, puppets—what Libby Tannenbaum described as the "furniture" of his paintings.[21] The drawing *Nude with Balustrade* (*Nu au balustre*; fig. 5) of 1880–85/1886–88 is a kaleidoscopic, almost hallucinatory drawing, superimposing a strange shell, a mysterious sea creature, and a nude female figure inexplicably adorned with monstrous faces on otherwise realistic furnishings. (In the bottom left-hand corner is a detail of a balustrade, very similar to a detail of an armoire in Ensor's Ostend home.)[22] Similarly, drawings such as *Hippogriff* (*Hippogriffe*, 1880–83/1886–88; plate 32) and *The Flea* (*La Puce*, 1880–83/1888; plate 34) were modified in the mid-1880s to include such elements as a horse with the head of an eagle—the mythical Hippogriff—and a jug with animated mask faces. These reworkings and distortions of recognizable reality have often been acknowledged as precursors of Surrealism.

Ensor's reworked drawings began as sketchbooklike pages peppered associatively with observed objects, laced often randomly together on a single sheet. Evolving through their bizarre additions, which often fill up all the available space, the crammed pages take on a surreal, impenetrable quality. The compositions seem to imply a coherence that is not present; Ensor has made wholes out of parts that are in fact quite disparate.

In the mid-1880s, Ensor was increasingly combining two distinct preoccupations by introducing fantastical elements, many of them recurring, into landscape paintings. In *Tribulations of Saint Anthony* (*Terribles Tribulations de Saint-Antoine*, 1887; plate 37), which Alfred H. Barr, Jr., founding director of The Museum of Modern Art, thought made Ensor "possibly the boldest living painter" of the time (when Paul Gauguin and Vincent van Gogh, for example, were also making radical work), an old Christian story fuses with a fully expressionist landscape as invented creatures populate the canvas.[23] Ensor, surely looking at the work of earlier Flemish artists like Pieter Brueghel and particularly Hieronymus Bosch,[24] began making landscapes and religious scenes that were irrational and otherworldly, fabricated from his imagination. Building on his earlier practice of combining multiple drawings on a single sheet, *Tribulations of Saint Anthony* sets disparate figures, objects, monsters, and animals in an abstract landscape, making the viewer digest what could be multiple works within a single canvas.

While much of the Belgian avant-garde was emulating the measured work of artists like Georges Seurat and the Neo-Impressionists, Ensor was determined to reconcile his interest in describing his compelling surroundings with his commitment to his own subjectivity, to being "personal through and through."[25] Paul Fierens aptly characterized his work as art in which "the logic of life gives way to dreams."[26] The relatively small number of truly academic paintings in his oeuvre (a small percentage of his entire seventy-six-year output, and generally confined to roughly 1873–79), and his self-conscious decision to modify existing drawings, as if unwilling to allow his legacy to include an inordinately high number of traditional works, point to his progressive ambition.

Ensor's work remains difficult to characterize, defying placement within the accepted movements and trajectories of late-nineteenth-century modern art. Like his Norwegian contemporary Edvard Munch, he functioned in Ostend separated from most of his art-world contemporaries and the traditional epicenters of avant-garde artmaking during this period, allowing him to create work persistently his own, both stylistically and conceptually. Some scholarship on Ensor has deemphasized his relationship to Ostend, the uninterrupted time he spent there, and the value the town held for him (he was its persistent advocate and defender),[27] perhaps in an attempt to avoid labeling him "provincial" or simply "the artist from Ostend." Like the distorting globe in his studio, Ensor appropriated and reenvisioned the material things present in his immediate environment: the masks and curiosities from his family shop, the familiar North Sea, and even his own family members. Ostend's intractable presence in his life and consciousness, and the physical separation it gave him from much of the art world, had a sophisticating and distinguishing effect on his work and provided the platform from which he began his venture into more ambitious territory. Ensor's decision to reexamine the world around him, a world not yet mined as progressively by other artists, through his personalized lens was a pivotal influence in his creation of startling compositions and a unique vocabulary and voice. The coherence of his perspective during the 1880s depended on this naturalistic foundation; for Ensor, creativity seems to have sprung from rattling about amid the familiar objects of his own existence.

NOTES

1. Paul Haesaerts, *Ensor* (New York: Harry N. Abrams, 1959), p. 50.
2. See, for example, Libby Tannenbaum, *James Ensor* (New York: The Museum of Modern Art, 1951), p. 35, and Anne Pingeot and Robert Hoozee, eds., *Paris–Bruxelles: Bruxelles-Paris: Réalisme, impressionnisme, symbolisme, art nouveau* (Antwerp: Fonds Mercator; Paris: Éditions de la Réunion des musées nationaux, 1997), p. 10.
3. Michel Draguet, *James Ensor ou la fantasmagorie* (Paris: Éditions Gallimard, 1999), p. 33. This and all other translations from French, unless otherwise noted, are by David Frankel.
4. James Ensor, letter to André De Ridder, August 2, 1928, in Ensor, *Lettres à André de Ridder* (Anvers: Librairie des Arts, 1960), p. 59.
5. See Peter Gay, *Modernism: The Lure of Heresy* (New York: W. W. Norton, 2008), p. 118.
6. *Sick Tramp Trying to Warm Himself* was destroyed during World War II. At the time it was in the collection of the Stedelijk Museum voor Schone Kunsten, Ostend.
7. Draguet, who calls the masklike face of the figure in *Sick Tramp Trying to Warm Himself* "the grotesque result of expressive distortion," links the work to *The Scandalized Masks* in *James Ensor*, p. 146.
8. Many critics have shared this interpretation of the seated figure in this painting. See Draguet, *James Ensor*, p. 145.
9. Ensor, letter to André De Ridder, September 30, 1928, in Ensor, *Lettres à André de Ridder*, p. 62.
10. In *Skeletons Trying to Warm Themselves* (*Squelettes voulant se chauffer*, 1889; plate 54), for example, the figures huddled around the stove, the stove itself, and the room and its wooden floorboards all seem borrowed from *Sick Tramp Warming Himself.*
11. See John David Farmer, *Ensor* (New York: George Braziller, 1976), p. 27.
12. See Diane Lesko, *James Ensor: The Creative Years* (Princeton: Princeton University Press, 1985), p. 24.
13. Robert Hoozee, "Drawings and Etchings" in Catherine de Zegher, ed., *Between Street and Mirror: The Drawings of James Ensor* (New York: The Drawing Center, 2001), p. 17.
14. See Herwig Todts, *James Ensor: Paintings and Drawings from the Collection of the Royal Museum of Fine Arts in Antwerp* (Antwerp: Koninklijk Museum voor Schone Kunsten and BAI, 2008), p. 52.
15. There has been much speculation on Ensor's reasons for turning away from the subject of his oppressive family. Farmer writes, "For relief from family anxieties, he turned to other models," presumably including invented subjects. *Ensor*, p. 19. In addition, Todts points out that when Ensor exhibited many of his "fictions of modern life," he gave them vague titles; they were not intended as portraits, regardless of who modeled for them. As examples Todts cites *The Land of Colors* (1882) and *After Lunch* (1881). See Todts, *James Ensor*, p. 52.
16. Farmer, *Ensor*, p. 21.
17. Émile Verhaeren, *Ensor*, p. 51, as quoted in Stephen H. Goddard, ed., *Les XX and the Belgian Avant-Garde: Prints, Drawings, and Books, c. 1890* (Lawrence, Kans.: Spencer Museum of Art, University of Kansas, 1992), p. 180.
18. Ensor himself identified the landscapes he painted from the window of his attic studio in a letter to de Ridder, August 2, 1928, in Ensor, *Lettres à Andre de Ridder*, p. 55.
19. "Septième Exposition de L'Essor," *L'Art moderne* 3, no. 2 (January 14, 1883): 10.
20. Ensor was not satisfied simply to add fantastical elements to the existing motifs. In *Hippogriff* (1880–83/1886–88), for example, "He entirely redrew the original composition, for example the horse on a page, and the dog's head above another." Sabine Bown-Taevernier, Robert Hoozee, and Jan Frederik Heijbroek, *Moi James Ensor* (Paris: Albin Michel, 1987), p. 104.
21. Tannenbaum, *James Ensor*, p. 31.
22. See Bown-Taevernier, Hoozee, and Heijbroek, *Moi James Ensor*, p. 103.
23. Alfred H. Barr, Jr., ed., *Masters of Modern Art* (New York: The Museum of Modern Art, 1955), p. 34.
24. Hieronymus Bosch painted an interpretation of the tribulations of Saint Anthony around 1500.
25. Gay, *Modernism*, p. 118. The Belgian artist Théo Van Rysselberghe, like Ensor a member of Les Vingt, is now known primarily for the relationship of his pointillist work to that of better-known artists such as Georges Seurat and Paul Signac.
26. Paul Fierens, "Preface," in Tannenbaum, *James Ensor*, p. 9.
27. See Frank Patrick Edebau, "James Ensor and Ostend" in Farmer, *Ensor*, p. 12. Ensor once wrote, "Poor old Ostend, at the mercy of the depredations of lame architects who see no farther than their noses. Down with those who are ruining our marvelous landmarks!" Patricia G. Berman, *James Ensor: Christ's Entry into Brussels in 1889* (Los Angeles: J. Paul Getty Museum, 2002), p. 34.

Ensor: A Theater of Matter

MICHEL DRAGUET

Yes, our actions are pictorial, our inventions are enormous, our thoughts are tragicomical, our temptations are burlesque, our desires are born of the flatlands, our paradises are made of dough and condensed milk, and our endearments are made of butter.

—*James Ensor, 1924*[1]

Throughout his writing, in both texts and correspondence, James Ensor shows a very acute sensitivity to matter and materiality. In a 1928 letter to his friend André de Ridder, he speaks of a passion for painting that took hold of him at the age of thirteen, describing his first two teachers, Michel Van Cuyck and Édouard Dubar, as "brined and oiled."[2] He would later employ a similar trope, speaking of the masks that are such an important motif in his work as "spiced with prettiness, purple, azure blue, mother-of-pearly, shell-like, oysterish, embossed, striped, turboty, bearded, coddy, floundery, rascally, imbued with imagination, they are exuberant to their hearts' content."[3]

Such subtle textures were rendered by Ensor with a technique that ran into criticism from very early on. What was seen as the "turpitude" of his early compositions was compounded by scatological effects that, beyond any iconography, exacerbated the offense against public taste.[4] His provocative technique, with its thick drips and impasto, was intended to be excremental in its very existentiality. In 1891 critics spoke out vociferously against Ensor—seeing nothing in his painting but "smears that seem randomly brushed on with hatchings of the palette."[5] According to Ernest Verlant, the artist was undertaking, "through a new dance of the human body, a crushing defeat of this microbial world that is nothing but coagulated nothingness."[6] Ensor's gesture seemed to spring from matter itself, with the force of an uncontrollable impulse.

A Northern Landscape

In 1875–76, to escape an oppressive familial universe,[7] Ensor entered into dialogue with nature and its lights, though without submitting to any sense of representational obligation. The painter displayed a true confidence in his atmospheric renderings of the Northern sky, in which the grays are modulated with little help from the sun (which shines rarely in this region). Light is not transparency; it would not appear in Ensor's work as such until 1885, when he began his series of drawings Visions: The Aureoles of Christ or the Sensibilities of Light (Visions: Les Auréoles du Christ ou les sensibilités de la lumière; plates 26 and 27). In his landscape paintings, from the "skies . . . low and heavy as a lid"[8] to the steel color of the menacing clouds, Ensor's brushstroke finds the nuances of all the gradations of gray. Here light is embodied in the matter that gives its texture to the landscape.

Ensor was an observer. But his gaze was fixed less on the object than on the substance of the spectacle before him. This "lyricism" of the brush comes primarily from his experience of the North Sea, with its opacity and the roughness of the elements brought in on the gray of its tides, which melds with the gray of the sky. The seascape is the perfect place for the meandering eye, which moves over the surface in a trajectory that recalls the traveler's journey. Everything here holds to a perfect flatness that focuses the gaze on the technique.

The sky establishes a relationship with the sea by providing a panoramic stretch of substantial emptiness (so important to the seascapes of Gustave Courbet, whose work Ensor studied with interest). Likewise, in Ensor's *Rooftops of Ostend* (*Grand View of Ostend*) (*La Grande Vue d'Ostende*, 1884; plate 20) the town is reduced to a frieze upon which the leaden sky weighs down. From the royal stables, visible in the foreground, to the Dominican church above which waves the Belgian flag, Ensor composes this marquetry of rooftops by modulating their colors, from sienna to pinkish-red. The heavy impasto emphasizes the solidity of this sea of tiles. The immutability is reconstructed, as if the sea had swallowed the city before mixing with the heavens. Ensor does not play with transparency by going from light to color; on the contrary, he spreads the impasto, first laying down his colors, which are never pure. The white that "taints" them obviates the dazzling illumination that would infiltrate the work of the Impressionists around the same period. Ensor remains faithful to his Northern sky: it provides a true painter's light, which brightens without making iridescent, illuminates without the aid of the sun. Ensor applies his shades of ocher, gray, and blue, forming a wall of matter that is both dense and opalescent, fierce and delicate. Spread with his palette knife, the impasto grabs on to the canvas and makes its imprint. Applying layer after layer, methodically varying his shades in harmonious contrasts, Ensor achieves the white that proves the opacity of a mist-filled sky. The work is also a harbinger: subtle strokes of orangey-red project reflections of the rooftops into the clouds, announcing the possibility of a hallucinatory swing into phantasmagoria.

Ensor offers the necrotic sociability of the city as a contrast to the vastness of the eternal, unchanging sea. He would continue to explore such techniques and qualities in his later landscapes.[9]

Matter and Tradition

Ensor's sensitivity to matter grew out of an artistic tradition that was deeply concerned with national identity in the years 1878–80. Belgium was then celebrating fifty years as an independent state and the debate about the nature of an "authentically" Belgian art was raging. Convinced of the organic power of color as matter, Ensor participated in these discussions. The painter found himself in the wake of the Société libre des beaux-arts,[10] founded in 1868, which brought together artists such as Charles Degroux, Constantin Meunier, Louis Dubois, Louis Artan, and Félicien Rops. Realism had been defined at the Société as a meeting of nature, the individual, and color. Light, it was believed, was the catalyst. For the writer Camille Lemonnier, this idea was "above all, landscapist and portraitist."[11] An instinctive painter, extremely aware of the senses, Ensor liked to think of himself as the agent of a tradition that fed into a nationalist discourse in the 1880s. Émile Verhaeren would return to this nationalist notion in a 1908 text:

> *Artistic aptitude is never knowledge, but a gift. It is subconscious and deaf. The man born without it, even as he sees, hears, smells, tastes, and touches, will never be an authentic artist. No amount of study will allow him to acquire it. Privileged races*

> *transmit it to their different schools, through the centuries. One of these races is the admirable race of the Netherlanders.*[12]

Fierce Troweling

In the early 1880s, Ensor was seeking a personal formula for his art. It would take shape through his association with two other painters, Périclès Pantazis and Guillaume Vogels, whose 1878 exhibition at Brussels's Cercle artistique et littéraire was a beacon for Ensor.[13] A disciple of Hippolyte Boulenger, Vogels established himself as the master of a new conception of landscape by rendering the fluidity of light with impastos. Emphasizing the qualities of immediacy and the effects of the season—rain, snow, fog—Vogels transformed the illusion of nature into a strictly pictorial demonstration. For reactionary critics, his painting appeared "impossible, thrown together, akin to that of whitewashers and poster hangers."[14] This emphasis on materiality would eventually begin to find critical favor in the mid-1880s. As one journalist put it in *L'Art moderne*, the landscape was transformed into a "reverie of nature, something like the lazy description of faraway feats, like softly soothing music whose vague, indecisive harmonies combine sensuously."[15]

In 1878–81, the schism between the older, naturalist generation and younger artists was widening, and knife-work was at the heart of their debate. Lemonnier denounced the use of a knife and palette as "fierce troweling."[16] Elsewhere, he elaborated:

> *A paintbrush is like a brain. But the knife is the dumb instrument of the laborer, it is unconscious, irresponsible, mechanical. It directs the hand, it collaborates with chance, even handled by a virtuoso, it keeps its inborn flaw, which is to turn everything it touches into matter. The knife invented the nearly-good-enough painting. The masons of art have found it convenient to perform their work with a trowel: it has simplified things, and they have been able to go without painting or drawing. It has been an enormous relief for lazy artists, who are numerous.*[17]

In his landscapes and still lifes, and in some lively portraits and self-portraits, Ensor became a master of knife-work. He emphasized the expressive power of action and revolutionized rough surface treatment. Light was no longer an exterior actor, but established as a material property. Applied with the knife, color adhered to the canvas in a body of matter. Ensor flattened space and negated perspective. He removed the sense of depth from his representations in order to better signify their solidity.

The Realist palette, dominated by grays and earth tones, gained luminosity under the influence of the work of Vogels and Pantazis, whose subtle harmonies and "pearly nuances of iridescent opal"[18] were greatly admired by Ensor. His impasto is worked over, twisted, kneaded to form an organism that seems to grow on the surface of the canvas. The paint is not spattered; the knife spreads it and smoothes it in large fields whose rough bumps allowed him to return with glazes, to modulate the gradations of color. The variations of light are not superimposed after the fact (as they were in the work of Claude Monet); they are instead juxtaposed in blotches that visually "create" the object and that interact chromatically until they compose a harmony of tones, culminating in the effect of a monochromatic ambiance.[19]

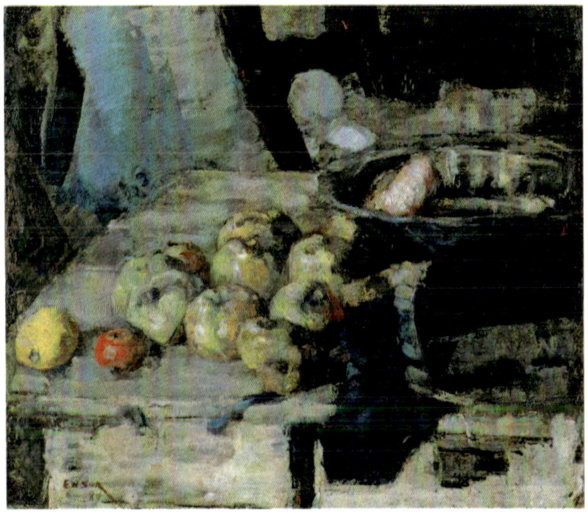

FIG. 1: JAMES ENSOR. *Apples*. 1880. Oil on canvas mounted on panel, 22 ¼ × 26 3/16" (56.5 × 66.5 cm). Staatsgalerie Stuttgart

From the Worker to the Object

In the world of the working man, Ensor discovered another focus that, like light, would serve as a vehicle with which to separate himself from the realm of bourgeois traditionalism. The rugged universe of fishermen, sailors, and other laborers seemed to the artist to be utterly without hypocrisy, and devoid of self-consciousness about appearances—and was thus able, in Ensor's view, to join the landscape and the still life as subjects of *pure presence*, disengaged from social theatricality.

In the early 1880s Ensor began to develop the raw style of painting for which he is best known. In *The Lamp-Lighter* (*Le Lampiste*, 1880; plate 3) he defines form by cutting the shadow out of the visual field, avoiding the obvious inscription of the body within space, negating perspective. This impulse to frame the entire image within the plane is even more emphasized by the painter's insistence on the materiality of his means—again, relying almost exclusively on his knife. The young ship's apprentice in this painting is for Ensor a pretext for an experiment with heaviness. Revealed by matter, shape exists independent of its illumination. As an integral part of matter, it is expressed in that "nameless mess" of technique about which *L'Art moderne* was still doubtful in 1883.[20] Ensor makes his black tones sing here, but does so without resorting to tonal effects: with only his knife-work, he brings out contrasts in the material itself.

Ensor never tried to achieve the objectivity that the Académie royale des beaux-arts in Brussels had attempted to inculcate in him. Everything was, for him, a pretext for painting to capture sensations and portray matter. His *Apples* (*Pommes*; fig. 1) presents red and green fruits arranged on a table next to a copper bowl. Nothing leads us to assign the composition any symbolic notation. The simplicity of the subject refers back to the painter's fixation on the conditions of sight. The colors allow him to structure the composition by playing with lighting and the sensuality of the materials. Form is inseparable from the sensation of volume that Ensor renders sculpturally. A few thick strokes sketch the object's essential geometry; the rest is organized into a dialogue of light and shadow. Ensor juxtaposes volumes, taking care to vary the way he paints them. The composition emphasizes the predominance of the layout: the table is treated formally and chromatically, in a way that frames the formal counterpoint. Without negating depth, Ensor reduces it: first by reinforcing the chromatic unity, then by underscoring it with knife-work, which draws out color whether it is in the foreground or the background. Unlike Paul Cézanne, Ensor does not link the solidity of the pictorial space with its transparency. The impasto affirms a flatness that weaves shadow and light into a dense web.

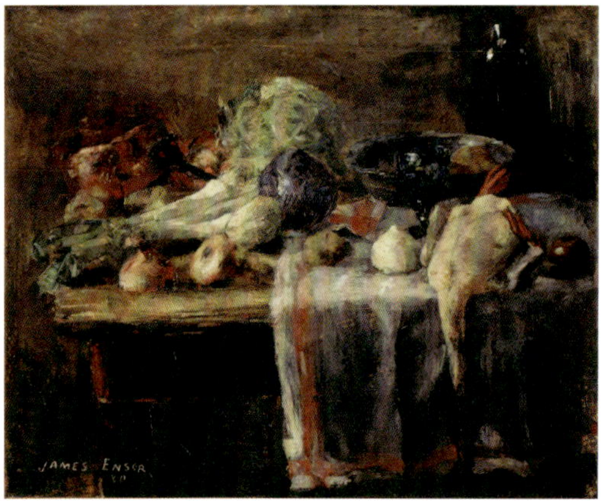

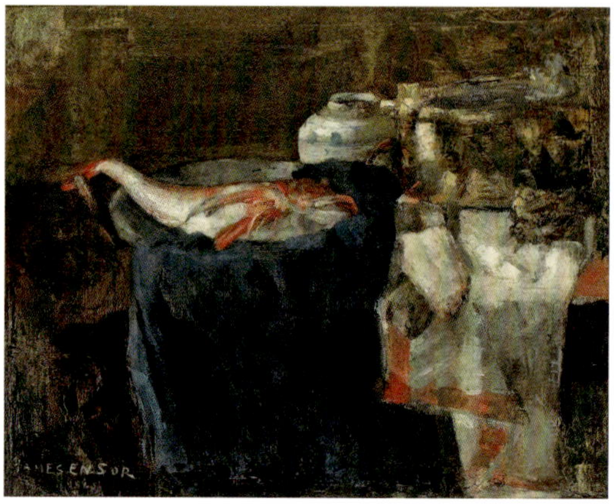

FIG. 2: JAMES ENSOR. *Still Life with Duck*. 1880. Oil on canvas, 31 ½ × 39 ⅜" (80 × 100 cm). Musée des beaux-arts, Tournai. Henri Van Cutsem Bequest, 1904

FIG. 3: JAMES ENSOR. *The Mullet*. 1880 or 1881. Oil on canvas, 31 ½ × 39 ⅜" (80 × 100 cm). Musée des arts décoratifs, Paris. Gift of Mrs. Paule Chardin in memory of her brother, Henri Chardin, 1986

The relationship that Ensor maintains with the visible world is not transformed into knowledge, but shows the way to an experiment in painting that restores its tactile dimension. The reality of things dissolves in the truth of the process that builds an image by playing with consistencies and textures. The relationships that the objects have with one another do not come from symbolic codes. Peaches on a white cloth, leeks beside a duck, a cabbage in the middle of a polyphony of vegetables: all find their meaning once the viewer's gaze touches them.

Light appears as an independent force that "irritates" color, forcing it to react. Objects have their own textures, independent of light's actions. Ensor portrays that sensation in a movement that progressively allows the shape to emerge from the background. His *Still Life with Duck* (*Nature morte au canard*; fig. 2) and *The Mullet* (*Le Rouget*; fig. 3) are perfect examples of this technique. In the former work, the brushstroke animates the still life without breaking its containment within the composition. Ensor contrasts the flickering light to the left with the muffled, funereal tones of the duck. Profusion and desolation come together here. In *The Mullet*, by radically breaking up the shapes, Ensor comes up against the limits of abstraction.

Double Vision

By first preparing his backgrounds with his knife, Ensor created an irregularity on the surface that would remain visible through subsequent work. The material and the design of the image face off; this confrontation is particularly charged in his self-portraits, which thus constitute a unique creative context.

For Ensor, painting offered a way to locate or found his identity in reaction to his family and society. This search for meaning was surely a reason for his prodigious number of self-portraits.[21] The self was nothing short of iconic for Ensor—as he put it: "The beautiful legend of Me, the unique Me, the corpulent Me, of the great verb To Be: I am, we are, you are, they are. . . ."[22] The self-portrait also offered him an unexpected laboratory for further experimentation with matter. While a landscape provides an inexhaustible horizon along which the viewer's gaze is carried, the self-portrait establishes a fixed point of view.[23] The viewer's eye comes closer to the painting to see its elements in detail. In so doing, it loses the sense of the piece as a whole, and hence creates a new relationship with the painting as matter.

Ensor achieved this give-and-take in three consecutive self-portraits. *Portrait of the Artist* (*The Big Head*) (*Portrait de l'artiste dit "grosse tête"*; fig. 4) is one example of this action: the viewer's gaze sheds its objective rationality, coming so close to the detail that the eye is almost touching it. The poeticism in this work does not stop at mimesis, but exerts a singular presence, dependent on the action that inscribes it on the canvas. This self-portrait is evidence of a physical experiment with matter that, between shadows and highlights, makes the body emerge as flesh much more than as ink or pencil marks. The drawing fades away, in a phenomenon that classical painters called the "madness" of close-up vision.[24] The system of perspective, which positions things at a distance to be recognized as objects, crumbles away and restores the body in its material immediacy. The "geometry of visibility" is followed by the tactile sensuality that emerges from the very depths of the painting.[25] Ensor elaborates his self-portrait blotch by blotch, from the ear worked in impasto to the luminous accent that comes to rest on the nose. The clothing is smeared impasto, the face a hastily built section of wall. There is no more distance. Self-representation is founded on the immediacy of the painter's awareness set against raw elements spread out on the palette, elements that must be fashioned into his likeness. This likeness no longer depends on a nominal outline to direct the line's shape on the canvas. On the contrary, it comes from a psychic drive to make the man—as the incarnation of will in action—emerge from the matter itself.

With this self-portrait, Ensor projects his self-awareness onto the canvas immediately and violently. The "close-up" he imposes on himself renounces the dignity of painting, which classical tradition established by distancing the subject and favoring the idea of the work over its matter.[26] This debate is addressed in two other Ensor self-portraits. *Portrait of the Artist* (*The Little Head*) (*Portrait de l'artiste dit "petite tête"*; fig. 5) restores a distance sufficient for the impasto work not to induce the dissolution

FIG. 4: JAMES ENSOR. *Portrait of the Artist* (*The Big Head*). 1879. Oil on panel, 6 11/16 × 5 1/8" (17 × 13 cm). Private collection

FIG. 5: JAMES ENSOR. *Portrait of the Artist* (*The Little Head*). 1879. Oil on panel, 7 7/8 × 5 1/2" (20 × 14 cm). Private collection

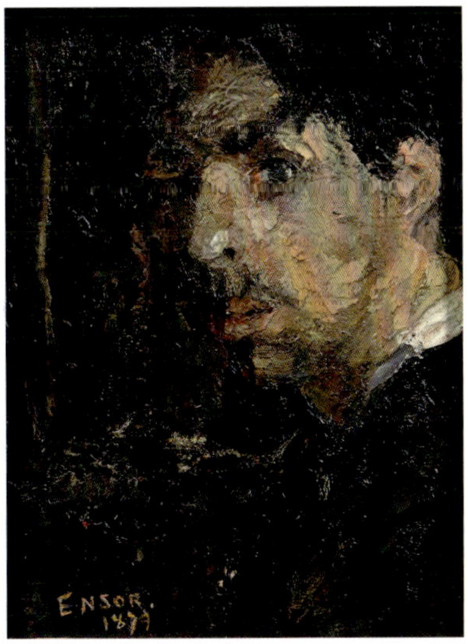

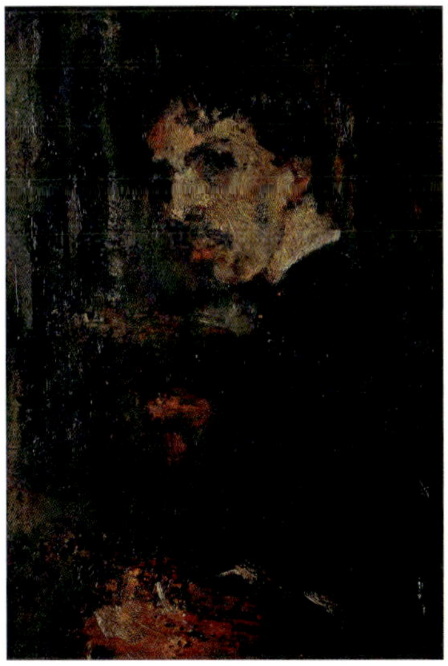

of visual representation. Into this game Ensor introduces a traditional element—the palette—that evidences his optical change. The presence of the palette signals to the viewer that this is not a man looking for himself but a painter in search of social status.

Painted the same year, *Portrait of the Artist at the Easel* (*Portrait de l'artiste au chevalet*) emphasizes this aspiration in a still more classical representation. In a tautological gesture, the painter, busy painting himself, offers himself up to view. The contemplation is both the act and the result of the act, both question and response. This traditional dynamic underscores a prescribed social status: painting is an art and a profession. From here derives Ensor's pretension in positioning himself in the scene like a modern-day Peter Paul Rubens,[27] a pretension manifested through a theater of gestures. (Ensor's 1884 *My Portrait* [*Mon Portrait*; plate 18] is another prime example of this impulse.) If painting defines humanity, it is humanity that gives meaning to the pictorial art. *Portrait of the Artist at the Easel* is a demonstration of a new kind of painting that cannot be seen *in* this image (the canvas placed on the easel is reduced to a sliver) but *through* the image—which is both the painting we see and the one that is hidden from us. Ensor concentrated his aesthetic ambition on two elements placed at the heart of this picture: the palette and the rag. The colors mix in measured harmonies and strident cries; the technique turns into blotches. On the rag—which is also canvas—the red accents have been placed without any attempt at realism. They are evidence of movement for its own sake, detached from any mimetic function. The action of painting has become the painting of action. Only a few years later, with Ensor's *The Skeleton Painter* (*Squelette peintre*, 1895 or 1896[?]; plate 89), it would become the painting of negation.

A Light from Within

Ensor's relationship with light determines his work. Throughout his life, the painter would tirelessly iterate this in his writings. Light renders great importance to his landscapes. It also places pressure on the social theater, the home torn apart by family conflicts—a muffled tragedy in which light represents a possible out, an alternative to the tensions that roil the familial unconscious. Light becomes a screen in a great number of painted works that critics have grouped into what they wrongly call Ensor's "bourgeois period." In works such as *The Bourgeois Salon* (*A Salon* [*Impression*]) (*Le Salon bourgeois*, 1881; p. 31, fig. 3), *Afternoon in Ostend* (*L'Après-dînée à Ostende*, 1881; plate 9), *The Somber Lady* (*La Dame sombre*, 1881; p. 17, fig. 2), and *The Lady in Distress* (*La Dame en détresse*, 1882; plate 10), no window ever opens on a landscape that might connect interior and exterior in a classical dialogue. Rather, light functions as a screen, keeping at bay that menacing "closed-off atmosphere,"[28] the tragedy of the quotidian. Behind closed doors, abandoned by reason, light touches everywhere, gnawing away at the object. It permeates every detail and transforms it until an interior life, which once seemed contained, erupts.

Built on chiaroscuro and on references to the paintings of Rembrandt van Rijn, Ensor's light-work evolves along the thread of canvases such as *A Colorist* (*Une Coloriste*, 1880; plate 6), the importance of which would be signaled by Verhaeren:

In "A Colorist," color is no longer [. . .] distributed in large areas. Far from it. It is divided, disseminated, sown. Without Ensor's tact, the multiplicity of greens, of reds, of blues, of yellows would end up in some blinding bedazzlement. The painted canvases would just be a collection of bursts of color and the painting wouldn't really be one. But the painter wanted the Colorist to show what a well-done painting should be. [. . .] The ensemble holds together from one end of the canvas to the other, and the subtle ties that unite the hues with one another like the notes on a sheet of music, wonderfully written, embrace each other and unite with each other all over.[29]

Light had a new existence. Under the influence of James McNeill Whistler,[30] it was now an agent of unification—a concept that would find its full revelation in the work of Joseph Mallord William Turner. The test of light would lead Ensor both to liberate the object from its realist anchor and to assimilate representation into a form of metaphysical impression.

It is not surprising that Ensor's original research into this concept was undertaken through drawing. By reducing his work to the movement of the pencil pressing down on the spotless paper, the painter could disengage from the weight of a dense impasto. Ensor discovered the line without having to construct his compositions anymore. The object no longer delivered itself sculpturally in its tactile presence, but emerged, freed of its nominal outline in a sensual movement that turns light into a revelation.

The Flesh of Masks

Throughout Ensor's 1885–86 Aureoles series, the line is returned to its mystical source and purpose: it creates a radiance that sets the paper ablaze. Here the object stands in for the subject to reveal an existence enclosed within the form: a life of shapes that transposes in imagination what bourgeois convention wanted to keep quiet. In 1882 Ensor described the process:

Vision is altered by observation. The first type of vision, the common kind, is the simple line—dry and with no attempt at colour. The second is where a keener eye makes out the value and delicacy of the different shades. This type is already less comprehensible to the common man. The final kind is where the artist discerns the subtleties and manifold effects of the light, its planes and gravitational fields. These progressive investigations alter primitive vision, undermining the line and rendering it subordinate. Such vision will not be widely understood. It requires long observation and attentive study. The common man will merely see disorder, chaos and impropriety. This is how art has evolved from the Gothic line through the colour and movement of the Renaissance to arrive at modern light.[31]

This path recaptures a mystical experiment. Rifling through matter to exalt its light, Ensor puts forth a principle that acts as a return to origins. His theater of masks is set up through a systematic exploration of biblical experience. This occupies him

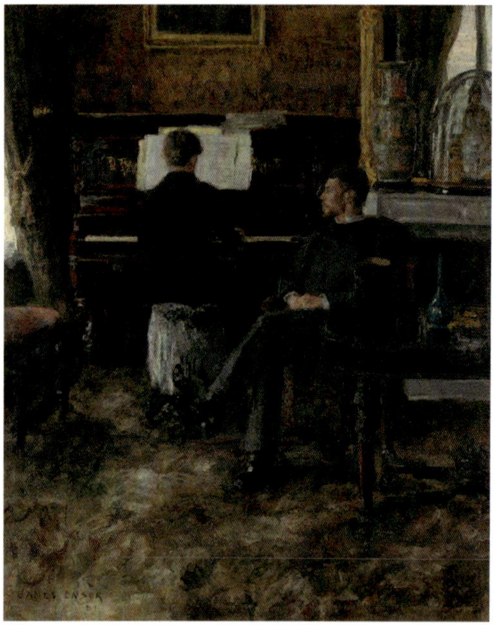

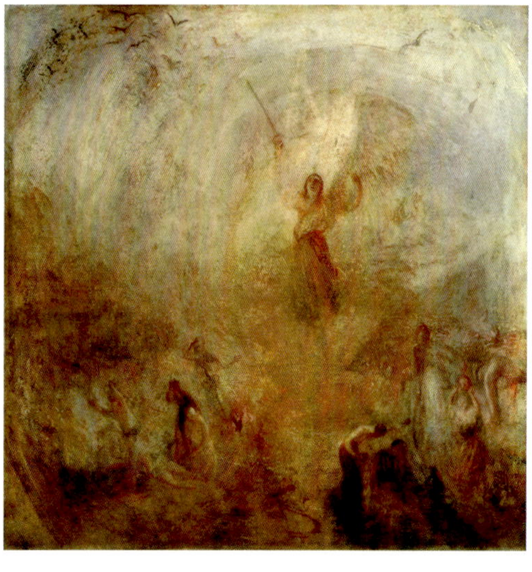

beginning in 1885 with the Aureoles series. Ensor plunges into an experiment from which painting will emerge transfigured. With *Adam and Eve Expelled from Paradise* (*Adam et Ève chassés du paradis terrestre*, 1887; plate 38) the "sensitivity of light" signals the triumph of an immaculate radiance that expels a reality reduced to a maelstrom of browns, ochers, and greens. This is a world as flat as the rug in a bourgeois salon in *Chez Miss* (*Russian Music*) (*Musique russe*; fig. 6).

As Turner does with *The Angel Standing in the Sun* (fig. 7), Ensor makes *Adam and Eve Expelled from Paradise* the expression of the symbolic struggle between the earthly world and celestial light. Deprived of light, matter is ruined, and by the same token, cedes its legitimacy to reality and to the social order. The restoration of light's sublime action is tantamount to the negation of society and the destruction of the mimetic principle of representation. Ensor engages in this radical perspective by mixing techniques and sources of inspiration—from Richard Wagner and Honoré de Balzac to the Bible—all linked by the same apocalyptic themes that are evident in Ensor's *The Ride of the Valkyries* (*Les Nuées ou les Walkures*, 1886–88; p. 109, fig. 7), *Tribulations of Saint Anthony* (*Terribles Tribulations de Saint-Antoine*, 1887; plate 37), and *The Fall of the Rebel Angels* (*The Rebel Angels and the Seven-Headed Dragon Struck by Lightning*) (*Foudroiement des anges rebelles et du dragon à sept têtes*, 1889[?]; p. 109, fig. 6).

Tribulations of Saint Anthony is a veritable exaltation of matter. The blaze of hues is almost hallucinatory, pouring over the theme, rooting itself in a new physics of color. The vision that would come to haunt the increasingly solitary Ensor is one of a shapeless mass of color that, under the gaze of Saint Anthony, seems to palpitate.[32] The painter confronts his own temptation by discovering—as Gustave Flaubert's Saint Anthony does—that "these images occur swiftly, percussively, showing up against the night like scarlet painted on ebony."[33] Flaubert's words sparkle like barbarian treasure; Ensor answers with colors that crackle on the surface of the canvas, beyond any illusion or any representation.[34] *Tribulations of Saint Anthony* enters a relationship with matter that explores life beyond form.

The Fall of the Rebel Angels is one of the most advanced articulations of the libertarian pictorial gesture in Ensor's work. An action painting that anticipates the Abstract Expressionism of Vasily Kandinsky and Willem de Kooning, it topples the order of mimetic representation, transforming painting into an act turned against itself.[35] The interchange between painter and image is represented by a raging crackle that shoots through the canvas. Ensor would only rarely achieve such violence in his representations.

FIG. 6: JAMES ENSOR. *Chez Miss* (*Russian Music*). 1881. Oil on canvas, 52 3/8 × 31 1/2" (133 × 110 cm). Musées royaux des Beaux-Arts de Belgique, Brussels

FIG. 7: JOSEPH MALLORD WILLIAM TURNER. *The Angel Standing in the Sun*. Exhibited 1846. Oil on canvas, 31 × 31" (78.7 × 78.7 cm). Tate, London. Accepted by the nation as part of the Turner Bequest, 1856

Form and outline seem abolished to make way for a general movement that allies color to an explosion of light. The painting becomes fireworks, following a poeticism that Ensor was exploring at the time. Explosive impastos, acidic contrasts, and suggestive drips all reflect an acceleration of movement. The sea and the sky are united; the boundaries are distinguished only by the brushstrokes (horizontal for the sea, vertical for the sky, circular for what looks like a rainbow).

Ensor turned painting into a form of chaos with the Edenic landscape of his 1890 *Domain of Arnheim* (*Le Domaine d'Arnheim*, 1890; plate 67). As Edgar Allan Poe wrote in the 1847 story that inspired the painting:

> *Let us imagine [. . .] a landscape whose combined vastness and definitiveness—whose united beauty, magnificence, and strangeness, shall convey the idea of care, or culture, or superintendence, on the part of beings superior, yet akin to humanity—the sentiment of interest is preserved, while the art intervolved is made to assume the air of an intermediate or secondary nature—a nature which is not God, nor an emanation from God, but which still is nature in the sense of the handiwork of the angels that hover between man and God.*[36]

In this phantasmic landscape, Ensor suggests depth without giving up his powerful gesturality. Color is the magma of light that the hand mixes, molds, exalts, excites. Outside the social realm, light is unfurled in a mythic infinity.

Ensor's radical experiment in "sensitivities of light" transformed painting. Matter is no longer merely a means of rendering the presence of forms and their tactile qualities. It embodies an absolute spirit from which form emerges, fully aware of itself. Brought back toward the light, matter is drawn to that white that makes up the very substance of *The Strange Masks* (*Les Masques singuliers*, 1892; plate 83). Indeed, it is because of that white that matter may exist in color. Like a demand for harmony, like a promise of unity, the immaculate impasto attests to an absolute from which Ensor composes his theater of masks and skeletons. With a cruel candor, they testify to what existence can be when it is not life.

Translated from the French by Elise Nussbaum

NOTES

1. James Ensor, "Discours prononcé à l'occasion de la Commémoration Bruegel à Bruxelles" (1924), in *James Ensor: Mes Écrits*, preface by Frans Hellens, 5th ed., enl. (Liège: Éditions nationales, 1974), p. 86. This and all other translations from French, unless otherwise noted, are by Elise Nussbaum.
2. See Anna Swinbourne, "Meeting James Ensor," in the present volume.
3. James Ensor, "Masques divers" (1937), in *Mes Écrits*, p. 201. Quoted (in English) in Ulrike Becks-Malorny, *James Ensor, 1860–1949*, trans. John Gabriel (Cologne: Taschen, 1999), p. 57.
4. See Susan M. Canning, "The Ordure of Anarchy: Scatological Signs of Self and Society in the Art of James Ensor," *Art Journal* 52, no. 3 (Fall 1993): 47–53.
5. Ernest Verlant, "Aux XX," *Le Journal de Bruxelles* (March 8, 1891): p. 285.
6. Ibid., p. 287.
7. See the discussion of Ensor's family, an issue crucial to understanding his work, in Michel Draguet, *James Ensor ou la fantasmagorie* (Paris: Gallimard, 1999), Part 1.
8. Charles Baudelaire, from "Spleen (IV)," in *Les Fleurs du mal*, trans. Richard Howard (Boston: David R. Godine, 1982), p. 76.
9. On Ensor's landscape techniques, see Robert Hoozee, "James Ensor's Vision of Nature," in the present volume.
10. See Jean-Paul Vanhove, "Le Réalisme dans la peinture au XIXe siècle en France et en Belgique," in Jan Dewilde and Jean-Marie Duvosquel, *Charles Degroux (1825–1870) et le réalisme en Belgique* (Brussels: Crédit communal, 1995), pp. 33–39.
11. Camille Lemonnier, *L'École belge de peinture, 1830–1905* (1906; Brussels: Éditions Labor, 1991), p. 133.
12. Émile Verhaeren, *James Ensor* (1908; Brussels: Éditions Complexe, 1990), p. 141.
13. Four decades later, Ensor would pay homage to the work of Pantazis and Vogels in "Six peintres belges dont la maîtrise s'est le mieux affirmée entre 1830 et 1900" (1920), in *Mes Écrits*, p. 49.
14. Anonymous, in *L'Art moderne* (February 19, 1888). Quoted in Serge Goyens de Heusch, *L'Impressionnisme et le fauvisme en Belgique* (Antwerp: Fonds Mercator, 1988), p. 63.
15. "Au cercle artistique: Exposition Vogels-Ensor-Storm de Gravesande," *L'Art moderne* 4, no. 11 (March 16, 1884): 87.
16. Camille Lemonnier, "Correspondance de Belgique: P. Pantazis," *La Chronique des arts* (March 16, 1878): 84.
17. Camille Lemonnier, *Gustave Courbet et son œuvre* (Paris: Alphonse Lemerre, 1868), p. 62.
18. Ensor, "Six peintres belges," p. 49.
19. This was, without question, a direct outcome of Ensor's encounter with James McNeill Whistler's work. See Draguet, *James Ensor ou la fantasmagorie.*
20. "Septième Exposition de L'Essor," *L'Art moderne* 3, no. 2 (January 14, 1883): 11.
21. See Gisèle Ollinger-Zinque, *Ensor par lui-même* (Brussels: Laconti, 1976).
22. Ensor, text prepared as a speech: "Discours pour la réception à l'Académie royale de Belgique" (1925), in *Mes Écrits*, p. 96.
23. For more on this subject, see Daniel Arasse, *Le Détail: Pour une histoire rapprochée de la peinture* (Paris: Flammarion, 1986), esp. pp. 248–60.
24. Ibid., p. 254.
25. The term "geometry of visibility" was coined by Michel Foucault, *Naissance de la clinique: Une Archéologie du regard médical*, 2nd ed. (Paris: Presses universitaires de France, 1963), p. 88. Cited in Hubert Damisch, *L'Origine de la perspective*, ed. Yves Bonnefoy (Paris: Flammarion, 1982), pp. 128–29, 132–34.
26. See, for example, Leonardo da Vinci's discussion of the topic in his *Treatise on Painting*, trans. John Francis Rigaud (London: George Bell, 1892), pp. 38–40, 58.
27. Ensor's *Self-Portrait with a Flowered Hat* (*Mon Portrait déguisé*, 1883/1888; plate 17) echoes the work of Rubens, and in so doing derides the master. See Marcel De Maeyer, "Ensor au chapeau fleuri," in *L'Art belge* (special issue dedicated to Ensor, December 1965): 41–45.
28. Paul Haesaerts, *James Ensor* (Brussels: Éditions et ateliers d'Art Graphique Elsevier, 1957), p. 56.
29. Verhaeren, *James Ensor*, p. 51.
30. For more on the (ambiguous) relationship between Ensor's work and Whistler's, see Draguet, *James Ensor ou la fantasmagorie*, pp. 85–89.
31. Ensor, "Réflexions sur l'art" (1882), in *Mes Écrits*, p. 50. Quoted (in English) in Michel Draguet, "The Looks of Pietje de Dood," in *Ensor*, trans. Ted Alkins (Brussels: Musées royaux des Beaux-Arts de Belgique, 1999), p. 48; and Patricia G. Berman, *James Ensor: Christ's Entry into Brussels in 1889* (Los Angeles: J. Paul Getty Museum, 2002), pp. 48–49.
32. See Marshall N. Myers, "James Ensor's 'The Tribulations of Saint Anthony': Permutations of the Excremental Vision," *Arts Magazine* 54, no. 4 (December 1979): 84.
33. Gustave Flaubert, "La Tentation de Saint Antoine," in *Œuvres complètes*, ed. A. Thibaudet and R. Dumesnil (Paris: Gallimard [Pléiade], 1951), p. 35.

34. The Devil says to the saint, "Form is perhaps an error of your senses, and Substance an image in your mind. Unless—the world being a perpetual flux of things—appearance on the contrary were to be all that is truest, and illusion the one reality." Flaubert, *The Temptation of Saint Anthony*, trans. Kitty Mrosovky (Ithaca, N.Y.: Cornell University Press, 1981), p. 212.
35. See Dore Ashton, *The New York School: A Cultural Reckoning* (Berkeley, Los Angeles, and Oxford: University of California Press, 1972), pp. 153–64; and Michael Leja, *Reframing Abstract Expressionism: Subjectivity and Painting in the 1940s* (New Haven and London: Yale University Press, 1993), pp. 265–66.
36. Edgar Allan Poe, "The Domain of Arnheim" (1847), in *The Collected Works of Edgar Allan Poe*, vol. 3 (Cambridge, Mass., and London: Belknap [Harvard University Press], 1978), p. 1276.

James Ensor's Vision of Nature

ROBERT HOOZEE

In the literature on James Ensor, landscapes are rarely granted much consideration. Yet the landscape was a constant factor for him, beginning with his formative years in the late 1870s up until around 1890—that is, throughout his most creative period. The evolution of Ensor's artistic output, from dark-hued realism and Impressionistic studies to brightly colored visionary art, can be witnessed not only in works depicting interiors and figures, but also in his interpretations of nature: landscapes, seascapes, and views across the roofs of Ostend, his hometown. These are not minor works, but highlights of Ensor's œuvre, many of which may be seen in this exhibition.

Painting by the Sea

For a Belgian artist of the late 1800s, it was only natural to take an interest in landscape painting. During the course of the nineteenth century, throughout Europe, landscape was a preeminent genre in art for experimentation and for expanding the limits of pictorial conventions. In Belgium, landscape painting was particularly vigorous. Following contemporary English and French examples and hearkening back to older Flemish and Dutch traditions, talented landscape painters had been working in Belgium since the mid-1800s, portraying the country's natural views from the Ardennes to the coast. Artists such as Théodore Fourmois, Paul Jean Clays, Hippolyte Boulenger, and Louis Artan, as well as many others who were often grouped into regional schools, developed a rich approach to the depiction of nature.[1] Inspired by the changeable Belgian climate, they often painted in dramatic weather conditions or under cloudy skies—thus giving rise to the appellation "Gray School" for their style: a robust and dynamic painterly mode that involved a heavy application of paint on the canvas.

The fact that Ensor's earliest work consists largely of landscapes and seascapes may be partly due to his seaside location: his studio was only a short walk from the beach. The explanation for his interest in these natural scenes also lies, however, in the status that landscape painting had at the time in Belgium and in the potential that this genre offered him as an artist. Furthermore, it is likely that Ensor knew at least some of the numerous artists who were coming to work at the Belgian seaside resorts in those days. Among them were the Realist painters Henri De Braekeleer and Félicien Rops; although landscape was not the primary focus of either of these artists, they came to the coast and painted the dunes and the sea as a pastime.

Ensor's early, small-scale studies of dunes and beaches are intensely observed, simply and straightforwardly depicted, sometimes dated to the very day. However, the young artist soon began to make use of the palette knife and darker, somewhat transparent paint—a style then common among landscape painters (fig. 1). By around 1880 he had mastered this rather sketchy style. Twenty years later, in a special issue of the French periodical *La Plume* devoted to Ensor, fellow artist Georges Lemmen rightly placed the young Ensor in the tradition of "the fine painters Artan, Boulenger and Louis Dubois."[2] The last of these, a painter of landscapes and portraits (and Gustave Courbet's most important follower in Belgium), was among the many who came to the coast to sketch, and it is said that on one of those occasions he met and encouraged the young Ensor.[3]

The style in which Ensor was working around 1880, based on the suggestive power of the paint stroke—made with brush or palette knife—has come to be known as "tachism" (a term also used internationally—applied, for example, to the work of the Scottish painters of the Glasgow School). It is not clear whether Ensor came to this style on his own or might have been influenced by the older painter Guillaume Vogels, a friend and associate (fig. 2). Whatever the case may be, Ensor and Vogels created works that are so similar in style as to be frequently indistinguishable. Numerous artists of Ensor's generation painted in this style as well, among them the Dutch painter Jan Toorop, and fellow Belgians Willy Finch, Théo Van Rysselberghe, and Guillaume Van Strydonck, all of whom Ensor knew in Brussels.

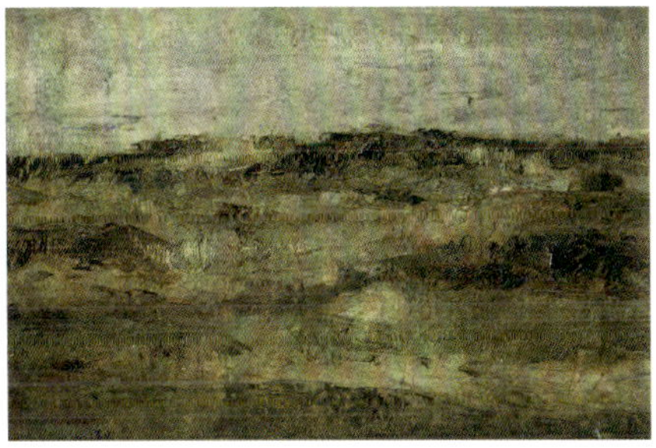

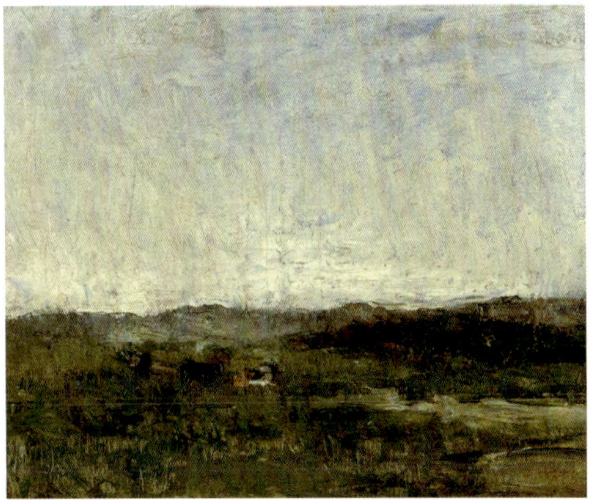

FIG. 1: JAMES ENSOR. *Dunes*. 1880. Oil on canvas, 8 7/8 × 13 3/8" (22.5 × 34 cm). Private collection

FIG. 2: GUILLAUME VOGELS. *Cows in the Dunes*. c. 1885. Oil on canvas, 15 15/16 × 19 7/8" (40.5 × 50.5 cm). Musées royaux des Beaux-Arts de Belgique, Brussels

Tachism was the modernist approach with which young Ensor would make a name for himself—although for many of his associates, the style was a short-lived phenomenon. After the artists of the Brussels art society Les Vingt (Les XX),[4] of which Ensor was a cofounding member, first encountered Pointillism through the work of Georges Seurat in 1887, they quickly adopted a radically Pointillist style. Ensor himself shunned what he called "the dry, repugnant processes of the Pointillists, already dead for light and for art."[5] He would remain fundamentally an artist who expressed himself through the substance of paint and the act of painting—a pictorial language in which he would venture to take increasing liberties.

Ensor's catalogue raisonné for the period up to 1880 reveals that landscapes, townscapes, and seascapes comprise the large majority of works. Most of these are small studies of the sea and the dunes, all painted presumably in Ostend and its environs. But despite the preponderance of these themes in Ensor's early oil paintings, he seems to have created scarcely any drawings or watercolors based on these motifs. Later in his life the artist attached considerable importance to these early studies, and even gave them a place in the illustrated catalogue of works that he compiled in later years.[6] The older Ensor often copied his own earlier efforts, including, somewhat surprisingly, some of these first unpretentious landscapes and seascapes.

In addition to his smaller studies, Ensor painted two seascapes and a landscape on a somewhat larger, more ambitious scale. One of the sea scenes, *The Rainbow* (*After the Storm*) (*L'Arc en ciel*, 1880; plate 1), is a very complex image; although ostensibly depicting a fleeting moment in the aftermath of a storm, it is far more than a simple impression.[7] The various visual elements—figures on the beach, a buoy, boats, a rainbow, clouds, and sunlight breaking through them—are all highly suggestive and dissolve completely in an almost abstract exploration of the canvas, by which the artist attempts to fathom and to render the play of light, color, and darkness. With this painting, one of Ensor's first symbolistic and gestural interpretations of a natural sight, he clearly leaves the other tachists far behind. And his distance from them as an artist would continue to widen. Years later, Ensor described the impact his own work now had on his fellow painters, starting with Vogels: "In 1884, Vogels, stewing in his own juice, an admirer of the Dutchman Maris, was surprised and influenced by my notes and my accents, and became carried away by my painting."[8]

Ensor never traveled far to see spectacular or picturesque natural settings: he found sufficient inspiration for a grand portrayal of nature in the dunes and the sea that were just outside his front door. This was equally true for his townscapes. The artist's studio was located in the attic of his parental home in Ostend, on the corner of Van Iseghemlaan and Vlaanderenstraat. As he later recalled: "My atelier there has five windows. [. . .] From the big window at the height of the balustrade one overlooks a large part of town, and a few views over the landscape supplement the wonderful panorama at will."[9]

Looking out from his studio, or from other rooms in that corner house, Ensor produced countless drawings of the streets and the activity below. Views down the streets were rendered in several oil sketches and paintings that demonstrate the degree to which he could employ his tachist style to subtly capture changing weather conditions (plates 4 and 5). In several paintings he directs the viewer's gaze upward, to the sky itself, so dramatically that the streets and houses appear to lose their identity beneath the atmospheric spectacle. The transition from a detailed study to a wide panorama is particularly striking in his 1884 *Rooftops of Ostend* (*Grand View of Ostend*) (*La Grande Vue d'Ostende*; plate 20). Depictions of views across rooftops were not uncommon throughout the nineteenth century, but they were invariably rendered on a smaller scale. Ensor, by contrast, opted for a canvas well over six and a half feet (two meters) in width. He painted the vista first with thin paint and then developed certain areas with his palette knife. As with the seascapes, it is evident here that Ensor was no longer content with the fluid, cohesive, and suggestive approach of the tachists. From a pictorial point of view, this work might be more aptly described as "stubborn": the eye is caught in the very substance of the painting. *Rooftops of Ostend* relates to the well-known cloud studies by such nineteenth-century masters as John Constable, Joseph Mallord William Turner, and Gustave Courbet. These artists, too, were only partly interested in the illusion of a cloudy sky: their deeper concern was for what they could achieve with the *idea* of a cloudy sky in terms of the substance of paint on the canvas itself.

Visions

In the trajectory of Ensor's career, the years 1885–87 constitute a turning point during which the artist explored new modes of expression and themes. This period began with a new focus on drawing. Prior to this era Ensor had drawn—passionately—on a smaller scale, but starting in 1885 he began to utilize sheets of paper, measuring four to seven feet (one and a half to two meters) in height, on which he drew massive scenes centered around the figure of Christ. In these works the artist obtained extremely nuanced effects of light and dark through the play of lines. Ensor exhibited this series of drawings with

Les Vingt under the title Visions: The Aureoles of Christ or the Sensibilities of Light (Visions: Les Auréoles du Christ ou les sensibilités de la lumière; plates 26 and 27). He referred to several other works from this period as "visions" and "light studies." These titles and subtitles collectively form a kind of manifesto, so to speak, of what Ensor was attempting to achieve with his art at that point. His goal was to render light not as an atmospheric suggestion (as the Impressionists did), but as a symbolic theme in itself, a means of expression—in line with the work of Rembrandt and Turner.

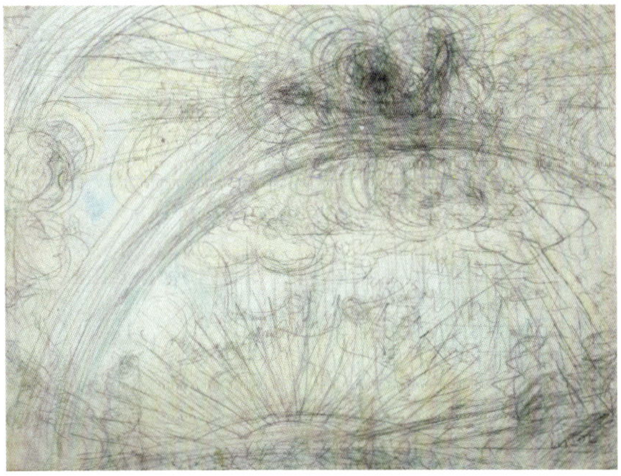

Through innovative graphic means, Ensor took a subject such as *The Creation of Light* (*La Creation de la lumière*; fig. 3) far beyond Gustave Doré's earlier, very suggestive interpretation of the same theme (an image that may have influenced the young artist; fig. 4); indeed, Ensor's drawing has a distinctly proto-Futurist sensibility. In other drawings he makes use of elegant curves that span an entire composition, as in *Christ Shown to the People and the Entry of Christ into Jerusalem* (*Le Christ montré au peuple et l'entrée du Christ à Jerusalem*, 1887; plate 24), a curious double composition involving two Christ figures in an abstract calligraphy of lines and accents that are scattered freely across the surface of the paper. These free drawings demonstrate the dynamic and broad "handwriting" that Ensor mastered in order to express space, light, and movement. This distinctive handwriting crops up again in several of his most important oil paintings from the same period.

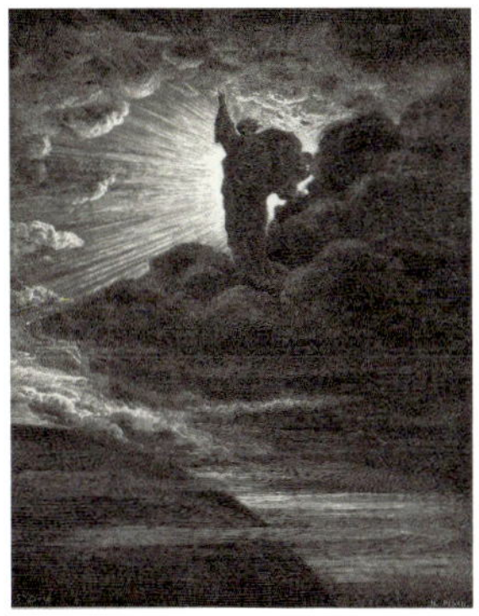

By the time Ensor was producing and exhibiting these large drawings, he had begun to make etchings. He described his turn to this medium poignantly:

> *I want to survive. The transiency of the pictorial material frightens me. Poor painting! An art exposed to the incompetence of restorers and the imperfections of reproduction. Yes, I desire to stir future generations for a long time to come. I want to survive—I think of hard copperplates, imperishable ink, easy reproduction. I therefore prefer the etching as a means of expression.*[10]

Ensor's chief period of etching-production was between 1886 and 1891;[11] not surprisingly, he focused upon the same themes that are found in his drawings and paintings. It is significant, though, that the landscape has such prominence in his prints: no fewer than thirty-six of his eighty-six etchings from this period represent landscapes, townscapes, or seascapes. In a letter to Emma Lambotte, one of his chief patrons, Ensor wrote of his landscape etchings:

> *How happy I am that you like my etchings. To oblige you, I have signed them and dated them. If you have a look at the dates, you will notice 1888 was a most productive year. It was a happy time of walks in the countryside, which were all the more pleasant because I took such delight in etching. Nature always seemed beautiful and benevolent.*[12]

FIG. 3: JAMES ENSOR. *The Creation of Light*. 1887. Pencil and colored pencil on paper, 6 3/8 × 8 11/16" (16.2 × 22 cm). Private collection

FIG. 4: HÉLIODORE-JOSEPH PISAN, after GUSTAVE DORÉ. "God Created Light," in *The Holy Bible*. Wood engraving. Plate I. Volume I. Tours: Alfred Mame et Fils, 1866. The Pierpont Morgan Library, New York

Although a few of Ensor's landscape etchings have an almost burlesque character—due to the introduction of comical figures into the scenes—and some allude to works by old masters, nearly all his etchings are faithful and modest studies from nature. They seem to form a parenthetical moment, as it were, in Ensor's œuvre, which at that time was undergoing a radical shift from realism to the grotesque and fantastic. His choice of subject matter was also limited and modest in his landscape etchings, in comparison with the more ambitious themes with which he was grappling in his paintings and drawings. He made etchings of the harbor near Ostend as well as of several villages along the coast: Mariakerke, Leffinge, Slykens, and Oudenburg. In Brussels he worked in Leopoldpark and in the nearby municipalities of Watermaal-Bosvoorde and Groenendaal. In both Ostend and Brussels he etched townscapes from the rooms in which he stayed.

It is clear from his correspondences of later years that Ensor was very attached to his landscape etchings.[13] In a 1925 letter to the collector Auguste Joye, Ensor makes it very clear that he drew directly onto the etching plate as he observed: "I etched all my landscapes from nature, for the most part without any retouching."[14] While it is not surprising, then, that there are no known preliminary studies for these works, it is striking that only a handful of drawn landscape studies have survived.[15] Those few drawings and the etched landscapes, seascapes, and townscapes are of an unusually high quality. They range from extremely subtle notations of light and atmosphere to compositions in which the artist's nervous scribbling renders a sense of great tension, particularly in his studies of trees and the edges of woods.

The years 1885–87 were pivotal in Ensor's artistic development. They are marked by a visionary approach to light and a new concentration on religious themes. These orientations are especially apparent in a series of landscapes and seascapes that Ensor began to paint, and that are imbued with a new depth of meaning. The earliest example is *Christ Walking on Water* (*Le Christ marchant sur la mer*; fig. 5), which Ensor showed in the same exhibition at Les Vingt that included his Aureoles series. The scene strongly resembles his sketchy seascapes from the early 1880s, but it is considerably larger and rendered in an even freer manner, with bright colors. It has been suggested that Ensor might have added the Christ figure to this painting after the initial scene was in place.[16] The figure of Christ, standing on the right, is indeed rendered in very thin paint on top of the broad strokes that make up the seascape, and there is thus a notable dichotomy between the painterly rendering of the natural elements and this biblical moment—which comes across as a mere detail.

This dichotomy is entirely absent from Ensor's monumental *Adam and Eve Expelled from Paradise* (*Adam et Ève chassés du paradis terrestre*, 1887; plate 38). In this large work, Ensor, for the first time in a painting, creates a synthesis of the problems that interest him: light, landscape, and biblical narrative.[17] *Adam and Eve Expelled from Paradise* is smaller than *Christ's Entry into Brussels in 1889* (*L'Entrée du Christ à Bruxelles en 1889*) of the same year (p. 29, fig. 1), but it is clear that Ensor wanted to obtain a similar effect of scale with *Adam and Eve*.[18] Here he is competing, in terms of dimensions, with the

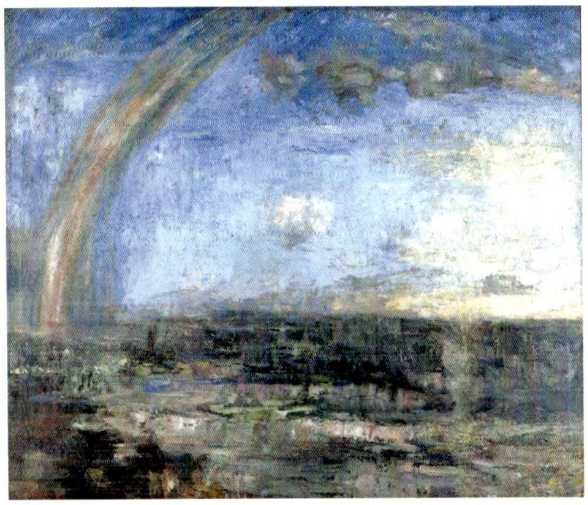

FIG. 5: JAMES ENSOR. *Christ Walking on Water*. 1885. Oil on canvas, 43 5/16 × 53 1/8" (110 × 135 cm). Museum Folkwang, Essen

apocalyptic landscapes of the Romantic artists such as John Martin or Turner. The painting shows a marshy landscape beneath a huge sky in which clouds and the figure of an angel form a heavenly canopy of light and color. On the right Adam and Eve are fleeing (and two other human figures seem to be standing at the far right as well—perhaps remnants of an initial composition).[19]

Adam and Eve Expelled from Paradise demonstrates, on a vast scale—indeed, the work seems almost to envelope the viewer—the free, painterly style that was taking shape in Ensor's smaller landscapes. The painting is also clearly related to drawings such as *The Creation of Light* (fig. 3) and the Aureoles works. Nearly identical fleeing figures can be seen in *The Intense: Christ Rising to the Sky* (*L'Intense: Le Christ montant au ciel*), the last drawing in the Aureoles series.[20] In *Christ Rising to the Sky*, they flee in panic from the blinding light of Christ's resurrection; in *Adam and Eve*, they are running away from the wrath of the angel. The painting evinces a highly graphic character due to the manner in which even the clouds and vegetation are drawn in the medium: sometimes the artist scraped into the paint, and other times he smeared globs of color, squirted directly from the tube.

This painting has, with good reason, been linked with the work of Turner. It is known that Ensor copied one of Turner's works from a book,[21] and it is fairly certain that he also saw actual works by Turner. Biographies of Ensor invariably mention a visit to London with Guillaume Vogels in 1886 (or 1887) to examine the Turners.[22] That purported trip, though cited repeatedly, is based on a hypothesis articulated in 1951 by the art historian Walther Vanbeselaere, who ventured: "Wouldn't the two have made a visit to London together? It must have been in 1886 or 1887."[23] It is true that during those years the works of Turner were on display at London's National Gallery, so it is certainly not impossible and—in view of both Ensor's origins (he was half English) and his location just across the Channel—quite likely that he did go to London and see Turner's golden landscapes there. Yet caution should be exercised here: not all the works from the Turner Bequest were on exhibit at the National Gallery at that time. One painting that is occasionally associated with Ensor, for example, Turner's *Angel Standing in the Sun* (first shown in 1846), was kept in storage, according to a museum guidebook of 1888. But there were many other works on view at the National Gallery that might have inspired the Belgian painter.[24] Ensor himself attested emphatically to his admiration for Turner: "I liked Rembrandt very much, but much later my sympathies went to Goya and Turner. I was charmed to find two masters so smitten with light and violence."[25]

There are of course others besides Turner who would likely have influenced Ensor in his development of an extremely free use of color and paint. The work of the French Impressionists, particularly Claude Monet, would surely have struck him when it was shown in Brussels. The exhibition held by Les Vingt in 1886 must have been a milestone for Ensor. That salon included the first presentation of work by Odilon Redon: an impressive selection of drawings and prints. Ensor's introduction to this work almost certainly set off his own quest for the fantastic, which began just at this point. At that same exhibition, work by Monet was also shown for the first time—no fewer than ten paintings, including several views of the Normandy coast, such as *The Church of Varengeville* (*L'Église de Varengeville*) and *The Manneporte (Étretat)* (1883).[26] In all these works Monet had gone very far in his informal handling of paint and his use of pure colors. Later Ensor (who rarely mentioned his own influences, or else played them down) would write disparagingly of Monet and the Impressionists. "My investigations [. . .] are far from the large, facile works of Claude Monet," he noted in 1899, calling the French master "a jovial, sensual painter, handler of thick pastes. Easy colorist. Crude maker of paintings. Rather vulgar vision. With the exception of the 'cathedrals.'"[27] Nonetheless, one can easily imagine that Ensor, who was still applying his medium heavily and tending toward darker colors (plate 20) in 1884, might have had a revelation on being faced with *The Manneporte (Étretat)* or *The Church of Varengeville*. He would have seen how Monet rendered the vegetation in individual flourishes and accents, the long lines drawn with the brush, the use of pure yellow and red, and how, in *The Manneporte (Étretat)*, the French artist modeled the rock's arch in colorful stripes.

This acquaintance must at least have stimulated Ensor to further his own free technique. He himself would soon begin to use paint more expressively, working less with transitions, deliberately counteracting and disrupting the fluid interplay of color strokes so that they would embody his emotion. In this sense it is easy to understand his dismissal of the French Impressionists as "*brosseurs superficiels*"—"superficial brushers."[28]

Whether because of external influences or inherent development, with *Adam and Eve Expelled from Paradise* Ensor began a series of works in which he portrays, with enormous pictorial freedom, a fantasized realm that may or may not be inhabited by angels and demons. This eruption is epitomized in *Fireworks* (*Feu d'artifice*, 1887; plate 36)—which could be considered a nod to Turner's *Burning of the Houses of Parliament*, although Ensor never saw either of the English painter's two versions of this scene (painted 1834 or 1835) with his own eyes.[29] *Fireworks* is unusual because, like its composition and its material structure, its content has been kept particularly "shallow" and simple as a pure act of painting, as a study of effect—which has nonetheless been carried out on a large scale. Dating from roughly the same time is another panorama, *The Tower of Lissewege* (*La Tour de Lisseweghe*, 1890; plate 55), which is reminiscent of the work of Jacob van Ruysdael in terms of concept. It does seem—with the painting's complicated cloudy sky and the striking accents suggesting a play of light on the landscape—as though Ensor wanted to yield an alternative to French Impressionism by adopting a style more in line with the work of artists such as Constable, Courbet, or Théodore Rousseau. It is curious that, during his most imaginative period, Ensor painted these two panoramas based not on fantasy but on reality. The setting of *Fireworks* is in the vicinity of Ostend, and shows the dark silhouettes of spectators scattered along the beach and in the dunes. In the background, to the left, we recognize the round shape of Fort Wellington.[30] *The Tower of Lissewege* is a topographical view of the polder landscape surrounding the prominent church tower of a village situated along the coast, about thirty-five kilometers east of Ostend. Ensor exhibited neither *Fireworks* nor *The Tower of Lissewege* with Les Vingt.[31]

Ensor's interest in nature and in spectacular natural phenomena at this stage is evident not only from these "pure" landscapes, but also from some of his most daring imaginary figure compositions. We can thereby link his oils *Tribulations of St. Anthony* (*Terribles Tribulations de Saint-Antoine*, 1887; plate 37) and *The Fall of the Rebel Angels* (*The Rebel Angels and the Seven-Headed Dragon Struck by Lightning*) (*Foudroiement des anges rebelles et du dragon à sept têtes*; fig. 6), as well as the watercolor *The Ride of the Valkyries* (*Les Nuées ou les Walkures*; fig. 7) with these landscape works. The vaulted compositions and the "writing" into the paint (sometimes in broad gestures, sometimes in uncontrolled scrawls) are elements of an expressionistic language of forms that Ensor was developing in his landscapes.

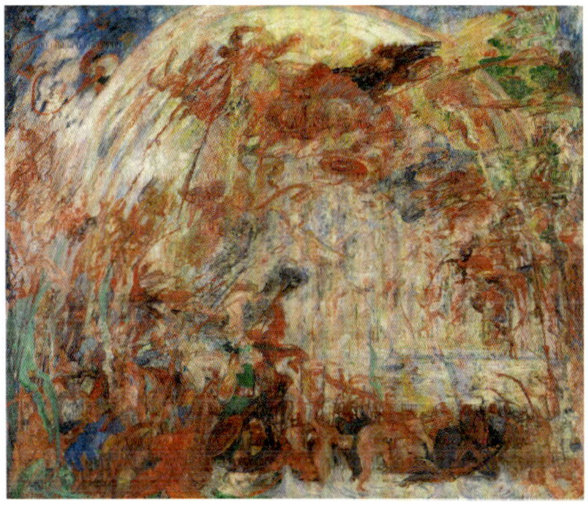

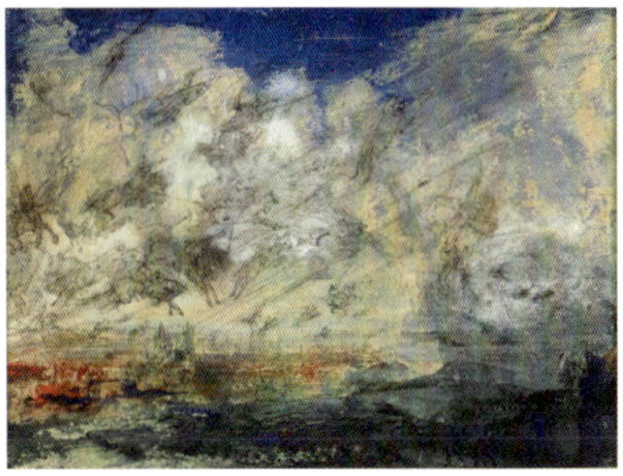

FIG. 6: JAMES ENSOR. *The Fall of the Rebel Angels* (*The Rebel Angels and the Seven-Headed Dragon Struck by Lightning*). 1889(?). Oil on canvas, 42 1/2 × 51 15/16" (108 × 132 cm). Koninklijk Museum voor Schone Kunsten, Antwerp

FIG. 7: JAMES ENSOR. *The Ride of the Valkyries*. 1886–88. Pencil and watercolor on paper, 8 × 11 1/4" (20.3 × 28.5 cm). Private collection

Expressionism

Two works constitute the high point as well as the end of this evolution: a landscape, *The Domain of Arnheim* (*Le Domaine d'Arnheim*, 1890; plate 67) and a seascape, *Christ Calming the Storm* (*Le Christ calmant la tempête*, 1891; plate 68). *The Domain of Arnheim* was inspired by the story of the same name by Edgar Allan Poe, first published in 1847 and available to Ensor in a translation by Charles Baudelaire. Poe's stories provided Ensor with inspiration for several drawings and etchings, but only this painting.[32] In "The Domain of Arnheim," Poe describes the ambition of the immensely rich Mr. Ellison, who spends his fortune on the creation of a visionary landscape that rivals the poetic aspirations of art. Poe describes how the visitor finds his way into this overwhelming natural setting, between the beautifully overgrown walls of a ravine and surrounded by lush vegetation through which the golden light of the setting sun shines. Although Ensor's painting is not a literal illustration, it does perhaps allude to the final passage of the tale, in which a light canoe of ivory enters through the doors of a golden gate:

> *The boat glides between them, and commences a rapid descent into a vast amphitheatre entirely begirt with purple mountains, whose bases are laved by a gleaming river throughout the full extent of their circuit. Meantime the whole Paradise of Arnheim bursts upon the view. There is a gush of entrancing melody; there is an oppressive sense of strange sweet odor;—there is a dream-like intermingling to the eye of tall slender Eastern trees—bosky shrubberies—flocks of golden and crimson birds—lily-fringed lakes—meadows of violets, tulips, poppies, hyacinths, and tuberoses—long intertangled lines of silver streamlets—and, uprising confusedly from amid all, a mass of semi-Gothic, semi-Saracenic architecture sustaining itself as if by miracle in mid-air; glittering in the red sunlight with a hundred oriels, minarets, and pinnacles.*[33]

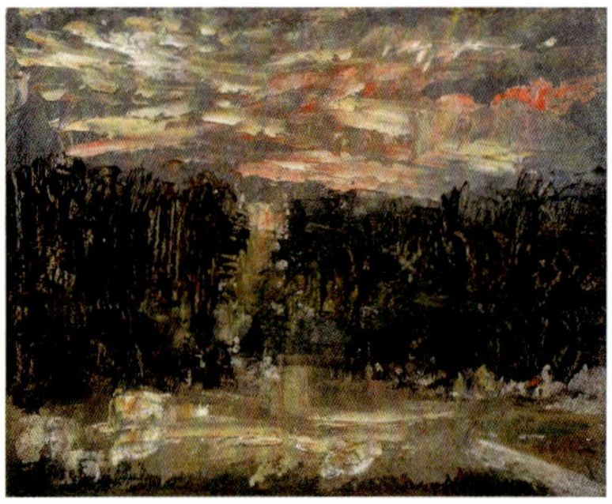

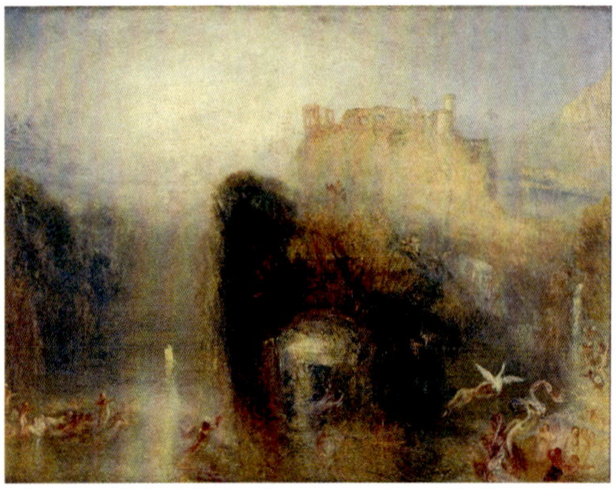

FIG. 8: JAMES ENSOR. *Forest Edge*. 1888–90. Oil on canvas, 7 7/8 × 9 13/16" (20 × 25 cm). Private collection

FIG. 9: JOSEPH MALLORD WILLIAM TURNER. *Queen Mab's Cave*. Exhibited 1846. Oil on canvas, 36 1/4 × 48 1/4" (92.1 × 122.6 cm). Tate, London. Accepted by the nation as part of the Turner Bequest, 1856

It is significant that Ensor not only takes grotesque figures from Poe's satires, but also is captivated by the description of an imaginary landscape. Later he would write: "I have dreamed above all before Poe, and like him, I loved to dream of certain landscapes of home."[34] In *The Domain of Arnheim* Ensor undoubtedly recognized his own fascination with a divine light that permeates and gives shape to everything. Perhaps Poe's narrative about a type of nature that is more sublime than real nature moreover affected the romantic nature-lover in Ensor, the man who would later rant frequently about the destruction of his beloved dunes and woods.

Inspired by Poe's vision, Ensor painted one of his most disconcerting landscapes. In 1892 he exhibited *The Domain of Arnheim* at Les Vingt, where it was purchased by the poet and critic Émile Verhaeren.[35] The depiction is fantastical but nonetheless brings to mind Ensor's earlier observations of nature. This marsh landscape with trees and edges of woods can be seen in various works, starting with the 1880 landscape *The Marsh* (*Le Marais*).[36] We also find this type of landscape in *Adam and Eve Expelled from Paradise* (plate 38) and in *The Edge of the Wood at Ostend* (*La Lisière du bois d'Ostende*), painted in 1886.[37] It appears also in the landscape etchings.[38] A small oil sketch dating from 1888–90 (fig. 8) might also have been based on observation; here we find all the essential ingredients that make up the "domain": a middle zone consisting of woods, the red glow above, and its reflection in the water below.[39] Ensor intensifies these elements in the painting. The red luminescence is painted heavily and dominates the landscape. Its reflection in the water has the effect of glowing lava. Between the two, trees and overgrown banks have merged into a mysterious vegetative substance that seems to float, or hover. Looming in the distance is a structure that has almost become part of the yellowish-red overcast sky. This work, too, evokes Turner, who in his later paintings often rendered the effect of rocks, boats, or buildings that loom up through the mist, against a golden light in the distance. There is a striking similarity between Ensor's *The Domain of Arnheim* and a popular work by Turner, which Ensor might have seen: *Queen Mab's Cave* (fig. 9). In the left part of Turner's painting is a composition highly reminiscent of *The Domain of Arnheim*—even the canoe is present.[40] With these elements, however, Ensor achieved an unusual degree of tension, delivering an emotional charge that makes the landscape as expressive as the grotesque grimaces and masks that he was also painting during this period.

Christ Calming the Storm, which Ensor did not immediately exhibit,[41] has a wholly different character. The artist had already dealt with this theme in 1886, in an etching[42] that relates stylistically and iconographically to the drawings of the Aureoles series. When he returned to the motif in 1891, he indulged himself one last time in an attempt to express the forces of nature while creating a painting on canvas. Again we see a circular composition—as in *The Fall of the Rebel Angels*—but the pictorial movement gives rise to no monsters here. It literally portrays a cyclical unity between the water, thrusting upward, and the atmosphere, rendered with parallel brushstrokes that call to mind Futurist techniques. In this work, too, the relationship with Turner is striking, specifically with the English painter's *Snow Storm–Boat off a Harbour's Mouth* (fig. 10), a work that Ensor might have seen. But more than anything we see, again, that obvious difference between Turner's fluid and illusionistic painterly style and Ensor's more explicit and autonomous use of paint.

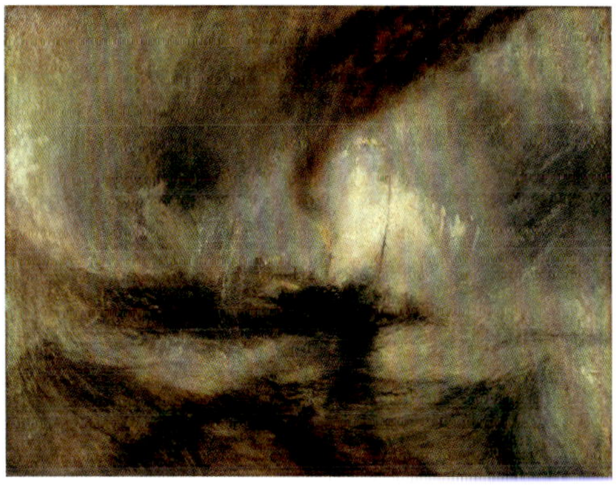

FIG. 10: JOSEPH MALLORD WILLIAM TURNER. *Snow Storm–Boat off a Harbour's Mouth.* Exhibited 1842. Oil on canvas, 36 × 48" (91.4 × 121.9 cm). Tate, London. Accepted by the nation as part of the Turner Bequest, 1856

In addressing Ensor's landscapes and seascapes, some authors have worn themselves out with lyrical descriptions, referring to Monet's later works as well as to Action painting. These references assume the character of clichés, but there is an element of validity to them. It is clear that Ensor's experience of nature was evolving toward a visionary one and that landscapes and seascapes stimulated him, by their lack of figurative content, to paint in a radically new way, as was being done only by Vincent van Gogh at the time.

It is, however, typical of the dynamics in Ensor's body of work throughout the period up to around 1890 that he never repeated or made variations of the extreme results he achieved in certain landscapes—that being indeed a common practice among many of his contemporaries. In his development of the landscape and the seascape, Ensor took a step forward, as it were, with every work. Because of that, masterpieces such as *Adam and Eve Expelled from Paradise* and *The Domain of Arnheim* remain lone highlights, separate stages in an experimental process that transpired within the span of a few years. Remarkably, Ensor never continued along this road at a later point. After 1891, the year of *Christ Calming the Storm*, he painted only a few topographical landscapes, mostly repetitions of earlier etchings. As mentioned earlier, Ensor had the habit of copying many of his own works later in life. Among these were his early landscapes, townscapes, and seascapes. He painted, for instance, replicas of *Rooftops of Ostend* and *Christ Calming the Storm*.[43] Most of his replicas, however, do not repeat the visionary landscapes that we have seen, but go back to older studies and even, as mentioned at the start of this essay, to the small landscapes and seascapes from his youth. In the extraordinary development from his first tachist works to his expressionistic visions from around 1890, it seems that Ensor followed a path of revelation and discovery—but lost track of it after 1891. It is as though, having emerged from a sort of trance, he was able to *recollect* his experiments with the imaginary, yet no longer wanted to (or could) proceed with them. On only a few occasions did the older artist venture to undertake a new landscape composition, as in *Moses and the Birds* (*The Finding of Moses*) (*Moïse et les oiseaux*, 1924; plate 96), but it is obvious that the landscape does not hold the same crucial importance in Ensor's later work as it did in the work prior to 1900.

Translated from the Dutch by Beth O'Brien

NOTES

I wish to thank Sabine Bown-Taevernier, Norbert Hostyn, Herwig Todts, Xavier Tricot, and Cathérine Verleysen for their help and advice.

1. See *Het landschap in de Belgische kunst, 1830–1914* (Antwerp: Koninklijk Museum voor Schone Kunsten, 1980).
2. Georges Lemmen, "James Ensor. Peintre et graveur, humoriste," *James Ensor, Peintre et graveur*, special issue of *La Plume*, no. 238 (December 15, 1898) This and all other translations from French, unless otherwise noted, are by Diana Stoll.
3. See *James Ensor: Lettres*, ed. Xavier Tricot, Archives du Futur (Brussels: Éditions Labor, 1999), p. 276.
4. On Les Vingt, see Anna Swinbourne, "Meeting James Ensor," and Susan Canning, "James Ensor: Carnival of the Modern," in the present volume.
5. James Ensor, "Réflexions sur quelques peintres et lanceurs d'éphémères" (1911), in *James Ensor: Mes Écrits*, preface by Frans Hellens, 5th ed. (Liège: Éditions nationales, 1974), p. 17.
6. James Ensor, *Liber Veritatis*, 1929–41, at the Art Institute of Chicago, inv. 1955.1021. Xavier Tricot's *James Ensor: Catalogue Raisonné of the Paintings*, 2 vols. (Antwerp: Pandora, 1992) contains references to all the landscapes and seascapes included in Ensor's *Liber Veritatis*.
7. The other two larger early paintings are *The Marsh* (*Le Marais*, 1880), now at the Musée des beaux-arts, Tournai; and *Grey Seascape* (*Marine grise*, 1880), at Antwerp's Koninklijk Museum voor Schone Kunsten.
8. Ensor, "Ma Vie en abrégé" (1934), in *Mes Écrits*, p. 206.
9. Ensor, letter to André De Ridder, August 2, 1928, in *James Ensor: Lettres*, p. 188. Eng. trans. in Ulrike Becks-Malorny, *James Ensor, 1860–1949* (Cologne: Taschen, 1999), p. 22.
10. Ensor, letter to Albert Croquez, 1934, quoted in Albert Croquez, *L'Œuvre gravé de James Ensor* (Geneva and Brussels: Pierre Cailler, 1947), p. 8. English translation by Dirk Verbiest, from Robert Hoozee, "Drawings and Etchings," in Catherine de Zegher, ed., *Between Street and Mirror: The Drawings of James Ensor* (New York: The Drawing Center; Minneapolis: University of Minnesota Press, 2001), p. 15.
11. See Robert Hoozee, Sabine Bown-Taevernier, and Jan Frederik Heijbroek, *Ik James Ensor: Tekeningen en prenten* (Antwerp: Mercatorfonds, 1987), p. 187.
12. Ensor, letter to Emma Lambotte, September 26, 1904, in Ensor, *Lettres à Emma Lambotte, 1904–1914*, ed. Danielle Derrey-Capon (Brussels: Centre internationale pour l'Étude du XIXe siècle and Renaissance du Livre, 1999), p. 62. Eng. trans. by Dirk Verbiest, in Hoozee, "Drawings and Etchings," p. 35.
13. See, for example, his letters to Pol de Mont, February 22, 1899, and June 21, 1900, in *James Ensor: Lettres*, pp. 143, 150.
14. Ensor, letter to Auguste Joye, July 26, 1925, in ibid., p. 453.
15. These drawings are located at the Koninklijk Museum voor Schone Kunsten in Antwerp. The collection also includes several Ensor drawings made in the Netherlands and in the Belgian Ardennes.
16. This has been surmised by Herwig Todts and Xavier Tricot. It is known that Ensor added figures to his 1887 oil *Carnival on the Beach* (*Carnaval sur la plage*), now at the Musées royaux des Beaux-Arts de Belgique, Brussels. See Marcel De Maeyer, "De genese van masker-, travestie- en skeletmotieven in het oeuvre van James Ensor," *Bulletin des Musées royaux des Beaux-Arts de Belgique* 10 (1963): 69–88.
17. This painting appears as number 2 on the list of Ensor's contributions to the salon held by Les Vingt in 1888. It is, however, not at all certain whether Ensor actually exhibited this work there. In a 1928 letter he states clearly that his entire contribution was refused that year (Ensor, letter to André De Ridder, September 30, 1928, in *James Ensor: Lettres*, p. 194). Yet in another letter, of 1894 or 1895, he writes: "1888. I show etchings and drawings at XX [Les Vingt]" (ibid., p. 127). From correspondence with Octave Maus, Secretary of Les Vingt, we know that Ensor was not able to send his works in, due to illness, and that he would send them later on ("Les Lettres de James Ensor à Octave Maus," ed. Francine-Claire Legrand, *Bulletin des Musées royaux des Beaux-Arts de Belgique* 15, nos. 1–2 [1966]: 33). Evidently his late submission included only drawings and etchings (this is confirmed by contemporary reports in the press). The fact that Ensor submitted *Adam and Eve Expelled from Paradise* for the 1889 exhibition suggests that he did not send the painting in 1888. I am grateful to Cathérine Verleysen and Xavier Tricot for their research on this matter.
18. See an interesting passage in a letter from Ensor to Max Gevers, December 12, 1927: "You consider that, after *Christ's Entry into Brussels*, *Adam and Eve Expelled from Paradise* is perhaps my most haunted, most poignant, and most human work. I have often had the same thought, and your kind appreciation emphasizes it further"; in *James Ensor: Lettres*, p. 404.

19. This possibility was first noted by Herwig Todts.
20. Ensor's black-chalk drawing *The Intense: Christ Rising to the Sky* (*L'Intense: Le Christ montant au ciel*; private collection) is illustrated in Hoozee et al., *James Ensor: Tekeningen en prenten*, pp. 117–18. On the Aureoles series, see Swinbourne, "Meeting James Ensor," and Canning, "Carnival of the Modern," in the present volume.
21. See Ensor's black-chalk-on-paper copy after Turner's 1829 *Ulysses Deriding Polyphemus*, KMSKA, inv. 2711/128. This copy (and another, after a work by John Constable) was probably made from a book: Ernest Chesneau's *La Peinture anglaise* (Paris: A. Quantin [printer], n.d.). The Antwerp museum has a large collection of copies, made from books and periodicals. See Lydia M. A. Schoonbaert and Dorine Cardyn-Oomen, *Tekeningen, Aquarellen en Prenten 19*de *en 20*ste *eeuw* (Antwerp: Koninklijk Museum voor Schone Kunsten Antwerpen, 1981), pp. 60 ff.
22. See, for example, Pierre Alechinsky et al., *Ensor* (Brussels: Musées royaux des Beaux-Arts de Belgique; Tournai: La Renaissance du livre, 1999), p. 335.
23. Walther Vanbeselaere, *James Ensor Retrospective*, exh. cat. (Antwerp: Koninklijk Museum voor Schone Kunsten Antwerpen, 1951), p. 15.
24. See Edward T. Cook, *A Popular Handbook to the National Gallery*, Appendix II, Index of Pictures (London and New York: Macmillan, 1888), pp. 687–89. For information related to London's National Gallery, I am grateful to Helen Simpson and Alan Crookham.
25. Ensor, letter to Pol de Mont, 1894 or 1895, *James Ensor: Lettres*, p. 132.
26. *Les XX Bruxelles: Catalogue des dix expositions annuelles* (Brussels: Centre international pour l'étude du XIXe siècle, 1981), p. 82. It is not known which version of Monet's *L'Église de Varengeville* was exhibited. *The Manneporte (Étretat)* is at The Metropolitan Museum of Art, New York. See also Daniel Wildenstein, *Monet: Catalogue raisonné*, vol. 2 (Cologne: Taschen/Wildenstein Institute, 1996), nos. 725–27, 832.
27. Ensor, note to Jules Du Jardin, *James Ensor: Lettres*, p. 272.
28. Ensor, "Réflexions sur quelques peintres et lanceurs d'éphémères" (1911), in *Mes Écrits*, p. 17.
29. Turner made two paintings of this event: one is at the Philadelphia Museum of Art, the other at the Cleveland Museum of Art.
30. This fort was located on the west side of Ostend and had a similar round shape to the Fort Napoléon, which still stands to the east of the town. (This information was kindly supplied by Norbert Hostyn.)
31. *Fireworks* was first exhibited in 1921; *The Tower of Lissewege* in 1920. See Tricot, *Ensor: Catalogue Raisonné*, nos. 270, 306.
32. See Hoozee, Bown-Taevernier, and Heijbroek, *Ik James Ensor*, pp. 136–38, 216–17.
33. Edgar Allan Poe, "The Domain of Arnheim" (1847), in *The Complete Poems and Tales of Edgar Allan Poe* (New York: Dorset, 1989), p. 683.
34. Ensor, letter to André De Ridder, August 2, 1928, in *James Ensor: Lettres*, p. 191.
35. See "Œuvres acquises pendant l'exposition," in *L'Art moderne* (March 12–13, 1892): 83.
36. *The Marsh* was one of Ensor's three large-scale nature studies of this period, along with *Grey Seascape* and *After the Storm* (see note 7).
37. *The Edge of the Wood at Ostend* is at the Musées royaux des Beaux-Arts de Belgique, Brussels, inv. 11.511.
38. For example, *The Pool with the Poplars* (*La Mare aux peupliers*, 1889). See Auguste Taevernier, *James Ensor: Illustrated Catalogue of His Engravings* (Ghent: Erasmus, 1973), no. 74.
39. Tricot, in *Ensor: Catalogue Raisonné*, no. 180, groups this work among the early landscapes, circa 1880, but it is more likely that this study has a later date.
40. According to Cook's 1888 *A Popular Handbook of the National Gallery*, this work was hanging in the museum, where Ensor might have seen it if he did indeed travel to London.
41. *Christ Calming the Storm* is thought to have been first shown at the art society Kunst van Heden in Antwerp in 1921.
42. *Christ Calming the Tempest* (*Le Christ apaisant la tempête*); see Taevernier, *James Ensor: Engravings*, no. 5.
43. The replicas are *Grand View of Ostend* (1906) and *Christ Calming the Storm* (c. 1906); both in private collections (Tricot, *Ensor: Catalogue Raisonné*, nos. 402, 406). In 1917 Ensor also painted a copy of the drawing *The Creation of Light*; private collection (Tricot, *Ensor: Catalogue Raisonné*, no. 478).

Ensor Is Eternal: The Painter and His Image

LAURENCE MADELINE

James Ensor once declared, "I've tried several times to paint my portrait, but I've never managed to capture the resemblance."[1] As of 1900 he had exhibited only one of his self-portraits, even though over the course of his life he would produce 112 such images. In his various discussions of his life and work, Ensor generally omitted mention of this chapter of his production. It is as if these works were so intimate that, according to Émile Verhaeren, "Up close, one could discern his psychology just by analyzing his self-portraits from different eras, and the elusive being that he is might be revealed better by this method than by examining the daily actions of his life."[2] Yet the portraits employ the same tools as those found in his richest, fiercest works, and can be seen as windows onto his state of mind as well as instruments of struggle.

In *Self-Portrait with a Flowered Hat* (*Mon Portrait déguisé*, 1883/1888; plate 17) Ensor appears decked out in a spectacular hat. We know that the painting was done in two stages: in 1883 he painted the bust and the frank gaze, and five years later he added the hat and the curling mustache. This was the only self-portrait that Ensor chose to exhibit during these years, at the Salon des Vingt (Salon des XX) in 1890. He went on to perfect this fastidious version of himself in two drawings, *My Portrait* (*Mon Portrait*, 1884; plate 18) and *My Sad and Splendid Portrait* (*Mon Portrait* [*Le Peintre triste et somptueux*]; fig. 1). In both of these he abolishes the paintbrushes that often are seen in his self-portraits, depicting Ensor the man rather than Ensor the artist. At the same time, in *Self-Portrait with a Flowered Hat*, a shift had taken place: by playing dress-up, Ensor was aligning himself with the Baroque Flemish master Peter Paul Rubens.[3]

In fact, Ensor did a number of self-portrayals inspired by other artists. The gesture in *My Portrait*, for example, is indebted to *Self-Portrait* (fig. 2) by Albrecht Dürer. Ensor's gesture, which was adopted from Dürer's work, could equally find precedent in Leonardo da Vinci's *Saint John the Baptist* (fig. 3). Another artist to whom Ensor pays homage is Jacques Callot. Ensor's etching *The Pisser* (*Le Pisseur*, 1887; plate 42), which shows a man from behind as he urinates against a wall, bears a striking resemblance to a drawing by Callot from about 1620.[4] Ensor's figure is surrounded by graffiti, including the inscription "Ensor est un fou" (Ensor is a madman), the artist's response to what he saw as an unrelenting barrage of unfair criticism.[5] By appropriating the critic's attack in this form, Ensor inverted it, making it something more than the introduction of a signature—it becomes a proud manifesto, a slogan.

These relatively naturalistic images were accompanied by self-portraits in various other guises. In *Peculiar Insects* (*Insectes singuliers*, 1888; plate 41) Ensor whimsically placed his head on the body of a large June bug.[6] Next to him his dear friend Mariette Rousseau assumes the form of a dragonfly. This fantastical composition alludes to the work of French artist Odilon Redon, but where Redon's bizarre grafts suggest evolutionary fantasies, something strange yet plausible, Ensor's tableau operates at the level of sarcasm. *Peculiar Insects* can be seen as an affectionate tribute to Rousseau, yet Ensor's

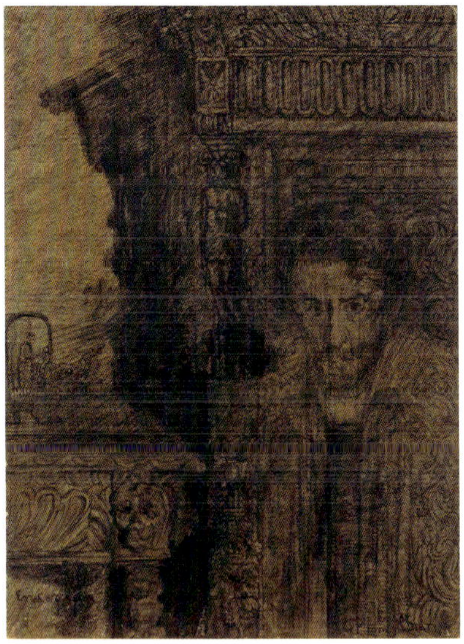

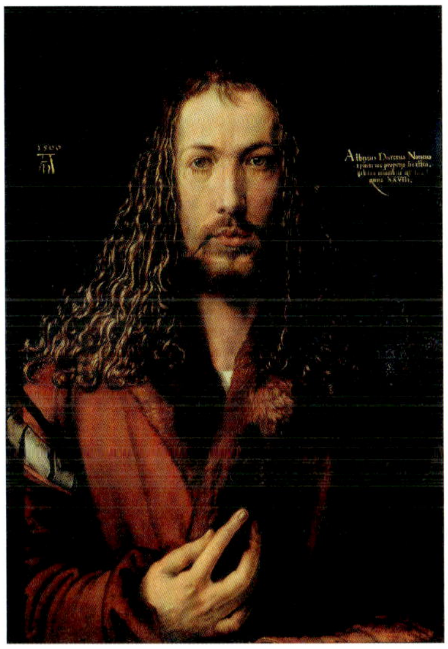

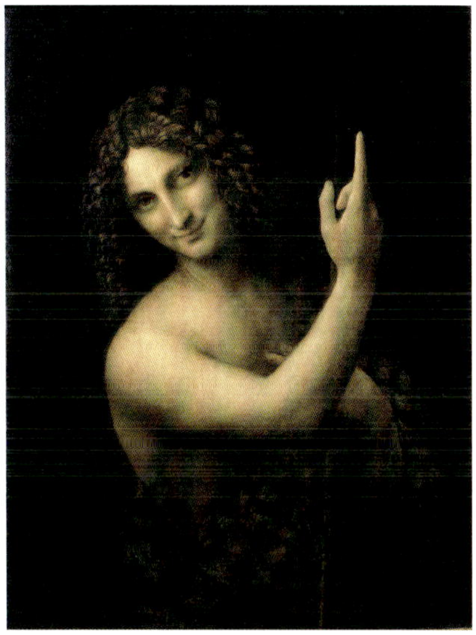

choice of the June bug—one of the most destructive pests in Europe at this time—for his own body is unsettling. (The bug's name is also linguistically related to insanity; in French, the expression "to have June bugs in one's roof" means to be insane.)

Again and again throughout his career Ensor cast himself in a very different role: that of Christ. This identification first appears in the 1884 work *My Portrait* and includes the remarkable series of drawings, begun in 1885, Visions: The Aureoles of Christ or the Sensibilities of Light (Visions: Les Auréoles du Christ ou les sensibilités de la lumière; plates 26 and 27).[7] Ensor clearly felt scorned by his contemporaries, and in fact he received criticism whose "viciousness," he once wrote, "goes beyond all known limits."[8] The identification of the artist with martyrs in general and with Christ in particular would remain constant through the 1880s and the beginning of the 1890s.[9] *The Man of Sorrows* (*L'Homme de douleurs*, 1891; plate 76) demonstrates both the extremity of his sense of martyrdom—nothing is spared in this fusion of Ensor's own face, the fixed, outraged expression of a Japanese Noh mask, and the "man of sorrows" of Isaiah 53—and its real consequence in psychic suffering. This message of torment reappears in less acute form in works such as *Ecce Homo* (*Christ and the Critics*) (*Le Christ et les critiques*, 1891; p. 39, fig. 8), in which Ensor, still as Christ, is flanked by two vociferating writers.

In the late 1880s and early 1890s, Ensor came up with a pair of devices that bore significance to his self-portraits. The first was the use of his own face, clearly identifiable with its mustache, goatee, and curls, as a form of self-caricature. This is how we find him in *Ecce Homo* (*Christ and the Critics*), *Ensor and Leman Discussing Painting* (*Ensor et Leman discutant peinture*, 1890; plate 71), and *The Virgin of Consolation* (*La Vierge consolatrice*, 1892; plate 81), in which his paintbrush and the palette are again his props. The second was the pun "art Ensor/hareng saur" (pickled herring), homophones in French. Ensor actually appropriated this phrase—an insult by an anonymous

FIG. 1: JAMES ENSOR. *My Sad and Splendid Portrait*. 1886. Black chalk on paper, 9 1/4 × 6 1/2" (23.5 × 16.5 cm). Private collection

FIG. 2: ALBRECHT DÜRER. *Self-Portrait*. 1500. Oil on panel, 26 7/16 × 19 3/16" (67.1 × 48.7 cm). Alte Pinakothek, Munich

FIG. 3: LEONARDO DA VINCI. *Saint John the Baptist*. c. 1513–16. Oil on panel, 27 3/16 × 22 7/16" (69 × 57 cm). Musée du Louvre, Paris

painter in 1885—turning it to his own use, just as he had done with the line "Ensor est un fou."[10] These two motifs join forces in *The Dangerous Cooks* (*Les Cuisiniers dangereux*, 1896; plate 88), which shows the painter's head served on a platter, alongside a herring and a label that reads "Art Ensor." The inscription and the pickled fish are at odds with the dramatic effect of the work's allusions to John the Baptist and Orpheus,[11] both stories with an iconography in art history, and to the mortuary mask, an ancient tradition revived in the nineteenth century. In this settling of accounts, Ensor creates a radically new tone in painting, mixing different registers—major and minor, painting and caricature.

From here it was perhaps a short step to Ensor's next invention. Posed for a photograph in his studio in about 1896 (p. 39, fig. 9), the artist is surrounded by painters' accessories: easel, palette, paintings, and a skull, an object that is often referenced by artists. From this photograph Ensor would create *The Skeleton Painter* (*Squelette peintre*, 1895 or 1896[?]; plate 89), in which he abandons his studio to a skeletal double. This was not Ensor's first such self-portrait; in *My Portrait in 1960* (*Mon Portrait en 1960*, 1888; plate 39), an etching from 1888, he appears as a skeleton, wearing only his shoes, but recognizable by his curling hair. Another etching, *My Skeletonized Portrait* (*Mon Portrait squelettisé*, 1889), is also based on a photograph (p. 24, fig. 9): the first version of the print (plate 57) is a straightforward portrait, a second state shows the artist as a man of bones (plate 58). Rather than anticipating death—the classic art-historical use of skeletal imagery—these works seem to intimate the parallel existence of a living man and his dead double.

Self-Portrait with Masks (*Ensor aux masques*, 1899; plate 91) presents a different, less macabre but perhaps more unnerving kind of symbolic death. Rather than show himself as a skeleton, here Ensor borrowed his own likeness, including headgear, from his *Self-Portrait with a Flowered Hat* of eleven years earlier and subjected it to an invasive advance of masks. The artist still resembles the proud young painter from the earlier work, elegantly Rubenesque, but he is no longer inventing anything, seemingly paralyzed and lost in a sea of frozen faces.

In Ensor's last self-portrait, titled *Self-Portrait with Masks* (*Mon Portrait aux masques*; plate 97), this time from 1937, the artist presents himself yet again in a new light: his hat is no longer flowered, he wears glasses, his hair and mustache are white. Compared to the unruly jumble of masks seen before, his studio is now nearly empty. The background is bright blue and red. Combative and mischievous, the aged painter brandishes his paintbrush like a whip and brings the masks to heel. Ensor invents his last self-image in which he is part painter, part venerable old man, and part eternal.

Translated from the French by Elise Nussbaum

NOTES

1. Ensor, letter to Pol de Mont, December 5, 1894, in *James Ensor: Lettres*, ed. Xavier Tricot, Archives du futur (Brussels: Éditions Labor, 1999), p. 122.
2. Émile Verhaeren, *Sur James Ensor* (1908; repr., Brussels: Le Regard Littéraire, Éditions Complexe, 1990), p. 74.
3. See, for example, Peter Paul Rubens, *Self-Portrait* (1639; Kunsthistorisches Museum, Vienna).
4. Jacques Callot, *Soldier, Viewed from Behind, Urinating on a Wall* (*Soldat vu en dos, en train d'uriner devant un mur*, c. 1620; Galleria degli Uffizi, Florence).
5. Jules Du Jardin, "James Ensor: La Réforme" (December 5, 1897), in *James Ensor: Lettres*, pp. 792–94.
6. In a letter to Valère Gille on December 4, 1890, Ensor referred to this engraved self-portrait as an "*hanneton*" ("June bug"). Michel Draguet calls the image a scarab. Draguet, *James Ensor ou la fantasmagorie* (Paris: Gallimard, 1999), p. 188.
7. Gisèle Ollinger-Zinque, "Le Christ-Ensor, ou l'identification au Christ dans l'œuvre d'Ensor," in *James Ensor* (Paris: Musée du Petit-Palais, 1990), pp. 27–34.
8. Ensor, letter to Jules Du Jardin, October 6, 1899, in, *James Ensor: Lettres*, p. 270.
9. Paul Gauguin, Vincent van Gogh, and Émile Bernard also painted themselves in this way. See *Rebels and Martyrs: The Image of the Artist in the Nineteenth Century* (London: National Gallery Company, 2006).
10. The association of Ensor with *hareng saur*—French for pickled herring—appeared in the catalogue of the Great Zwanze Exhibition, organized in 1885 by the avant-garde society L'Essor, when a painter using the pseudonym Franc Masson exhibited a work titled *L'Har-Engsor*.
11. See, for example, Andrea Solario's painting *The Head of John the Baptist* (*La Tête de saint Jean-Baptiste* c. 1506–07; Musée du Louvre, Paris) and Gustave Moreau's *Young Thracian Woman Discovering the Head of Orpheus* (*Orphée ou Jeune fille thrace portant la tête d'Orphée*, 1866; Musée d'Orsay, Paris).

"Make Way for the Old Ones! Respect Defunct Schools!" Ensor and the Art-Historical Canon

HERWIG TODTS

At seventeen I aspired to the Prix de Rome, but at twenty I exclaimed magnanimously as an extreme revolutionary and belligerent trouble-maker: Make way for the old ones! Respect defunct schools! [. . .] Driven by often contrasting winds I went in search of adventure in fabulous lands. This brought me to the delights of horizons populated by endlessly nuanced dreams.

—*James Ensor, from a speech prepared for the Académie royale de Belgique, 1925*[1]

Copies and "Chef's Secrets"

In 1951, shortly after James Ensor's death, the Koninklijk Museum voor Schone Kunsten in Antwerp organized the first posthumous retrospective exhibition of the artist's work. In that show a number of drawings, copied after works by other artists, old and modern, were presented to the public for the first time. The works were lent to the museum by the collector Jacques Janssens, who after the exhibition sold them to the institution, along with more than three hundred other drawings.[2] This entire collection was catalogued by curator Lydia M. A. Schoonbaert, who managed to identify a large number of the images.[3]

Some three hundred of the drawings are considered to be copies after works by other artists. While most of these drawings were rendered in Conté crayon, around forty were drawn in pencil: these seem to be copies of genre paintings in the style of Adriaan Van Ostade or Ferdinand De Braekeleer. Ensor probably made these pencil drawings before entering the Académie royale des beaux-arts in Brussels, where he studied from 1877 to 1880. A group of forty Conté drawings of Spanish soldiers (probably from 1879 or 1880) have long been misidentified as illustrations for Miguel de Cervantes's *Don Quixote* (fig. 1). Although the figures in these depictions feature traditional costumes and equipment of sixteenth- and seventeenth-century Spanish soldiers—and one drawing is definitely a strange mirror-image copy of an illustration by Gustave Doré for *Don Quixote*—there is no other situation or character in the group that refers concretely to Cervantes's story. For the time being we cannot say whether these are copies after illustrations (some figures seem to be abruptly cut from larger scenes) or representations thought up by Ensor, or a combination of the two.[4]

Finally, there is a group of around 220 drawings that are considered to be copies after works by artists from the sixteenth to the end of the late nineteenth century.[5] They include three sketches that Ensor probably made during a visit to the Palais des Beaux-Arts in Lille in November 1884. In a letter to his friend Darío de Regoyos, Ensor testifies to his admiration for the paintings ascribed to Goya, which he copied in Lille, where he also made a sketch after a version of *Malle Babbe* (1633–35), at the time attributed to Frans Hals.[6] Two copies were based on works that during Ensor's Académie years were in the collection of the Musées royaux des Beaux-Arts

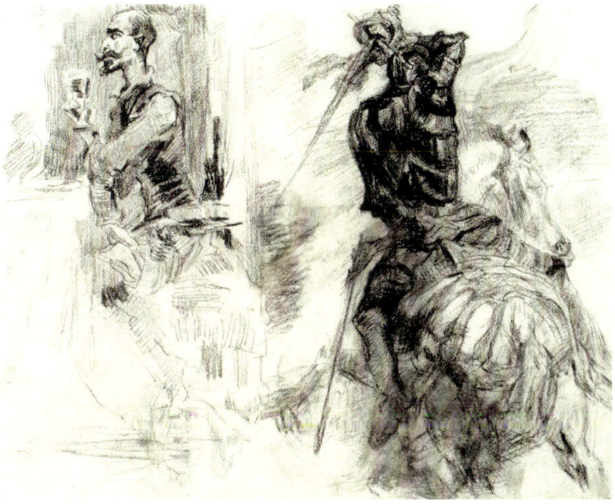

FIG. 1: JAMES ENSOR. *A Don at a Table* (*the Duke of Alva?*) and *Rear View of a Caballero over Copies of Genre Figures* (*Don Quixote?*). 1877/1879 and 1880(?). Pencil and Conté crayon on paper, 7 11/16 × 10 3/16" (19.6 × 25.9 cm). Koninklijk Museum voor Schone Kunsten, Antwerp

de Belgique in Brussels: Rembrandt van Rijn's 1641 portrait of Nicolaas van Bambeek (from which Ensor copied only the head and shoulders) and two heads from *Virgil Reading from the Aeneid before Augustus and Livia* (*Virgile lisant l'Enéïde devant Auguste et Livie*, 1812) by Jean-Auguste-Dominique Ingres.

Whether Ensor actually went to the museum to draw or worked from reproductions is not absolutely clear, but it is believed that virtually all the copies were most likely redrawn from reproductions in magazines such as *Le Magasin pittoresque*, *La Gazette des beaux-arts*, *L'Art*, and *La Vie moderne*, or in illustrated catalogues from Salons in Brussels and Paris. Many of his sources remain unidentified. He copied works by a wide range of masters, from Michelangelo to John Constable, Albrecht Dürer to Hokusai. He made twenty-three copies after portraits, by artists including Rembrandt, Eugène Delacroix, Gustave Courbet, Édouard Manet, and Pierre Puvis de Chavanne. Apparently Ensor owned a copy of the 1880 illustrated catalogue of an exhibition of Belgian art and works in the collection of the Musée moderne de Bruxelles with illustrations based on original drawings by the masters themselves; many of Ensor's copies are based on images from this publication.[7]

Few of Ensor's copies are dated, but we do know some specifics. In the course of 1885 he had access to a small volume of Hokusai's *manga* (sketches), from which Ensor copied several pages. Following Schoonbaert, we generally accept the publication date of the probable visual source as the earliest possible date of Ensor's copy. Thus his drawing after a scene from Honoré Daumier's series of lithographs *The Bachelor's Day* (*La Journée du célibataire*, 1839) might have been rendered anytime after Daumier's work was reproduced in the *Gazette des Beaux-Arts* in 1878.[8] I believe that this and most of Ensor's other copies were made between 1880 and 1890, although there is scant solid evidence of their dates.

Because this rich collection of copies was unknown until after Ensor's death, an impression arose in the scholarly community that the artist wished to carefully preserve his "chef's secrets."[9] And yet Ensor never kept his love for the work of many old and modern masters hidden. In early January 1895 Pol de Mont, author, critic, and the first curator of the Museum voor Schone Kunsten in Antwerp, asked Ensor to provide a statement for a study de Mont planned to publish in the Dutch-language magazine *De Vlaamse School*. Ensor responded with a summary of his views and the main facts about his artistic career. Asked whether he was particularly devoted to a specific master, Ensor answered:

> *Initially I very much liked Rembrandt, but much later I became attracted to Goya and Turner. I was fascinated by the discovery of two masters who were obsessed with light*

and ferocity. The extravagant inventions of Hieronymus Bosch and Pieter Bruegel also pleased me tremendously. I thought their works were better than those of other masters from the Flemish School.[10]

In magazine articles and texts for speeches that appeared in various publications beginning in 1921, Ensor wrote about artists of his own time and of earlier eras in sometimes seemingly contradictory ways. For example, he spoke proudly of his admiration for the art of Ingres,[11] but (the above-mentioned copy notwithstanding) there would seem to be few or no similarities between the two artists' styles. In 1896 Ensor published a scathing attack in the monthly journal *Le Coq rouge*[12] about the art critic Arthur Stevens and his brother, the painter Alfred Stevens—and yet Ensor made copies of at least three of Alfred Stevens's works.[13] To add to the confusion, while Ensor's writings and letters contain a trove of information, the obliquity of his language has taxed more than one critical reader's patience.[14]

Ever since Ensor's earliest participation in exhibitions at Les Vingt (Les XX) in 1884, faultfinders, admirers, and researchers have cited old and modern artists whose work he may have imitated, quoted, or made use of in some other way. Thus far, unfortunately, no effort has been made to systematically and critically study the parallels among Ensor's writings, his hundreds of copies, and his art as such; this is an open subject for future research. Here, however, we will endeavor to place Ensor's interest in "defunct schools" in the context of the rapid modernization of the art-historical canon, which occurred during the course of the nineteenth century.

Establishing and Updating the Art-Historical Canon

In Francis Haskell's 1976 study *Rediscoveries in Art*, the author describes a consensus regarding the hierarchy of Western artists, which was reached over the course of the seventeenth and eighteenth centuries.[15] This "art-historical canon" was gradually modified and updated, starting in the late eighteenth century. Taste and artistic notions changed; great masters who had once been considered "immortal"—such as Otto Van Veen, Pietro da Cortona, and Eustache Le Sueur (esteemed by eighteenth-century art historians as greater than Giorgione, Michelangelo, or Caravaggio)[16]—eventually disappeared from prominence, and the reassessment of long-forgotten artists began. However, many nineteenth-century academies and art schools still held stubbornly to the classical art-historical canon as it had been initially established.

Western art, from roughly the fifteenth to the nineteenth century, focused primarily on naturalistic representation—although even great skill at figuration was by no means enough. The classical, or "humanistic" theory of art (as Rensselaer Wright Lee termed it in his seminal 1967 treatise *Ut pictura poesis*)[17] makes clear why, until well into the nineteenth century, "realism" as such was considered insufficient and even objectionable. The task of the artist, it was thought, is larger and more serious than mere rendering (no matter how skillful); not only does he have to give people pleasure, he must also—like the poet and the philosopher—offer insight and wisdom. It was believed that this could be accomplished only if the artist chose to portray lofty themes and noble characters from devotional and secular history.

Thus the quality of a work of art was seen as contingent upon the degree to which it depicted "important" figures and situations in a dignified and genuine way. As for the choice of the themes to be depicted, it was the artist's task to make a distinction between the particular and the universal—even while striving to unite the beautiful, the true, and the good in a single objective representation. The preeminent example of universal beauty was to be found in Greco-Roman art. The objectivity of an image, it was thought, was guaranteed by the proper application of tried-and-true techniques: linear precision, perspective (by means of converging lines and color), and the suggestion of volume (by means of light and shadow).

Classical values, notions, and techniques were still adamantly taught at European academies in the nineteenth century. The historical compositions, paintings, and drawings that Ensor made (or began) while at the Académie comply with the classical artistic rules (consider, for example, the central section of *The Mystic Death of a Theologian* [*Elated Monks Claim the Body of Theologian Sus Ovis, in Spite of the Resisting Bishop Friton or Friston*] [*La Mort mystique d'un théologien* (*Moines exaltés réclamant le corps du Théologien Sus-Ovis malgré l'opposition de l'évêque Friton ou Friston*), 1880/1885–86(?); plate 22]). If the series of depictions of Spanish soldiers mentioned above (fig. 1) are free creations and not copies, these vivid drawings may be counted among the few works by Ensor that still fully connect with classical Western European artistic tradition in terms of both concept and execution.

In 1884, however, Ensor published a striking satire on academic education in the journal *L'Art moderne* in which he ridiculed one professor's random preference for "correct design" against another's equally random advocacy for the true "Flemish palette."[18] Apparently, the time-honored discussion about the value of the palette and verisimilitude vis-à-vis the rendering of an ideal—*disegno* versus *colore*, *ancien* versus *moderne*, or "Poussinists" versus "Rubenists"—was still relevant among nineteenth-century academy teachers.

According to some art historians, anti-academicism was the fundamental common principle for the art of the nineteenth- and twentieth-century modernists. This may explain why Ensor was praised by Emil Nolde and Paul Klee on the one hand, but was also admired by many far less progressive artists and critics, such as the Antwerp museum curators Pol de Mont and Walther Vanbeselaere.

But—just as Realism as such was considered inadequate for the followers of the classical or humanistic theory of art—mere anti-academicism was seen as insufficient as an impulse for the modernist artist. In 1909 Klee wrote in his diary: "A work of art can only leave behind the true-to-life if the line, as in the drawings and paintings by Van Gogh or in the graphic art of Ensor, occurs as an independent pictorial element. In Ensor's work the parallel position of the lines in his graphic art is striking."[19] In his 1960 essay "Modernist Painting," Clement Greenberg summarized the basic task of the modernist artist: to locate the essence of his artistic media—the flat plane, forms, colors, paint, gesture, and even the (suppressed) emotions of the painter. Greenberg explained that "the task [. . .] to eliminate from the effects of each art any and every effect that might conceivably be borrowed from or by the medium of any other art" influenced the modernization of the art-historical canon:

> *Modernism may have had something to do with the revival of the reputations of Uccello, Piero, El Greco, Georges de la Tour, and even Vermeer and it certainly confirmed if it did not start other revivals like that of Giotto; but modernism has not lowered thereby the standing of Leonardo, Raphael, Titian, Rubens, Rembrandt or Watteau. What modernism has made clear is that though the past did appreciate masters like these justly, it often gave wrong or irrelevant reasons for doing so.*[20]

Rembrandt and the Credo of the Plein-Air Artist

Ensor did not develop his artistic views and commit them to paper in any systematic way. Still, he left behind a wealth of material, the coherence of which is often underestimated. His essay "Réflexions sur l'art," written in 1882, was first cited by Eugène Demolder (plate 86) in 1892. Ensor seems to have set much stock by this relatively short text: in 1895 he advised Pol de Mont to consult it (and de Mont quotes important passages from it in his piece for *De Vlaamse School*).[21] "Réflexions" was also published in the last of five issues of the journal *La Plume* that were dedicated to Ensor on the occasion of his solo exhibition in Paris in 1898. The artist included the essay in the publication of his collected writings, and an expanded version of it appeared as the introduction to the catalogue of his works presented at Ostend's Galerie Studio in August 1933.

In "Réflexions sur l'art," Ensor outlines the evolution of the art of painting in three stages. This evolution begins with what he calls the "primitive view": the Gothic style, which he describes as simple, dry, and easily accessible to most people. With progressive study and observation, painting then develops into a second stage: the Renaissance, when artists (i.e., the masters of the classical art-historical canon), with their well-trained eyes, learned to distinguish the values and nuances of tonalities. After more attentive study and patient observation, finally, the modern artist comes to understand that the line (the *correct* line) is secondary to the subtle play of light. According to Ensor, most people cannot perceive this at all and see in modern art only chaos and mistakes.

"Réflexions sur l'art" may be considered both an apology and a credo: when academics, critics, or other viewers reproach Ensor for not drawing "correctly," it is due to the fact that they themselves look at reality only superficially—like "primitive" Gothic artists; or (in the case of more experienced art lovers) they expect that the artist should adhere to Renaissance techniques and values. But the modern artist practices observation and studies reality; he is a researcher. Fundamental artistic changes through the eras are thus explained as the progress of the artist as an observer.

Ensor stated clearly that he was an advocate of plein-air painting. For Ensor—as opposed to the followers of the classical (and academic) theory of art—realism, observation, and representation are valid objectives in themselves. In this, he shared the views of the influential French critic and art-historian Théophile Thoré, better known by his pen name, Wilhelm Bürger. Bürger did not hesitate to call Raphael and Rubens artists of the past, artists that force us to look backward. The heroes of the plein-air artists and the Realists were Rembrandt and Hals, who, according to Bürger, were much greater artists than Raphael or Rubens, for they were artists of the *future*, artists of the free human being.[22]

After his visit to the Lille museum in November 1884, Ensor wrote to Darío de Regoyos some thoughts in a similar vein: "Courbet amazed me, without exaggeration, he is as good as Rembrandt. [. . .] Jordaens is magnificent [. . .] Delacroix has great qualities but a pity that there is much too much [influence of] Rubens [in his work]."[23] This appreciation is confirmed by the many copies that Ensor made after Rembrandt and Hals.

The reassessment of Rembrandt occurred in three stages over the course of the nineteenth century. Early on, French Romantic artists and writers admired the Dutch master's enigmatic and dramatic chiaroscuro. For Bürger and artists such as Courbet (and later Ensor), Rembrandt was the preeminent example of an anticlassical, decidedly human aesthetic ideal. The new interest in the potentials of the graphic arts of the "peintre-graveur" was also influenced by Rembrandt's work (Ensor copied several etchings by Rembrandt [figs. 3 and 4]). Toward the end of the nineteenth century, Rembrandt would inspire artists as diverse as Gustave Moreau, Odilon Redon, Lovis Corinth, and Emil Nolde.[24]

Jacob Burckhardt, the great cultural historian and a very reserved admirer of Rembrandt, provides insight into why a third wave of artists turned to Rembrandt's work around the turn of the century. Burckhardt was of the opinion that Rembrandt was the greatest Dutch painter, and yet he believed that his art was not an example to be followed by the modern artist. In the first place, Rembrandt disregarded the classical aesthetic ideal and refused to follow correct proportions. Second, his altogether too-human approach to religious subjects was seen as generally improper and sometimes even vulgar. And last, the use of pictorial means was insufficiently functional in Rembrandt's art. According to Burckhardt, "with him everything becomes a problem of light" and his models and figures are "purely a substrate for a light experiment"; therefore "the insignificant and the unsightly are also mystically transfigured."[25]

Such warnings were undoubtedly wasted on Ensor. Burckhardt's assessment of Rembrandt may be applied to Ensor's *The Mystic Death of a Theologian* (and to other extremely Rembrandtesque works, such as Ensor's series of drawings Visions: The Aureoles of Christ or the Sensibilities of Light [Visions: Les Auréoles du Christ ou les sensibilités de la lumière; plates 26 and 27]). Initially the *Mystic Death* drawing, owned for many years by Jean Portaels, director of the Académie in Brussels, had the extraordinary title *Elated Monks Claim the Body of the Theologian Sus Ovis, in Spite of the Resisting Bishop Friton or Friston* (*Moines exaltés réclamant le corps du Théologien Sus-Ovis malgré l'opposition de l'évêque Friton ou Friston*).[26] As Marcel De Maeyer has made clear, this was a crucial

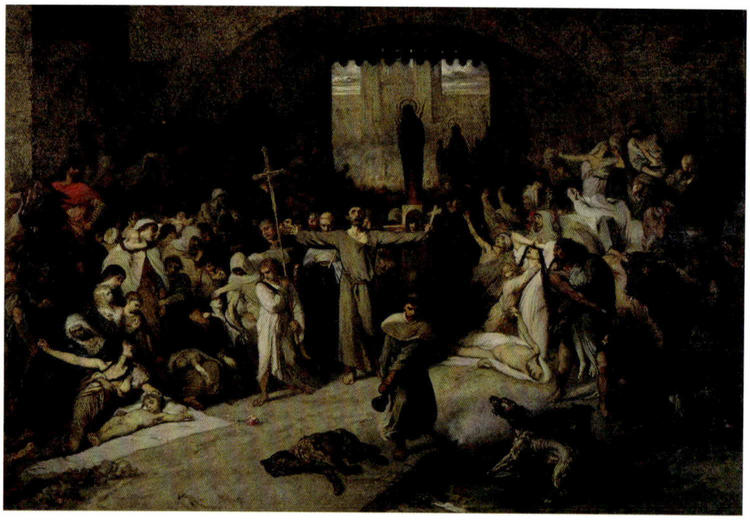

FIG. 2: LOUIS GALLAIT. *The Plague of Tournai*. 1882. Oil on canvas, 17' 8 5/8" × 27' 4 3/4" (540 × 835 cm). Musées royaux des Beaux-Arts de Belgique, Brussels. On deposit with Musée des Beaux-Arts, Tournai

work in Ensor's œuvre. De Maeyer discovered that, probably in 1886, Ensor enlarged an older drawing, made during his time at the Académie, of a group of barefoot men in long shirts; to this he added other figures and architectural elements, transforming it into an enigmatic and mystical scene. The drawing was thus created during two separate sessions.[27]

The bald man with a beard and moustache in the image seems to be dressed as a mendicant friar. This figure may represent Peter the Hermit, summoning the faithful to take part in the First Crusade to the Holy Land. (Peter the Hermit was a popular character from Belgian history who often played a leading part in Académie composition exercises.) In the later, expanded state of the drawing, Ensor relocated the procession of simply attired men and children into a church building. There is a pillar with an enormous crucifix on the left, and above are indications of a Gothic church vault, an orating priest, a statue of a female saint, and a group of figures on a balcony. The "elated" or frenzied monks enter from the right. On the left a second group is arriving, carrying on their shoulders the monumental statue of a male saint and preceded by a man with a bishop's staff and miter—this is "Friton or Friston," apparently the opponent of the monks.[28] In the foreground, a group of kneeling men is praying at the deathbed of the theologian, whose hands are also folded as in prayer.

The composition of *The Mystic Death of a Theologian* (church building, procession, statue of female saint, recumbent figures in the foreground) is reminiscent of Louis Gallait's *The Plague of Tournai* (*La Peste de Tournai*; fig. 2). The Belgian historical painter Gallait began work in the 1850s on the preparation of this painting, but the monumental canvas was exhibited for the first time, amid great public interest, in the summer of 1884 at the Exposition triennale de Bruxelles. Critic August Vermeylen later rightly called this work "the last word on romantic painting in Belgium."[29] Perhaps during a visit to the Brussels Salon in 1884 Ensor was struck by the coincidental similarity between his group of monks and those by Gallait. Patrick Florizoone thinks that Ensor based both the first and second state of the entire drawing on Gallait's painting, carried out in 1880 and at a second around 1886; indeed, Florizoone contends that *The Mystic Death of a Theologian* is one of Ensor's many homages to Gallait.[30] In my opinion, the rather disrespectful tone of the original title (a tone that is echoed in more than one visual detail) indicates that Ensor's drawing may be a malicious caricature of Gallait's outstanding academic canvas.

Ensor's drawing also obviously testifies to his renewed interest in Rembrandt. The group of praying figures is perhaps a mirrored retake of a copy of a number of figures from Rembrandt's etching *The Triumph of Mordecai* (c. 1639–43) (fig. 3). The young girl who is running away on the right may originate from the Dutch master's *The Night Watch* (1642), but Ensor copied a similar figure from Rembrandt's etching *The Pancake Woman* (1635) (fig. 4). Indeed, Ensor's admiration for Rembrandt's work is so patent that even forgers of Ensor's work seem to hope that a reference to the old master in their counterfeits will remove any doubts about provenance. A very active (and easy to identify) "pseudo-Ensor" thus created an Ensoresque variation on Rembrandt's 1639 etching *Death Appearing to a Wedded Couple from an Open Grave*; the forger added the skeleton of a horseman on the skeleton of a horse, an Ensor-style surprised sun, and, to be absolutely sure there would be no mistake, the text: "Death appearing to a married couple after Rembrandt / James Ensor / Ensor."[31]

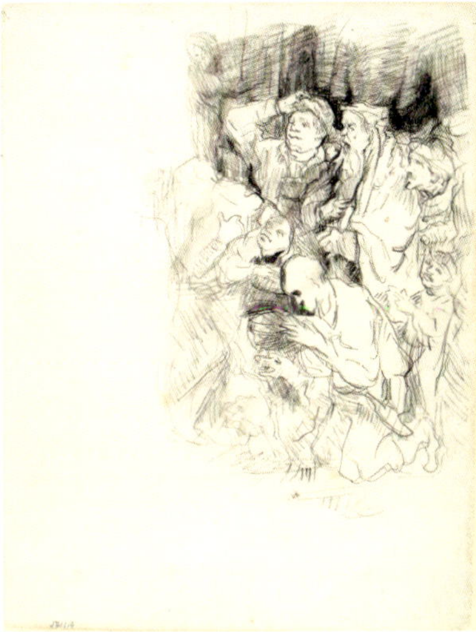

FIG. 3: JAMES ENSOR. *Copy after a Fragment of the Rembrandt Etching "The Triumph of Mordecai"*. c. 1885(?). Conté crayon on paper, 8 7/8 × 6 11/16" (22.5 × 17 cm). Koninklijk Museum voor Schone Kunsten, Antwerp

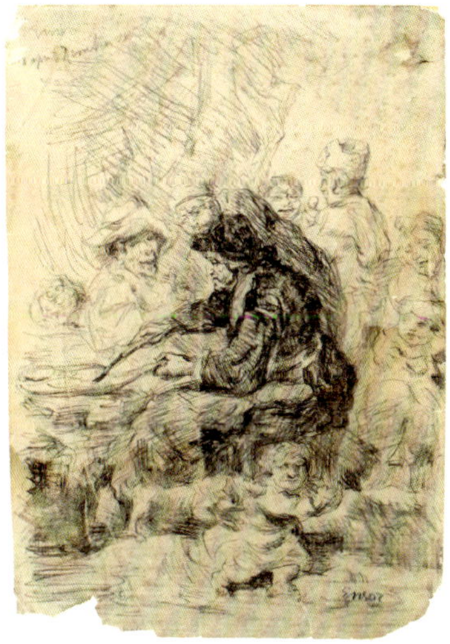

FIG. 4: JAMES ENSOR. *Copy after the Rembrandt Etching "The Pancake Woman"*. c. 1885. Conté crayon on paper, 8 7/8 × 6 11/16" (22.5 × 17 cm). Koninklijk Museum voor Schone Kunsten, Antwerp

The Mystic Death of a Theologian reveals how important this return to Rembrandt was for Ensor. Rembrandt's works taught him how to give a new turn to the "very attentive study and patient observation of light" that Ensor pursued as a plein-air painter, and how he could use light itself as an expressive pictorial medium. The Aureoles series of drawings of 1885–86 were given striking subtitles in which Ensor tried to characterize the quality of the light: "tranquil and serene," "gay," "alive and radiant," "intense," "sad and broken." In the second definitive state of *The Mystic Death of a Theologian,* Ensor represented light as an overwhelming, ominous force.

Almost as a matter of course, this drawing also reveals the "preference for the extraordinary and the abnormal always combined with or altered by the study of light" about which Ensor wrote in an 1899 letter to the critic Jules Du Jardin.[32] The figure of Christ and the bizarre, devilish creatures in the architectural decoration at the top and at the ends of the chandelier were clearly drawn by a lover of "primitive" art forms.

Indeed, there was a return in the nineteenth century to the "gothic" or "primitive" painters. The reevaluation of the artists of the Italian quattrocento and the "Flemish primitives" transpired over time and in stages, and was defended with a variety of arguments. Historical curiosity, nationalist pride, nostalgia for a time of uncomplicated religious devotion, sincere admiration for the charms of naïveté, and (not least) the "cult" of art-historical reevaluation all complemented one another. After the mid-nineteenth century, Charles Baudelaire and Joris-Karl Huysmans would express their admiration for the anti-classical aesthetic and the intense expressiveness of the "primitives" (among whom were included Bosch and Bruegel).[33] In his 1895 letter to Pol de Mont, Ensor too confessed: "The excessive inventions of Hieronymus Bosch and

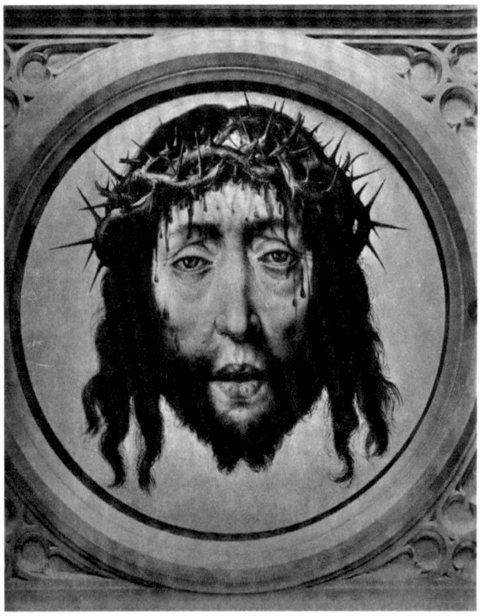

FIG. 5: ALBRECHT BOUTS. *Man of Sorrows*. c. 1490–1500. Oil on panel, 11 7/16 × 11 7/16" (29 × 29 cm). Koninklijk Museum voor Schone Kunsten, Antwerp. Gift of Florent Van Ertborn 1841

Pieter Bruegel [please me] tremendously. [. . .] I thought their works were better than those of the other masters of the Flemish school."[34] Ensor considered them superior to Rubens and the heroes of the classical art-historical canon. (Ensor also made several noteworthy statements about the modernization of the Flemish variant of the classical art-historical canon, including the summary statement: "Flemish art is no longer: it is dead, truly dead.")[35]

Does the appreciation of Bosch and Bruegel conflict with Ensor's aversion to the "dry, primitive, gothic line (and design)"? Unlike several of his Belgian colleagues (such as Eugène Laermans, Gustave Van de Woestyne, Valerius De Saedeleer, and later George Minne), Ensor was clearly not concerned with the simplified design and the colorful palette of the primitives. In a letter from 1900 to de Mont, he mocks "the particularly perverted" taste of some current English artists "dedicated to the obsequious imitation of the old Italian masters."[36] Ensor's love of Bruegel and the primitives was based on what he called his "love of the extraordinary and the abnormal." This is apparent from the crucifix in *The Mystic Death of a Theologian*. It can also be seen in his 1891 *The Man of Sorrows* (*L'Homme de douleurs*; plate 76), in which he shockingly combined a devil's mask from the Japanese Noh theater and the bleeding face of Christ—the latter based on a fifteenth-century representation by Albrecht Bouts (fig. 5). (Ensor had used the same Bouts image earlier, with his 1887 drawing *The Temptation of Saint Anthony* [*La Tentation de Saint-Antoine*; p. 21, fig. 7].)

Gunners to Your Cannons

Might Ensor have developed these new artistic insights and aesthetic preferences through reading Bürger, Baudelaire, or Huysmans? Other critics and art historians—including his friend, the writer and artist Théo Hannon—might certainly have played important roles in the development of Ensor's "theory of art." Did he speak with Maurice Maeterlinck about their shared interest in the "mystic" medieval world? What were the literary and visual sources available to Ensor: did he really have firsthand knowledge of the work of Joseph Mallord William Turner or the French Impressionists? All these questions present possibilities for further research.

As we attempt to determine the sense and significance of Ensor's remarks on old and contemporary art, we obviously have to account for the circumstances in which he expressed his opinions. In a long explanation on "the crisis in painting," written in 1922, the sixty-two-year-old painter wryly praised the versatility of art, and played on the different connotations of the French word *canon*: "Let us encourage the art of the painter and his various canons. Heavenly art: canon. Hindu art: canon. Greek art: canon. [. . .] Gothic art: canon. Academic: canon, canon [. . .] art really clears a path by means of cannon shots."[37] In a polemical contribution to the journal *La Ligue artistique* of June 1896 about the organization and curation of the Musée moderne in

Brussels, Ensor took to task those among his contemporaries who already belonged to the national collection and demanded to know why older Belgian masters had been ignored: "Respect defunct schools!" he urged.[38] In 1921 in Antwerp he championed the work of Henri Leys, De Braekeleer, and Jan Stobbaerts. "Give our young art what is young art's and to the old [art] what is the old's." Saying that he was "driven by an inexplicable need for artistic balance," Ensor reiterated his injunction: "Respect defunct schools! Make way for the old ones!"[39] He would repeat the statement in 1925 when he addressed the members of the Académie royale de Belgique, who had condescended to give him a place at their side.[40]

According to art-historian Robert Delevoy, Ensor chose his artistic examples "without horizon," and in this was often "naïve, in the absence of a yardstick for opinion or even for bias."[41] But in fact Ensor's artistic opinions were, all in all, far less noncommittal, pluralistic, or paradoxical than is generally claimed. The internal coherence of Ensor's understanding of past masters seems unequivocal and very meaningful, based as it was at least partly on a desire to establish his personal position in the larger trajectory of art history's canon.

NOTES

1. James Ensor, "Discours pour la réception à l'Académie royale de Belgique" (1925), in *Mes Écrits ou les suffisances matamoresques*, ed. Hugo Martin, rev. and enl. 6th ed. (Brussels: Éditions Labor, 1999), pp. 20–21. (This and all other translations from French, unless otherwise noted, are by Stephen Windrose and the author.)
2. According to reports, Janssens purchased this collection directly from James Ensor's heir, Alexandrine Daveluy, the daughter of Ensor's deceased sister Marie ("Mitche").
3. Lydia M. A. Schoonbaert and Dorine Cardyn-Oomen, *Tekeningen, aquarellen en prenten 19de en 20ste eeuw* (Antwerp: Koninklijk Museum voor Schone Kunsten Antwerpen, 1982), pp. 60–159, nos. 2708/1–66, 2709/1–50, 2709 A/1–15, 2710/1–15, 2711/1–165, 2712/1–239. Richard Thomson, Review: "*Tekeningen, aquarellen en prenten 19de en 20ste eeuw, Koninklijk Museum voor Schone Kunsten, Antwerp,* by Lydia M. A. Schoonbaert and Dorine Cardyn-Oomen," *Master Drawings* 22, no. 1 (1984): 82–85, contains important corrections and supplements.
4. Together with some copies in the collection of the Museum voor Schone Kunsten in Ostend (now with the Kunstmuseum aan zee, Ostend), the drawings are part of a single album. An online publication at http://www.vlaamsekunstcollectie.be/ is presently under construction. For further discussion, see Herwig Todts, *James Ensor: De noche cartografiaba mis sueños. Obras en las colecciones del Koninklijk Museum voor Schone Kunsten de Amberes (KMSKA) y del Museum voor Schone Kunsten de Ostende (MSKO)* (Salamanca: Caja Duero; Seville: Caja San Fernando; Antwerp: Koninklijk Museum voor Schone Kunsten, 2004), pp. 31–43.
5. Ensor copied work by the following artists: Michelangelo, Albrecht Dürer, Frans Hals (of whose work Ensor made nine copies), Rembrandt (sixteen copies), Jan Steen, Jacques Callot (three copies), Antoine Watteau, Thomas Rowlandson, John Constable, Joseph Mallord William Turner, Hokusai (ten copies), Eugène Delacroix (twenty-five copies), Honoré Daumier, Édouard Manet, Alfred Grévin, Edgar Degas, Jules Bastien-Lepage (two copies), and Jean-François Raffaelli.
6. *James Ensor: Lettres*, ed. Xavier Tricot, Archives du futur (Brussels: Éditions Labor, 1999), pp. 153–56; and Todts, *Ensor: De noche cartografiaba mis sueños,* pp. 78–82.
7. *1830–1880 Catalogue illustré de l'exposition historique de l'art belge et du museé moderne de Bruxelles, d'après les dessins originaux des artistes* (Brussels, Paris, 1880).
8. Schoonbaert, *Tekeningen, aquarellen,* no. 2711/46.
9. See Walther Vanbeselaere, *Rétrospective James Ensor* (Antwerp: Koninklijk Museum voor Schone Kunsten Antwerpen, 1951), p. 8. Lydia M. A. Schoonbaert, *Tekeningen van James Ensor*, exh. cat. (Antwerp: Koninklijk Museum voor Schone Kunsten Antwerpen, 1977), p. 14.
10. Ensor, letter to Pol de Mont, 1895, in *James Ensor: Lettres*, p. 132. See Pol de Mont, "De schilder en etser James Ensor. Een bijdrage tot de geschiedenis der kunst van den laatsten tijd," *De Vlaamse School* 8 (1895): 110–19. Ensor was happy with the publication and thanked de Mont (see his letter of July 31, 1895, in *James Ensor: Lettres,* pp. 134–35). In a letter of July 14, 1898, Ensor asked whether de Mont would translate "Réflexions sur l'art" free of charge for publication in *La Plume* (*James Ensor: Lettres,* p. 137ff). See "James Ensor: Peintre et aquafortiste," *James Ensor: Peintre et graveur,* special edition of *La Plume* (Paris 1899): 85–90.
11. Ensor, "Discours" (1925), in *Mes Écrits*, p. 20.
12. See *Le Coq rouge* 1, nos. 11–12 (March–April 1896): 550–52; see also Ensor, "Les Frères Stevens" (1896), in *Mes Écrits*, pp. 28–31.
13. Ensor's Stevens copies are: no. 2711/138b (after Stevens's *A Passionate Song*) and no. 2711/158a (after *The Baby*) in the Koninklijk Museum voor Schone Kunsten in Antwerp; his copy after *The Parisian Sphinx* is in a private collection.
14. See Rudolf Schmitz, "'You Words without Rhyme and Reason, I Love You, I Love You': The Deregulated Language of James Ensor," in Ingrid Pfeiffer and Max Hollein, eds., *James Ensor* (Frankfurt: Schirn Kunsthalle Frankfurt, 2005), p. 149ff.
15. Francis Haskell, *Rediscoveries in Art: Some Aspects of Taste, Fashion and Collecting in England and France* (Ithaca, N.Y.: Cornell University Press, 1976).
16. Roger de Piles's *Cours de peinture par principes* (Paris, 1708), an exemplary source for the classical art-historical canon, includes a table that scores, on a scale from one to twenty, the "57 best-known artists" in terms of their abilities and talents in composition, drawing, palette, expression, etc.
17. Rensselaer Wright Lee, *The Humanistic Theory of Painting* (New York: Norton, 1967), pp. 67–69. Rev. ed.: *Ut pictura poesis: Humanisme et théorie de la peinture, XVe–XVIIIe siècles*, trans. to French by Maurice Brock (Paris: Macula, 1991).
18. Ensor, "Trois semaines à l'académie" (1884), in *Mes Écrits*, pp. 50–53. For a translation into English and Spanish of the complete

text, see Todts, *Ensor: De noche cartografiaba mis sueños*, pp. 25–26 and 233. The manuscript of Ensor's text is preserved in the Museum Plantin-Moretus / Stedelijk Prentenkabinet Antwerpen: Fonds Vandevoir no. 261 / 1.

19. *Tagebücher von Paul Klee 1898–1918*, ed. Felix Klee (Cologne: Dumont Schauberg, 1957), p. 242. English: *The Diaries of Paul Klee, 1898–1918*, ed. Felix Klee (Berkeley and Los Angeles: University of California Press), p. 232.
20. Clement Greenberg, "Modernist Painting," *Arts Yearbook* 4 (1961).
21. Ensor, letter to Pol de Mont, 1895, in *James Ensor: Lettres*, pp. 795–96.
22. See Haskell, *Rediscoveries in Art*, pp. 146–51.
23. Ensor, letter to Darío de Regoyos, 1884, in *James Ensor: Lettres*, pp. 153–55.
24. See Johannes Stückelberger, *Rembrandt und die Moderne: Der Dialog mit Rembrandt in der deutschen Kunst um 1900* (Munich: W. Fink, 1996), pp. 9–26.
25. Jacob Burckhardt, cited in ibid., pp. 236–41.
26. It is not known when or how the drawing came to be the property of Portaels: Ensor may have given or "lent" it to him after leaving the Académie in 1880, or it may have come to Portaels only after being reworked in 1886 (or later). In an 1894 letter, Ensor asked Portaels whether he would like to lend the drawing for an exhibition that Demolder was organizing for Brussels late that year. *James Ensor: Lettres*, pp. 610–11.
27. Marcel De Maeyer, "De mystieke dood van een godgeleerde van James Ensor," *Jaarboek van het Koninklijk Museum voor Schone Kunsten Antwerpen* (1962–63): 151–58. See also De Maeyer, "Mystic Death of a Theologian," in Catherine de Zegher, ed., *Between Street and Mirror: The Drawings of James Ensor* (New York: The Drawing Center; Minneapolis: University of Minnesota Press, 2001), pp. 187–202.
28. Cognoscenti readers of Cervantes's *Don Quixote* may recognize the reference to a character referred to by Quixote's interlocutor as "Frestón or Fritón; all I know is that his name ended in a *tón*." Miguel de Cervantes, *Don Quixote*, trans. Samuel Putnam, part 1, chap. 7 (New York, Viking, 1949), p. 60. Yoko Fukumitsa discovered this passage in Cervantes and shared it with me in 1995.
29. "De Belgische Schilderkunst sedert 1830," in Hendrik Enno van Gelder, *Kunstgeschiedenis der Nederlanden* (Utrecht: W. de Haan, 1936). Vermeylen's writings may be referenced online at: http://www.dbnl.org/tekst/verm036verz04_01/verm036verz04_01_0031.htm
30. Patrick Florizoone and I discovered independently that the similarities between Ensor's *Mystic Death of a Theologian* and Gallait's *Plague of Tournai* are more than coincidental. We discussed our findings in March 1999. See Florizoone, "Negentiende-eeuwse historische thema's en onbekende bronnen in het œuvre van James Ensor: Over copie, interpretatie en originaliteit," in *Ensorgrafiek in confrontatie* (Ghent: Snoeck-Ducaju; Antwerp: Pandora, 1999), p. 17.
31. In Pfeiffer and Hollein, eds., *James Ensor*, pp. 78, 324. The drawing was removed from the exhibition. See also *Ensor* (Brussels: Musées royaux des Beaux-Arts de Belgique; Tournai: La Renaissance du Livre), no. 293, a fraudulent drawing for a lithograph from Ensor's *La Gamme d'amour*, and no. 294 titled *La Monteuse d'éléphants* (The elephant rider), are by the same hand. The members of the Ensor Advisory Committee (Robert Hoozee, Sabine Bown-Taevernier, Xavier Tricot, Herwig Todts) gather several times a year to discuss the authenticity of certain works attributed to Ensor. On those occasions forgeries have frequently been identified by the hand of the same "pseudo-Ensor" (including other fraudulent copies after Rembrandt). This pseudo-Ensor was exposed in the late 1960s by Marcel De Maeyer.
32. Ensor, letter to Jules Du Jardin, 1899, in *James Ensor: Lettres*, p. 262.
33. Haskell, *Rediscoveries in Art*. W. E. Krul, "Realisme, renaissance en nationalisme: Cultuurhistorische opvattingen over de Oudnederlandse schilderkunst tussen 1860 en 1920," in Bernhard Ridderbos and Henk van Veen, *Om iets te weten van de oude meesters: De Vlaamse primitieven–Herontdekking, waardering en onderzoek* (Heerlen and Nijmegen: Open Universiteit; SUN, 1995), pp. 236–84.
34. Ensor, letter to Pol de Mont, 1895, in *James Ensor: Lettres*, pp. 795–96.
35. Ensor, "Une Réaction artistique au pays de Narquoisie" (1900), in *Mes Écrits*, pp. 23–27.
36. Ensor, letter to Pol de Mont, 1900, in *James Ensor: Lettres*, pp. 151–52.
37. Ensor, "Sur la crise de la peinture" (1932), in *Mes Écrits*, pp. 105–6.
38. Ensor, "Au musée moderne" (1896). This text is not included in the 1999 edition of *Mes Écrits*, but in *James Ensor: Mes Écrits*, preface by Frans Hellens, fifth ed., enl. (Liège: Éditions nationales, 1974), pp. 42–43.
39. Ensor, "Discours prononcé au banquet Ensor offert par les peintres d'Anvers" (1922), in *Mes Écrits*, pp. 156–60.
40. Ensor, "Discours" (1925), in *Mes Écrits*, p. 20.
41. Robert L. Delevoy, *Ensor* (Antwerp: Mercatorfonds, 1981), p. 243.

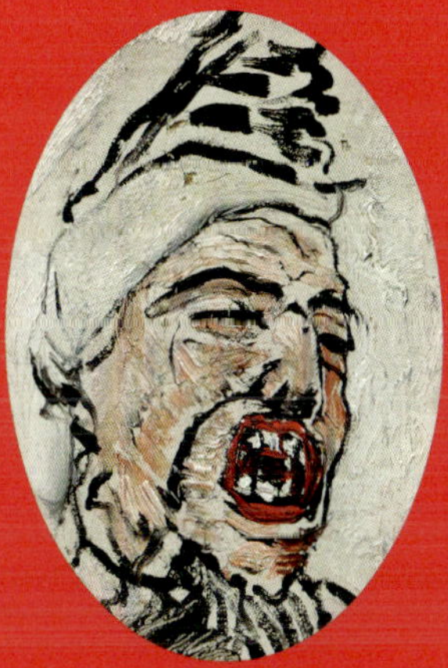

PLATES

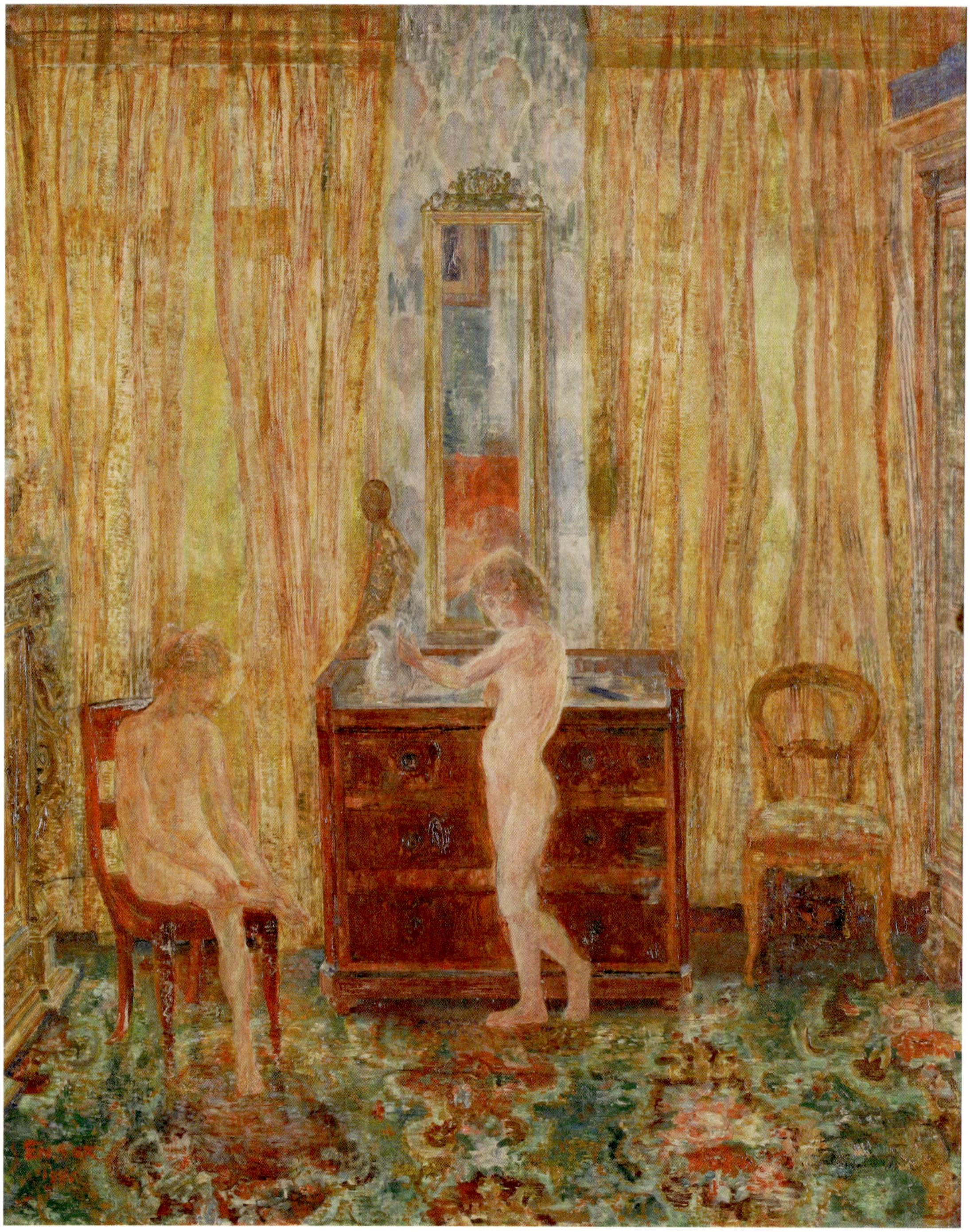

35. *Children Dressing.* 1886
Oil on canvas, 53 1/8 × 43 1/4" (136 × 110 cm)

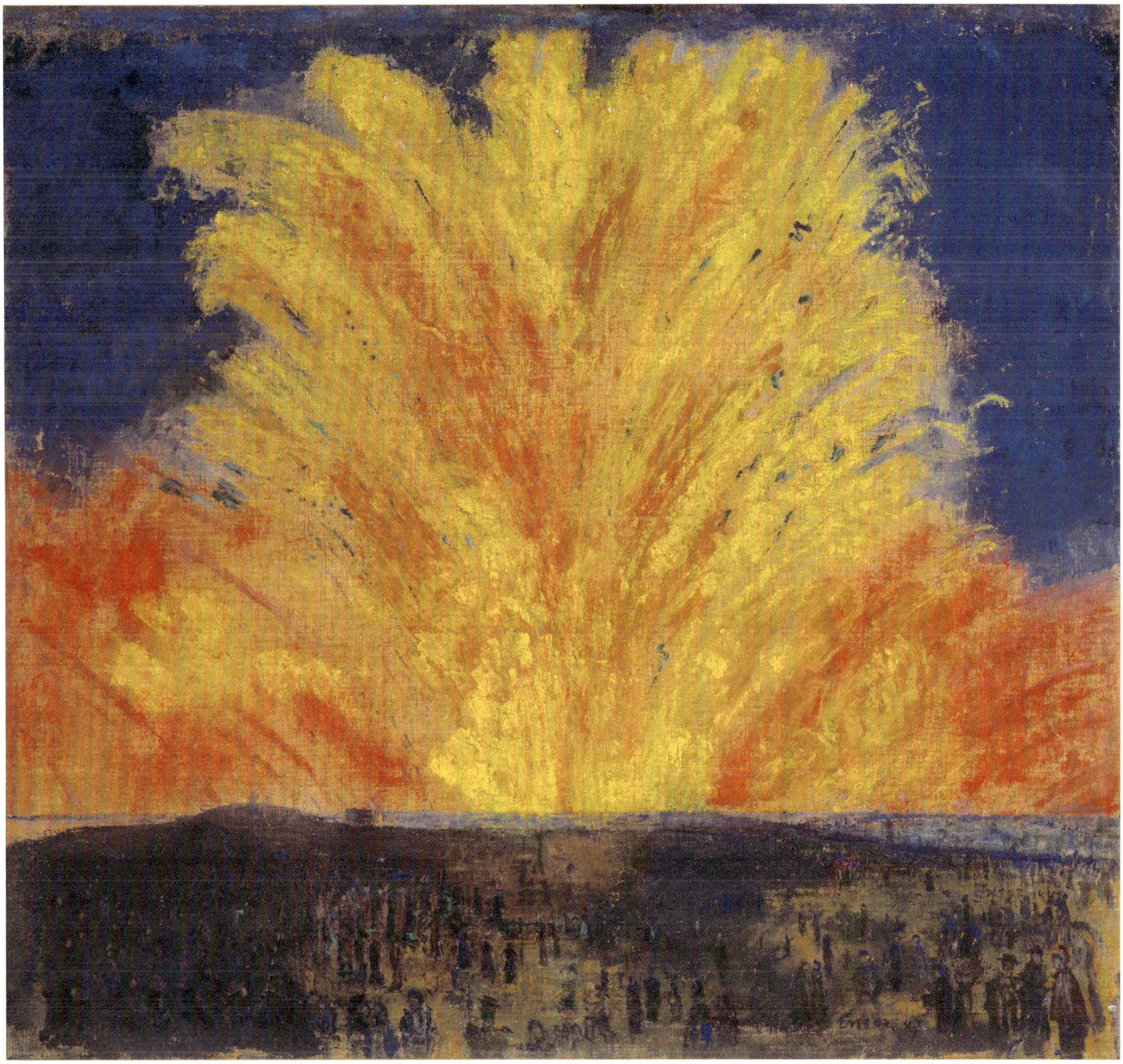

36. *Fireworks.* 1887
Oil and encaustic on canvas, 40 ¼ × 44 ¼"
(102.2 × 112.4 cm)

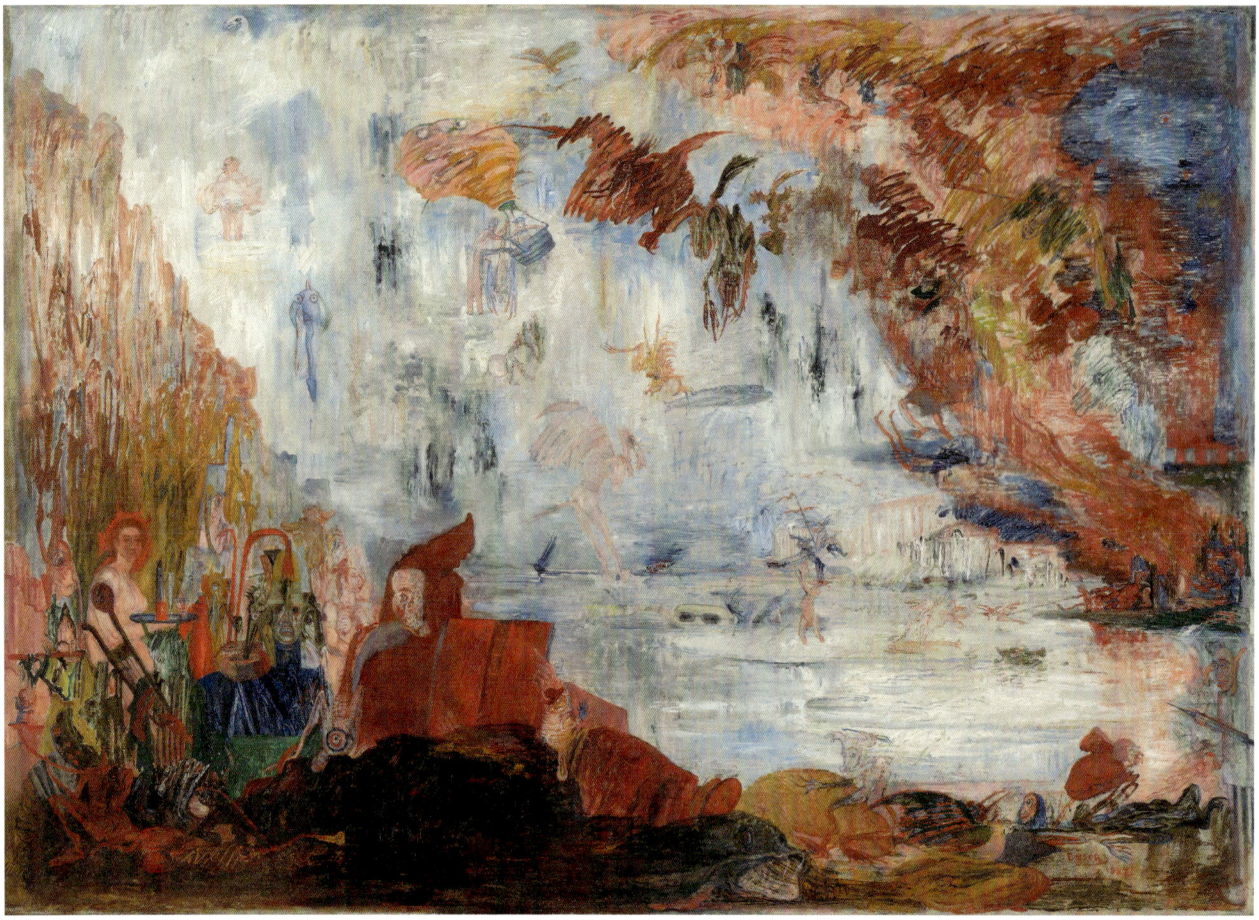

37. *Tribulations of Saint Anthony.* 1887
Oil on canvas, 46 3/8 × 66" (117.8 × 167.6 cm)

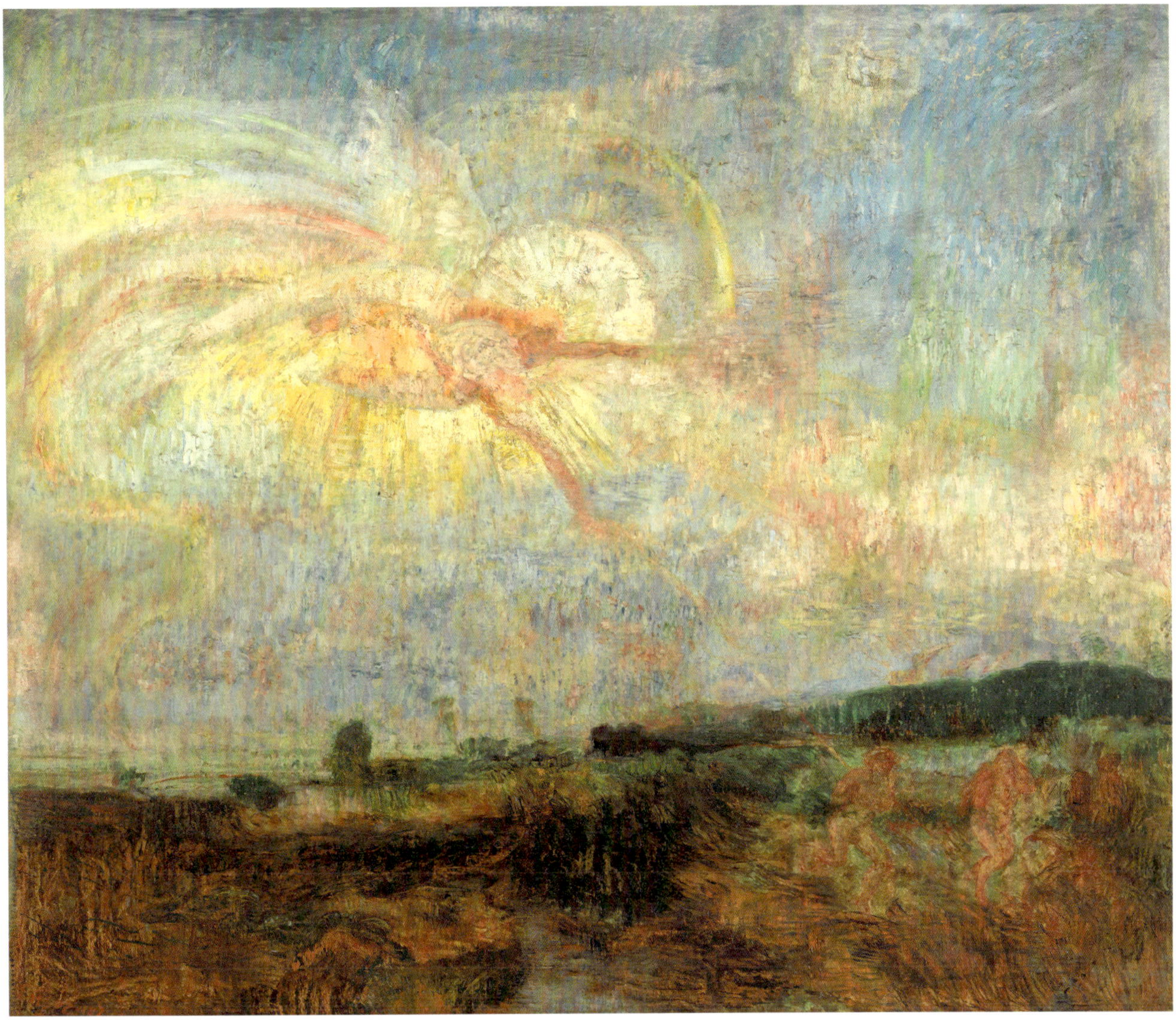

38. *Adam and Eve Expelled from Paradise.* 1887
Oil on canvas, 80 11/16 × 96 7/16" (205 × 245 cm)

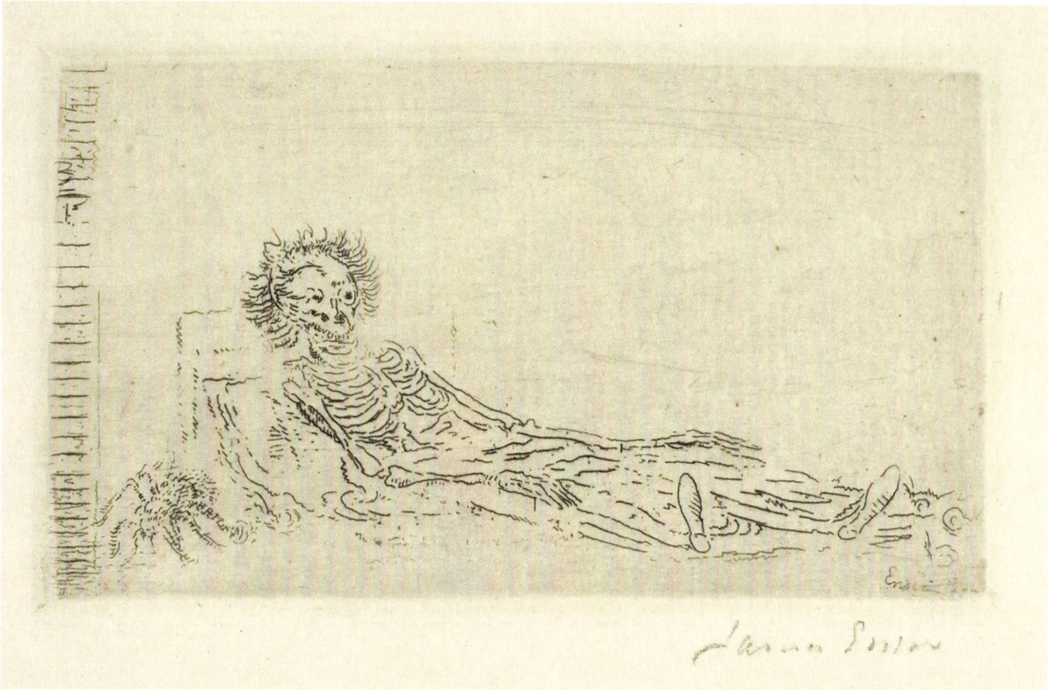

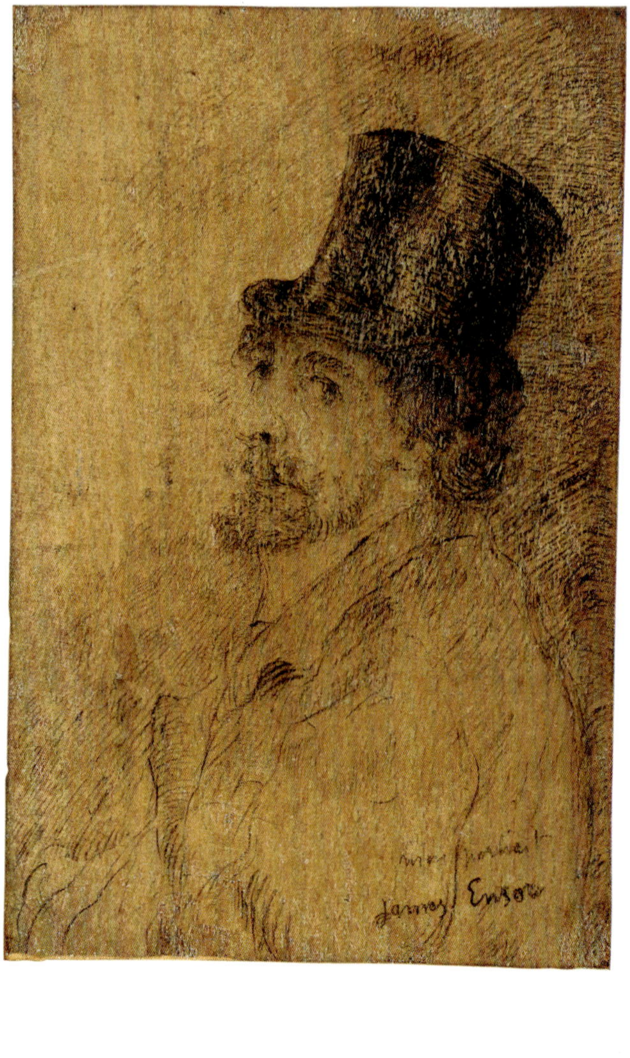

39. *My Portrait in 1960.* State II. 1888
Etching on wove paper, plate: 2 3⁄4 × 4 11⁄16" (7.0 × 11.9 cm)

40. *Self-Portrait.* c. 1888
Pencil on panel, 6 3⁄8 × 4 1⁄4" (16.3 × 10.8 cm)

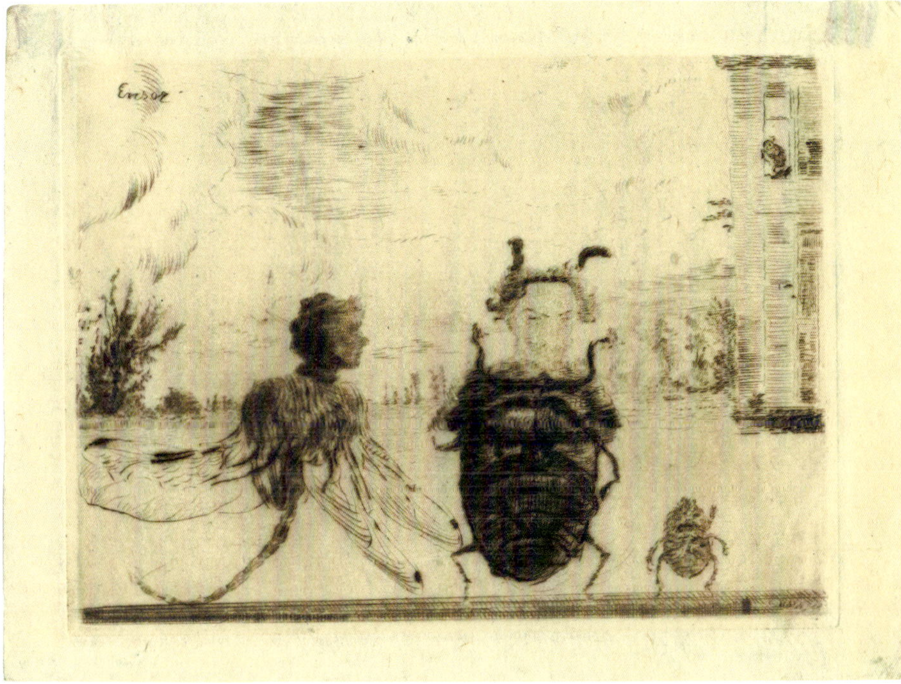

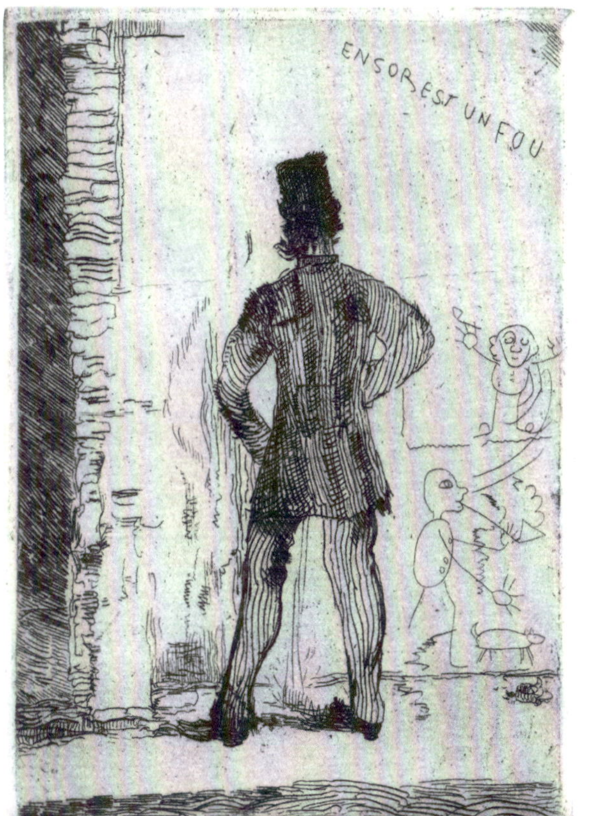

41. *Peculiar Insects.* State III, proof no. 8. 1888
Drypoint on laid Japan paper, plate: 4 ½ × 6 ⅛"
(11.4 × 15.4 cm)

42. *The Pisser.* Only state. 1887
Etching on simili-Japan paper, plate: 5 11/16 × 4 ⅛"
(14.5 × 10.5 cm)

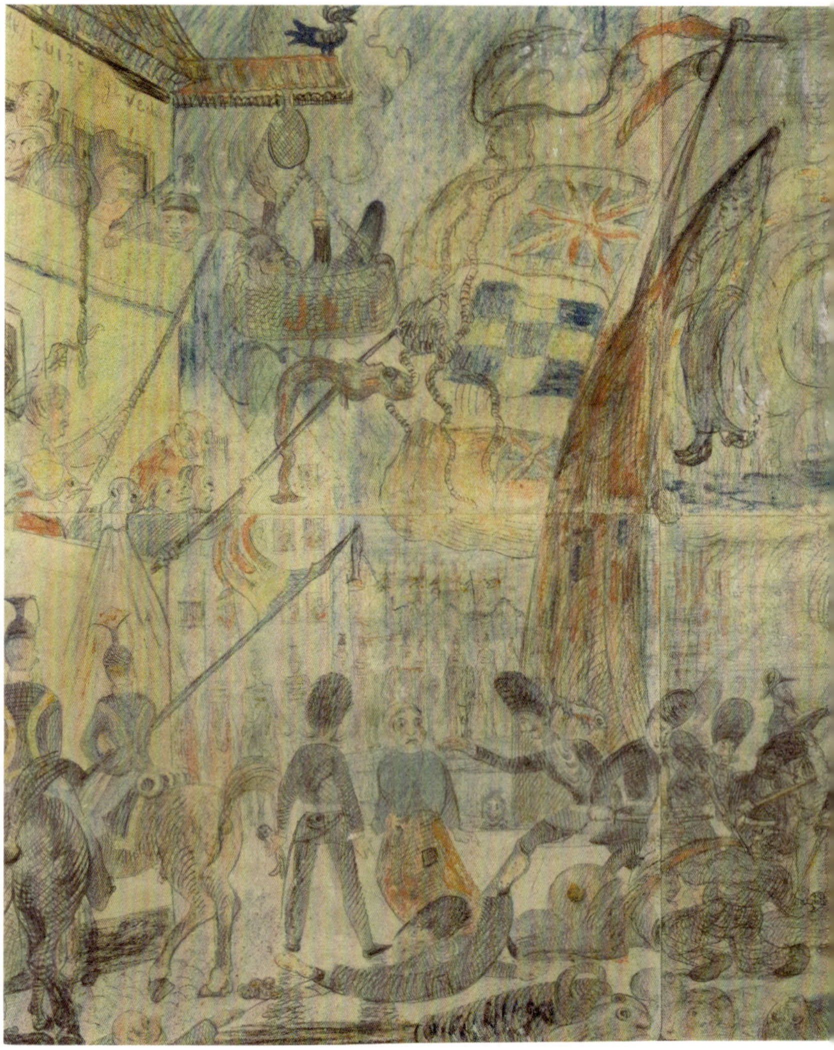

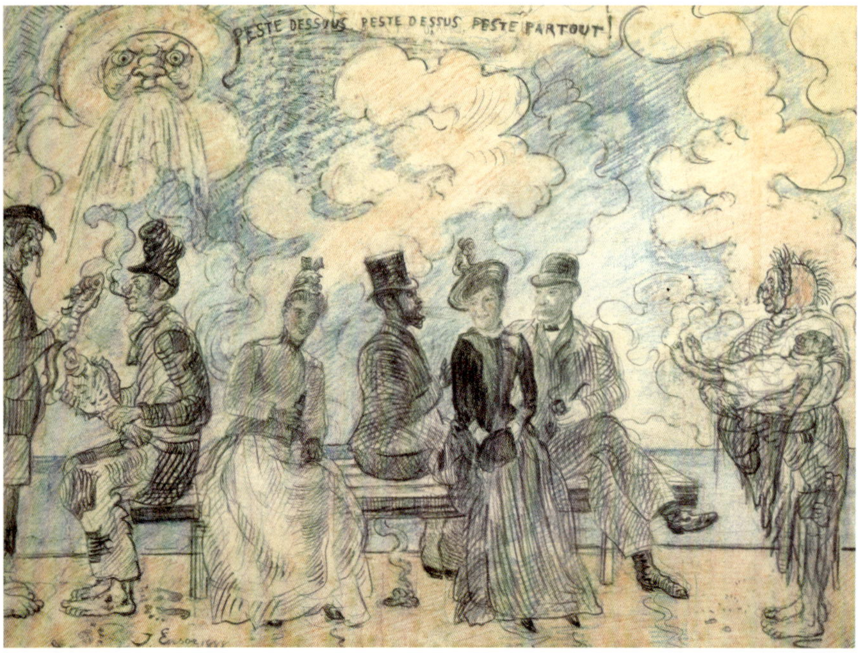
PESTE DESSUS PESTE DESSUS PESTE PARTOUT!

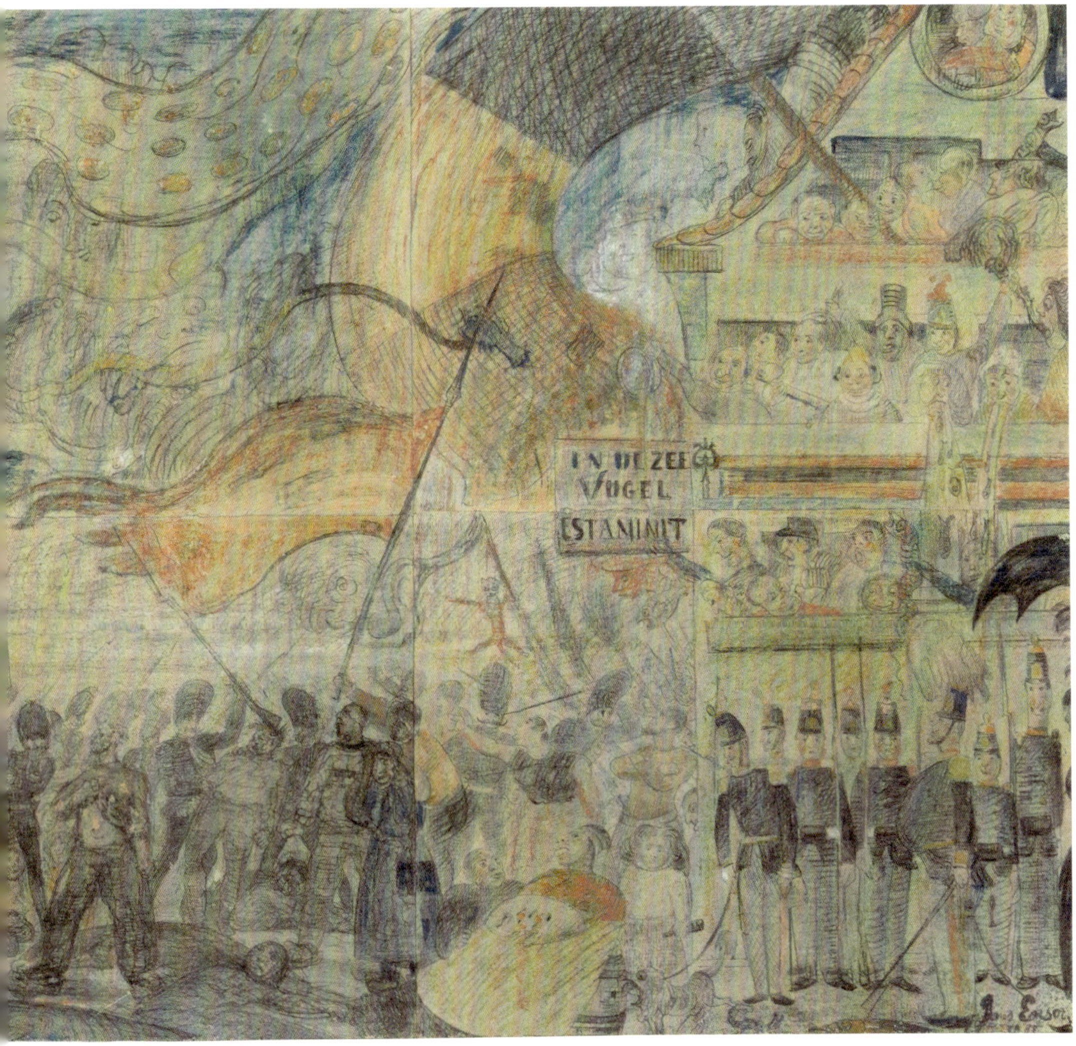

43. *The Strike* (*The Slaughter of the Ostend Fishermen [August 1887]*). 1888
Pencil and colored pencil on paper, mounted on board, 13 3/8 × 26 9/16" (34 × 67.5 cm)

44. *Plague Above, Plague Below, Plague All Around!* 1888
Conté crayon and colored pencil on paper, 8 7/8 × 11 13/16" (22.5 × 30 cm)

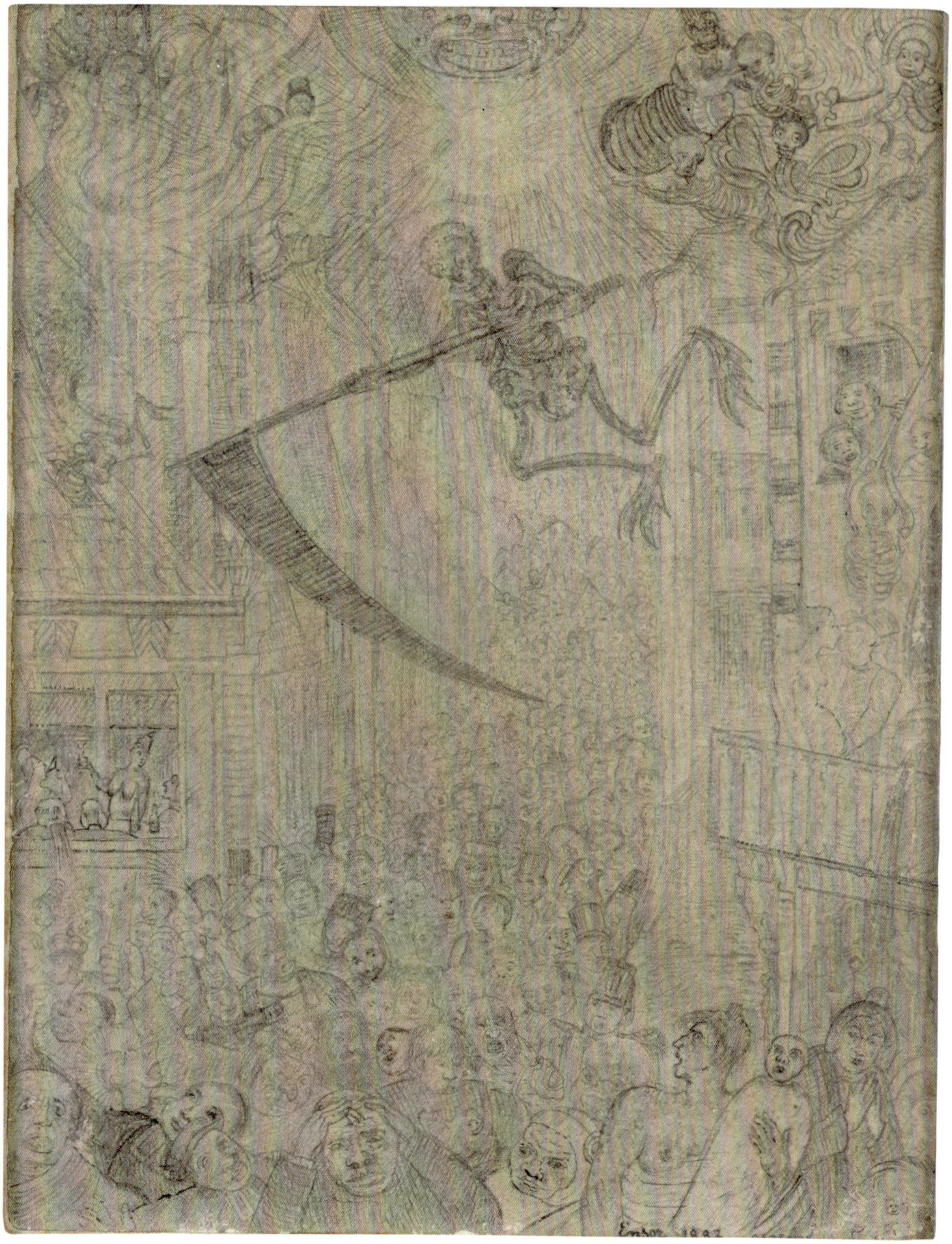

45. *Death Pursuing the Human Flock* (*Triumph of Death*). 1887
Black crayon, ink, and colored pencil on paper, mounted on board, 8 7/8 × 6 11/16" (22.5 × 17 cm)

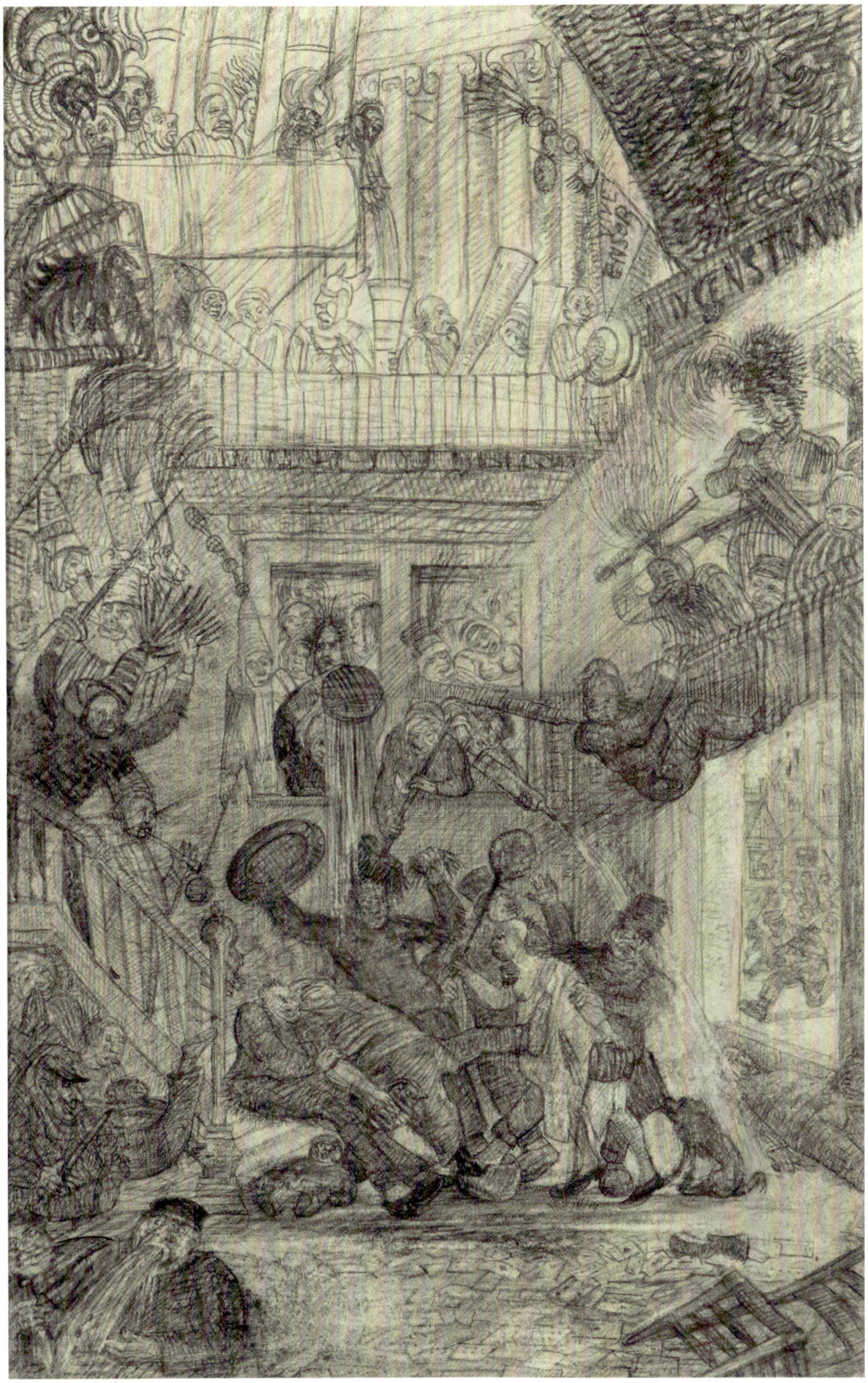

46. *Fight of the Down-and-Outs.* 1887
Black pencil on paper, mounted on board,
13 9⁄16 × 8 7⁄8" (34.5 × 22.5 cm)

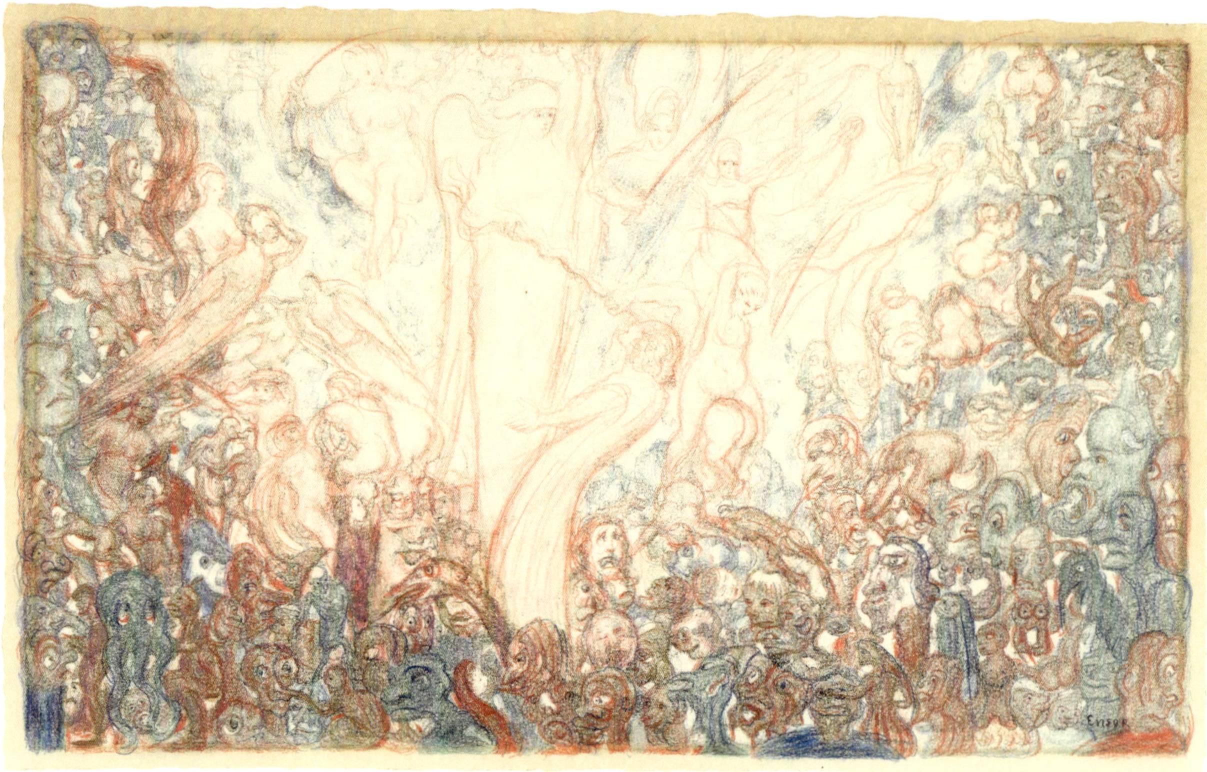

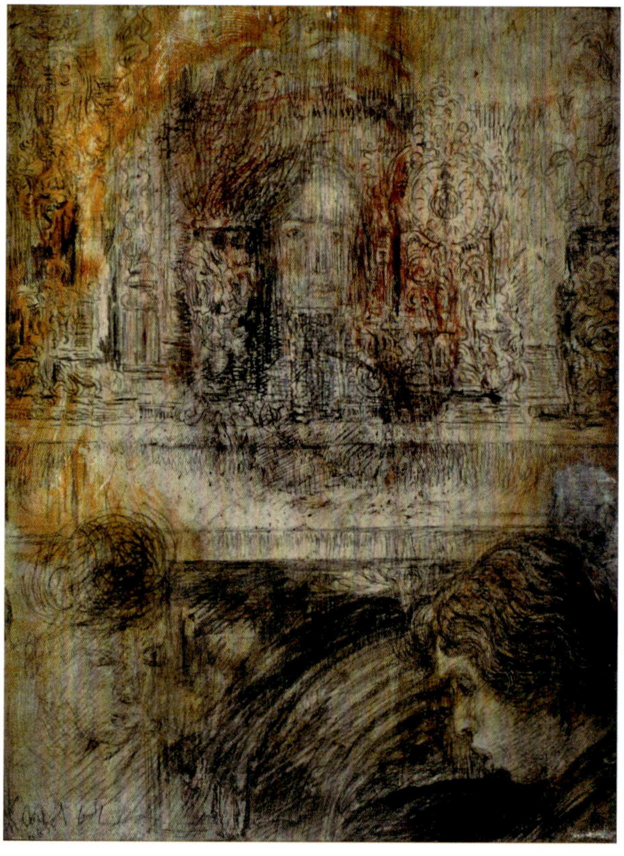

47. *The Fight of the Angels and the Demons.* 1888
Colored crayon on paper, 10 7/16 × 17 5/16" (26.5 × 44 cm)

48. *The Haunted Fireplace.* 1888
Crayon and colored pencil on panel, 9 7/16 × 6 5/16" (24 × 16 cm)

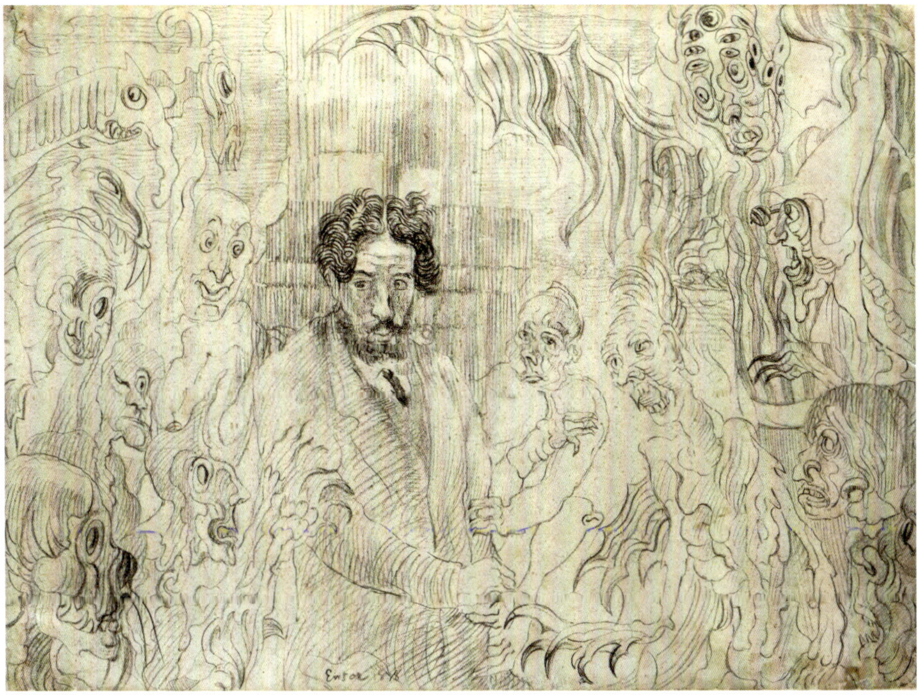

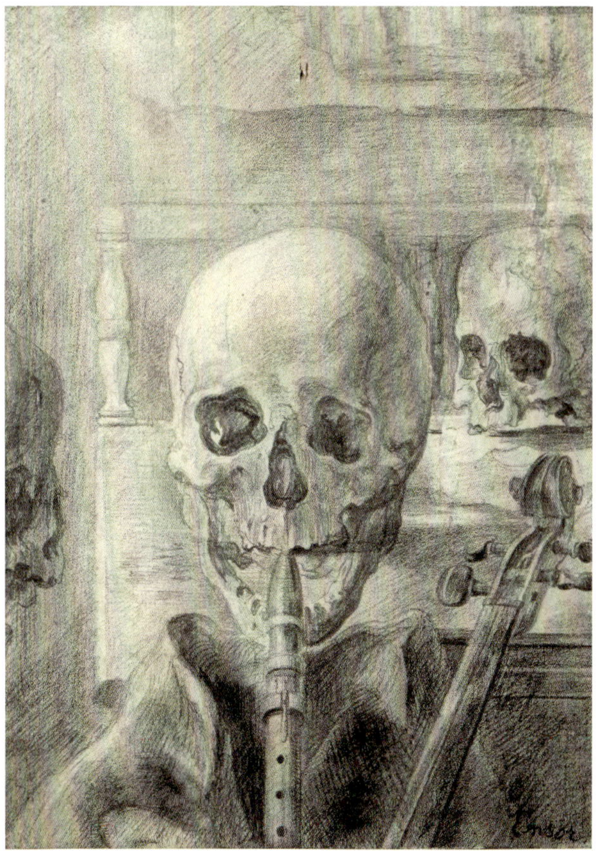

49. *Demons Tormenting Me.* 1888
Graphite and black chalk on wove paper,
8 9/16 × 11 3/4" (21.8 × 29.8 cm)

50. *Skeleton Musicians.* 1888
Black pencil and brown chalk on paper, mounted
on panel, 8 1/4 × 6 5/16" (21 × 16 cm)

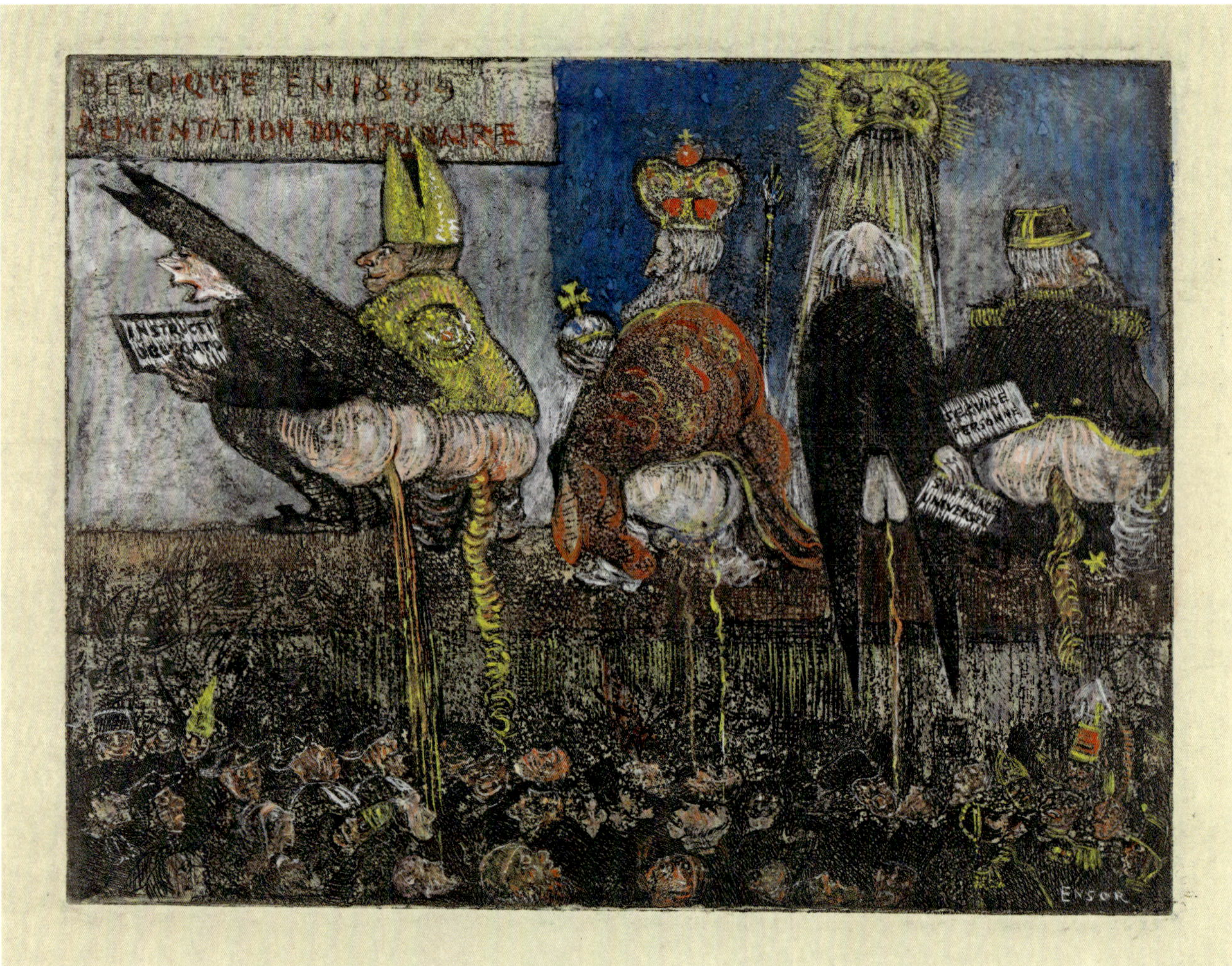

51. *Doctrinaire Nourishment.* Plate I, state II. 1889
Etching heightened with watercolor and gouache on Japan paper, plate: 7 1/16 × 9 3/8" (18 × 23.8 cm)

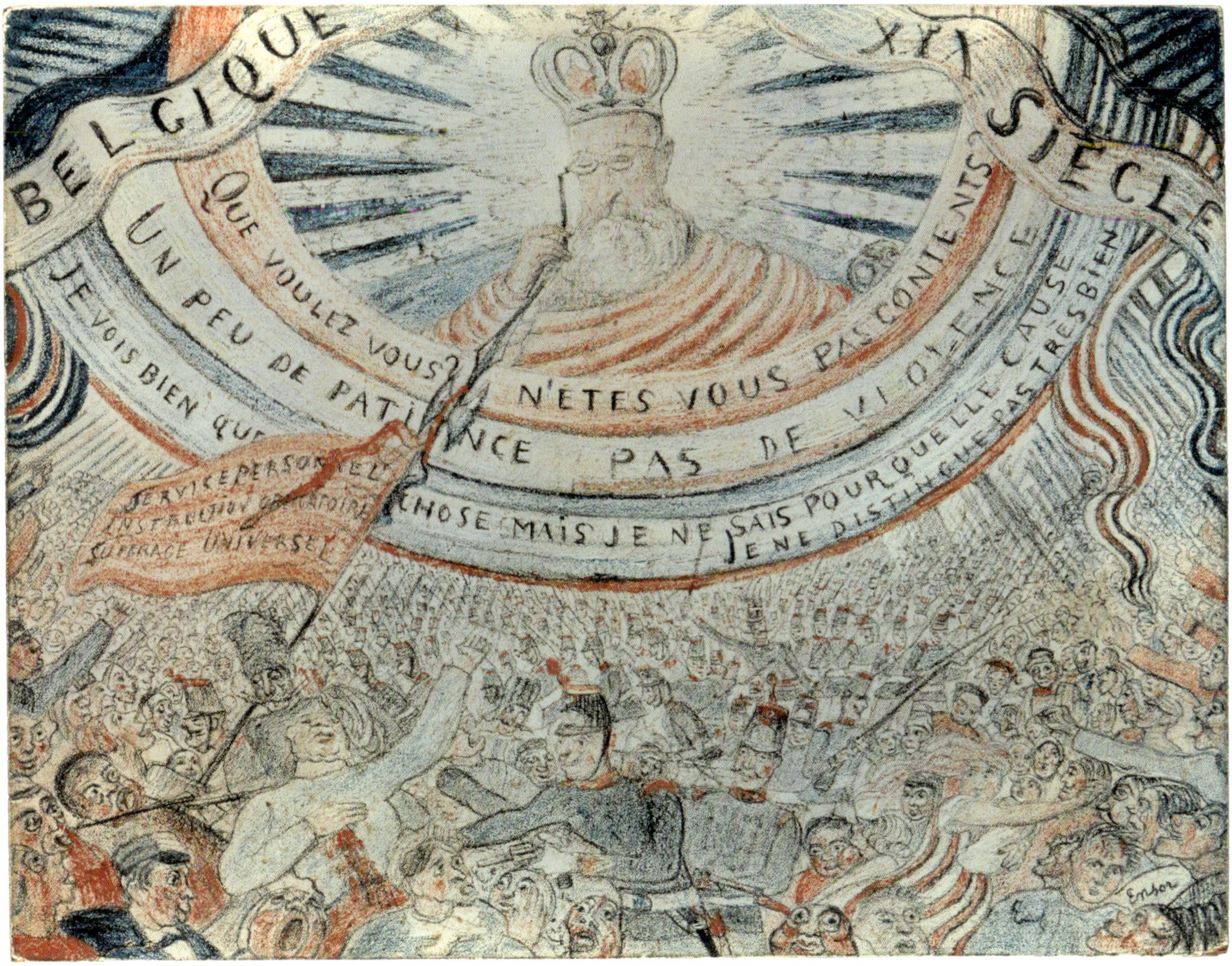

52. *Belgium in the Nineteenth Century.* 1889
Pencil and colored pencil on paper, mounted on panel, 8 9/16 × 11 11/16" (16.3 × 21.4 cm)

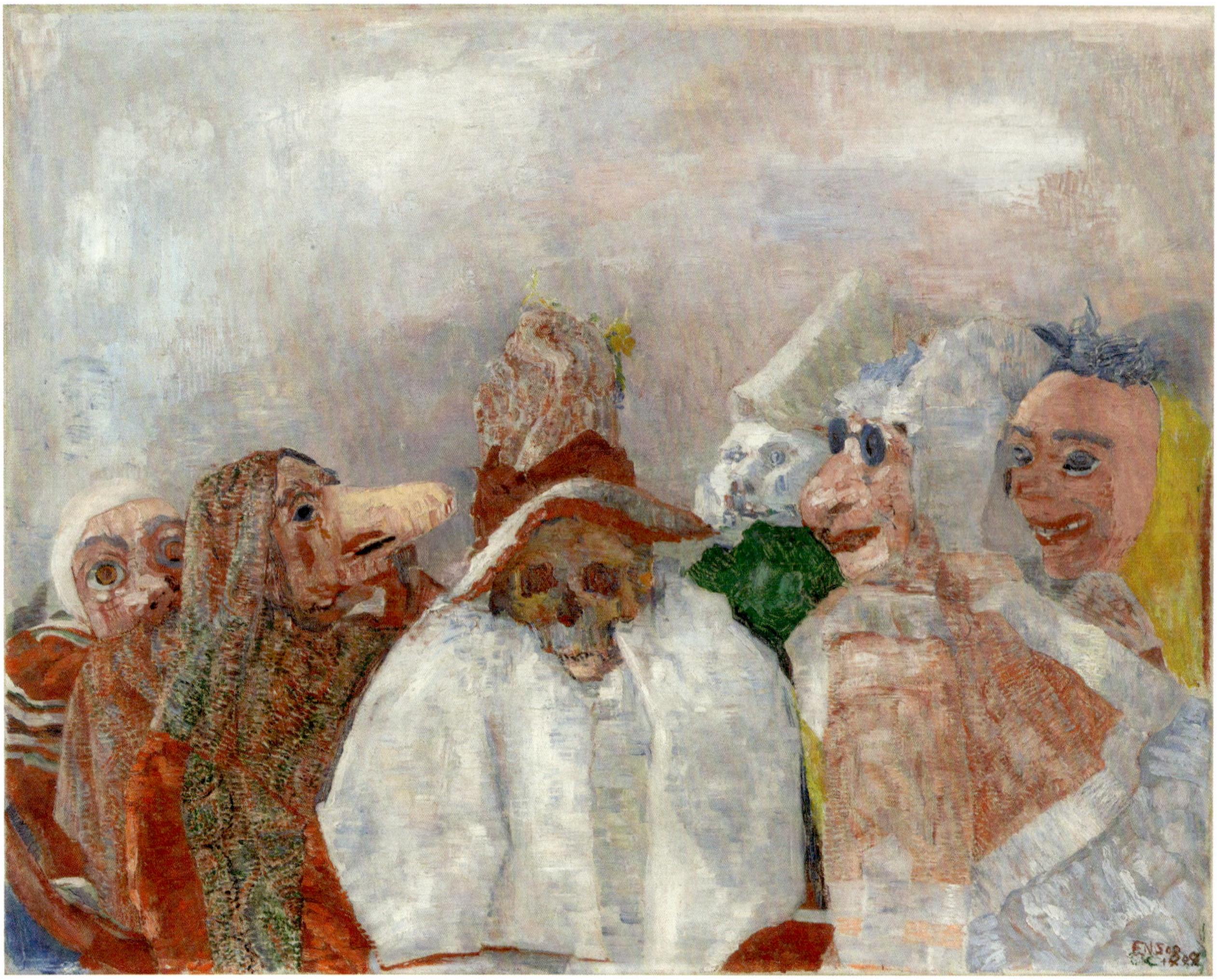

53. *Masks Mocking Death* (*Masks Confronting Death*). 1888
Oil on canvas, 32 × 39 ½" (81.3 × 100.3 cm)

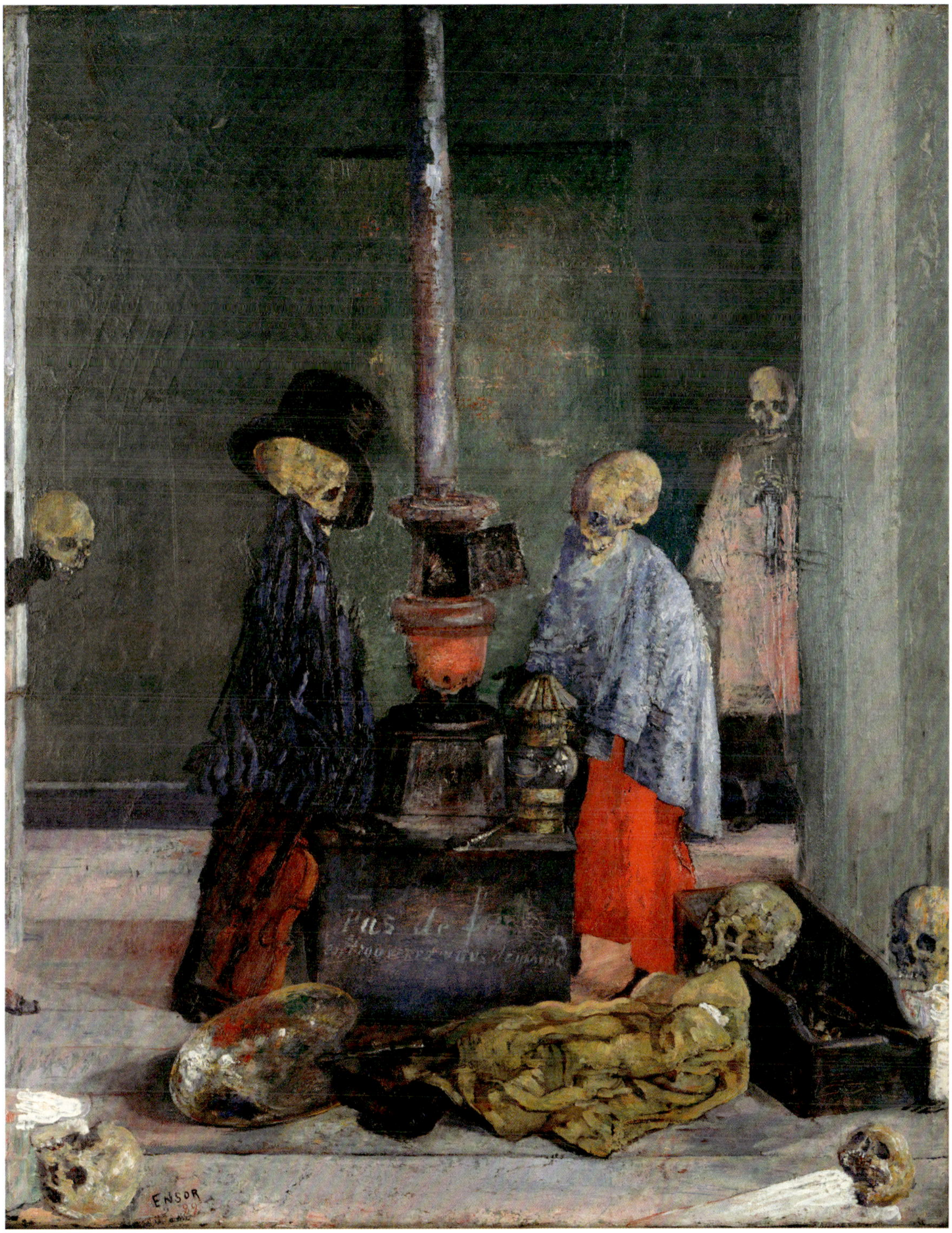

54. *Skeletons Trying to Warm Themselves.* 1889
Oil on canvas, 29 ½ × 23 ⅝" (74.8 × 60 cm)

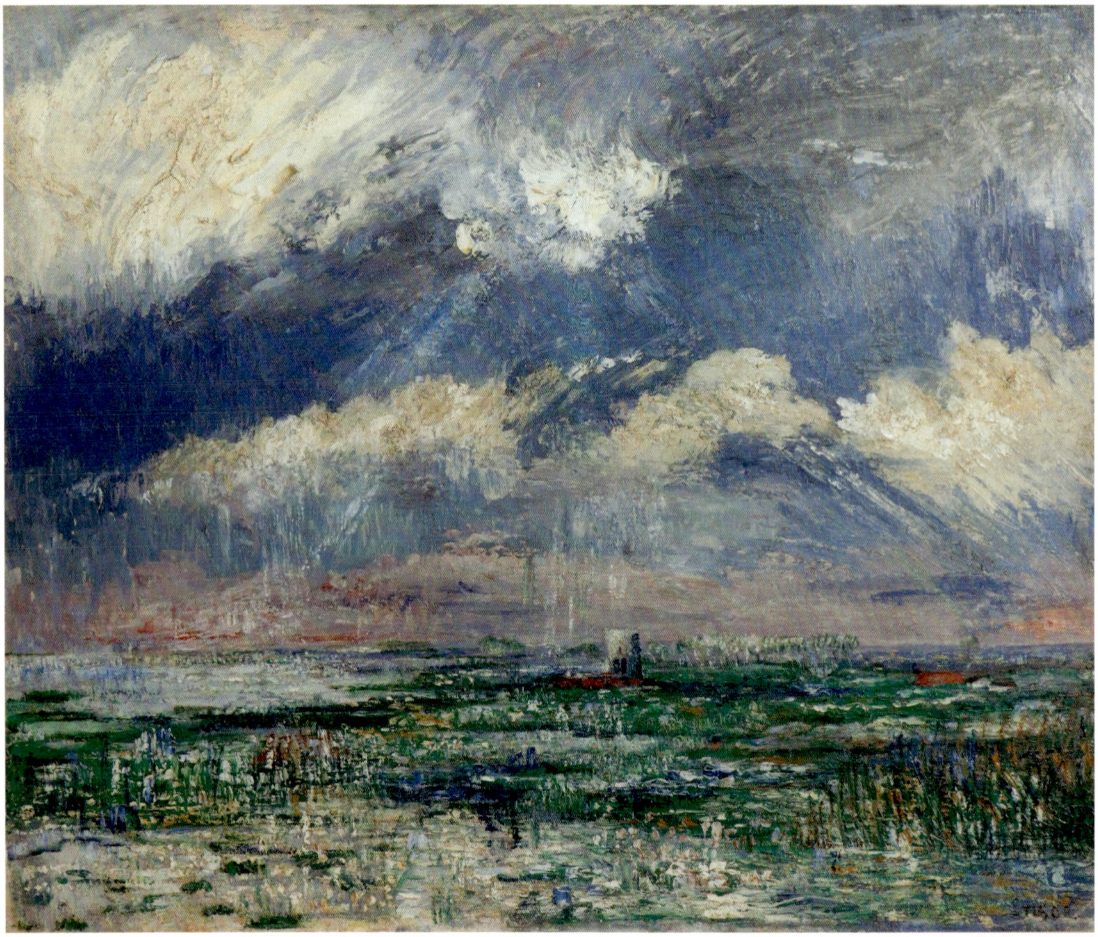

55. *The Tower of Lissewege.* 1890
Oil on canvas, 23 1/4 × 29 1/8" (59 × 74 cm)

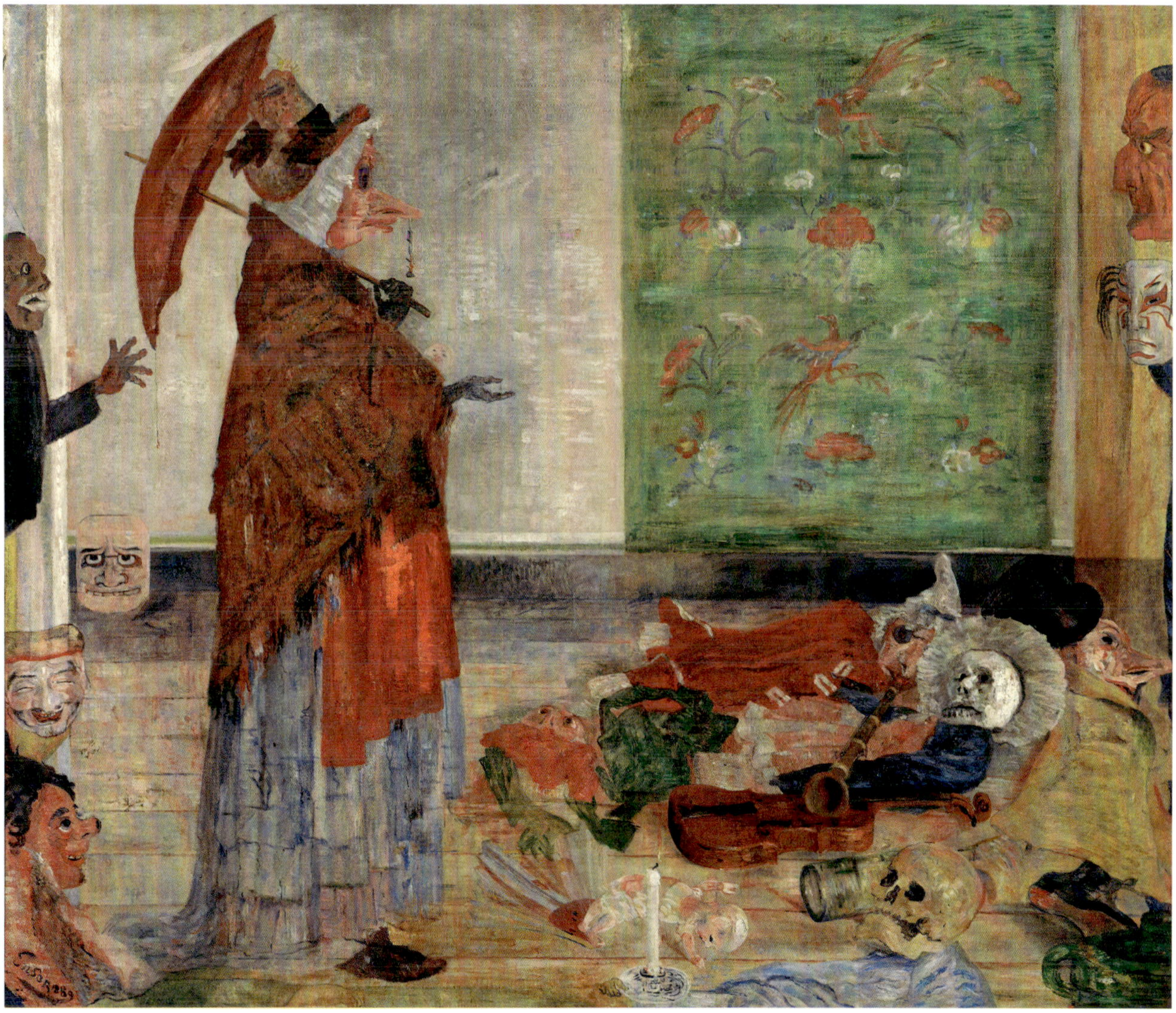

56. *The Astonishment of the Mask Wouse.* 1889
Oil on canvas, 42 5/16 × 51 9/16" (109 × 131 cm)

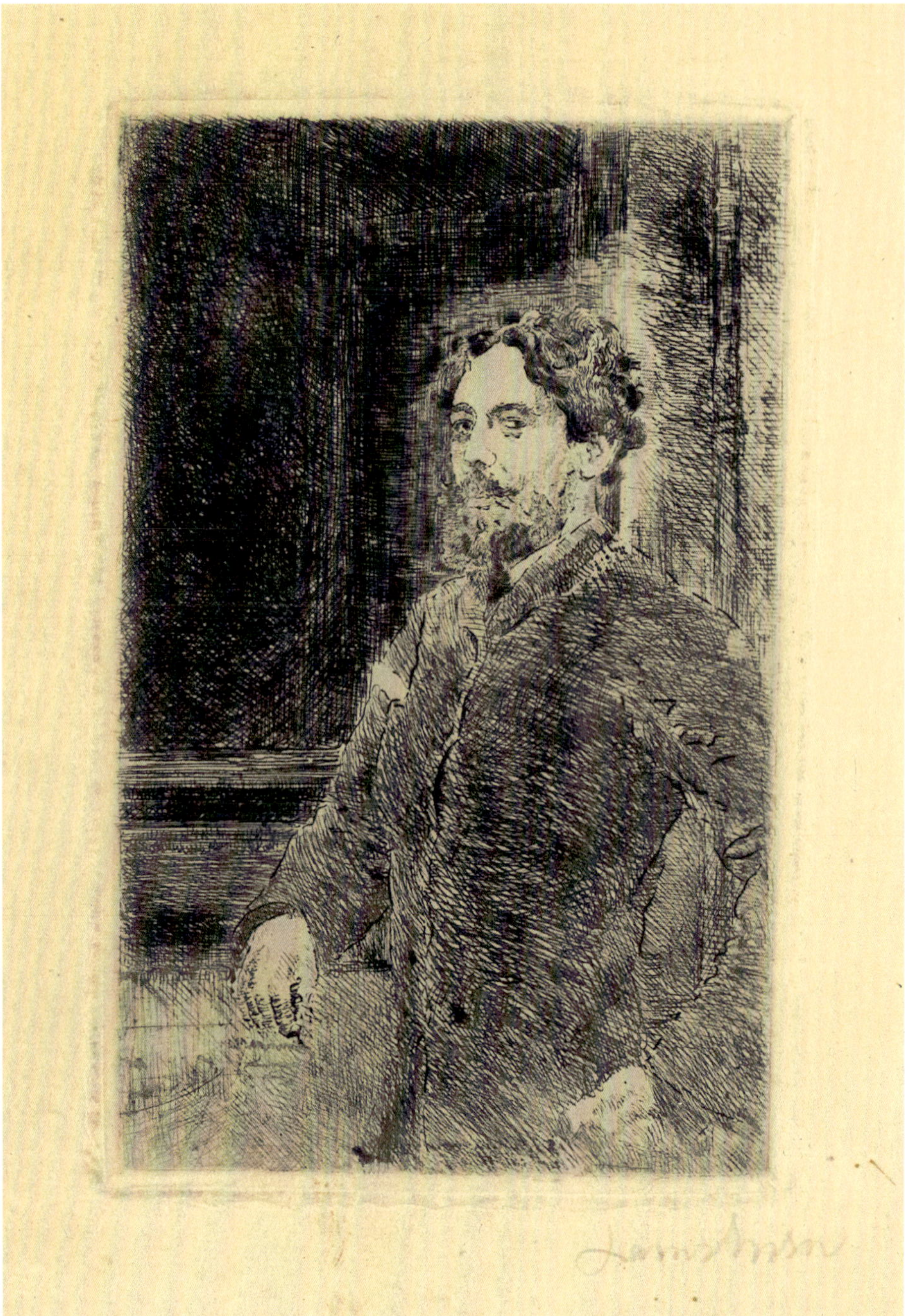

57. *My Skeletonized Portrait.* State I, unique impression. 1889
Etching on wove paper, plate: 4 9/16 × 2 15/16"
(11.6 × 7.5 cm)

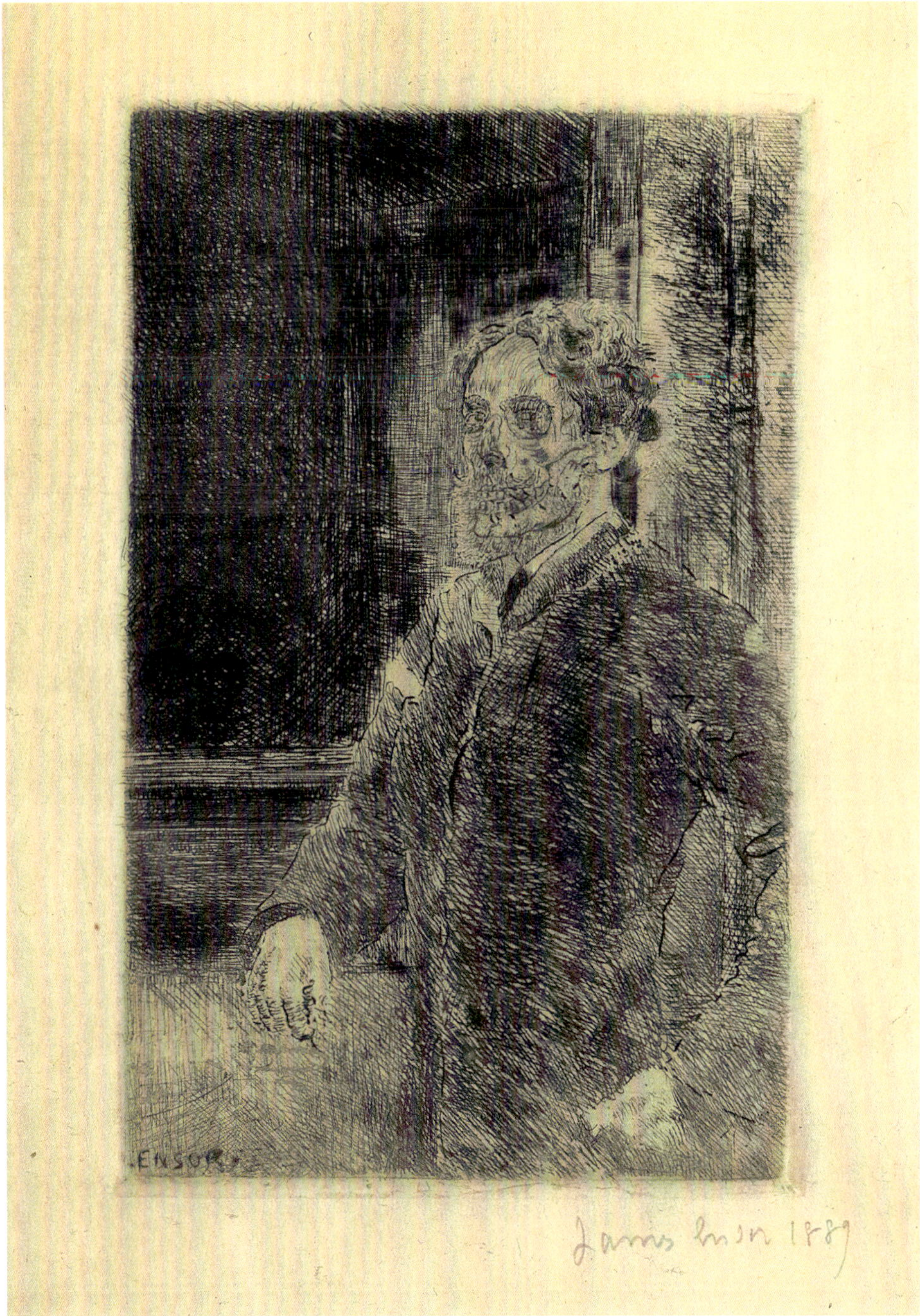

58. *My Skeletonized Portrait.* State II. 1889
Etching and drypoint on wove paper, plate:
4 9/16 × 2 15/16" (11.6 × 7.5 cm)

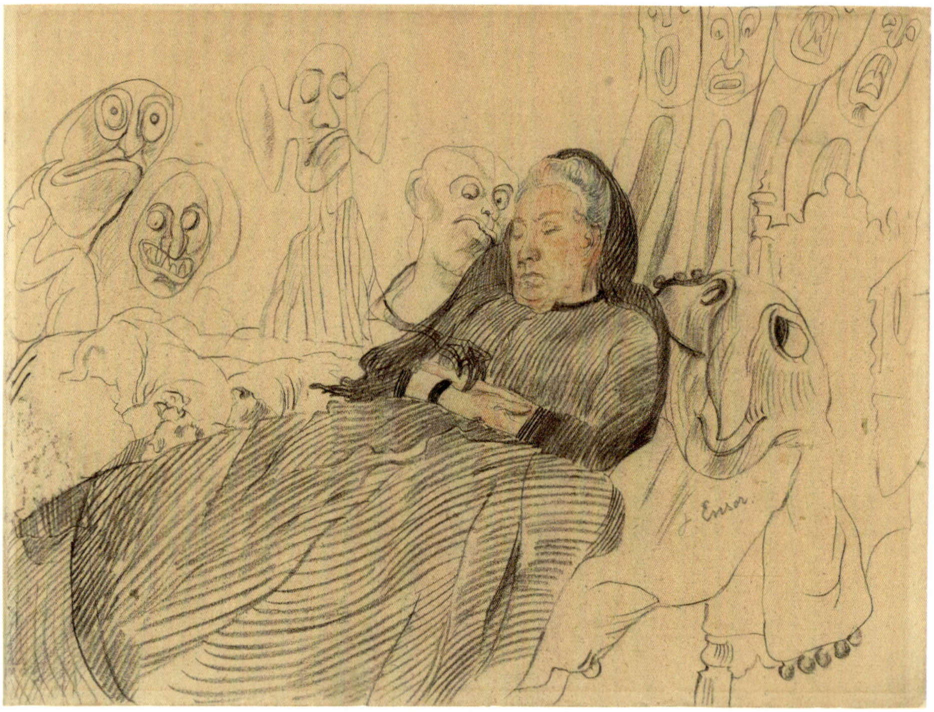

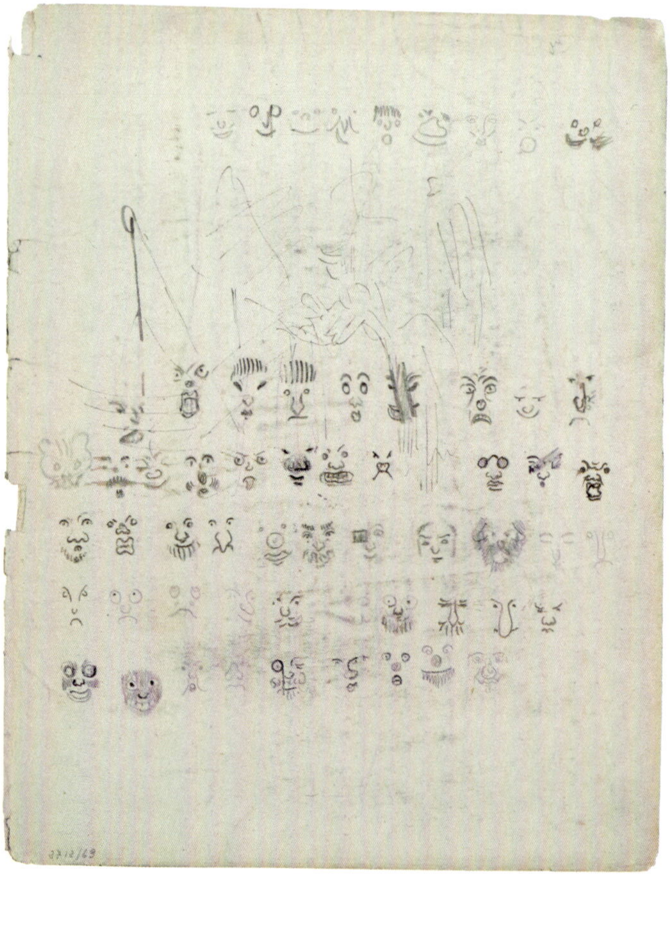

59. *My Aunt Asleep Dreaming of Monsters.* c. 1888
Pencil, Conté crayon, and colored pencil on paper, 8 5/8 × 11 13/16" (21.9 × 30 cm)

60. *Series of Small Masks.* c. 1890(?)
Conté crayon on paper, 8 13/16 × 6 7/8" (22.4 × 17.5 cm)

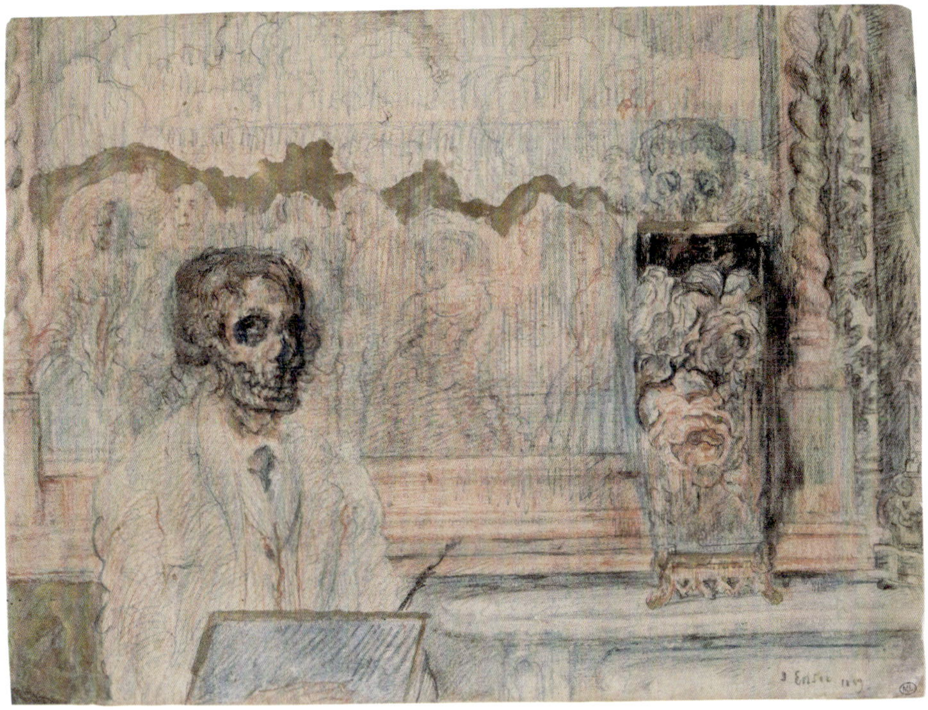

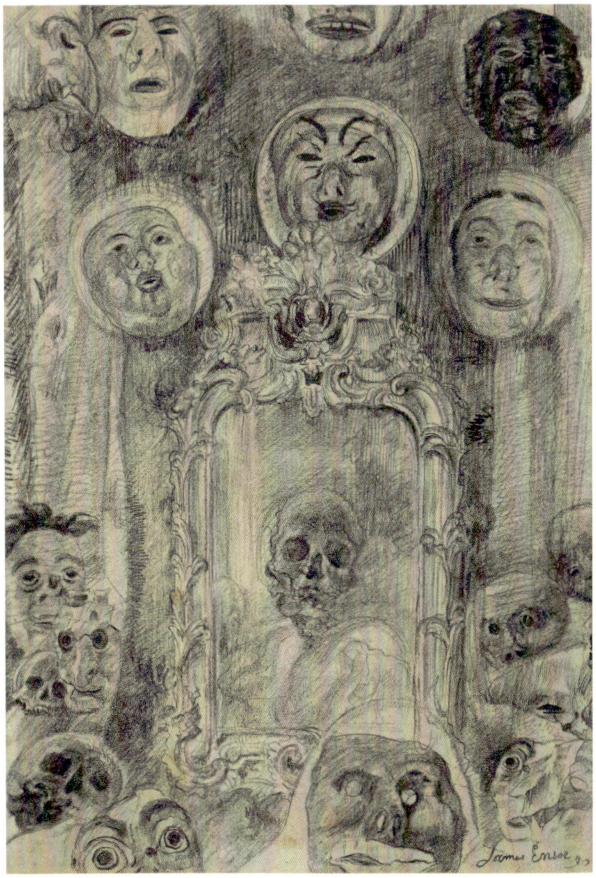

61. *Skeleton Drawing Fine Pranks.* c. 1889
Black chalk, colored pencil, and gold paint on paper, $8\frac{1}{2} \times 11\frac{5}{8}$" (21.6 × 29.6 cm)

62. *Skeleton in the Mirror.* 1890
Black crayon on paper, $11\frac{13}{16} \times 8\frac{11}{16}$" (30 × 22 cm)

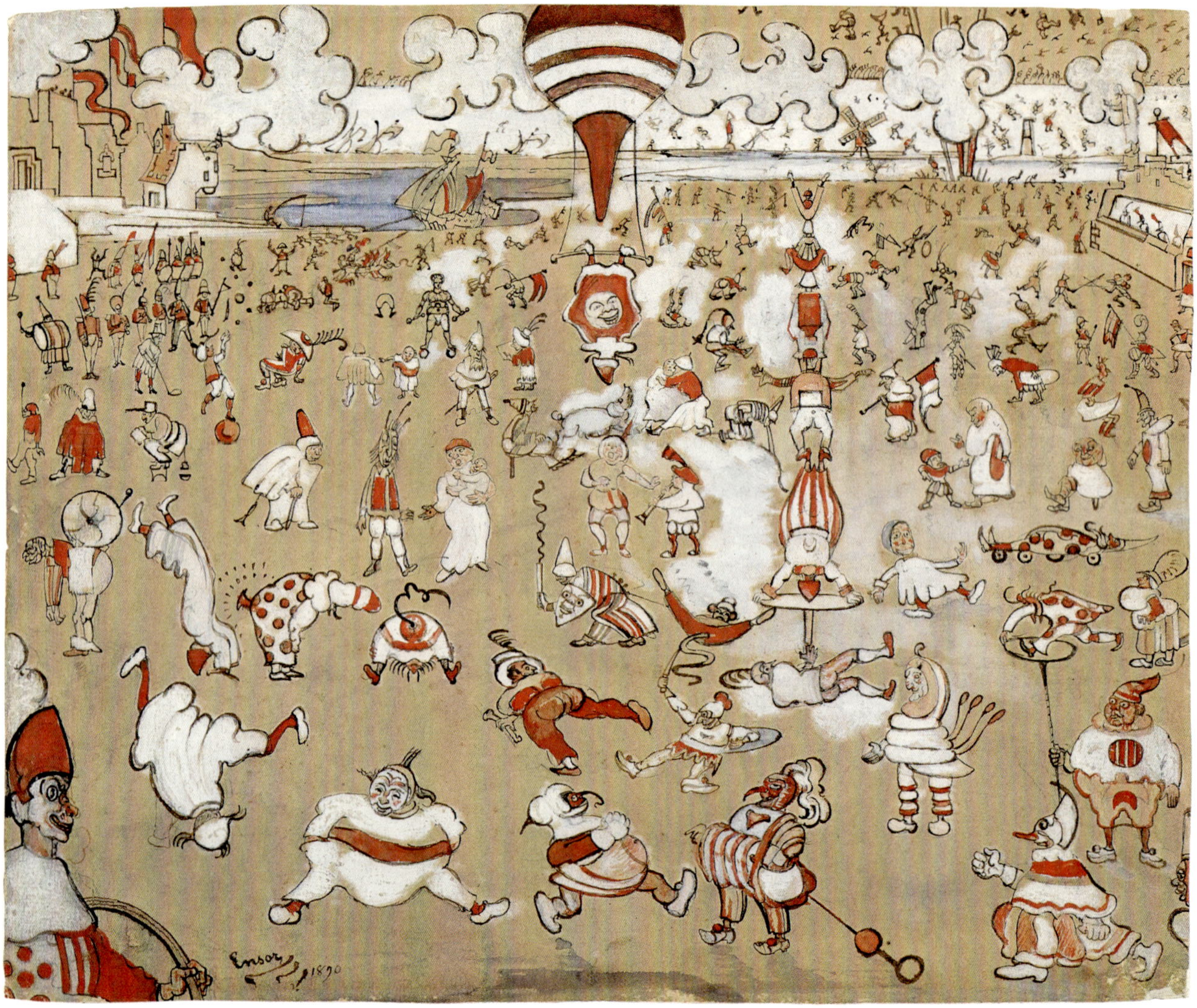

63. *White and Red Clowns Evolving.* 1890
Pencil, ink, and gouache on paper, 9 1/2 × 11 11/16"
(24.1 × 29.7 cm)

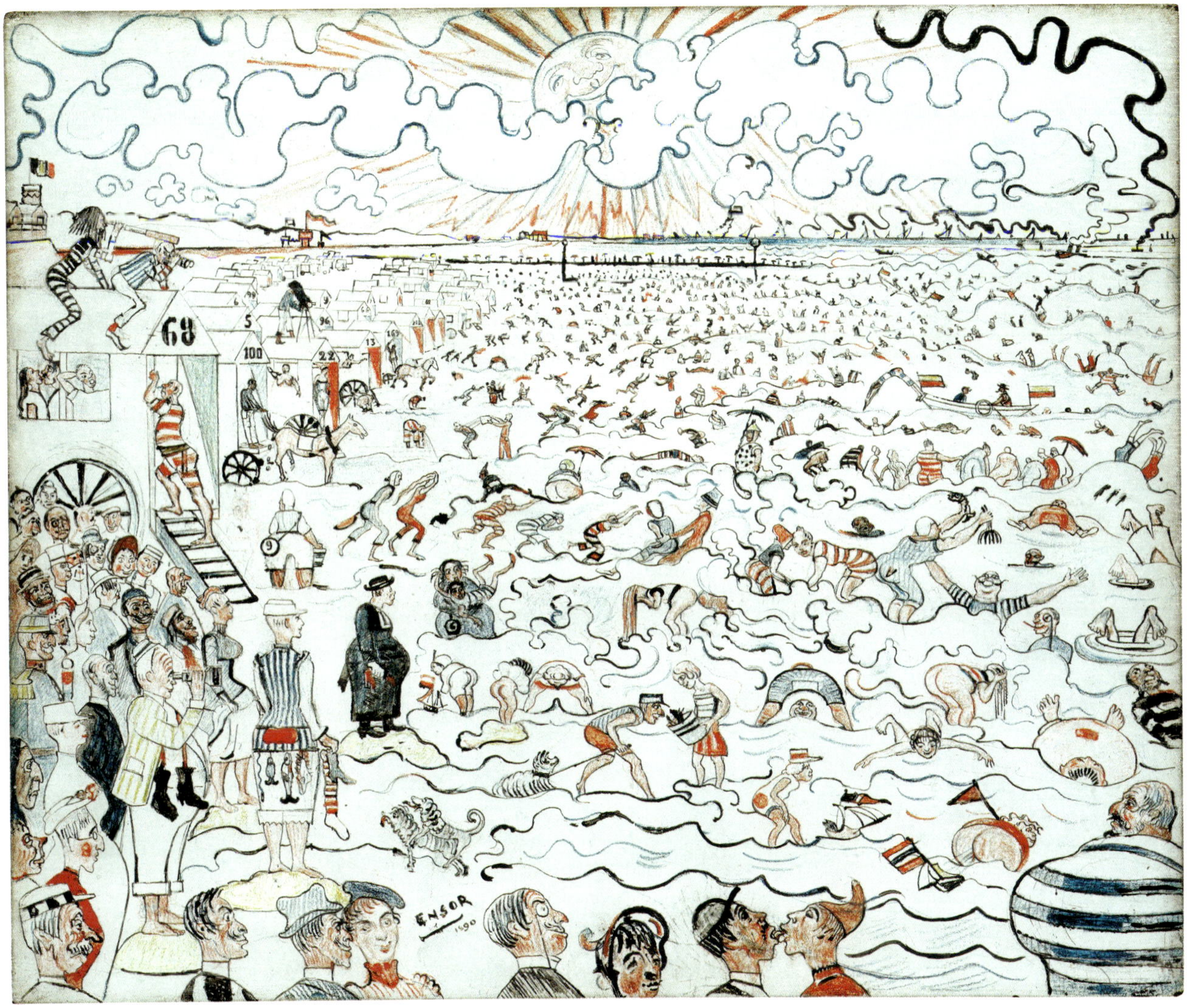

64. *The Baths at Ostend.* 1890.
Black crayon, colored pencil, and oil on panel,
14 3/4 × 17 15/16" (37.5 × 45.5 cm)

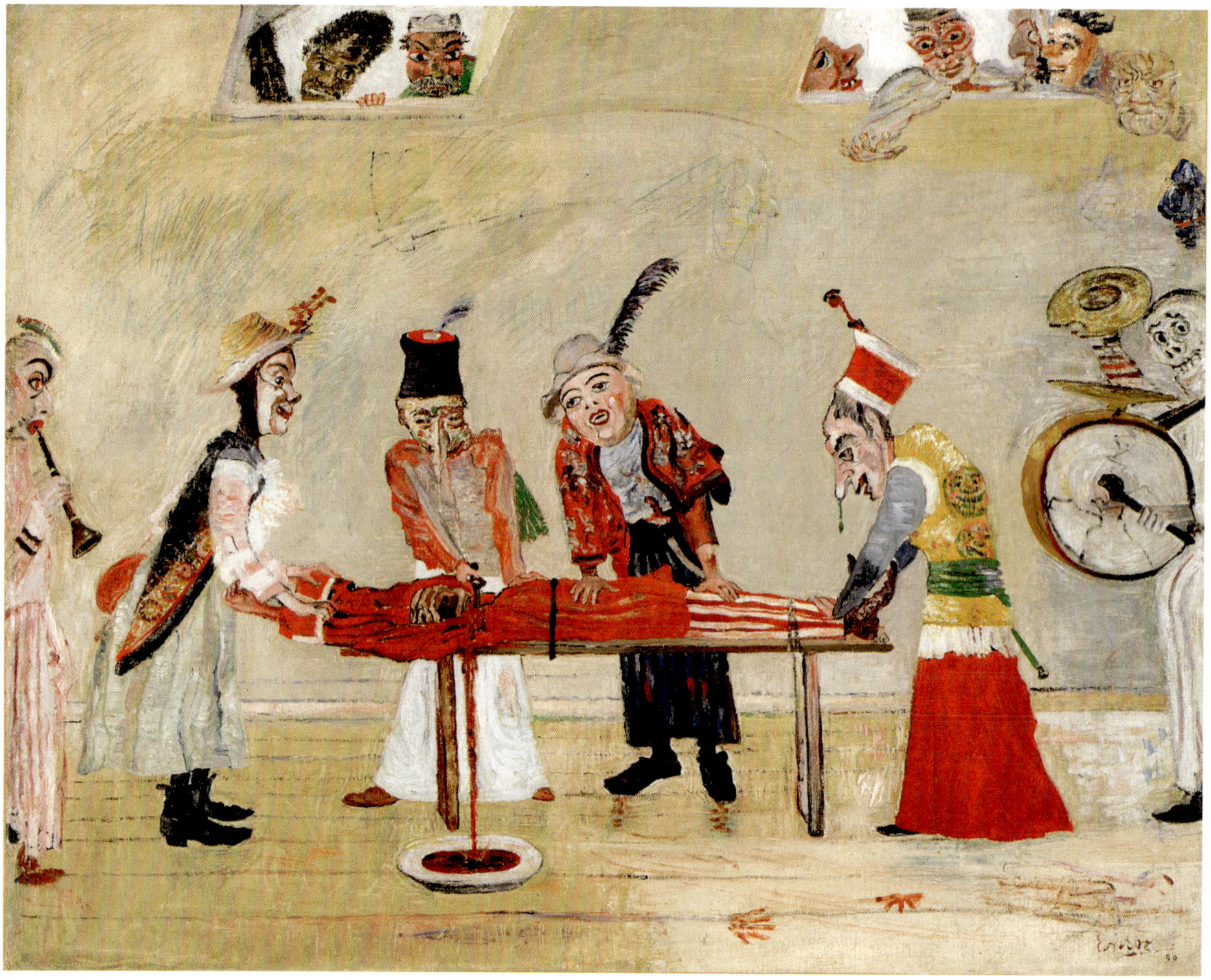

65. *The Assassination.* 1890
Oil on canvas, 23 13⁄16 × 30 3⁄8" (60.5 × 77.2 cm)

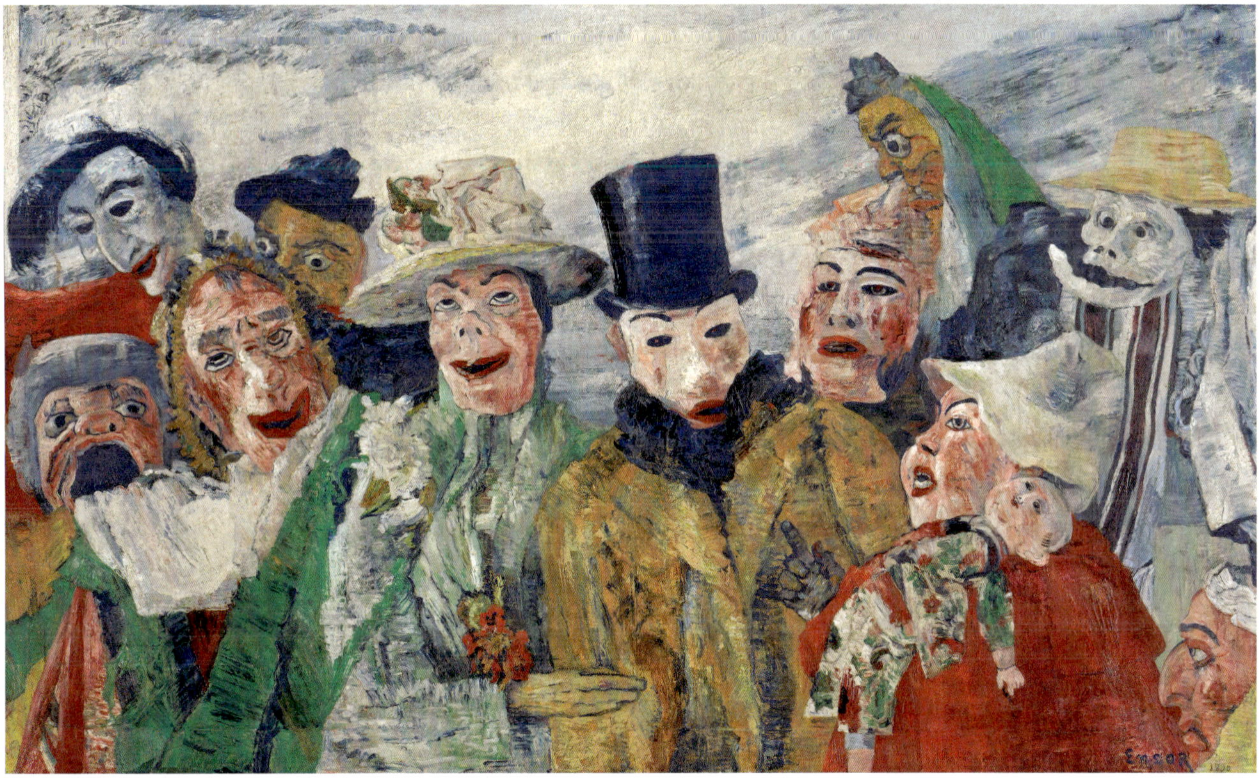

66. *The Intrigue.* 1890
Oil on canvas, 35 7/16 × 59 1/16" (90 × 150 cm)

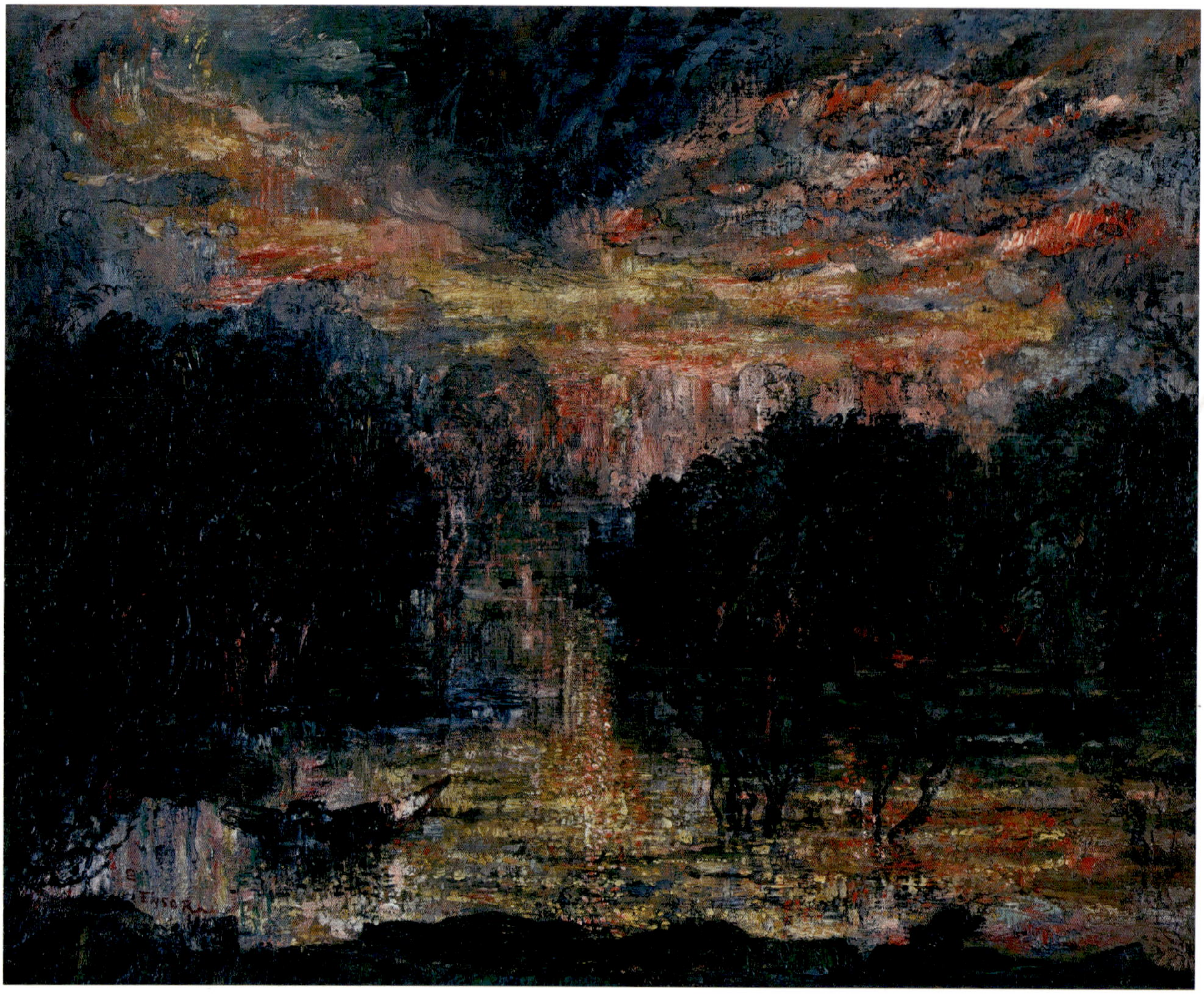

67. *The Domain of Arnheim.* 1890
Oil on canvas, 31 1/2 × 39 3/8" (80 × 100 cm)

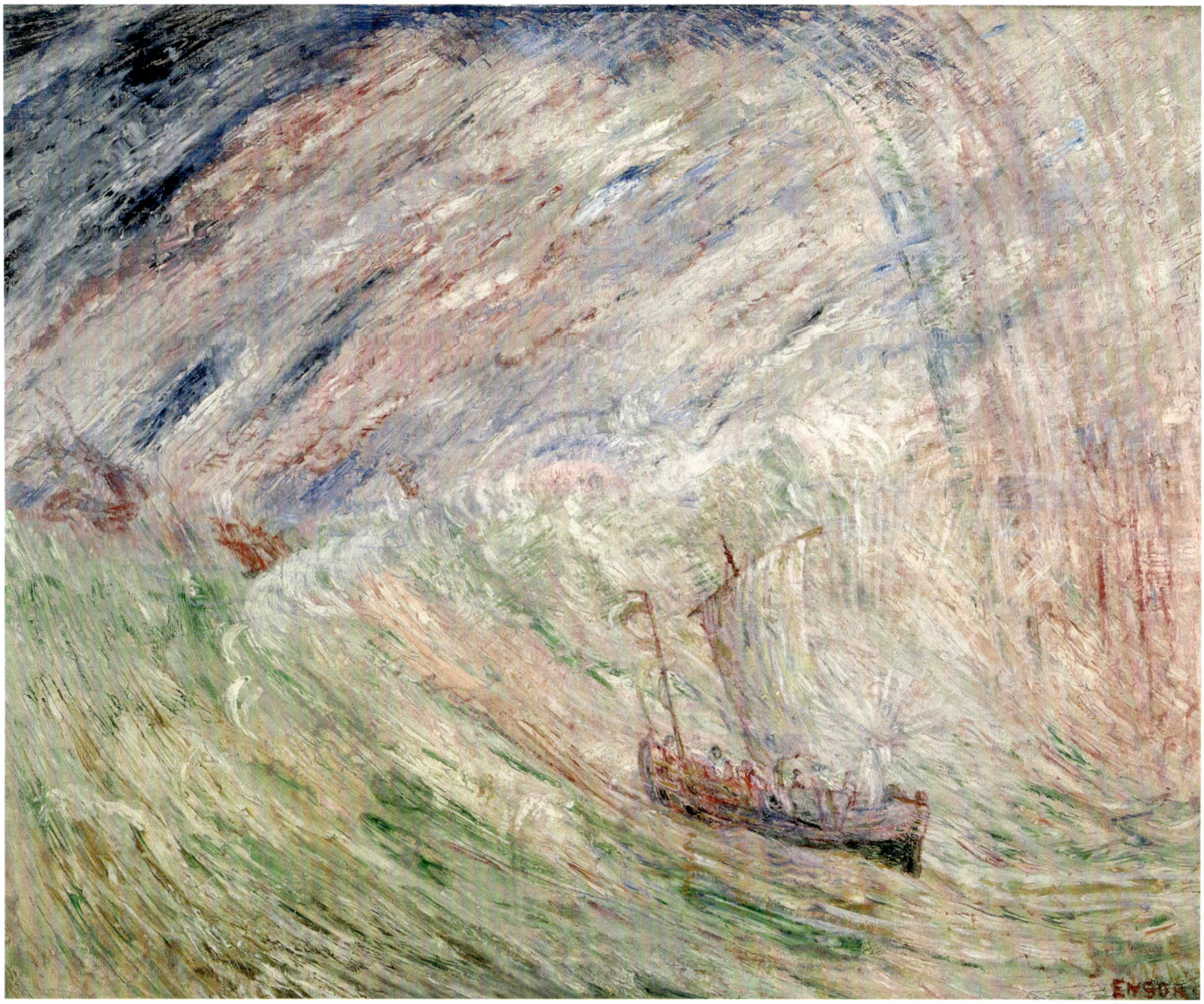

68. *Christ Calming the Storm.* 1891
Oil on canvas, 31 ½ × 39 ⅜" (80 × 100 cm)

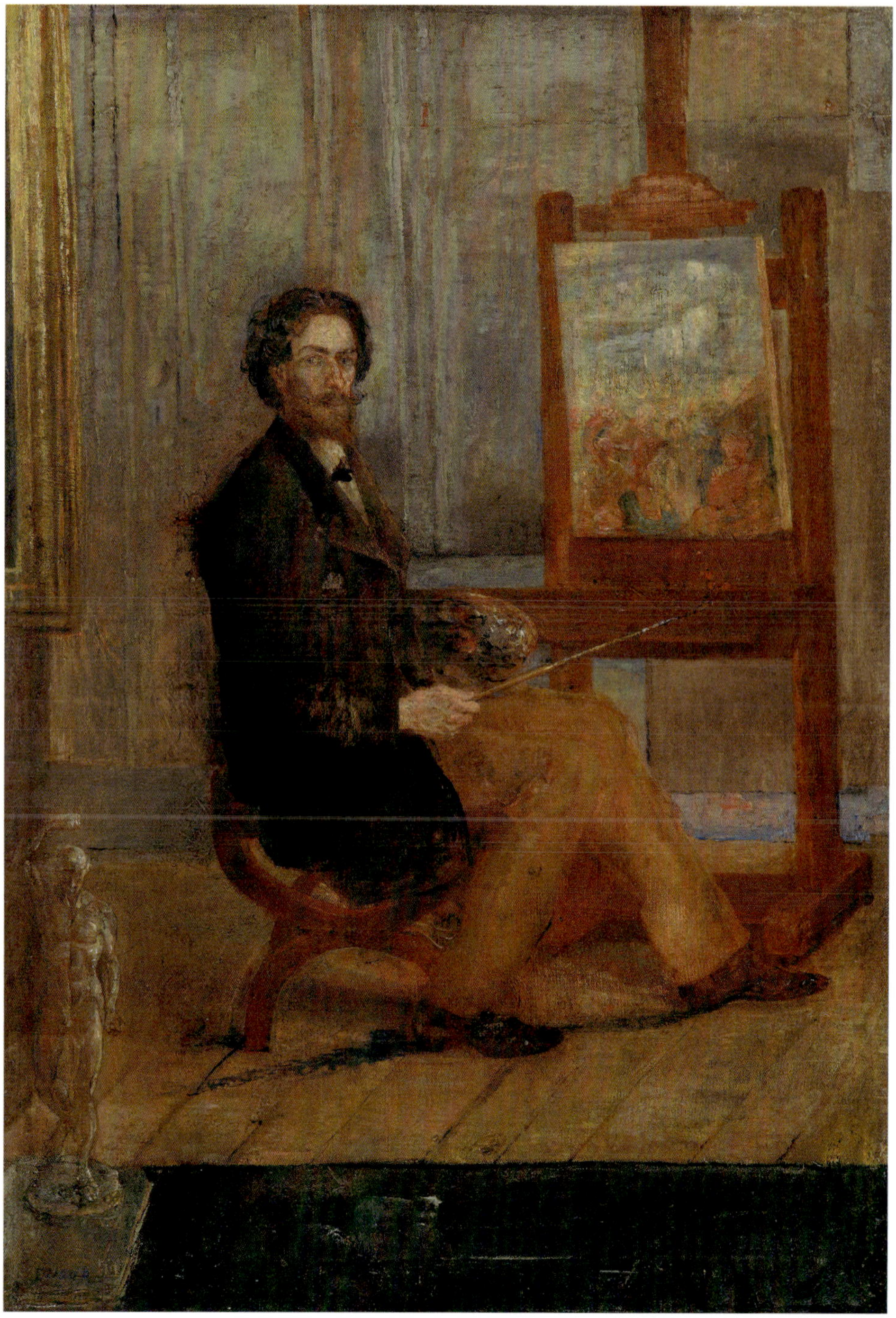

69. *Self-Portrait at the Easel.* 1890
Oil on canvas, 23 7/16 × 16 1/8" (59.5 × 41 cm)

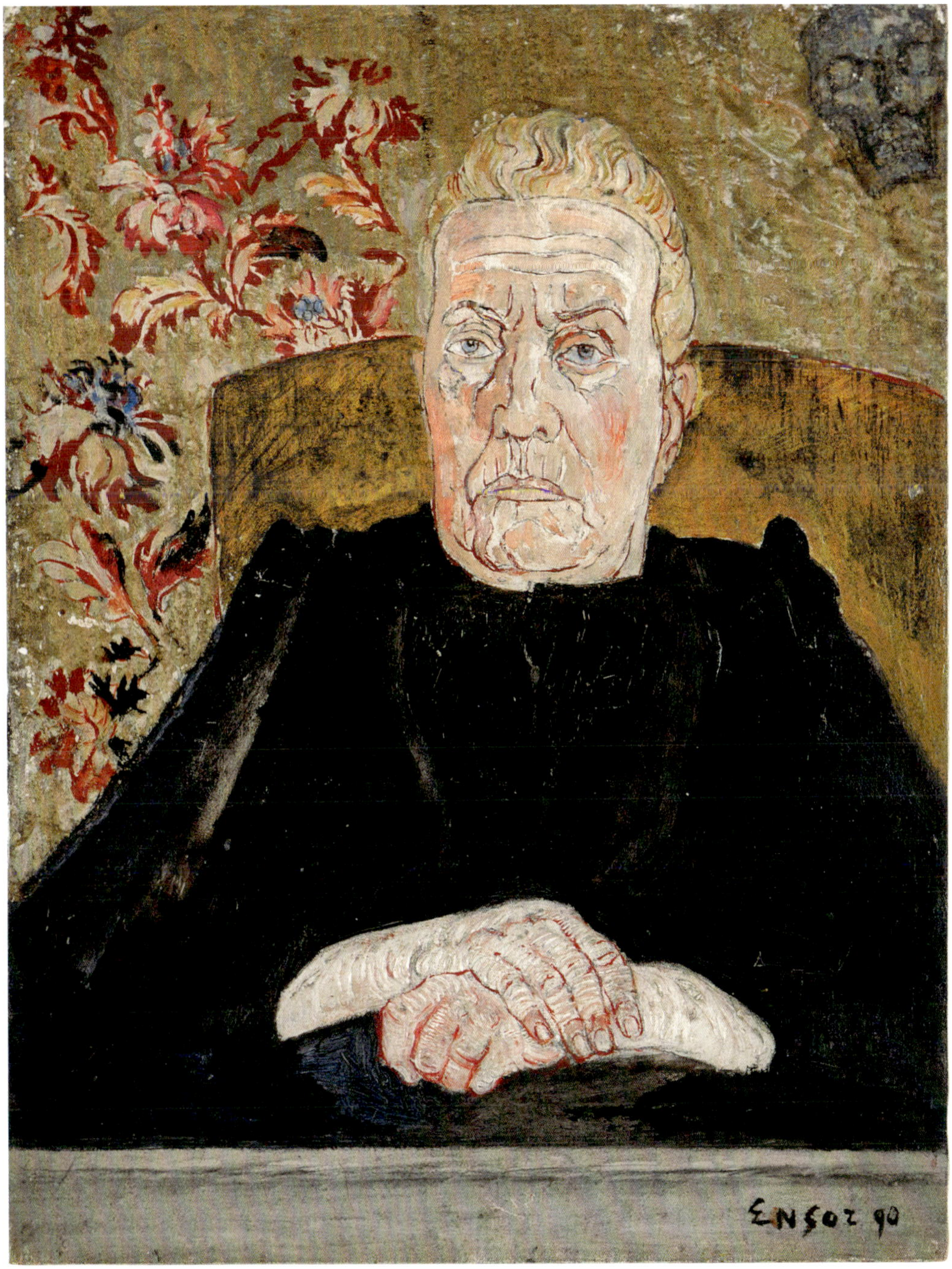

70. *Surly Countenance.* 1890
Oil on panel, 9 5/8 × 7 1/2" (24.5 × 19 cm)

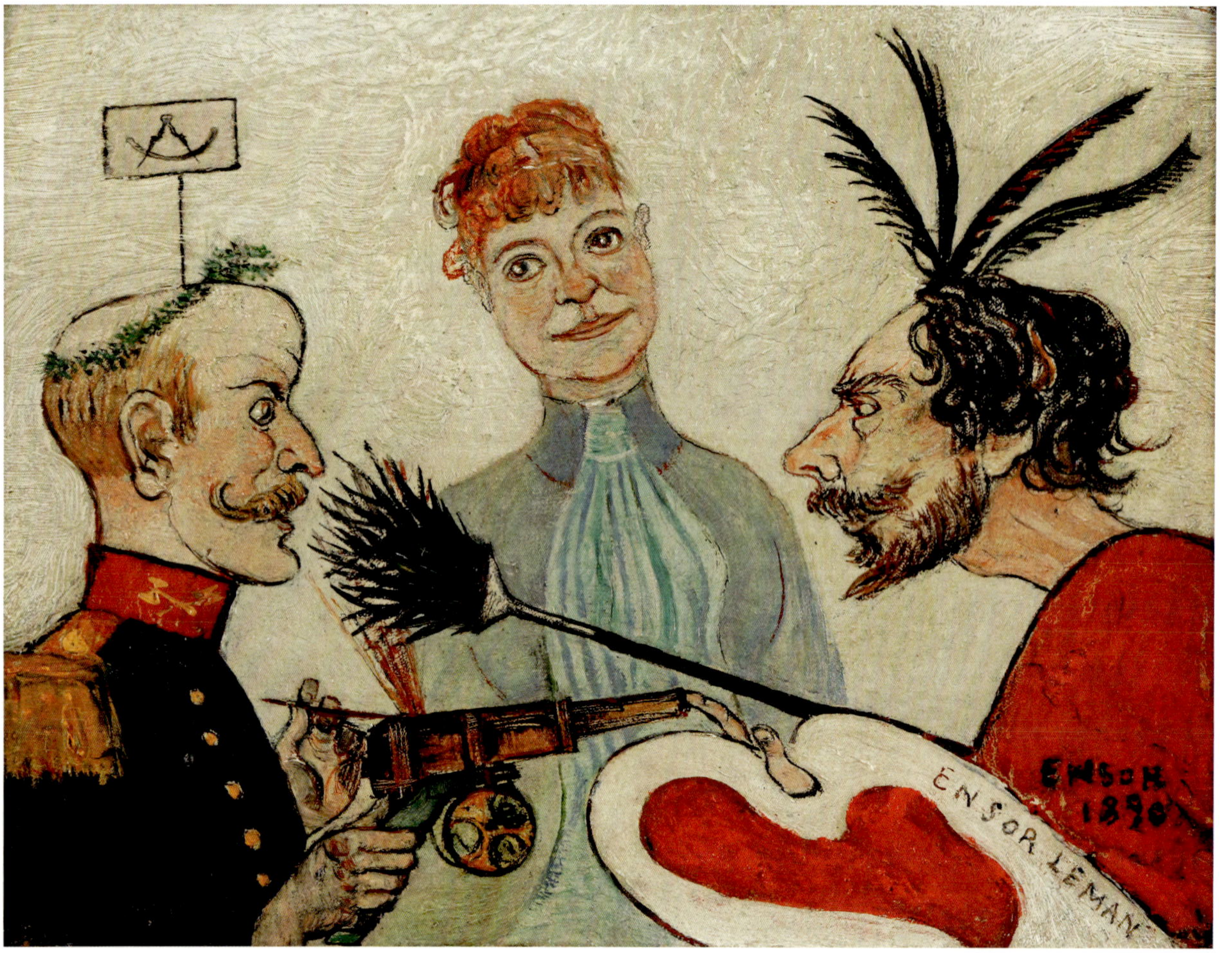

71. *Ensor and Leman Discussing Painting.* 1890
Oil on panel, 4 3/4 × 6 5/16" (12 × 16 cm)

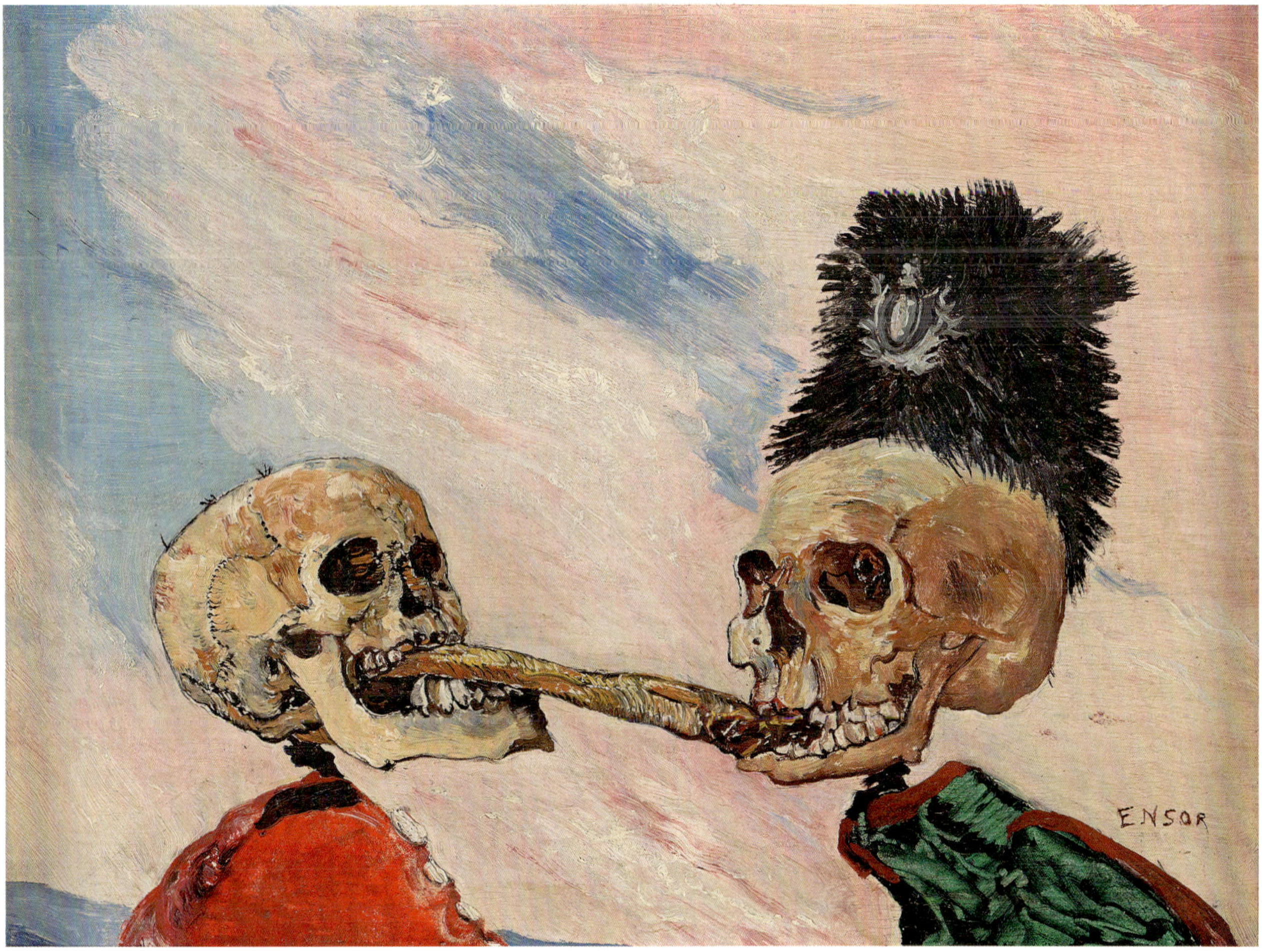

72. *Skeletons Fighting Over a Pickled Herring.* 1891
Oil on panel, 6 5⁄16 × 8 7⁄16" (16 × 21.5 cm)

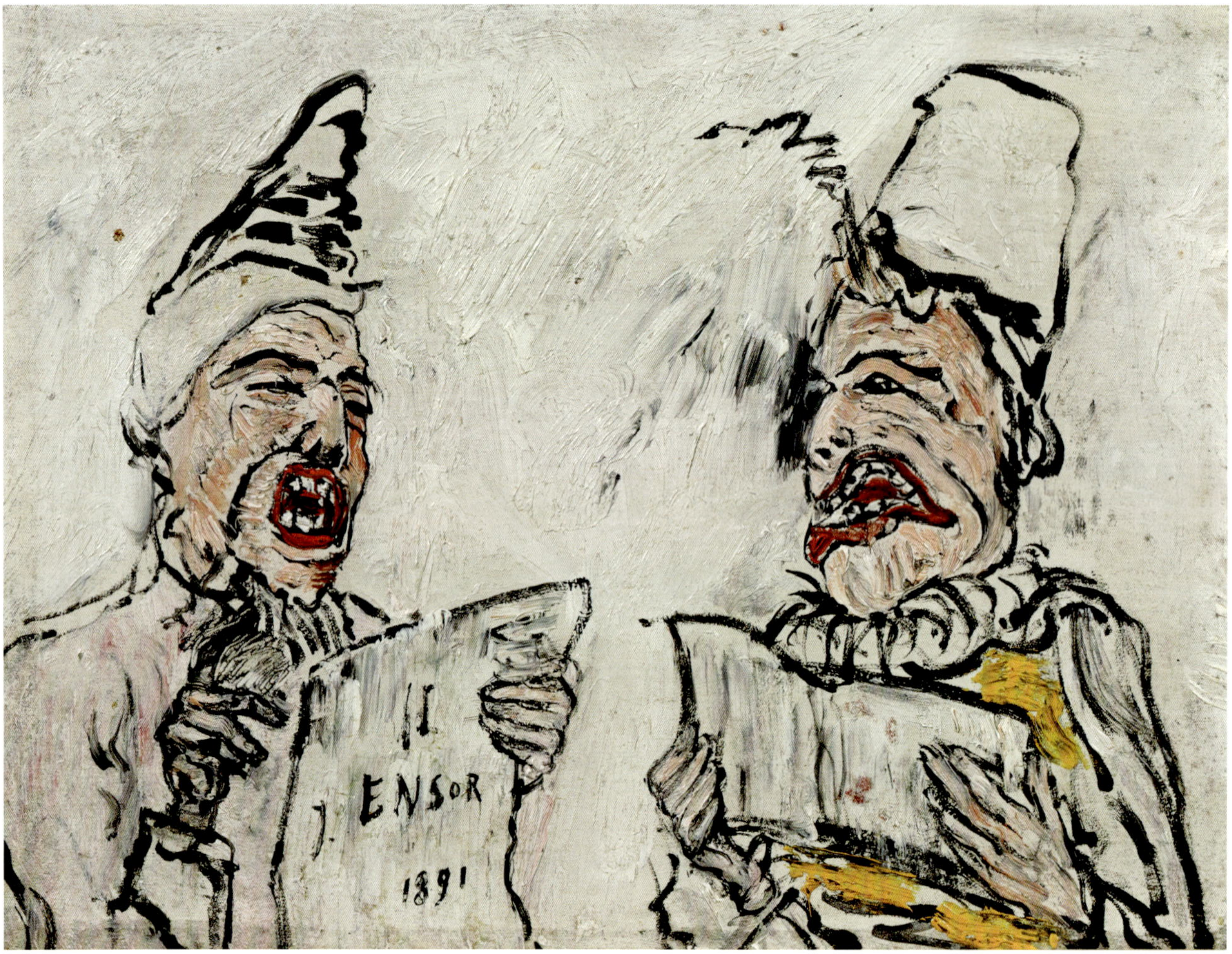

73. *The Grotesque Singers.* 1891
Oil on panel, 6 5/16 × 8 11/16" (16 × 22 cm)

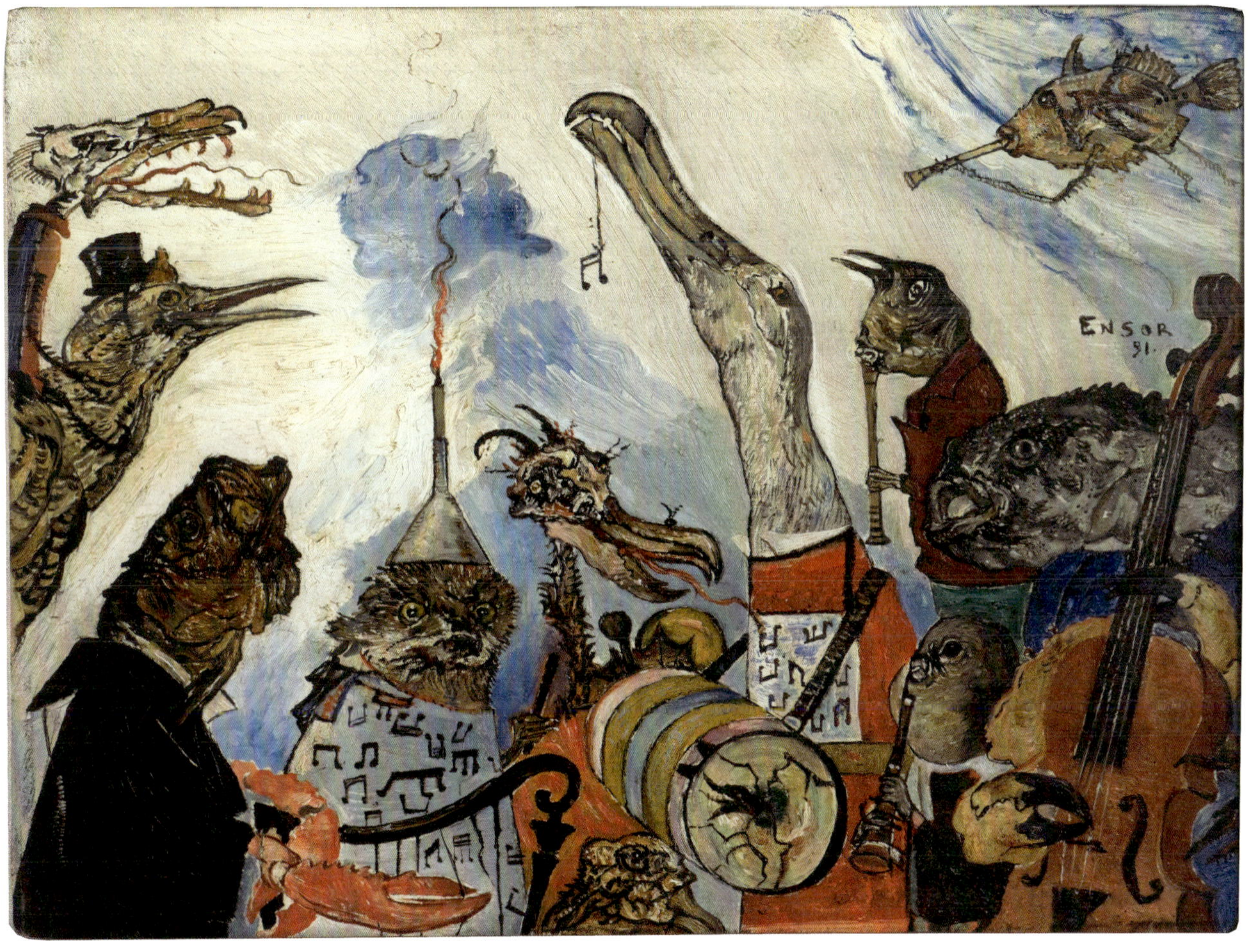

74. *The Frightful Musicians.* 1891
Oil on panel, 6 5⁄16 × 8 1⁄4" (16 × 21 cm)

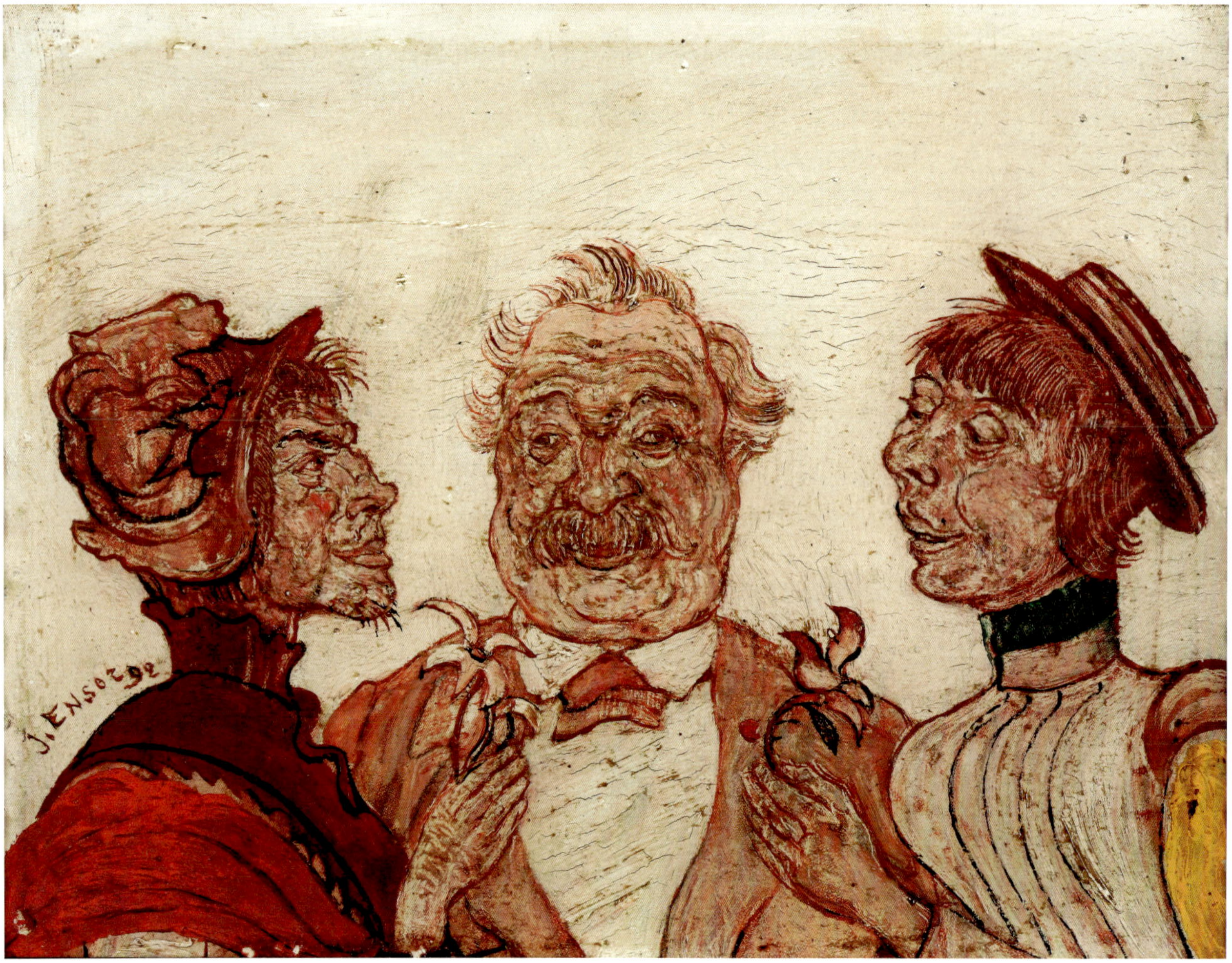

75. *Monsieur and Madame Rousseau Speaking with Sophie Yoteko.* 1892
Oil on panel, 4 3/4 × 6 5/16" (12 × 16 cm)

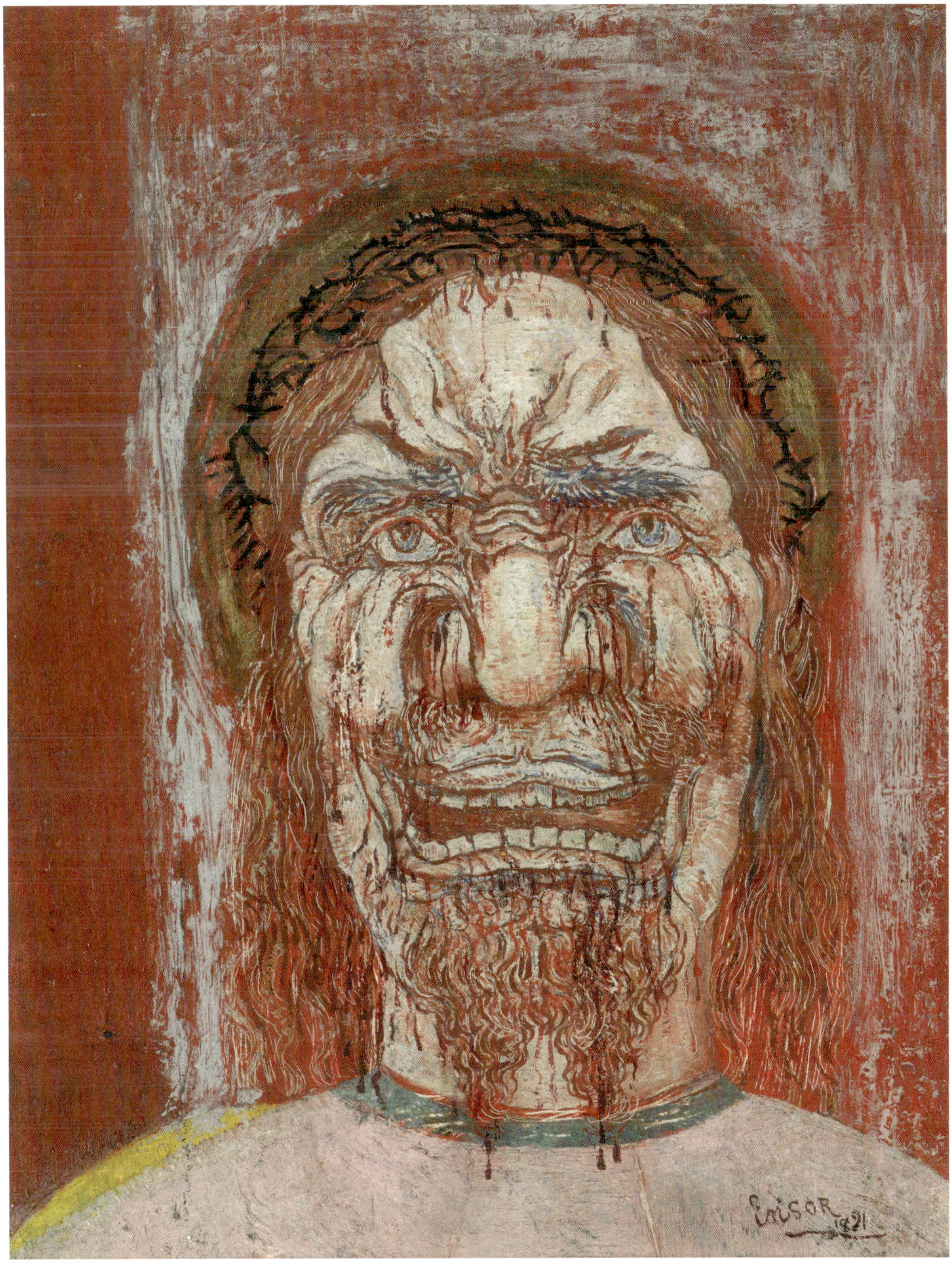

76. *The Man of Sorrows.* 1891
Oil on panel, 8 5/8 × 6 5/16" (21.9 × 16 cm)

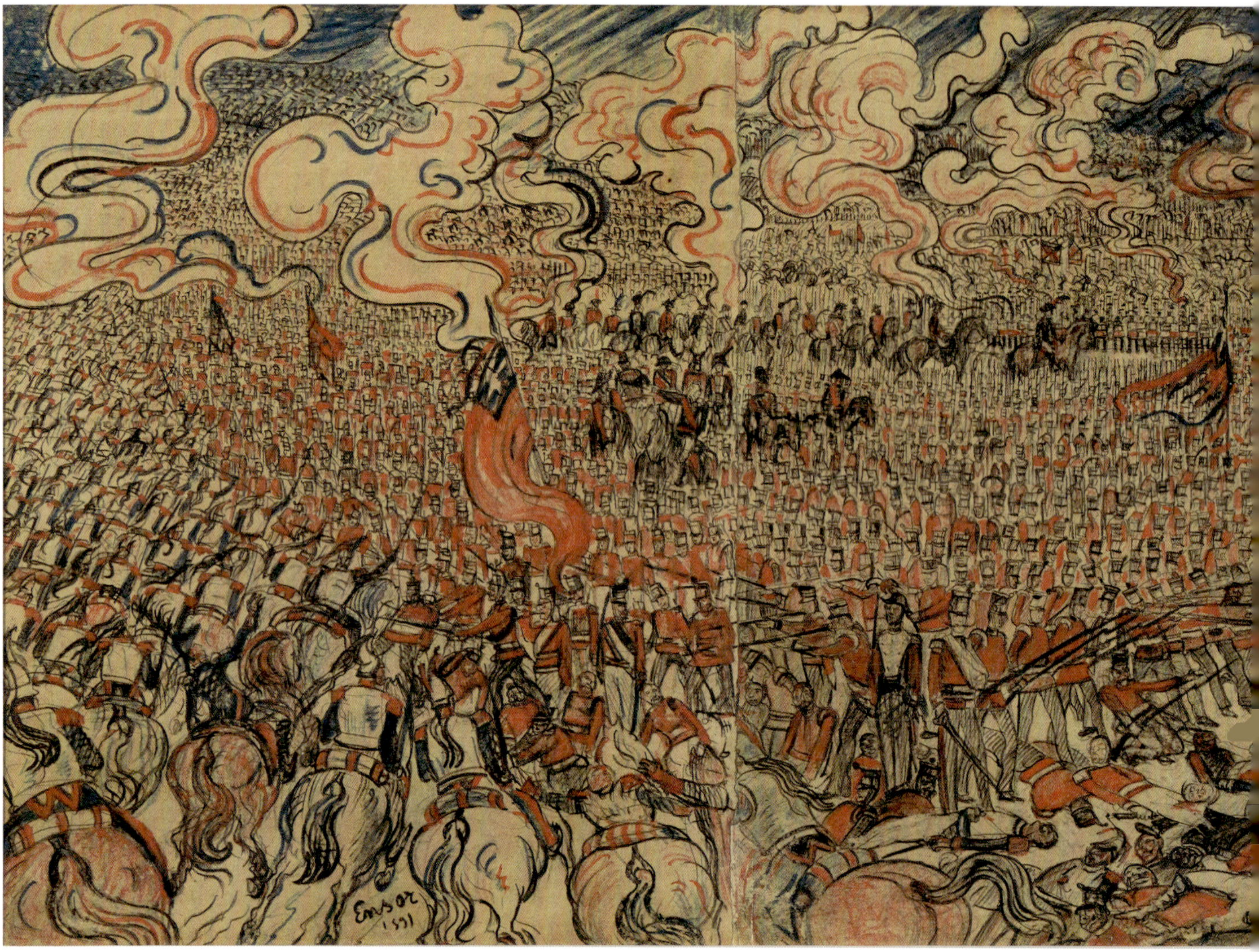

77. *The Cuirassiers at Waterloo.* 1891
India ink, crayon, colored pencil, and pastel on three sheets of paper, mounted on board, 8 7/8 × 24 5/8" (22.5 × 62.5 cm)

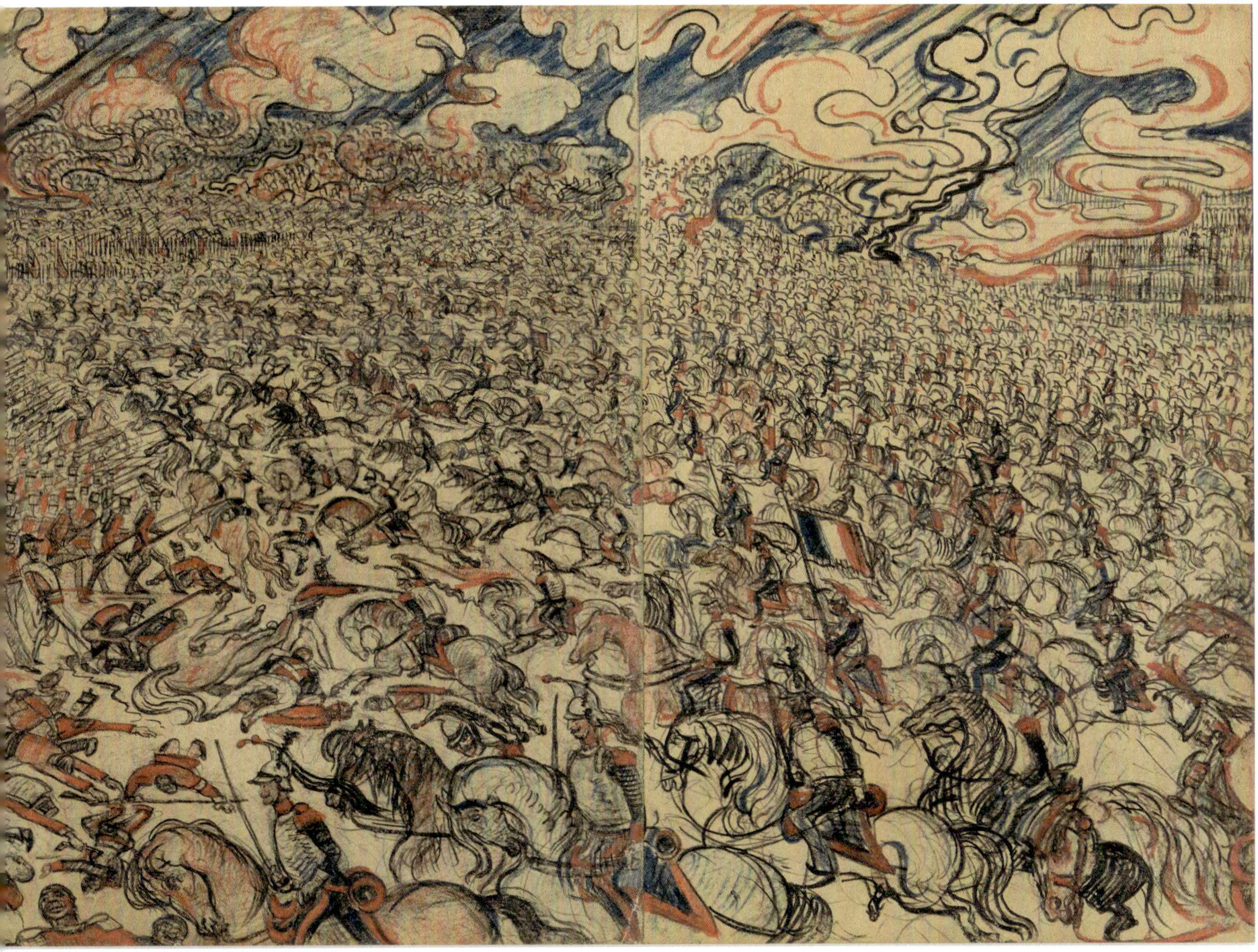

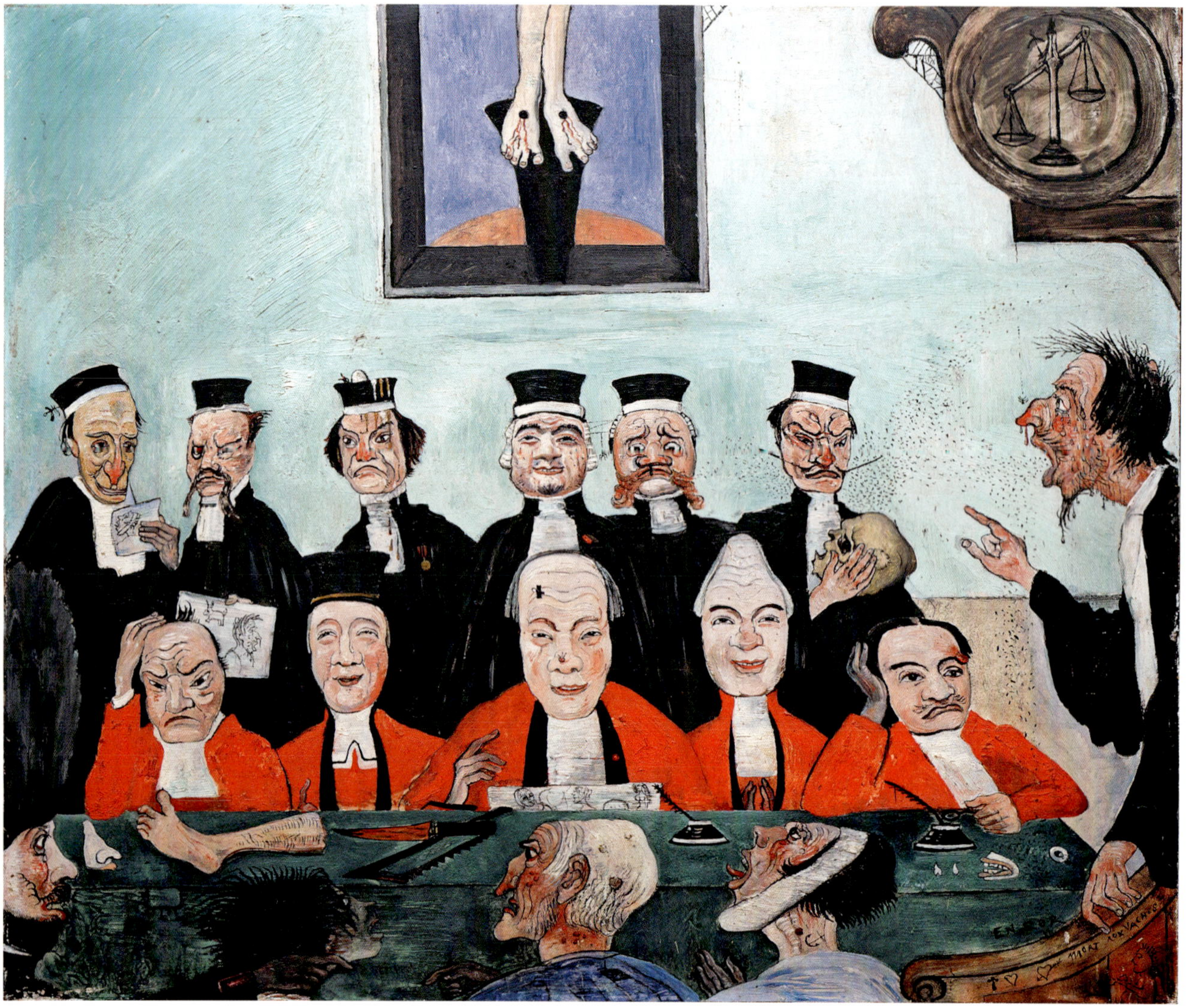

78. *The Wise Judges.* 1891
Oil on panel, 14 15/16 × 18 1/8" (38 × 46 cm)

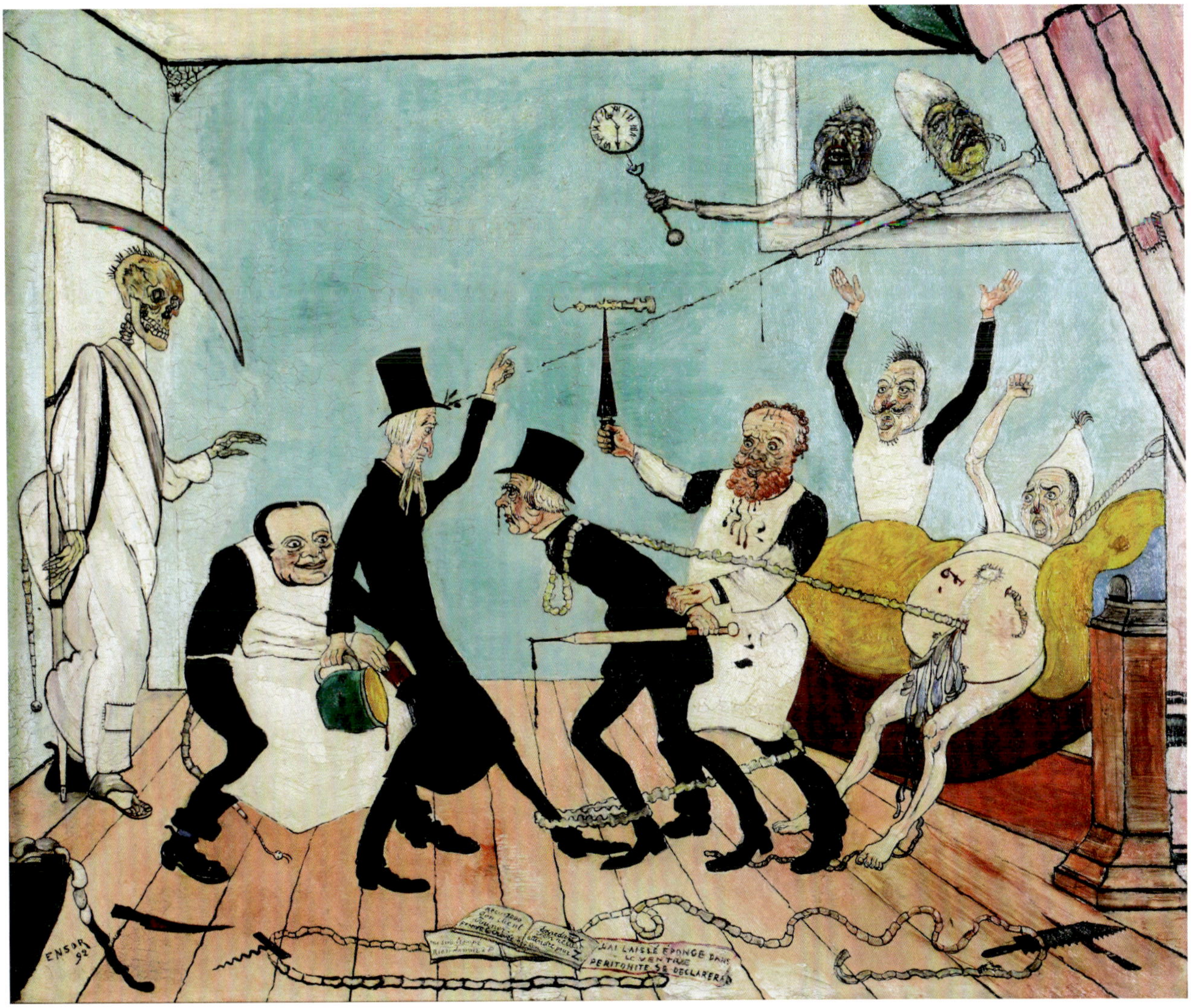

79. *The Bad Doctors*. 1892
Oil on panel, 19 11/16 × 24" (50 × 61 cm)

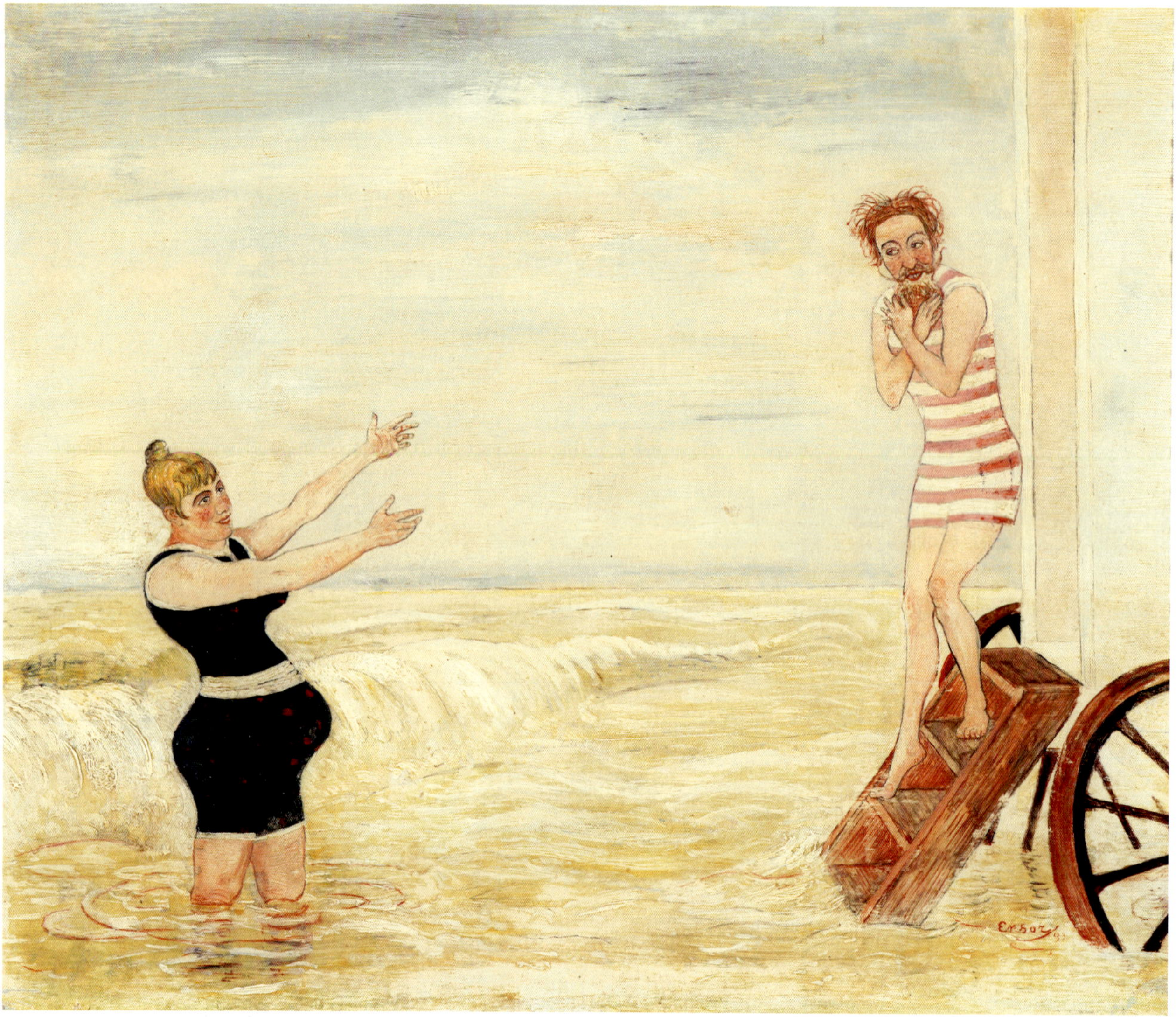

80. *The Call of the Siren.* 1891 or 1893
Oil on panel, 14 15/16 × 18 1/8" (38 × 46 cm)

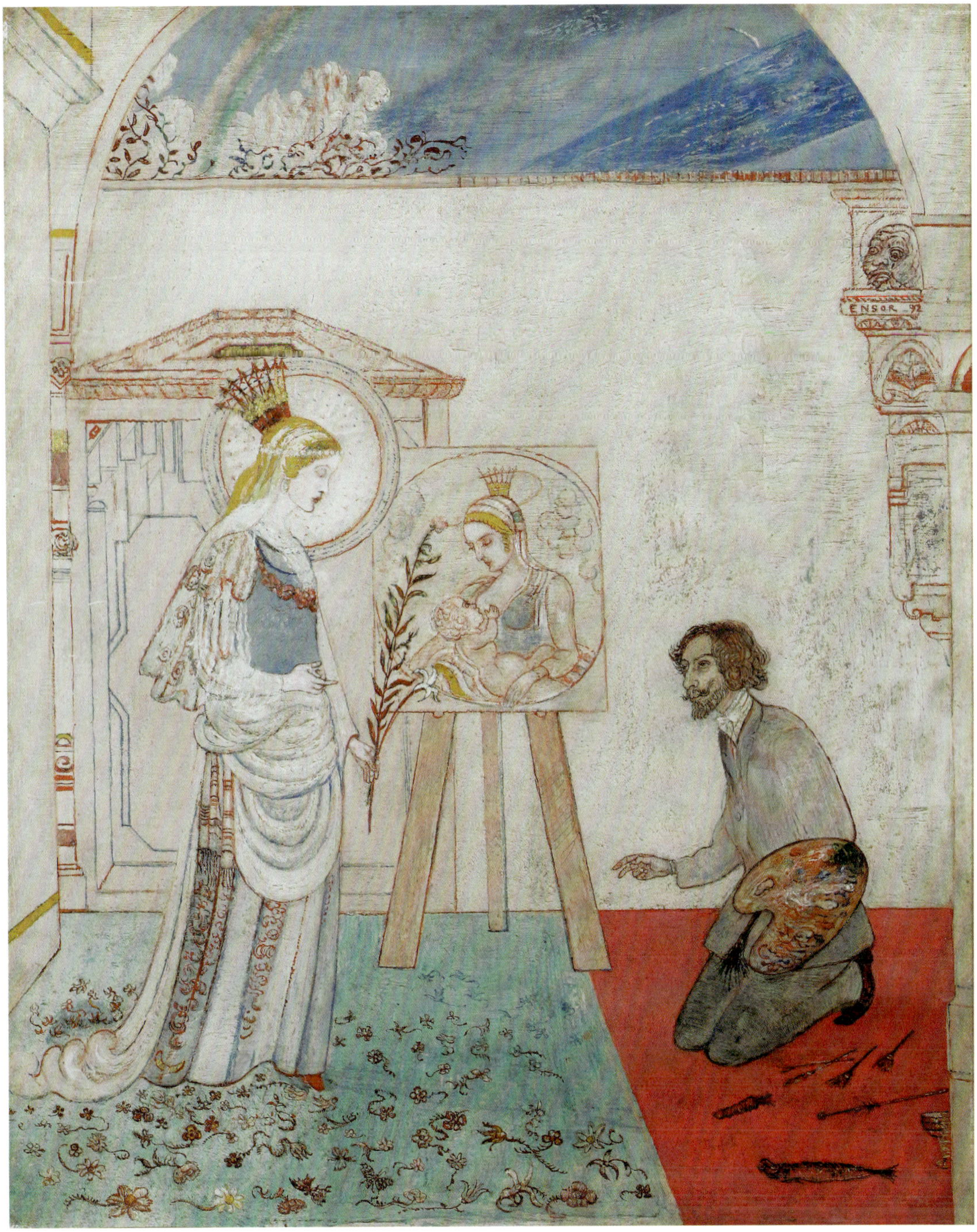

81. *The Virgin of Consolation.* 1892
Oil on panel, 15 3/4 × 14 15/16" (40 × 38 cm)

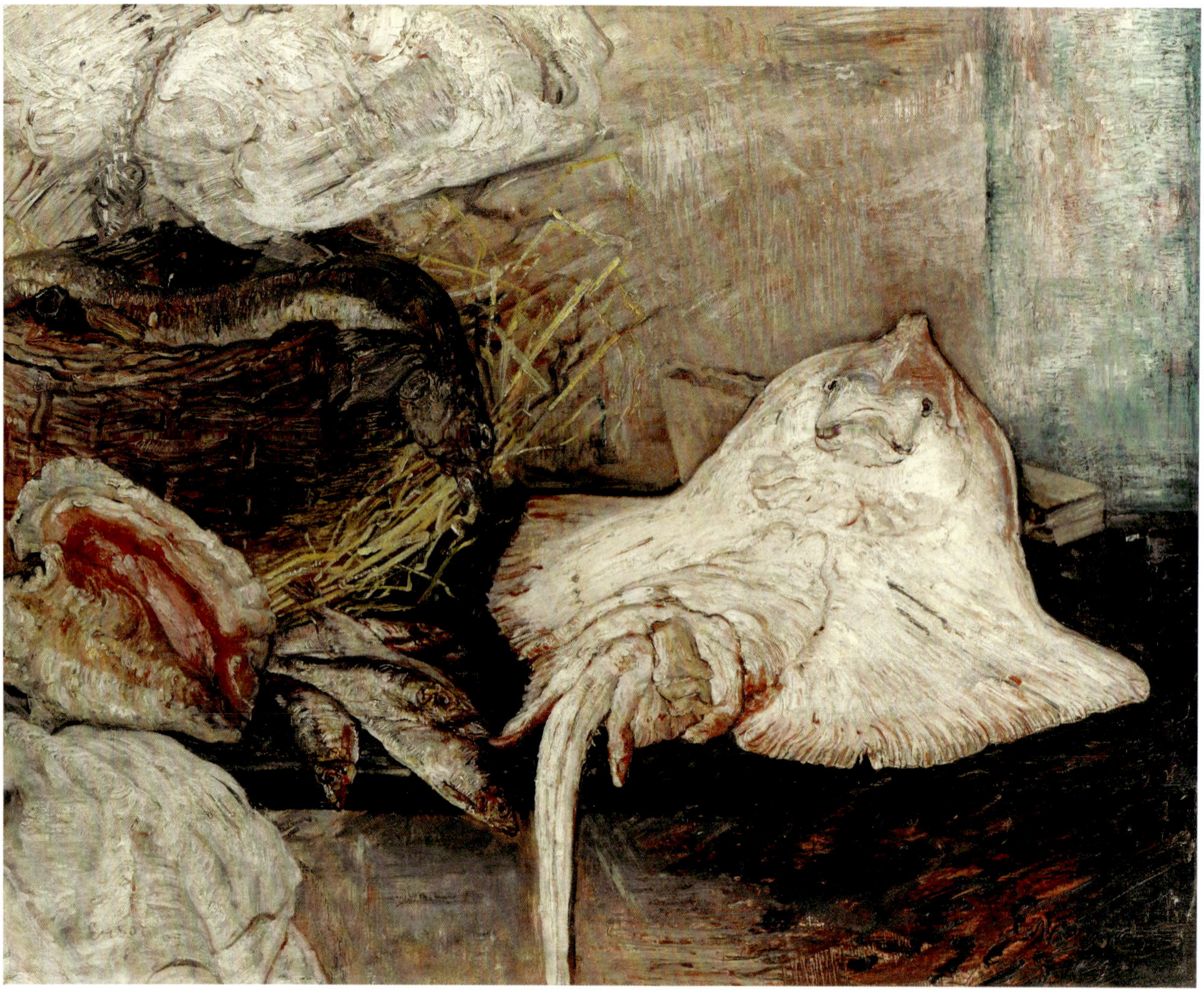

82. *The Skate.* 1892
Oil on canvas, 31 ½ × 39 ⅜" (80 × 100 cm)

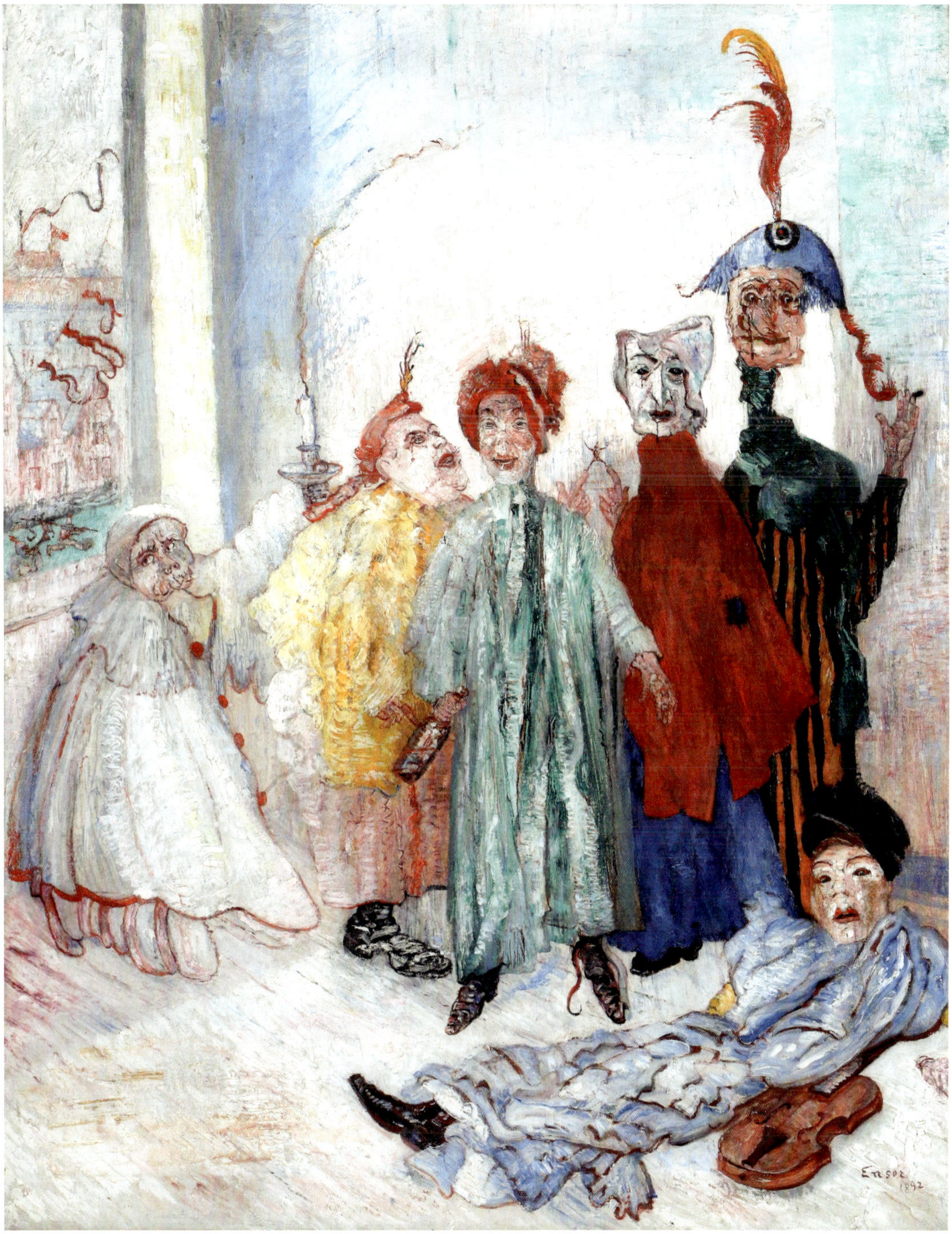

83. *The Strange Masks*. 1892
Oil on canvas, 39 3/8 × 31 1/2" (100 × 80 cm)

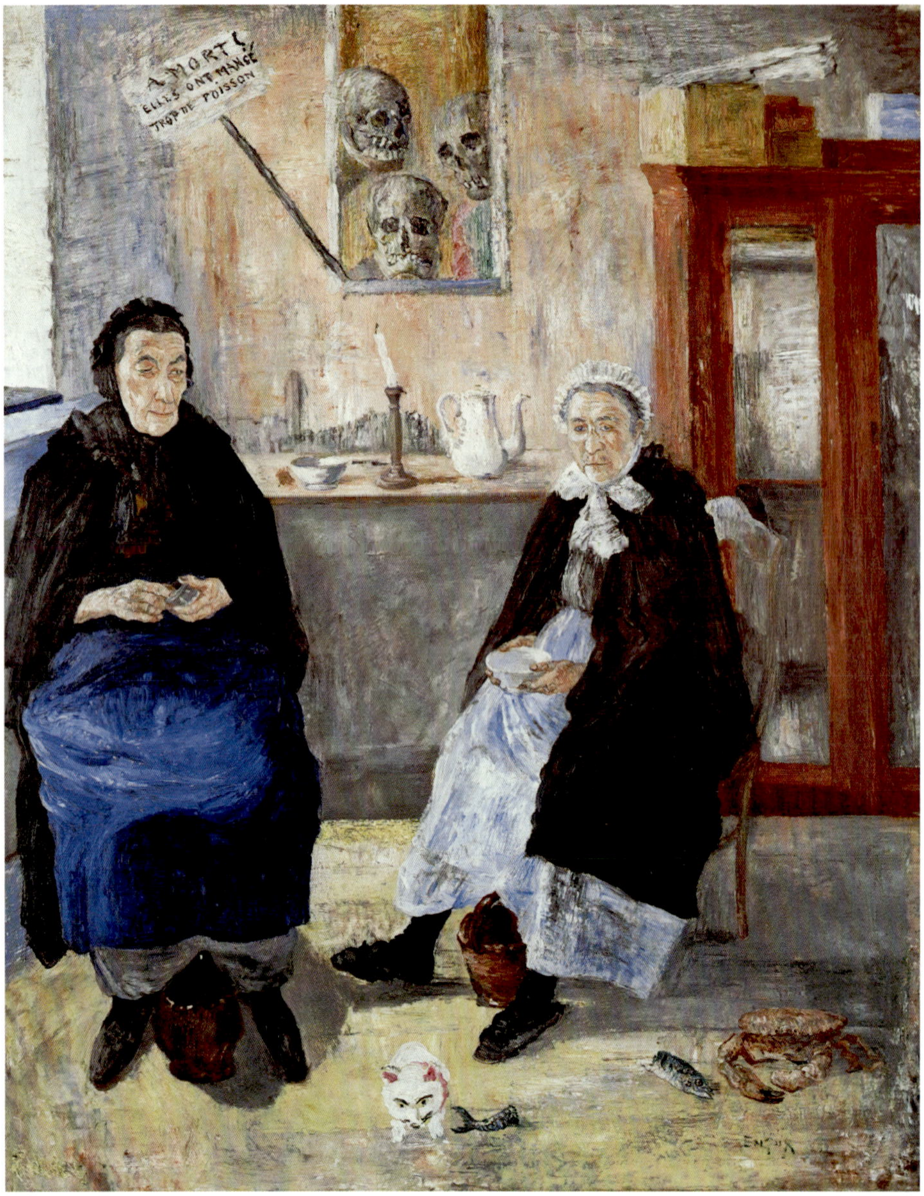

84. *The Melancholy Fishwives.* 1892
Oil on canvas, 39 3/8 × 31 1/2" (100 × 80 cm)

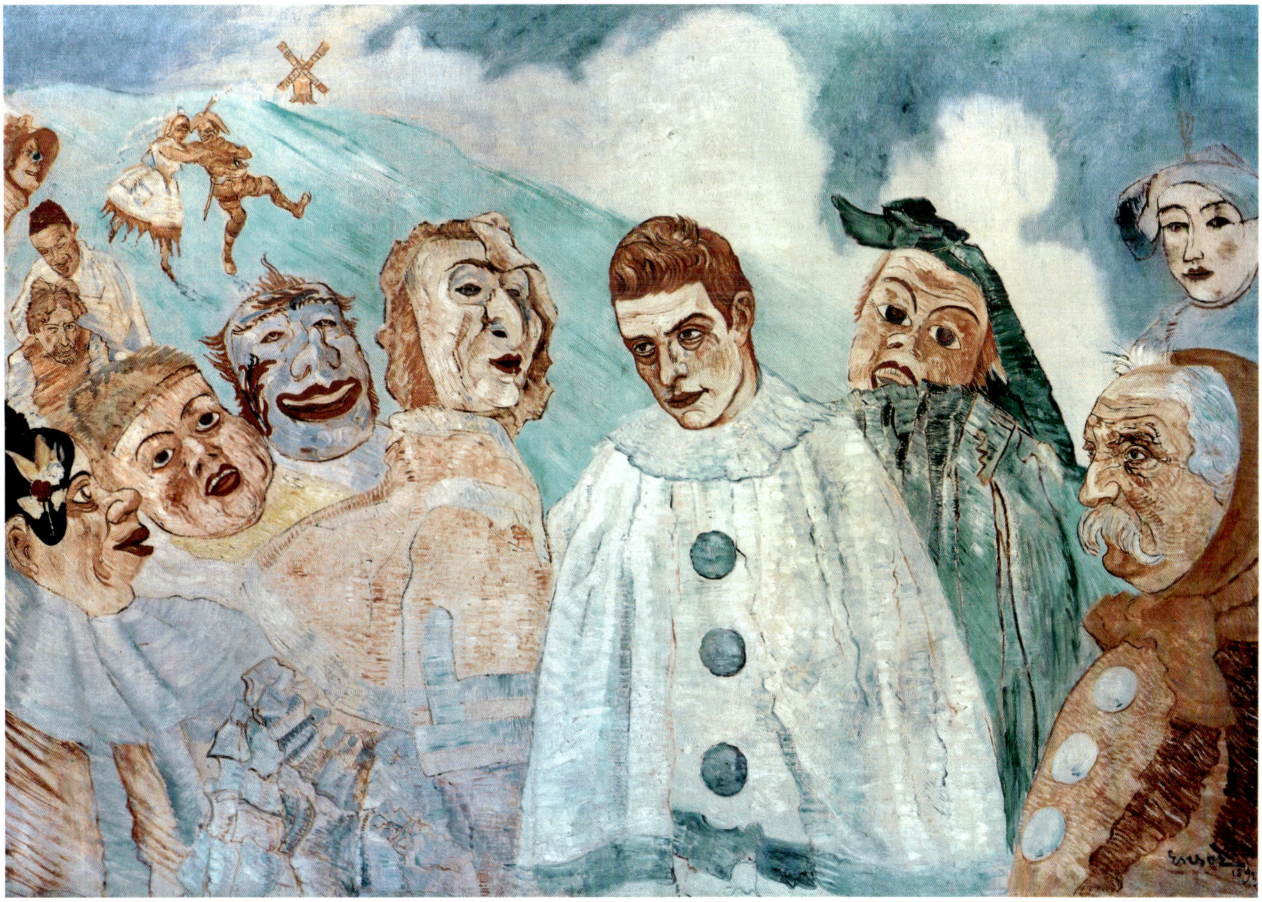

85. *The Despair of Pierrot.* 1892
Oil on canvas, 56 7/8 × 76 9/16" (144.5 × 194.5 cm)

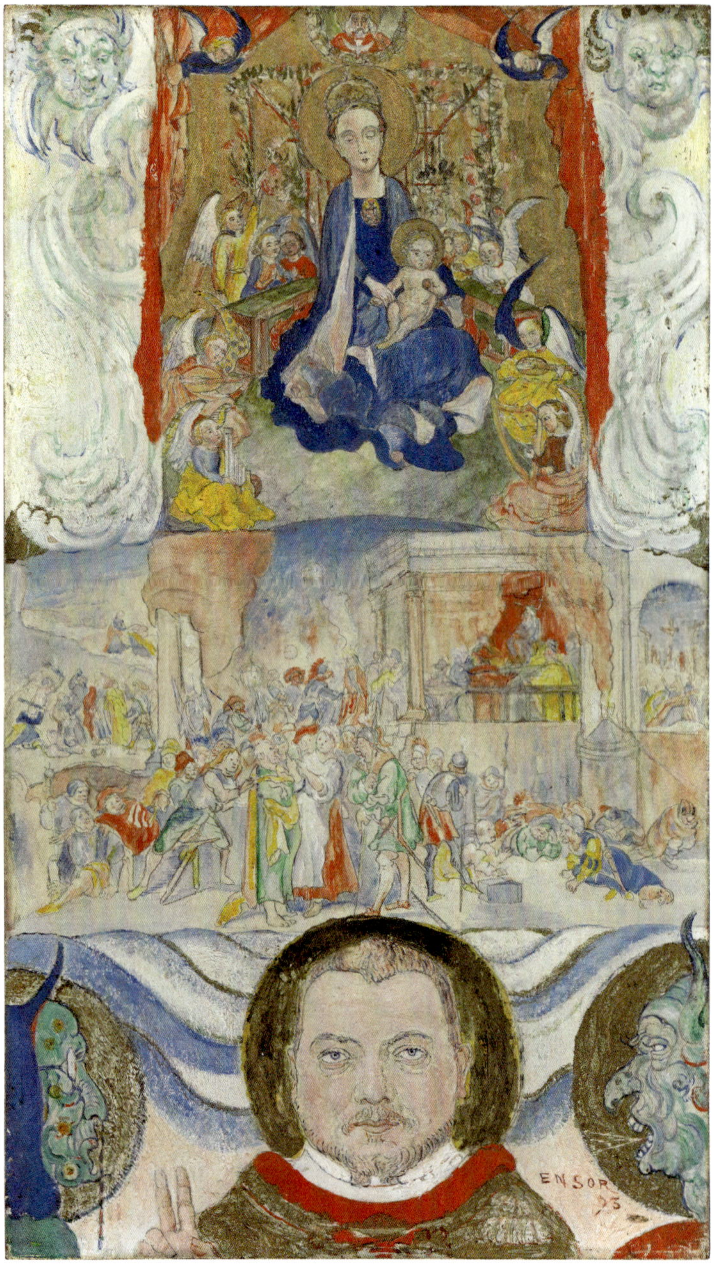

86. *Icon* (*Portrait of Eugène Demolder*). 1893
Oil, pencil, and gouache on panel, 14 3/16 × 8 1/4"
(36 × 21 cm)

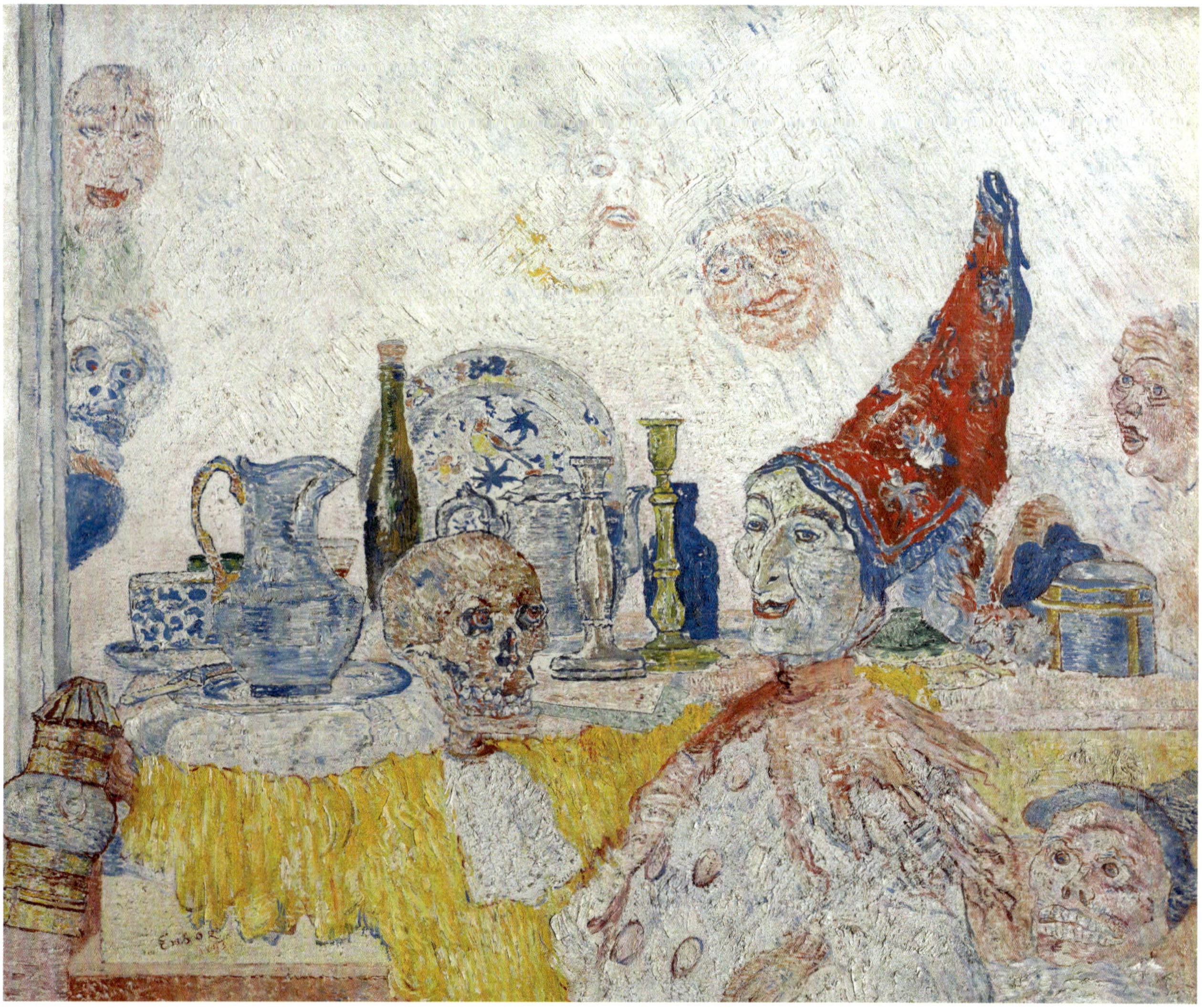

87. *Pierrot and Skeleton in a Yellow Robe.* 1893
Oil on panel, 14 15/16 × 18 7/8" (38 × 48 cm)

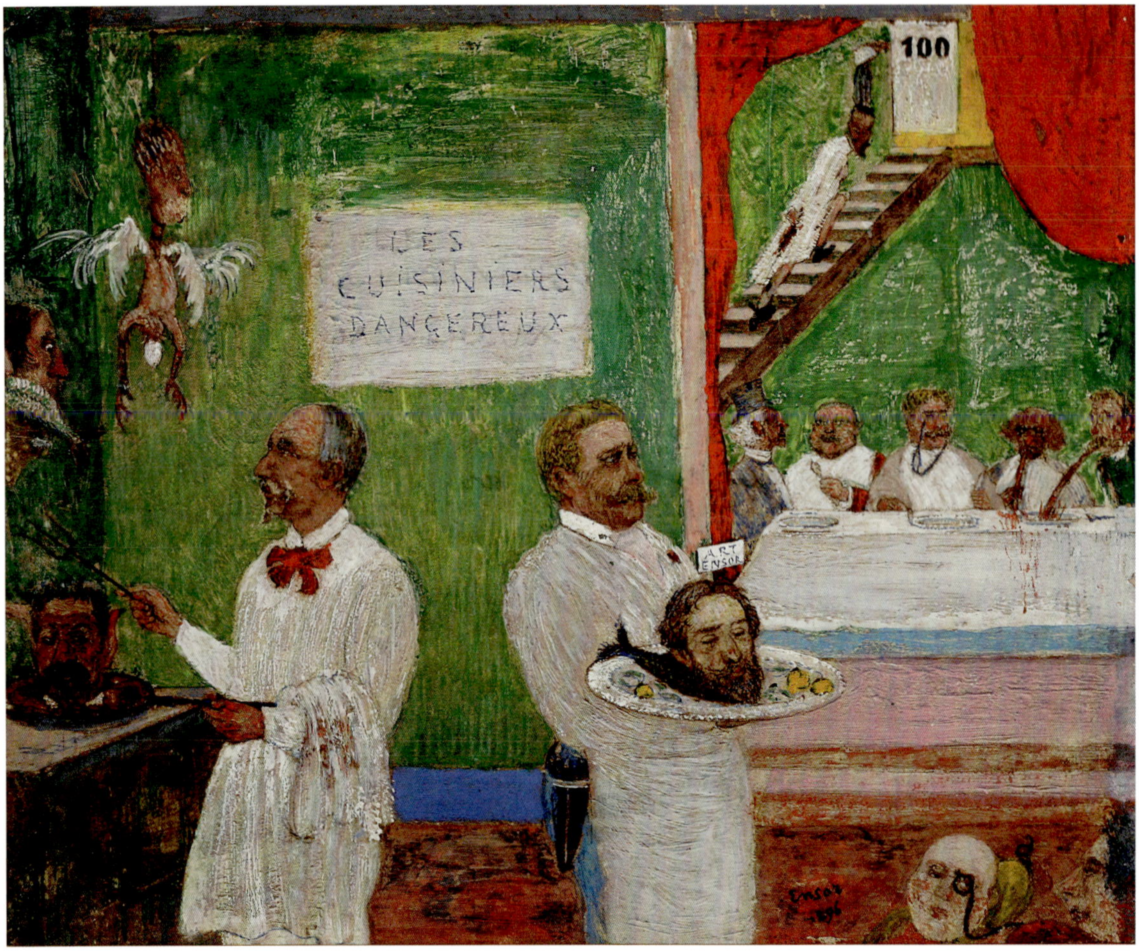

88. *The Dangerous Cooks.* 1896
Pencil, gouache, and oil on board, 7 7/8 × 9 13/16"
(20 × 25 cm)

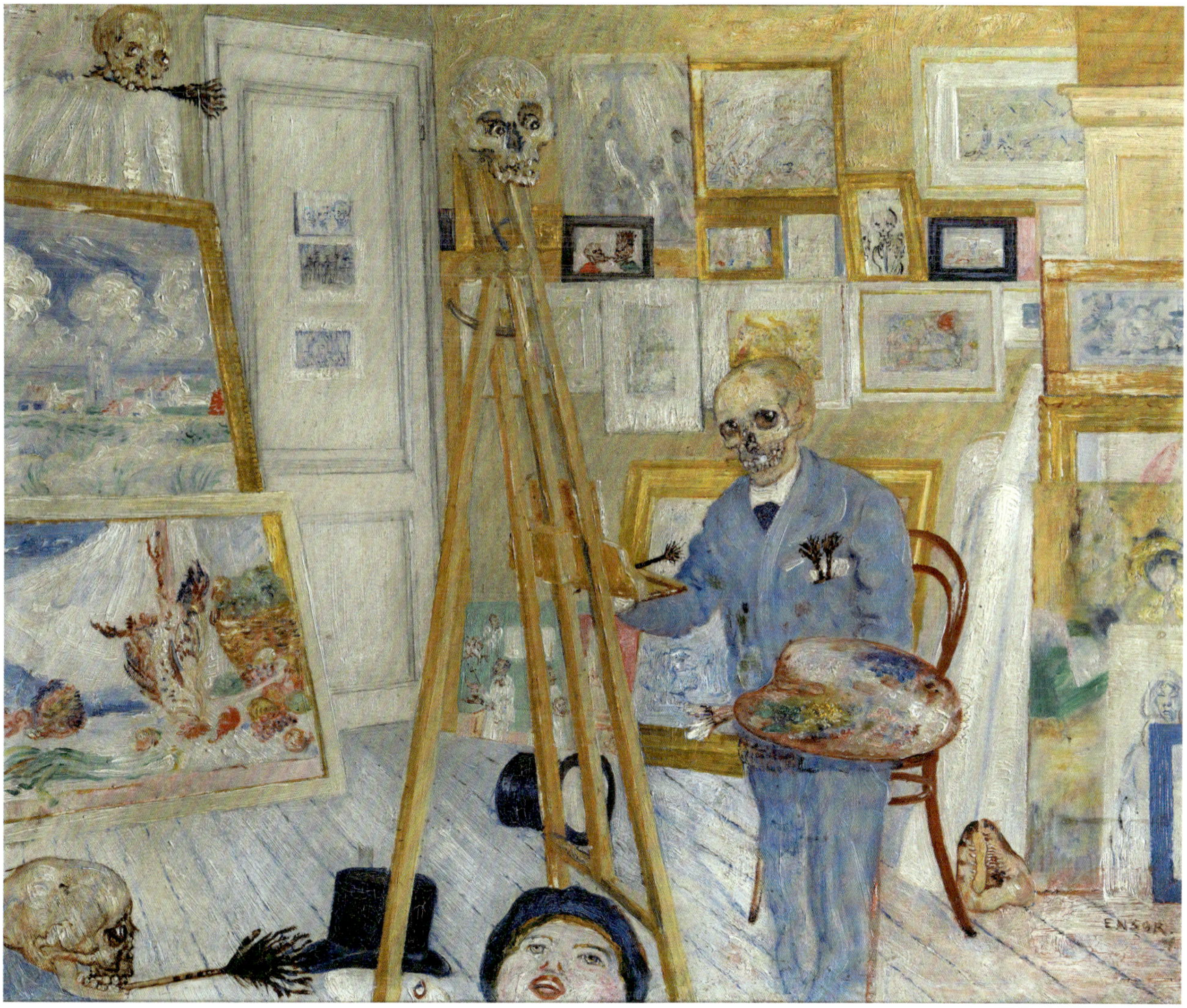

89. *The Skeleton Painter.* 1895 or 1896(?)
Oil on panel, 14 13/16 × 18 1/8" (37.7 × 46 cm)

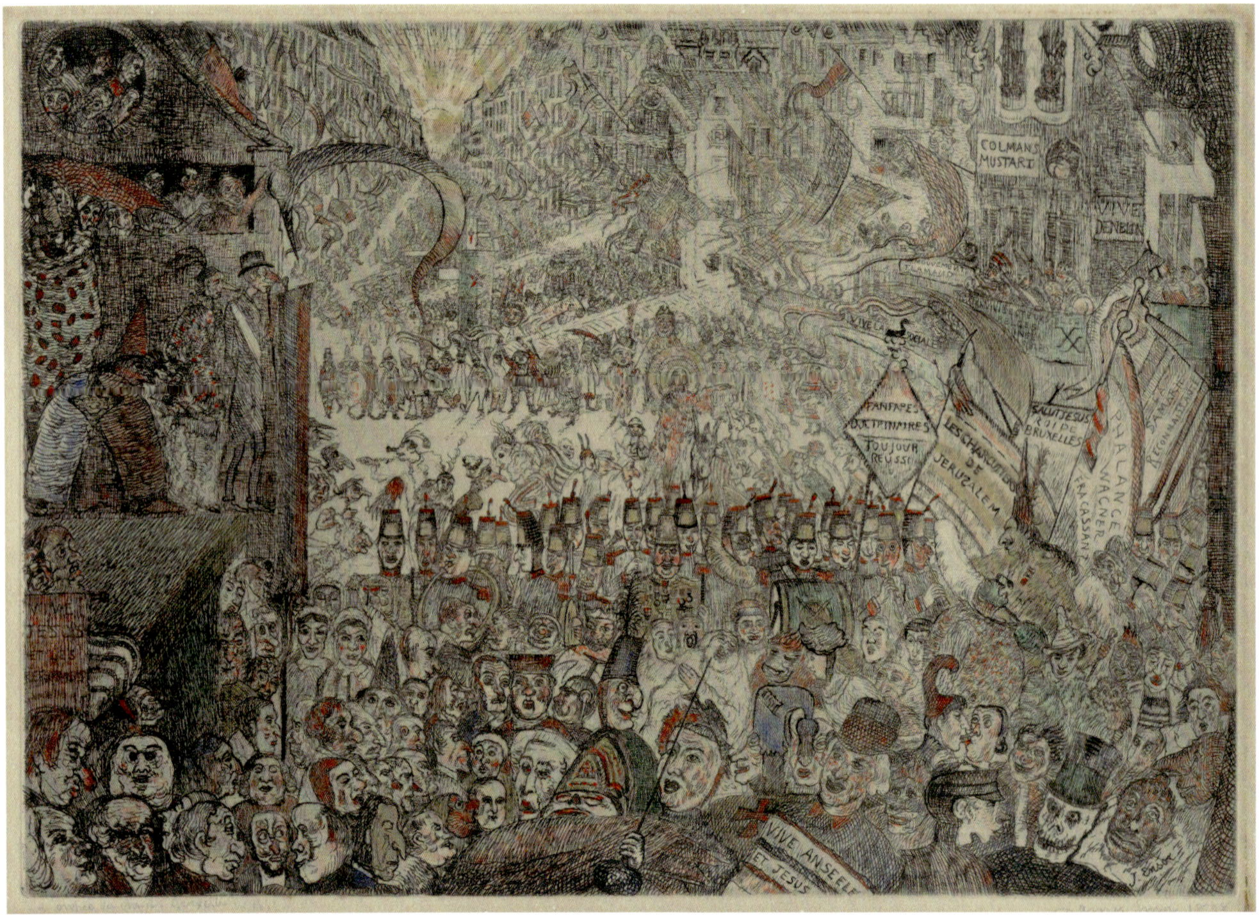

90. *The Entry of Christ into Brussels.* State III. 1898
Etching heightened with watercolor on Arches
laid paper, plate: 9 ¾ × 14" (24.8 × 35.5 cm)

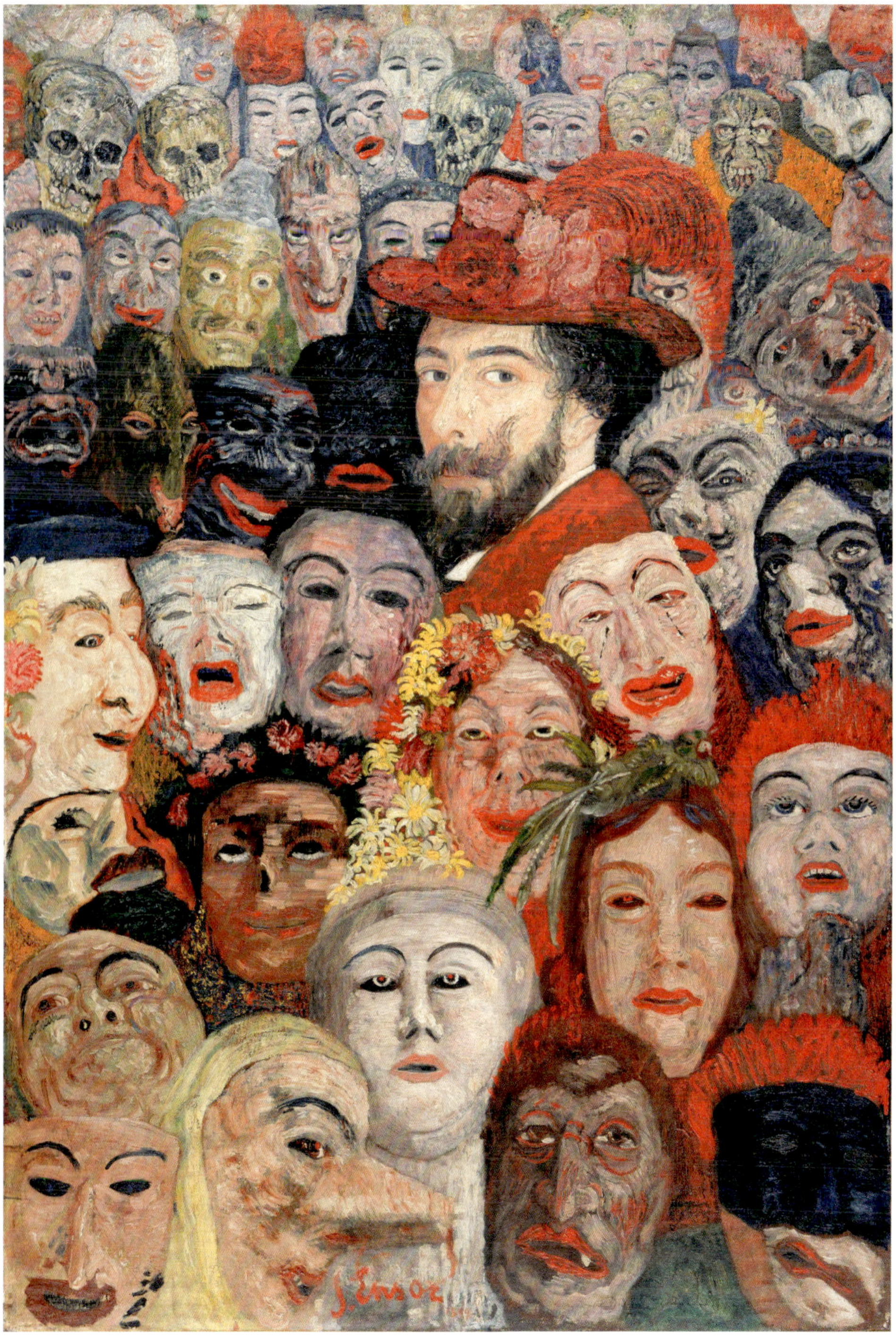

91. *Self-Portrait with Masks.* 1899
Oil on canvas, 47 1/4 × 31 1/2" (120 × 80 cm)

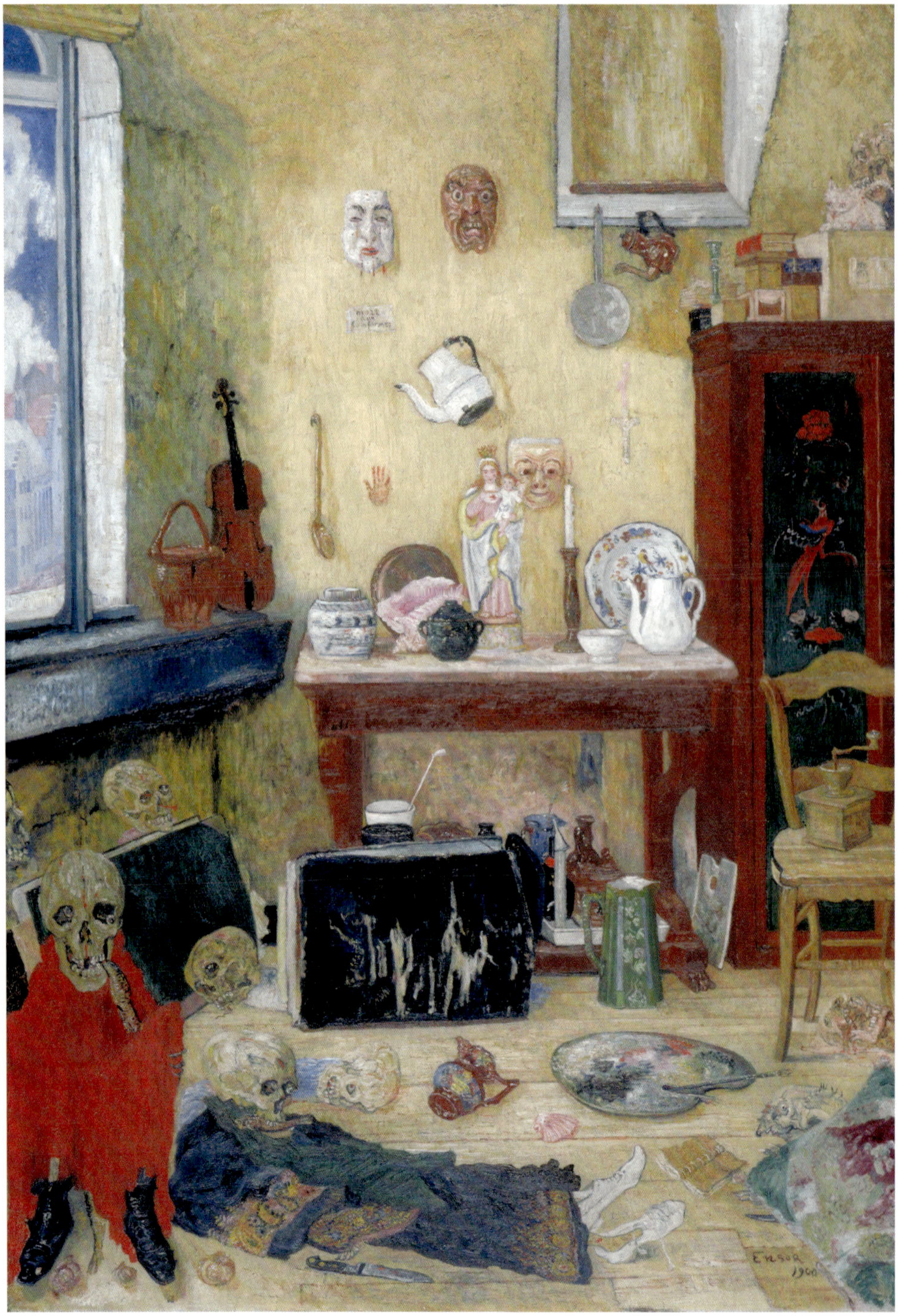

92. *Skeletons in the Studio.* 1900
Oil on canvas, 43 11/16 × 31 5/16" (111 × 79.5 cm)

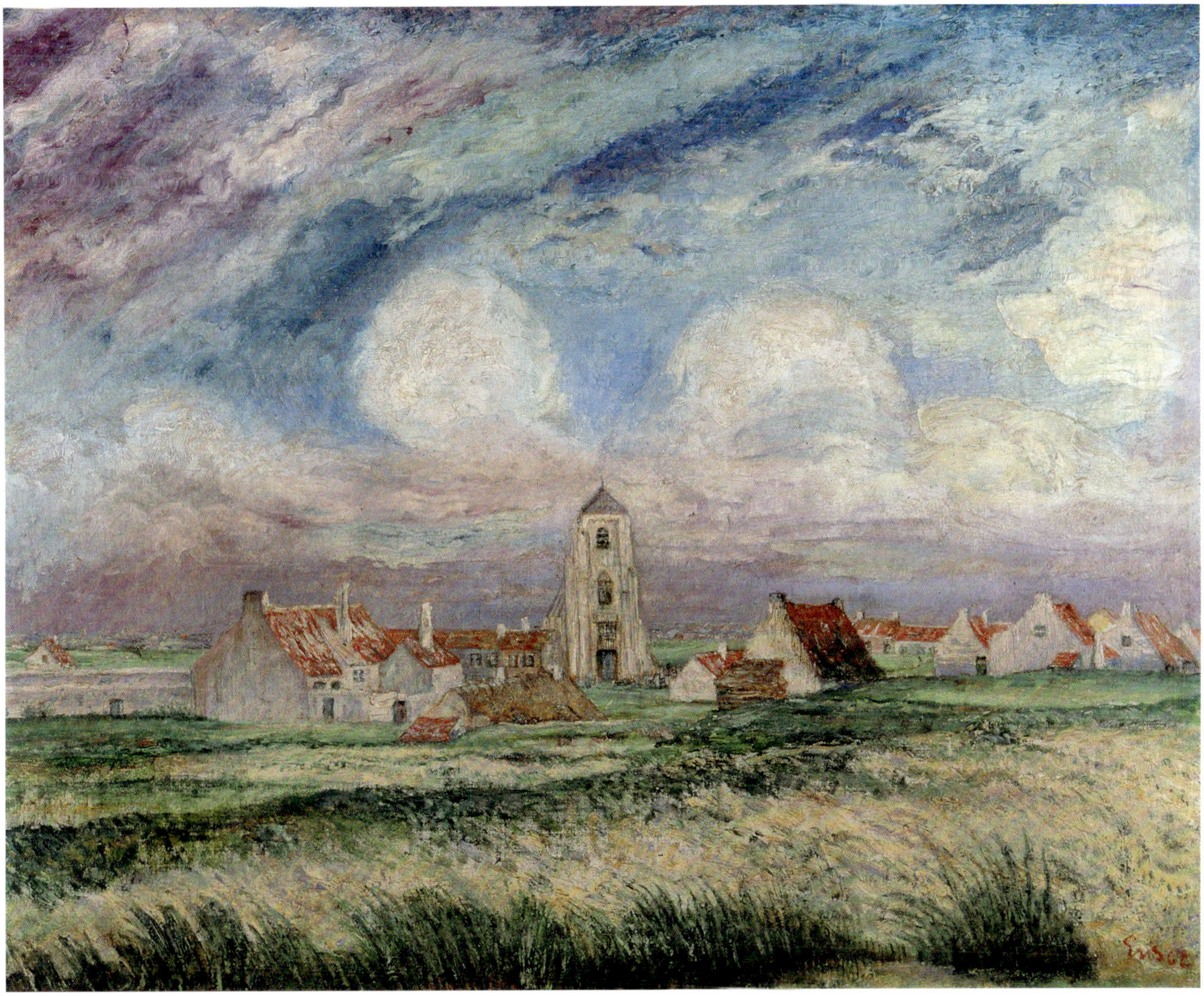

93. *View of Mariakerke.* 1901
Oil on canvas, 21 1/4 × 26 3/8" (54 × 67 cm)

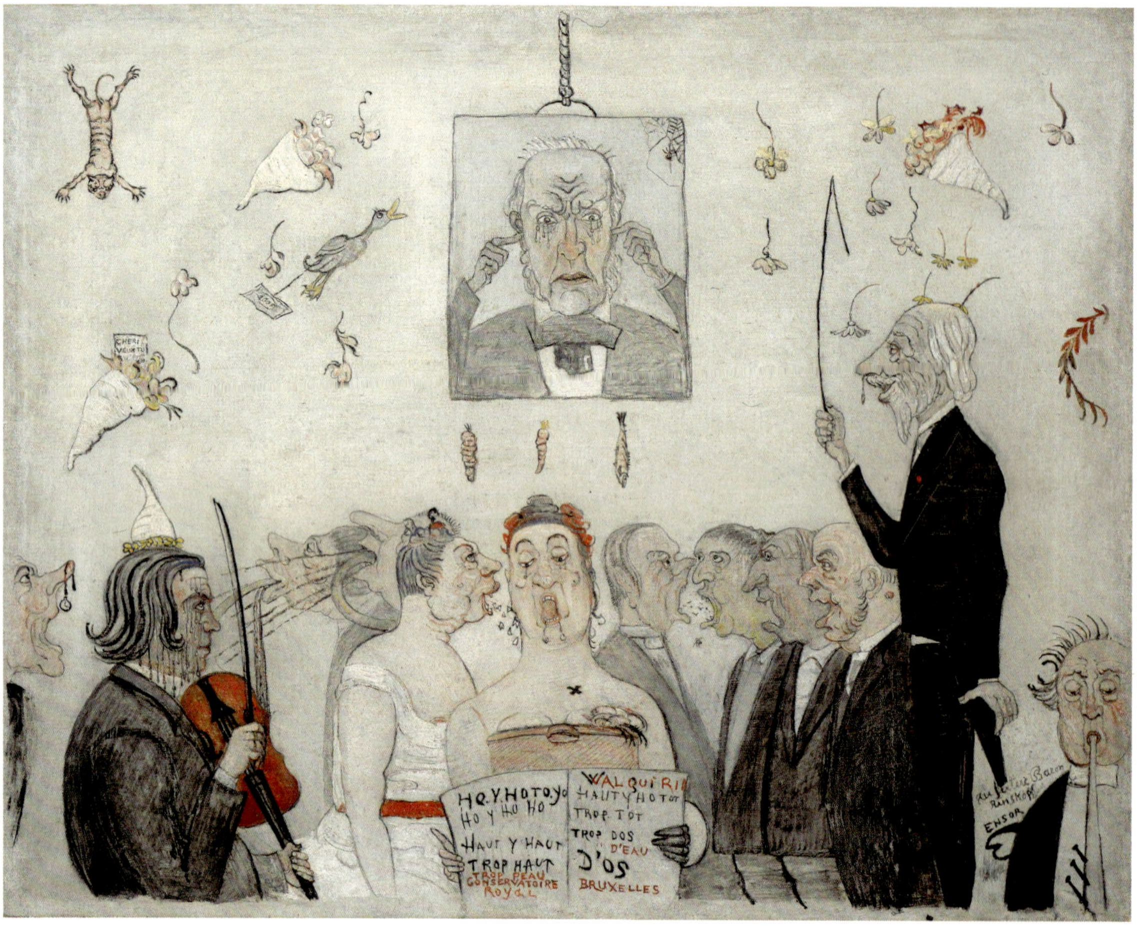

94. *At the Conservatory.* 1902
Oil on canvas, mounted on panel, 22 1/16 × 28 1/8"
(56 × 71.5 cm)

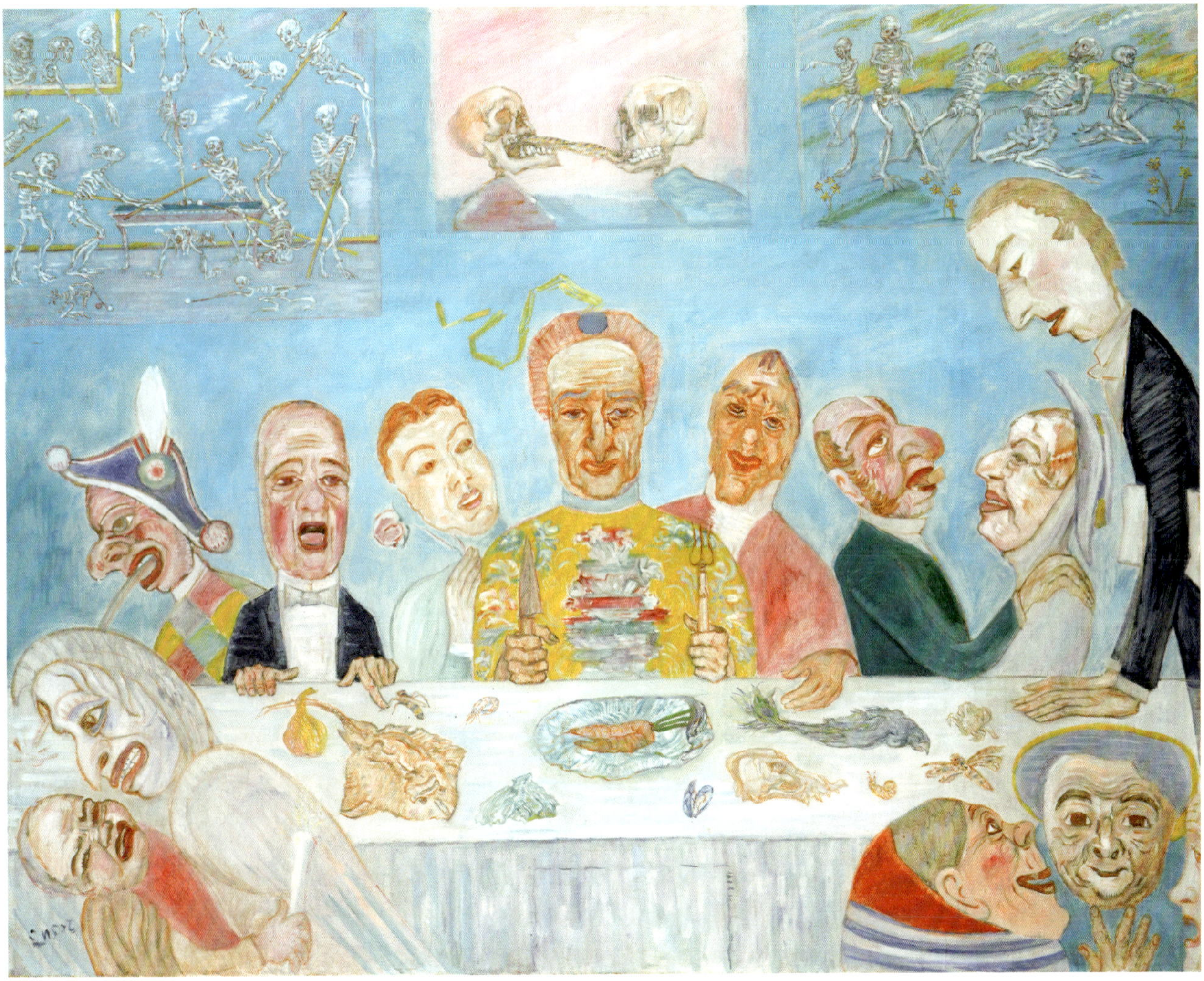

95. *The Banquet of the Starved.* 1915
Oil on canvas, 45 1/2 × 57 1/4" (115.6 × 145.4 cm)

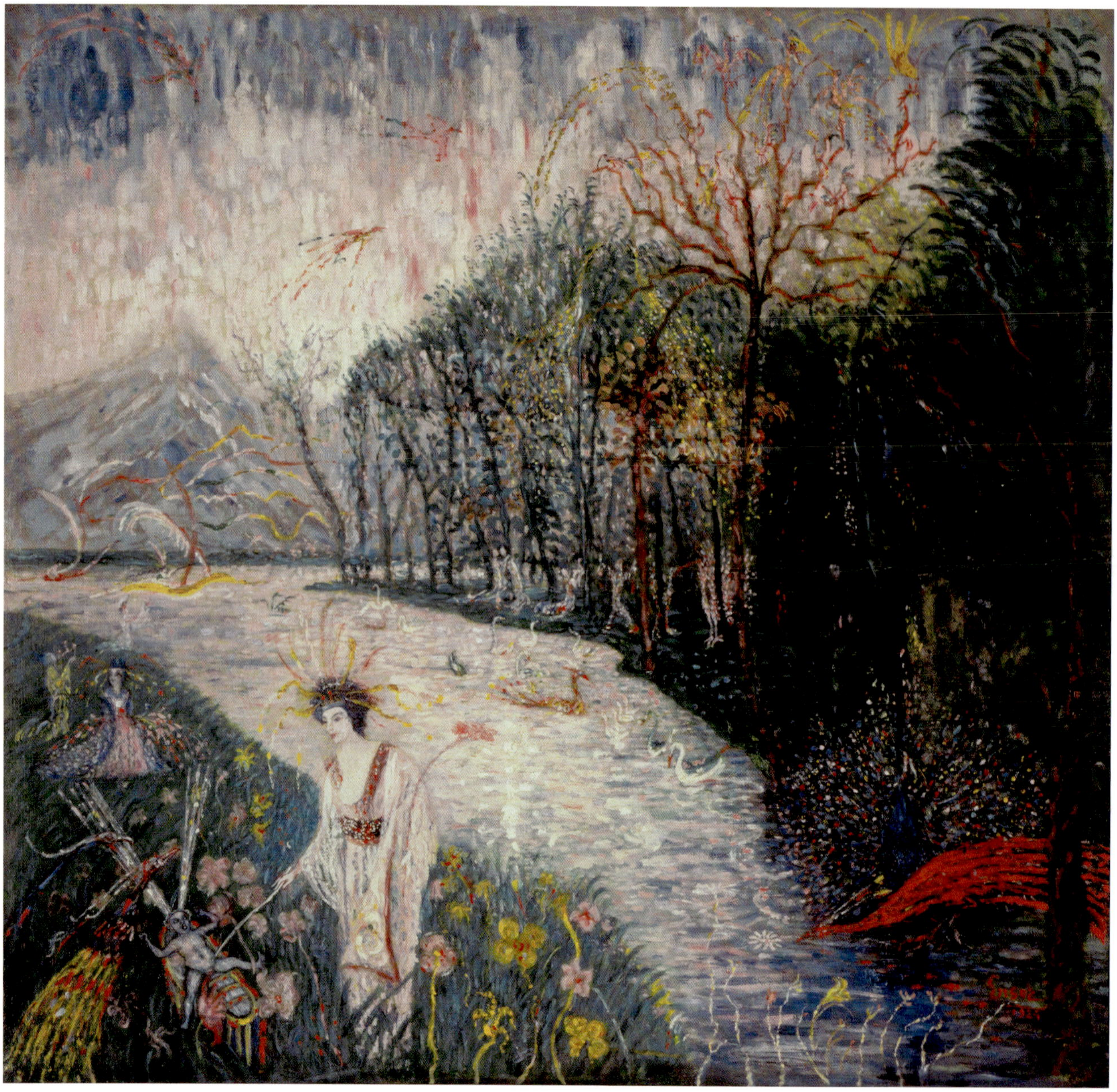

96. *Moses and the Birds* (*The Finding of Moses*). 1924
Oil on canvas, 47 × 50 ½" (119.4 × 128.3 cm)

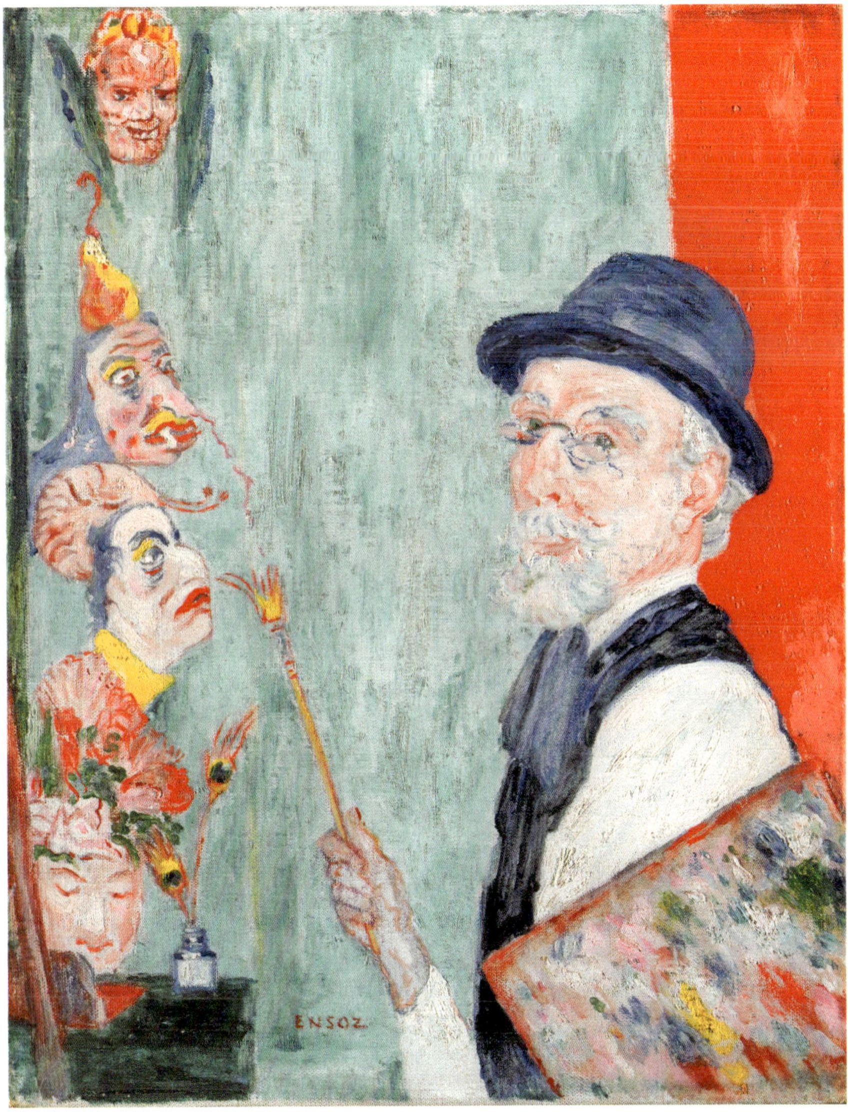

97. *Self-Portrait with Masks.* 1937
Oil on canvas, 12 ¼ × 9 ⅝" (31.1 × 24.4 cm)

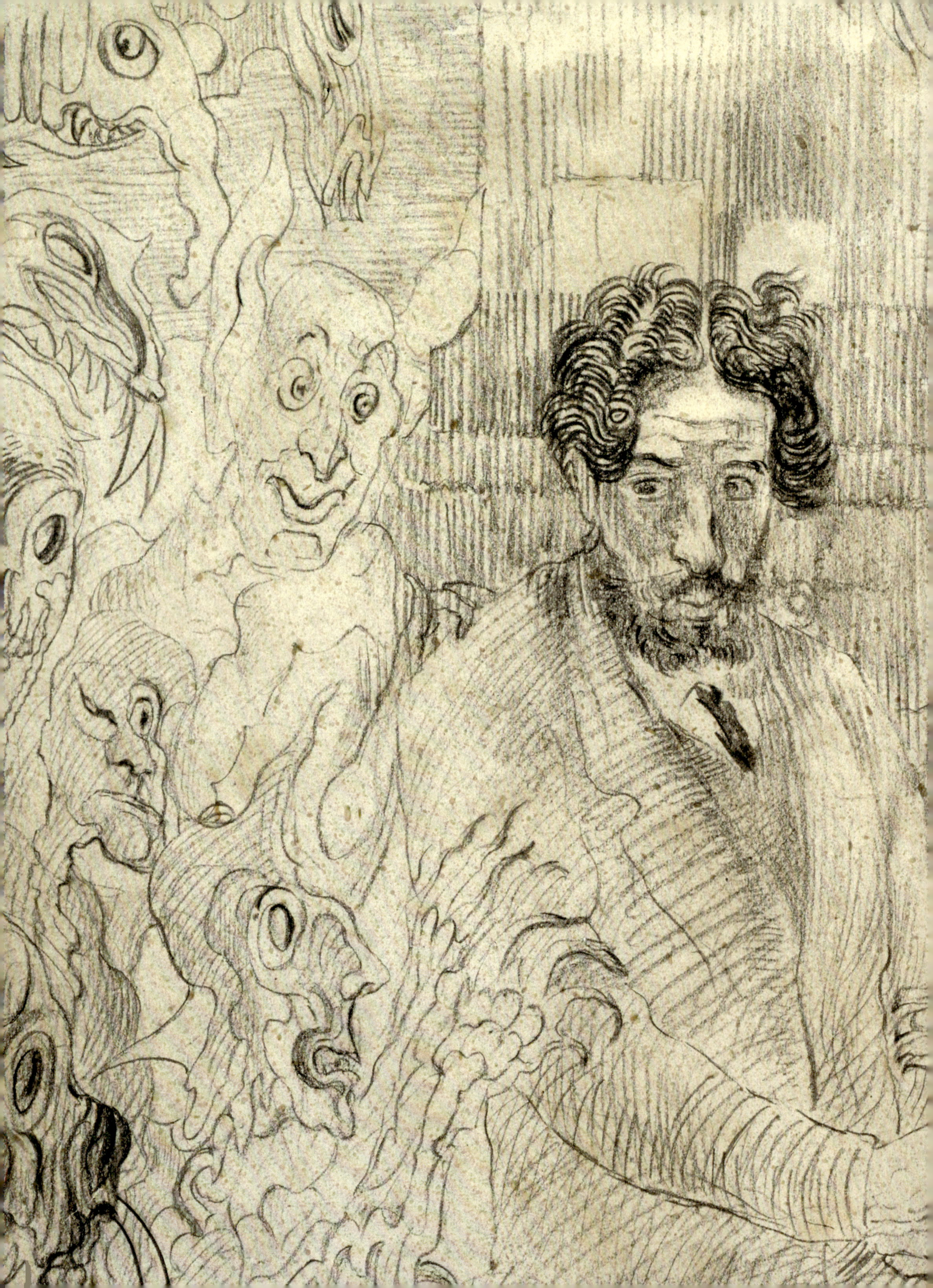

CATALOGUE OF THE EXHIBITION

Compiled by Blair Hartzell

The English titles provided, listed here in alphabetical order, represent how the works are best known in the language. An additional title, especially if in common use, is noted in parentheses.

Whenever possible, the French titles provided revert to Ensor's original usage in primary documents. In instances when a French title could not be confirmed in Ensor's letters or his earliest exhibition catalogues, the title most widely accepted by scholars is included.

Medium, dimensions, and dates of execution have been provided by the owners or custodians of the works, in some cases augmented by additional research carried out by curatorial staff at The Museum of Modern Art. Measurements are given in inches followed by centimeters; height precedes width. Works included in the exhibition at The Museum of Modern Art but not illustrated in the plate section of the present volume are marked by an asterisk (*).

Adam and Eve Expelled from Paradise (*Adam et Ève chassés du paradis terrestre*) 1887. Oil on canvas, 80 11/16 × 96 7/16" (205 × 245 cm). Koninklijk Museum voor Schone Kunsten, Antwerp
Plate 38

Afternoon in Ostend (*L'Après-dînée à Ostende*). 1881. Oil on canvas, 43 9/16 × 52 15/16" (110.7 × 134.5 cm). Koninklijk Museum voor Schone Kunsten, Antwerp
Plate 9

The Assassination (*L'Assassinat*). 1890. Oil on canvas, 23 13/16 × 30 3/8" (60.5 × 77.2 cm). Columbus Museum of Art, Ohio: Gift of Howard D. and Babette L. Sirak, the Donors to the Campaign for Enduring Excellence, and the Derby Fund
Plate 65

The Astonishment of the Mask Wouse (*Étonnement du masque Wouse*). 1889. Oil on canvas, 42 5/16 × 51 9/16" (109 × 131 cm). Koninklijk Museum voor Schone Kunsten, Antwerp
Plate 56

At the Conservatory (*Au conservatoire*). 1902. Oil on canvas, mounted on panel, 22 1/16 × 28 1/8" (56 × 71.5 cm). Musée d'Orsay, Paris
Plate 94

The Bad Doctors (*Les Mauvais Médecins*). 1892. Oil on panel, 19 11/16 × 24" (50 × 61 cm). Université libre de Bruxelles
Plate 79

* *The Bad Doctors* (*Les Mauvais Médecins*). Only state. 1895. Etching heightened with chalk and watercolor on simili-Japan paper, plate: 7 × 10" (17.2 × 24.6 cm), sheet: 13 11/16 × 17 5/16" (34.8 × 43.9 cm). Collection Thomas and Lore Firman

The Banquet of the Starved (*Le Repas des maigres*). 1915. Oil on canvas, 45 1/2 × 57 1/4" (115.6 × 145.4 cm). The Metropolitan Museum of Art, New York. Bequest of Miss Adelaide Milton de Groot, 1967
Plate 95

The Baths at Ostend (*Les Bains à Ostende*). 1890. Black crayon, colored pencil, and oil on panel, 14 3/4 × 17 15/16" (37.5 × 45.5 cm). Fondation Challenges, The Netherlands
Plate 64

* *Battle of the Golden Spurs* (*Bataille des éperons d'or*). Only state. 1895. Etching with hand-coloring on simili-Japan paper, plate: 9 1/2 × 11" (17.3 × 23.7 cm), sheet: 11 5/16 × 14 11/16" (28.8 × 37.3 cm). Collection Thomas and Lore Firman

Belgium in the Nineteenth Century (*La Belgique au XIXe siècle*). 1889. Pencil and colored pencil on paper, mounted on panel, 8 9/16 × 11 11/16" (16.3 × 21.4 cm). Bibliothèque royale de Belgique, Brussels. Cabinet des Estampes
Plate 52

* *Boats Aground* (*The Stranded Boats*) (*Les Barques échouées*). State I. 1888. Etching on Chine, plate: 7 × 9 3/8" (17.6 × 23.7 cm), sheet: 9 1/2 × 11 5/8" (24.2 × 29.6 cm). Collection Thomas and Lore Firman

Boulevard Van Iseghem in the Rain (*Boulevard Van Iseghem sous la pluie*). 1880. Oil on cardboard, 9 1/4 × 6 1/2" (23.5 × 16.5 cm). Private collection
Plate 5

Brussels Town Hall (*Hôtel de Ville de Bruxelles*). 1885. Oil on canvas, 39 3/8 × 31 7/8" (100 × 81 cm). Musée d'Art moderne et d'Art contemporain de la Ville de Liège
Plate 23

The Call of the Siren (*L'Appel de la Sirène*). 1891 or 1893. Oil on panel, 14 15/16 × 18 1/8" (38 × 46 cm). Private collection, Belgium
Plate 80

Calvary (*Calvaire*). 1886. Pencil, crayon, and oil on paper, 6 3/4 × 8 3/4" (17.2 × 22.2 cm) Private collection, Belgium
Plate 29

The Cathedral (*La Cathédrale*). Plate I, state III. 1886. Etching on Japan paper, plate: 9 5/16 × 7" (23.6 × 17.7 cm), sheet: 11 1/4 × 8 5/8" (28.5 × 22.7 cm). Collection Thomas and Lore Firman
Plate 31

Children Dressing (*Les Enfants à la toilette*). 1886. Oil on canvas, 53 1/8 × 43 1/4" (136 × 110 cm). Museum voor Schone Kunsten, Ghent. On long-term loan from the Flemish Community
Plate 35

Child with Doll (*Enfant à la poupée*). 1884/1886–89(?). Oil on canvas, 58 11/16 × 35 13/16" (149 × 91 cm). Wallraf-Richartz-Museum & Fondation Corboud, Cologne
Plate 19

Chinoiseries with Fans (*Chinoiseries aux éventails*). 1880. Oil on canvas, 31 1/2 × 39 3/8" (80 × 100 cm). Musées royaux des Beaux-Arts de Belgique, Brussels
Plate 2

Christ Calming the Storm (*Le Christ calmant la tempête*). 1891. Oil on canvas, 31 1/2 × 39 3/8" (80 × 100 cm). Kunstmuseum aan zee, Ostend
Plate 68

* *Christ Mocked* (*Le Christ insulté*). State II. 1886. Etching on simili-Japan paper, plate: 9 7/16 × 6 5/16" (23 × 15.5 cm), sheet: 12 9/16 × 8 7/8" (31.9 × 22.5 cm). Collection Thomas and Lore Firman

Christ's Entry into Jerusalem (recto). *Christ Bearing the Cross* (verso) (*Étude pour "L'Entrée du Christ à Jérusalem"*). 1885. Graphite and Conté crayon on wove paper, 8 7/8 × 6 1/2" (22.5 × 16.5 cm). The J. Paul Getty Museum, Los Angeles
Plate 25

Christ Shown to the People and the Entry of Christ into Jerusalem (*Le Christ montré au peuple et l'entrée du Christ à Jérusalem*). 1887. Black chalk on paper, 6 13/16 × 8 11/16" (17.3 × 22.1 cm). Museum voor Schone Kunsten, Ghent
Plate 24

Christ Watched Over by Angels (*Le Christ pleuré par les anges*). 1886. Black chalk on panel, 6 1/2 × 8 7/16" (16.5 × 21.4 cm). Private collection
Plate 28

A Colorist (_Une Coloriste_). 1880. Oil on canvas, 40 3/16 × 32 5/16" (102 × 82 cm). Musées royaux des Beaux-Arts de Belgique, Brussels
Plate 6

The Cuirassiers at Waterloo (_Bataille à Waterloo_). 1891. India ink, crayon, colored pencil, and pastel on three sheets of paper, mounted on board, 8 7/8 × 24 5/8" (22.5 × 62.5 cm). Koninklijk Museum voor Schone Kunsten, Antwerp
Plate 77

The Dangerous Cooks (_Les Cuisiniers dangereux_). 1896. Pencil, gouache, and oil on board, 7 7/8 × 9 13/16" (20 × 25 cm). Private collection
Plate 88

*_The Deadly Sins Dominated by Death_ (_Les Péchés capitaux dominés par la mort_). Only state. 1904. Etching with hand-coloring on Japan paper, plate: 3 1/2 × 5 1/4" (8.4 × 13.4 cm), sheet: 8 7/8 × 11 1/8" (22.5 × 28.3 cm). Collection Thomas and Lore Firman

Death Pursuing the Human Flock (_Triumph of Death_) (_La Triomphe de la Mort_). 1887. Black crayon, ink, and colored pencil on paper, mounted on board, 8 7/8 × 6 11/16" (22.5 × 17 cm). Koninklijk Museum voor Schone Kunsten, Antwerp
Plate 45

*_Death Pursuing the Human Flock_ (_La Mort poursuivant le troupeau des humains_). State II. 1896. Etching on laid paper, plate: 9 1/2 × 7 1/8" (23.5 × 17.5 cm), sheet: 19 × 13 1/8" (48.3 × 33.3 cm). Collection Thomas and Lore Firman

Demons Tormenting Me (_Démons me turlupinant_). 1888. Graphite and black chalk on wove paper, 8 9/16 × 11 3/4" (21.8 × 29.8 cm). The Art Institute of Chicago. Ada Turnbull Hertle Fund
Plate 49

The Despair of Pierrot (_Pierrot jaloux_). 1892. Oil on canvas, 56 7/8 × 76 9/16" (144.5 × 194.5 cm). Courtesy Christie's, Inc.
Plate 85

The Devils Dzitts and Hihahox, Led by Crazon, Riding a Wild Cat, Leading Christ into Hell (_Les Diables Dzitts et Hihahox commandés par Crazon, montant un chat furieux, conduisent le Christ aux enfers_). 1886. Pencil, Conté crayon, black chalk, brown India ink, pen, and white gouache on paper, mounted on panel, 6 13/16 × 8 15/16" (17.3 × 22.7 cm). Musées royaux des Beaux-Arts de Belgique, Brussels
Plate 30

*_The Devils Dzitts and Hihahox, Led by Crazon, Riding a Wild Cat, Leading Christ into Hell_ (_Les Diables Dzitts et Hihahox commandés par Crazon, montant un chat furieux, conduisent le Christ aux Enfers_). Only state, proof no. 6. 1895. Etching on Japan paper, plate: 5 1/2 × 7" (13.3 × 17.2 cm), sheet: 6 11/16 × 7 7/8" (17 × 20 cm). Collection Thomas and Lore Firman

*_Devils Thrashing Angels and Archangels_ (_Diables rossant anges et archanges_). Only state. 1888. Etching on simili-Japan paper, plate 9 7/16 × 11 9/16" (25 × 29.3 cm), sheet: 14 3/8 × 18 13/16" (36.5 × 47.8 cm). Collection Thomas and Lore Firman

Doctrinaire Nourishment (_Alimentation doctrinaire_). Plate I, state II. 1889. Etching heightened with watercolor and gouache on Japan paper, plate: 7 1/16 × 9 3/8" (18 × 23.8 cm), sheet: 9 1/4 × 11 5/8" (23.5 × 29.53 cm). Museum voor Schone Kunsten, Ghent
Plate 51

The Domain of Arnheim (_Le Domaine d'Arnheim_). 1890. Oil on canvas, 31 1/2 × 39 3/8" (80 × 100 cm). Private collection. On long-term loan to Musées royaux des Beaux-Arts de Belgique, Brussels
Plate 67

The Drunkards (_Les Pochards_). 1883. Oil on canvas, 45 1/4 × 64 15/16" (115 × 165 cm). Dexia Collection, Brussels
Plate 14

*_The Elephant's Joke_ (_La Blague d'éléphant_). Only state. 1888. Etching with hand-coloring on Japan paper, plate: 7 1/16 × 9 3/8" (18 × 23.7 cm), sheet: 14 1/8 × 18 7/8" (35.8 × 47.9 cm). Collection Thomas and Lore Firman

Ensor and Leman Discussing Painting (_Ensor et Leman discutant peinture_). 1890. Oil on panel, 4 3/4 × 6 5/16" (12 × 16 cm). Private collection
Plate 71

The Entry of Christ into Brussels (_L'Entrée du Christ à Bruxelles_). State III. 1898. Etching heightened with watercolor on Arches laid paper, plate: 9 3/4 × 14" (24.8 × 35.5 cm), sheet: 14 3/16 × 18 11/16" (36 × 47.5 cm). Collection Thomas and Lore Firman
Plate 90

The Fight of the Angels and the Demons (_Le Combat des anges et démons_). 1888. Colored crayon on paper, 10 7/16 × 17 5/16" (26.5 × 44 cm). Staatsgalerie Stuttgart. Graphische Sammlung
Plate 47

Fight of the Down-and-Outs (_Le Combat des pouilleux_). 1887. Black pencil on paper, mounted on board, 13 9/16 × 8 7/8" (34.5 × 22.5 cm). Fondation Challenges, The Netherlands
Plate 46

*_The Fight of the Down-and-Outs Désir and Rissolé_ (_Le Combat des pouilleux Désir et Rissolé_). State II. 1888. Etching heightened with gouache and colored pencil on Japan paper, plate: 9 1/4 × 11 7/16" (22.9 × 28 cm), sheet: 13 3/8 × 15" (33.9 × 38.1 cm). Collection Thomas and Lore Firman

Fireworks (_Feu d'artifice_). 1887. Oil and encaustic on canvas, 40 1/4 × 44 1/4" (102.2 × 112.4 cm). Albright-Knox Art Gallery, Buffalo. George B. and Jenny R. Mathews Fund, 1970
Plate 36

The Flea (_La Puce_). 1880–83/1888. Black crayon on paper, mounted on board, 8 7/8 × 6 5/8" (22.6 × 16.8 cm). Private collection
Plate 34

The Frightful Musicians (_Les Musiciens terribles_). 1891. Oil on panel, 6 5/16 × 8 1/4" (16 × 21 cm). Courtesy Patrick Derom Gallery, Brussels
Plate 74

*_The Gendarmes_ (_Les Gendarmes_). State II. 1888. Etching with hand-coloring on Van Gelder paper, plate: 7 × 9 3/8" (17.9 × 23.8 cm), sheet: 13 7/16 × 19 11/16" (34.1 × 50 cm). Collection Thomas and Lore Firman

The Grotesque Singers (_Les Chanteurs grotesques_). 1891. Oil on panel, 6 5/16 × 8 11/16" (16 × 22 cm). Private collection
Plate 73

The Haunted Fireplace (*La Cheminée hantée*). 1888. Crayon and colored pencil on panel, 9 7/16 × 6 5/16" (24 × 16 cm). Private collection
Plate 40

Hippogriff (*Hippogriffe*). 1880–83 / 1886–88
Black chalk on two sheets of paper, mounted on board, 8 7/8 × 6 11/16" (22.5 × 17 cm). Museum voor Schone Kunsten, Ghent
Plate 32

**Hop-Frog's Revenge* (*La Vengeance de Hop-Frog*). State II. 1898. Etching with hand-coloring on Japan paper, plate: 14 1/8 × 9 7/8" (35 × 24.2 cm), sheet: 20 13/16 × 15 13/16" (52.8 × 40.1 cm). Collection Thomas and Lore Firman

**House on the Boulevard Anspach* (*Maison du Boulevard Anspach*). State II. 1888. Drypoint with hand-coloring on simili-Japan paper, plate: 5 1/2 × 3 5/8" (13.4 × 8.5 cm), sheet: 9 13/16 × 6 5/16" (25 × 16 cm). Collection Thomas and Lore Firman

Icon (*Portrait of Eugène Demolder*) (*Icône*). 1893. Oil, pencil, and gouache on panel, 14 3/16 × 8 1/4" (36 × 21 cm). Groeningemuseum, Bruges
Plate 86

The Intrigue (*L'Intrigue*). 1890. Oil on canvas, 35 7/16 × 59 1/16" (90 × 150 cm). Koninklijk Museum voor Schone Kunsten, Antwerp
Plate 66

**Iston, Pouffmatus, Cracozie, and Transmouff, Famous Persian Physicians, Examining the Stool of King Darius after the Battle of Arbela* (*Persian Physicians*) (*Iston, Pouffamatus, Cracozie et Transmouffe, célèbres médecins persans examinant les selles du roi Darius après la bataille d'Arbelles* [*Médecins persans*]). State III. 1886. Etching on simili-Japan paper, plate: 9 3/4 × 7 1/2" (23.7 × 17.8 cm), sheet: 12 3/8 × 8 3/4" (31.5 × 22.2 cm). Collection Thomas and Lore Firman

The Lady in Distress (*La Dame en détresse*). 1882. Oil on canvas, 39 9/16 × 31 1/2" (100.5 × 80 cm). Musée d'Orsay, Paris
Plate 10

The Lamp-Lighter (*Le Lampiste*). 1880. Oil on canvas, 59 7/16 × 35 13/16" (151.5 × 91 cm). Musées royaux des Beaux-Arts de Belgique, Brussels
Plate 3

The Lively and Radiant: The Entry of Christ into Jerusalem (*La Vive et rayonnante: L'Entrée à Jérusalem*). 1885. Black and brown crayon, with collaged paper, mounted on canvas, 6' 9 1/8" × 59 3/16" (206 × 150.3 cm). Museum voor Schone Kunsten, Ghent
Plate 27

**Lust* (*La Luxure*). State II. 1888. Etching heightened with gouache on Japan paper, plate: 3 7/8 × 5 1/2" (9.2 × 13.1 cm), sheet: 9 5/16 × 11 9/16" (23.7 × 29.3). Collection Thomas and Lore Firman

The Man of Sorrows (*L'Homme de douleurs*). 1891. Oil on panel, 8 5/8 × 6 5/16" (21.9 × 16 cm). Koninklijk Museum voor Schone Kunsten, Antwerp.
Plate 76

Masks Mocking Death (*Masks Confronting Death*) (*Masques raillant la mort*). 1888. Oil on canvas, 32 × 39 1/2" (81.3 × 100.3 cm). The Museum of Modern Art, New York. Mrs. Simon Guggenheim Fund
Plate 53

The Melancholy Fishwives (*Les Poissardes mélancoliques*). 1892. Oil on canvas, 39 3/8 × 31 1/2" (100 × 80 cm). Fondation Socindec. Courtesy Fondation Pierre Gianadda, Martigny
Plate 84

Monsieur and Madame Rousseau Speaking with Sophie Yoteko (*Monsieur et Madame Rousseau parlant avec Sophie Yoteko*). 1892. Oil on panel, 4 3/4 × 6 5/16" (12 × 16 cm). Private collection, Belgium
Plate 75

Moses and the Birds (*The Finding of Moses*) (*Moïse et les oiseaux*). 1924. Oil on canvas, 47 × 50 1/2" (119.4 × 128.3 cm). University of California, Berkeley Art Museum and Pacific Film Archive. Gift of Joachim Jean Aberbach
Plate 96

My Aunt Asleep Dreaming of Monsters (*Ma Tante endormie rêvant de monstres*). c. 1888. Pencil, Conté crayon, and colored pencil on paper, 8 5/8 × 11 13/16" (21.9 × 30 cm). Musées royaux des Beaux-Arts de Belgique, Brussels. Alla Goldschmidt-Safieva Bequest
Plate 59

**My Father in Death* (*Mon Père mort*). 1887. Pencil and gouache on paper, 6 3/4 × 8 15/16" (17.1 × 22.7 cm). Collection Thomas and Lore Firman

My Portrait (*Mon Portrait*). 1884. Charcoal and white chalk on paper, 29 3/4 × 22 3/4" (75.5 × 57.8 cm). Musées royaux des Beaux-Arts de Belgique, Brussels
Plate 18

My Portrait in 1960 (*Mon Portrait en 1960*). State II. 1888. Etching on wove paper, plate: 2 3/4 × 4 11/16" (7.0 × 11.9 cm), sheet: 6 5/16 × 9 7/8" (16 × 25.1 cm). The Art Institute of Chicago. Charles Deering Collection Fund
Plate 39

My Skeletonized Portrait (*Mon Portrait squelettisé*). State I, unique impression. 1889. Etching on wove paper, plate: 4 9/16 × 2 15/16" (11.6 × 7.5 cm), sheet: 11 3/8 × 9 3/8" (28.8 × 23.8 cm). Kunstmuseum aan zee, Ostend
Plate 57

My Skeletonized Portrait (*Mon Portrait squelettisé*). State II. 1889. Etching and drypoint on wove paper, plate: 4 9/16 × 2 15/16" (11.6 × 7.5 cm), sheet: 11 3/8 × 9 3/8" (28.8 × 23.8 cm). Kunstmuseum aan zee, Ostend
Plate 58

The Mystic Death of a Theologian (*Elated Monks Claim the Body of the Theologian Sus Ovis, in Spite of the Resisting Bishop Friton or Friston*) (*La Mort mystique d'un théologien* [*Moines exaltés réclamant le corps du Théologien Sus-Ovis malgré l'opposition de l'évêque Friton ou Friston*]). 1880 / 1885–86(?). Pencil, charcoal, and black crayon on paper, mounted on canvas, 38 3/16 × 32 11/16" (97 × 83 cm). Koninklijk Museum voor Schone Kunsten, Antwerp
Plate 22

Nude with Curtain (*Le Nu au rideau*). 1880–85 / 1886–88. Pencil and black chalk on paper, mounted on board, 8 7/8 × 6 7/16" (22.5 × 16.4 cm). museum kunst palast, Dusseldorf. Graphische Sammlung
Plate 33

The Oyster Eater (*La Mangeuse d'huîtres*). 1882. Oil on canvas, 81 1/2 × 59 1/16" (207 × 150 cm). Koninklijk Museum voor Schone Kunsten, Antwerp
Plate 13

Peculiar Insects (*Insectes singuliers*). State III, proof no. 8. 1888. Drypoint on laid Japan paper, plate: 4 1/2 × 6 1/8" (11.4 × 15.4 cm), sheet: 5 1/2 × 7 3/8" (13.8 × 18.7 cm). Collection Thomas and Lore Firman
Plate 41

*_Perplexed Masks_ (_Masks intrigués_). Only state. 1904. Etching on laid paper, plate: 3 ¼ × 4 ¾" (7.4 × 11.4 cm), sheet: 8 ⅞ × 11 13/16" (22.5 × 30 cm). Collection Thomas and Lore Firman

Pierrot and Skeleton in a Yellow Robe (_Pierrot et squelette en jaune_). 1893. Oil on panel, 14 15/16 × 18 ⅞" (38 × 48 cm). Museum voor Schone Kunsten, Ghent. On long-term loan from the Flemish Community
Plate 87

The Pisser (_Le Pisseur_). Only state. 1887. Etching on simili-Japan paper, plate: 5 11/16 × 4 ⅛" (14.5 × 10.5 cm), sheet: 11 ¾ × 9 ½" (29.8 × 24.0 cm). Collection Thomas and Lore Firman
Plate 42

Plague Above, Plague Below, Plague All Around! (_Peste dessous, peste dessus, peste partout!_). 1888. Conté crayon and colored pencil on paper, 8 ⅞ × 11 13/16" (22.5 × 30 cm). Koninklijk Museum voor Schone Kunsten, Antwerp
Plate 44

*_Plague Above, Plague Below, Plague All Around!_ (_Peste dessous, peste dessus, peste partout!_). Only state. 1904. Etching on Japan paper, plate: 3 ½ × 5 ¼" (84 × 13.4 cm), sheet: 10 5/16 × 15 7/16" (26.2 × 39.2 cm). Collection Thomas and Lore Firman

*_The Pool of the Poplars_ (_La Mare aux peupliers_). Only state. 1889. Etching on Japan paper, plate: 6 5/16 × 9 ⅜" (15.5 × 23.3 cm), sheet: 7 × 10 ⅛" (17.8 × 25.7 cm). Collection Thomas and Lore Firman

*_Portrait of Ernest Rousseau_ (_Portrait d'Ernest Rousseau_). State III. 1887. Drypoint on Japan paper, plate: 9 7/16 × 7 ¼" (22.8 × 16.8 cm), sheet: 12 ⅝ × 8 13/16" (32 × 22.4 cm). Collection Thomas and Lore Firman

Portrait of the Artist's Father (_Portrait du père de l'artiste_). 1881. Oil on canvas, 39 ⅜ × 31 ½" (100 × 80 cm). Musées royaux des Beaux-Arts de Belgique, Brussels
Plate 7

Portrait of the Artist's Sister, Marie (_La Soeur de l'artiste_). 1881. Charcoal on wove paper, mounted on board, on stretcher, 29 ¾ × 23 7/16" (75.5 × 59.5 cm). The Art Institute of Chicago. Margaret Day Blake Collection
Plate 8

Portrait of Willy Finch (_Portrait du peintre W. Finch_). 1882. Oil on canvas, 43 5/16 × 37 ⅜" (110 × 95 cm). Kunstmuseum aan zee, Ostend
Plate 11

The Rainbow (_After the Storm_) (_L'Arc en ciel_). 1880. Oil on canvas, 20 11/16 × 24 ⅝" (52.5 × 62.5 cm). Kunstmuseum aan zee, Ostend
Plate 1

*_The Red Apples_ (_Les Pommes rouges_). 1883. Oil on canvas, 23 ⅝ × 18 ⅞" (60 × 75 cm). Group Verbaet, Belgium

The Rising: Christ Shown to the People (_La Crue: Jésus montré au peuple_). 1885. Black crayon and watercolor on paper, mounted on canvas, 61 × 40 3/16" (155 × 102 cm). Museum voor Schone Kunsten, Ghent. On long-term loan from the Flemish Community
Plate 26

Rooftops of Ostend (_Grand View of Ostend_) (_La Grande Vue d'Ostende_). 1884. Oil on canvas, 58 11/16 × 81 ⅛" (149 × 206 cm). Koninklijk Museum voor Schone Kunsten, Antwerp
Plate 20

Rue de Flandre in the Snow (_La Rue de Flandre, neige_). 1880. Oil on canvas, 18 ⅛ × 10 1/16" (46 × 25.5 cm). Fondation Socindec
Plate 4

The Scandalized Masks (_Les Masques scandalisés_). 1883. Oil on canvas, 53 ⅛ × 44 ⅛" (135 × 112 cm). Musées royaux des Beaux-Arts de Belgique, Brussels
Plate 15

Self-Portrait (_Autoportrait_). c. 1888. Pencil on panel, 6 ⅜ × 4 ¼" (16.3 × 10.8 cm). Gallery Ronny Van de Velde, Antwerp
Plate 40

Self-Portrait at the Easel (_Portrait de James Ensor_). 1890. Oil on canvas, 23 7/16 × 16 ⅛" (59.5 × 41 cm). Koninklijk Museum voor Schone Kunsten, Antwerp
Plate 69

Self-Portrait with a Flowered Hat (_Mon Portrait déguisé_). 1883/1888. Oil on canvas, 30 ⅛ × 24 3/16" (76.5 × 61.5 cm). Kunstmuseum aan zee, Ostend
Plate 17

Self-Portrait with Masks (_Ensor aux masques_). 1899. Oil on canvas, 47 ¼ × 31 ½" (120 × 80 cm). Menard Art Museum, Komaki City
Plate 91

Self-Portrait with Masks (_Mon Portrait aux masques_). 1937. Oil on canvas, 12 ¼ × 9 ⅝" (31.1 × 24.4 cm). Philadelphia Museum of Art. The Louis E. Stern Collection, 1963
Plate 97

Series of Small Masks (_Série de masques réunis en théâtre d'expression_). c. 1890(?). Conté crayon on paper, 8 13/16 × 6 ⅞" (22.4 × 17.5 cm). Koninklijk Museum voor Schone Kunsten, Antwerp
Plate 60

The Skate (_La Raie_). 1892. Oil on canvas, 31 ½ × 39 ⅜" (80 × 100 cm). Musées royaux des Beaux-Arts de Belgique, Brussels
Plate 82

Skeleton Drawing Fine Pranks (_Squelette dessinant fines puérilitiés_). c. 1889. Black chalk, colored pencil, and gold paint on paper, 8 ½ × 11 ⅝" (21.6 × 29.6 cm). Musée d'Orsay, Paris. On deposit with the Département des Arts graphiques du Musée du Louvre. Gift of the artist, 1932
Plate 61

Skeleton in the Mirror (_Le Miroir au squelette_). 1890. Black crayon on paper, 11 13/16 × 8 11/16" (30 × 22 cm). Private collection
Plate 62

Skeleton Looking at Chinoiseries (_Squelette regardant chinoiseries_). 1885/1888. Oil on canvas, 39 ⅜ × 23 ⅝" (100 × 60 cm). Museum voor Schone Kunsten, Ghent. On long-term loan from the Koning Boudewijnstichting, Brussels
Plate 21

Skeleton Musicians (_Squelettes musiciens_). 1888. Black pencil and brown chalk on paper, mounted on panel, 8 ¼ × 6 5/16" (21 × 16 cm). Private collection
Plate 50

The Skeleton Painter (_Squelette peintre_). 1895 or 1896(?). Oil on panel, 14 13/16 × 18 ⅛" (37.7 × 46 cm). Koninklijk Museum voor Schone Kunsten, Antwerp
Plate 89

Skeletons Fighting Over a Pickled Herring (_Squelettes se disputant un hareng saur_). 1891. Oil on panel, 6 5/16 × 8 7/16" (16 × 21.5 cm). Musées royaux des Beaux-Arts de Belgique, Brussels
Plate 72

Skeletons in the Studio (*Squelettes à l'atelier*). 1900. Oil on canvas, 43 11/16 × 31 5/16" (111 × 79.5 cm). National Gallery of Canada, Ottawa. Purchased 1981
Plate 92

Skeletons Trying to Warm Themselves (*Squelettes voulant se chauffer*). 1889. Oil on canvas, 29 1/2 × 23 5/8" (71.8 × 60 cm). Kimbell Art Museum, Fort Worth
Plate 54

* *Skeletons Trying to Warm Themselves* (*Squelettes voulant se chauffer*). State I. 1895. Etching heightened with ink, colored chalk, and wash on wove paper, used as proof envelope, sheet: 5 11/16 × 4 1/2" (14.5 × 11.4 cm). Collection Thomas and Lore Firman

Sketchbook (*Carnet Rousseau*). 1883–96. India ink, pen, Conté crayon, graphite, and black chalk on paper, 11 5/16 × 16 3/16" (28.7 × 41.1 cm). fifty-three bound drawings, seven additional loose drawings, and one visiting card. Musées royaux des Beaux-Arts de Belgique, Brussels
Plate 16

* *The Small Boats* (*Les Petites Barques*). Only state, proof no. 4. 1894. Etching on Chine, plate: 3 3/8 × 5 1/2" (8.3 × 11.6 cm), sheet: 5 1/2 × 7 5/16" (13.9 × 18.5 cm). Collection Thomas and Lore Firman

* *The Stars in the Cemetery (Les Étoiles au cimetière)*. Only state. 1888. Etching with drypoint on simili-Japan paper, plate: 5 1/2 × 7 1/16" (14 x 17.9 cm), sheet: 9 7/16 × 12 1/16" (23.9 × 30.7 cm). Collection Thomas and Lore Firman

Still Life with Vegetables (*Nature morte*). 1882. Oil on canvas, 31 1/2 × 39 3/8" (80 × 100 cm). Musée d'Art moderne et d'Art contemporain de la Ville de Liège
Plate 12

The Strange Masks (*Les Masques singuliers*). 1892. Oil on canvas, 39 3/8 × 31 1/2" (100 × 80 cm). Musées royaux des Beaux-Arts de Belgique, Brussels
Plate 83

The Strike (*The Slaughter of the Ostend Fishermen [August 1887]*) (*Massacre des pêcheurs ostendais [août 1887]*). 1888. Pencil and colored pencil on paper, mounted on board, 13 3/8 × 26 9/16" (34 × 67.5 cm). Koninklijk Museum voor Schone Kunsten, Antwerp
Plate 43

Surly Countenance (*Figure revêche*). 1890. Oil on panel, 9 5/8 × 7 1/2" (24.5 × 19 cm). Private collection
Plate 70

* *The Thunderstorm* (*L'Orage*). State II. 1889. Etching on simili-Japan paper, plate: 3 1/8 × 4 3/4" (7.9 × 12.1 cm), sheet: 5 1/4 × 7 13/16" (13.3 × 19.8 cm). Collection Thomas and Lore Firman

The Tower of Lissewege (*La Tour de Lisseweghe*). 1890. Oil on canvas, 23 1/4 × 29 1/8" (59 × 74 cm). Fondation Socindec
Plate 55

Tribulations of Saint Anthony (*Terribles Tribulations de Saint-Antoine*). 1887. Oil on canvas, 46 3/8 × 66" (117.8 × 167.6 cm). The Museum of Modern Art, New York. Purchase
Plate 37

View of Mariakerke (*La Vue de Mariakerke*). 1901. Oil on canvas, 21 1/4 × 26 3/8" (54 × 67 cm). Kunstmuseum aan zee, Ostend
Plate 93

* *Village Fair at the Windmill* (*La Kermesse au moulin*). Only state. 1889. Etching on satin, plate: 5 3/8 × 7" (13.5 × 17.4 cm), sheet: 6 15/16 × 8 3/8" (17.6 × 21.3 cm). Collection Thomas and Lore Firman

The Virgin of Consolation (*La Vierge consolatrice*). 1892. Oil on panel, 15 3/4 × 14 15/16" (40 × 38 cm). Private collection
Plate 81

White and Red Clowns Evolving (*Clowns blanc et rouge évoluant*). 1890. Pencil, ink, and gouache on paper, 9 1/2 × 11 11/16" (24.1 × 29.7 cm). Musées royaux des Beaux-Arts de Belgique, Brussels. Alla Goldschmidt-Safieva Bequest
Plate 63

The Wise Judges (*Les Bons Juges*). 1891. Oil on panel, 14 15/16 × 18 1/8" (38 × 46 cm). Private collection
Plate 78

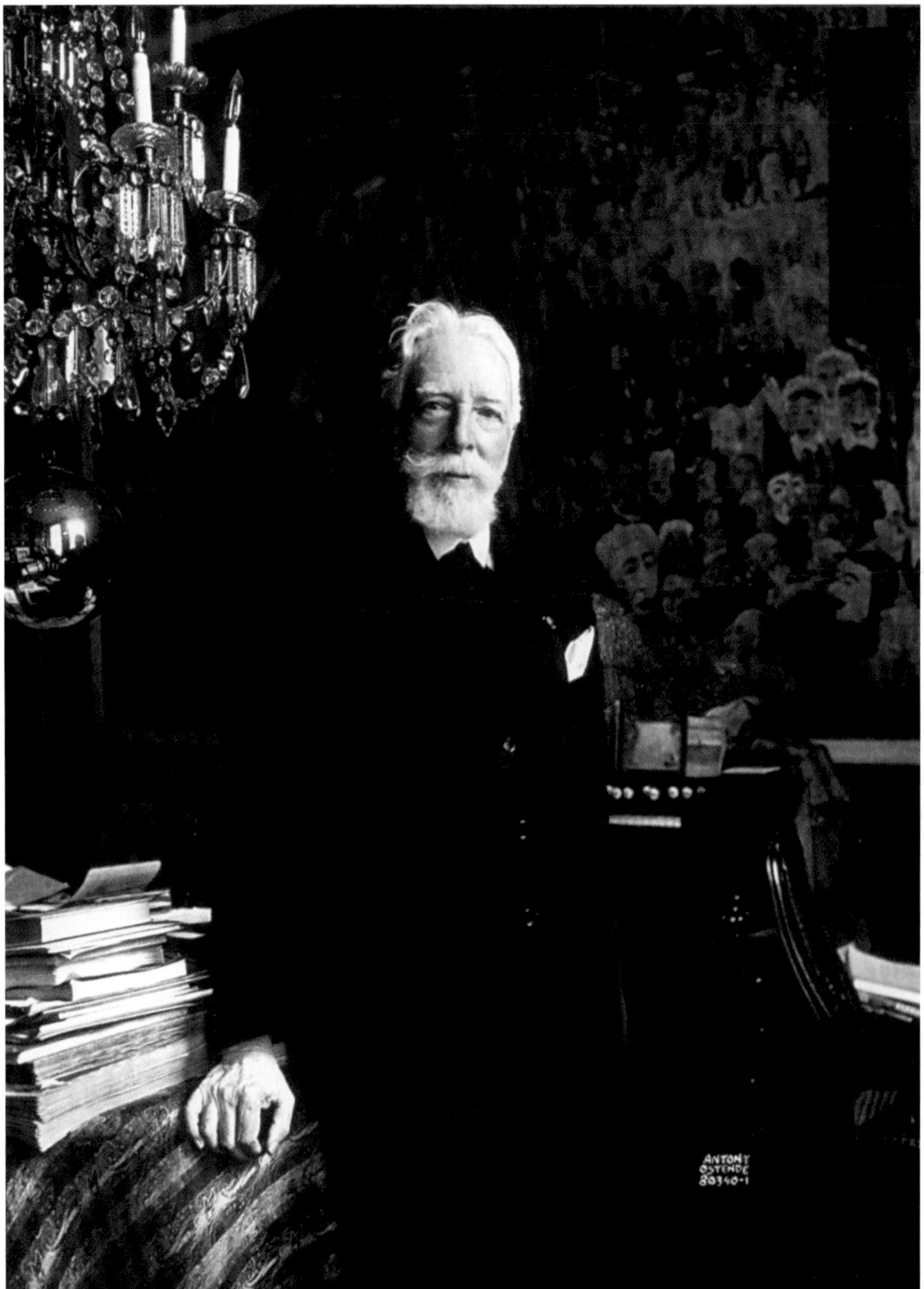

James Ensor in his drawing room in front of his harmonium and *Christ's Entry into Brussels in 1889* (1888; p. 29, fig. 1). Ostend, 1940. Photograph by Maurice Antony

CHRONOLOGY

Compiled by Jane Panetta

1860
James Sidney Édouard Ensor is born on April 13 at 44 Langestraat (now 26) in Ostend, on the Belgian coast, to James Frederic Ensor, an Englishman educated as an engineer, and Maria Catharina Haegheman, an Ostendaise from a family of shopkeepers. His mother's family maintains a curio business in Ostend that sells carnival masks, shells, china, and stuffed animals.

1861
Ensor's sister and only sibling, Marie Carolina Emma Ensor, nicknamed "Mitche" by Ensor, is born on August 29. She serves as a frequent model for Ensor.

1873
Ensor and his family move to 13 Weststratt (now Adolf Biylstraat) on the corner of Christinastraat. Ensor enrolls at the Collège Notre-Dame in Ostend and begins to take lessons from local painters Édouard Dubar and Michel Van Cuyck.

1875
Ensor's family declares bankruptcy and relocates to 66 Langestraat (now 44).

1876
Leaves the Collège and enrolls at the Académie des beaux-arts in Ostend. The family moves again to 23 Vlaanderenstraat (now Vlaanderenhelling) at the corner of Noordstraat (now Van Iseghemlaan).

1877
In October enrolls at the Académie royale des beaux-arts in Brussels and rents a room at 12 Rue Saint-Jean. At the Académie, he studies with Alexandre Robert, Joseph Stallaert, and Joseph Van Severdonck. Here Ensor meets fellow artists Paul Dubois, Alfred William "Willy" Finch, Fernand Khnopff, Willy Schlobach, Guillaume Van Strydonck, Darío de Regoyos, and Rudolph Wystman, all of whom, along with Ensor, would become part of the avant-garde group Les Vingt (Les XX), founded in 1883.

1879
Meets writer, critic, and fellow art student Théo Hannon. Hannon introduces Ensor to the Rousseau family in Brussels, who would provide Ensor with an important and supportive intellectual base with progressive leanings. Ernest Rousseau works as a professor at the Université Libre de Bruxelles, specializing in physics and geometry, and serves as the university rector from 1884 until 1886. His wife, Mariette, Hannon's sister, is an amateur mycologist, or biologist who specializes in the study of mushrooms. Ensor would remain close to her in the years to come; the Rousseau's son, Ernest Jr., would also become one of Ensor's closest friends. Through the Rousseau family, Ensor later meets the artist Félicien Rops and the lawyer and art writer Eugène Demolder.

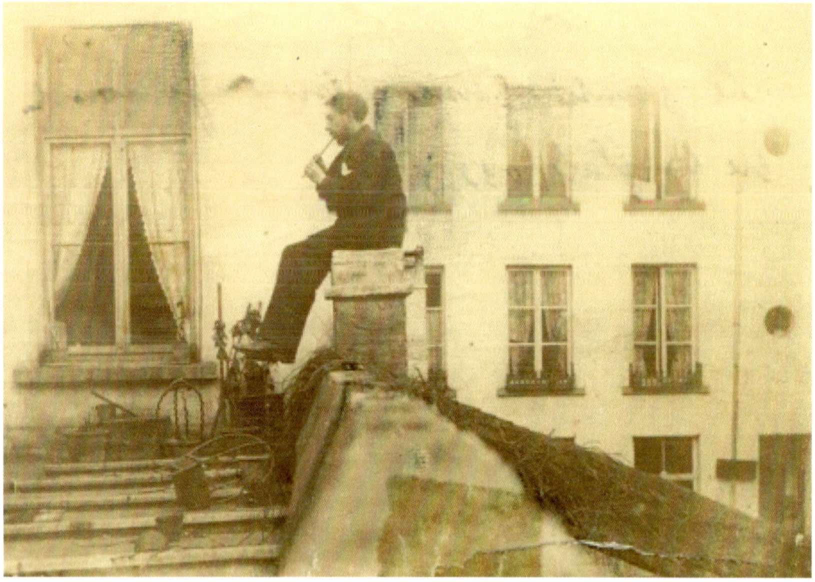

James Ensor playing the flute on a rooftop chimney. Ostend, c. 1881

1880
Leaves the Académie in Brussels and returns to Ostend, moving back into the family home at 23 Vlaanderenstraat; the family's curiosity shop is located on the ground floor and Ensor sets up his studio in the attic. He continues to travel to Brussels regularly to visit the Rousseau family.

1881
Exhibits his work publicly for the first time and sends three paintings to the salon of La Chrysalide and one work to the Exposition générale des beaux-arts in Brussels.

1882
Joins the group L'Essor, established in 1876, and presents works in several exhibitions organized by the group's salon. Ensor also shows his work with the Cercle artistique et littéraire in Brussels and sends two works to the Paris Salon des beaux-arts. His monumental painting *The Oyster Eater* (*La Mangeuse d'huîtres*, 1882; plate 13) is refused by the Antwerp Salon.

1883
On October 28 Ensor cofounds the avant-garde group Les Vingt with the artists Khnopff, Finch, Théo Van Rysselberghe, and Guillaume Vogels, and several others; Ensor would exhibit with this group at their annual salon, held in February. The group would prove critically important for Ensor's artistic development, although certain members would later become unsupportive of his work. Lawyer and writer Octave Maus is selected as Secretary of Les Vingt. Ensor's submissions to the Cercle artistique et littéraire and L'Essor are rejected. In October he visits The Netherlands with Belgian painters Vogels and Charles-Louis Bellis.

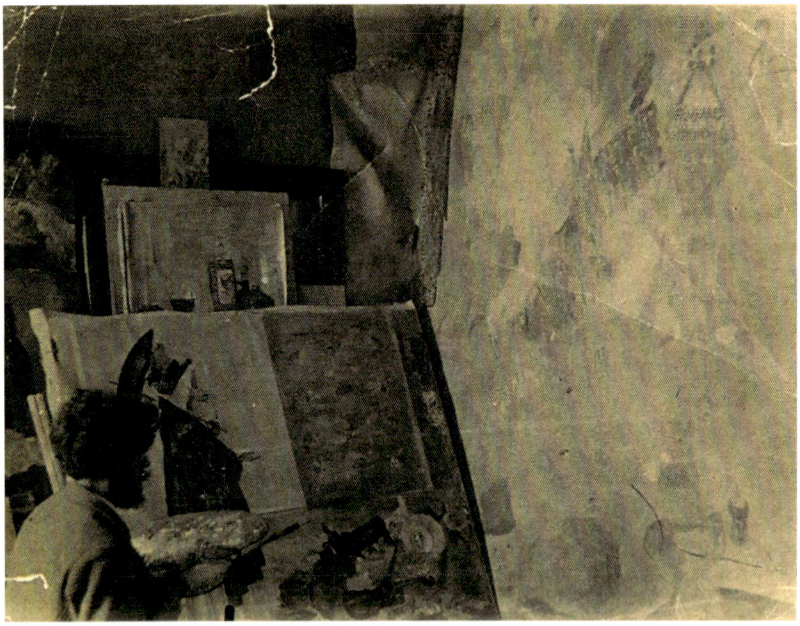

James Ensor in his studio working on *Christ's Entry into Brussels in 1889* (1888; p. 29, fig. 1); visible to Ensor's left is *The Astonishment of the Mask Wouse* (1889; plate 56). Ostend, c. 1888–89

1884
Participates in the first annual exhibition of Les Vingt in Brussels and exhibits six paintings. Auguste Rodin and James Abbott McNeill Whistler are also invited to exhibit with the group. Ensor's short essay, "Trois semaines à l'Academie," a parody of his time spent at the Brussels Académie, is published in *L'Art moderne*. Ensor exhibits with the Cercle artistique et littéraire but his entry for the Brussels Salon is refused. Travels to Paris with the Dutch painter Jan Toorop.

1885
Becomes ill during the winter of 1884–85, suffering from severe intestinal problems. Exhibits with both L'Essor and Les Vingt but has a disagreement with Maus and Khnopff over his painting *Chez Miss* (*Russian Music*, 1881; p. 98, fig. 6) which he believes is plagiarized by Khnopff in his work *On Listening to Schumann* (1883). Ensor works on his seminal series of drawings, Visions: The Aureoles of Christ or the Sensibilities of Light (Visions: Les Auréoles du Christ ou les sensibilités de la lumière; plates 26 and 27). Beginning in December, Ensor briefly moves to Brussels with his mother, sister, and aunt, where they live at 1 Rue Borgval for three months.

1886
At the exhibition of Les Vingt presents twenty works, including *The Oyster Eater*, the work's first public appearance. Claude Monet and Pierre-Auguste Renoir are also invited to exhibit with the group. Tensions continue to mount within Les Vingt, and Ensor is increasingly ostracized; he opposes the election of Whistler to the group. Begins to produce his first etchings. May have traveled to London with Vogels (or perhaps in 1887) and seen the work of Joseph Mallord William Turner.

1887
Ensor's father, probably an alcoholic, is found dead, likely from exposure, at age fifty-two; his maternal grandmother also dies. Exhibits his Aureoles series at the exhibition of Les Vingt, where Georges Seurat exhibits *A Sunday on La Grande Jatte–1884* (1884–86; p. 19, fig. 4). Presents work in an exhibition titled *L'Art zwanze,* an irreverent salon in Brussels that parodied existing styles and artists. Again becomes ill in the winter of 1887–88 while renting a room in Brussels at 123 Boulevard Anspach.

1888
Becomes too ill to submit works to the annual exhibition of Les Vingt, though twenty-two works were mistakenly included in the accompanying catalogue. Begins painting his monumental masterpiece *Christ's Entry into Brussels in 1889* (*L'Entrée du Christ à Bruxelles en 1889*, 1888; p. 29, fig. 1). Produces forty-four etchings, approximately one-third of his entire output. Meets Augusta Boogaerts, the daughter of a local hotel owner, whom he nicknames "La Sirène." Ensor would portray her in future works and she would become his lifelong companion.

1889
Participates in the exhibition of Les Vingt. Though Ensor does not complete *Christ's Entry into Brussels in 1889* in time for submission, the work is included in the exhibition catalogue. Visits Paris.

1890
Participates in the exhibition of Les Vingt, where he exhibits eighteen works; Paul Cézanne, Paul Signac, and Vincent Van Gogh are also invited to exhibit with the group.

1891
The first monographic exhibition of Ensor's graphic work is held at the Galerie Dietrich in Brussels. Ensor participates in the exhibition of Les Vingt and exhibits fifteen works. His etching *The Cathedral* is reproduced on the cover of *La Jeune Belgique*. Visits the Dutch province of Zeeland with Eugène Demolder, now a close friend of the artist.

1892
The first monograph on Ensor is published, written by Demolder. Ensor participates in the exhibition of Les Vingt, exhibiting fifteen works. His sister, Mitche, marries Alfred John Taen Hee Tseu, a Chinese salesman and dealer of chinoiserie from Germany, whom she may have met in the family shop in Ostend; he leaves her within the year. Ensor falls ills with pneumonia. Makes a brief visit to London.

1893
Participates in the tenth and final exhibition of Les Vingt. Despite Ensor's protests, the group is disbanded by Maus

and other members so as to establish its successor, La Libre Esthétique. Perhaps discouraged by the end of Les Vingt, Ensor puts his studio and its contents up for sale for 8,500 Belgian francs; no offers are made. The Brussels Cabinet des estampes purchases a large number of the artist's etchings. Ensor's niece Mariette Alexandrine Jeanne, or "Alex," is born on March 26, and she and Mitche move in with Ensor; Mitche and Ensor would live together until her death in 1945.

1894
Participates in the first exhibition of La Libre Esthétique. Along with Vogels, Ensor founds the Cercle des beaux-arts d'Ostende, a group that would produce only two exhibitions. Demolder organizes the first one-man exhibition of Ensor's work, held at Demolder's father's shop, the Comptoir des arts industriels la royale in Brussels, which brings together the artist's paintings, drawings, and etchings publicly for the first time.

1895
In March the Belgian government purchases *The Lamp-Lighter* (*Le Lampiste*, 1880; plate 3) for 2,500 Belgian francs for the Musées royaux des Beaux-Arts de Belgique in Brussels, the first public purchase of a work by Ensor. The artist returns to Zeeland with Demolder.

1896
Brussels printer Van Campenhout publishes a fifty-edition series of twelve of Ensor's etchings, *Douze eaux-fortes*.

1898
In December, with the support of Demolder, Ensor's first one-man exhibition of drawings and prints abroad opens in Paris, organized by the periodical *La Plume* and held at the Salon des cent. In addition, *La Plume* publishes a special issue titled "James Ensor. Peintre et graveur" entirely devoted to Ensor.

1899
The Cercle artistique et littéraire organizes a one-man exhibition of Ensor's work. In September the Graphische Sammlung Albertina in Vienna purchases one hundred etchings by the artist.

1901
Becomes a member of Libre Académie de Belgique, a group founded by Edmond Picard. The City of Ostend purchases a series of 188 etchings by Ensor.

1903
Is named Chevalier de l'ordre de Léopold by King Leopold II, and the occasion is celebrated in Ostend by the Ensor-led satirical society Le Rat mort. Ensor meets poet, critic, and future patron Emma Lambotte, who publishes several articles on Ensor under the pen name Emaël. She and her husband, Dr. Albin Lambotte, would later purchase several important works by Ensor, including *The Oyster Eater* and *Self-Portrait with Masks* (*Ensor aux masques*, 1899; plate 91).

1904
The Deadly Sins (*Les Péchés capitaux*), an album of etchings, is published by Van Campenhout with a preface written by Demolder. Joins the group Vie et lumière, founded by Cyriel Buysse, Émile Claus, and George Morren.

1905
Through Mrs. Lambotte, meets important Antwerp collector François Franck, who would eventually purchase many important works by Ensor. A new group called Kunst van Heden / L'Art contemporain is founded in Antwerp by Ensor, Franck, and Franck's brothers. Ensor subsequently exhibits twenty paintings in the group's inaugural salon. The Ensor family hires August Van Yeper, known as "Gustje," to work as a butler; he remains with Ensor until the end of his life.

1906
The Lambottes present Ensor with a harmonium and he begins to compose music for *La Gamme d'amour*, also known as *Flirt des marionettes*, a ballet that he would complete by 1911. In addition to writing the music, Ensor designs sets and costumes for the ballet. Begins making replicas of his existing paintings.

1907
Exhibits three paintings at the Salon d'automne in Paris.

1908
A monograph on Ensor is published, written by poet and art critic Émile Verhaeren. With the assistance of Franck, the Koninklijk Museum voor Schone Kunsten in Antwerp acquires eight paintings by Ensor. On September 26 Ensor's niece, Alex, age fifteen, marries Richard Daveluy, later a croupier at the Ostend Casino. This union greatly disappoints Ensor; the couple, along with Ensor's Aunt Mimi, move into the house with Ensor and Mitche.

1909
Jules Daveluy, son of Alex and Richard Daveluy, is born on July 17. The three subsequently move out of Ensor's house.

1910
A retrospective of Ensor's work is held at the Rotterdamsche Kunstkring in Rotterdam. An exhibition is also held at the Cercle royal artistique et littéraire in Antwerp.

1911
Completes his ballet *La Gamme d'amour*. German artist Emil Nolde visits Ensor in Ostend.

1913
A catalogue raisonné of Ensor's prints is published by collector Herbert von Garvens-Garvensburg. Belgian artist Rik Wouters sculpts a bust in Ensor's honor.

1914
World War I breaks out; Ensor remains in Ostend throughout the war.

1915
Ensor's mother dies on March 8 at the age of eighty.

1916
Ensor's Aunt Mimi dies on April 11. Ensor remains at 23 Vlaanderenstraat with his sister and two servants.

1917
Moves down the street to 17 Vlaanderenstraat (now 27) to a house he inherits from his uncle, Leopold Haegheman, his mother's brother, where he will remain until his death. (This building is now the Ensor-Museum.)

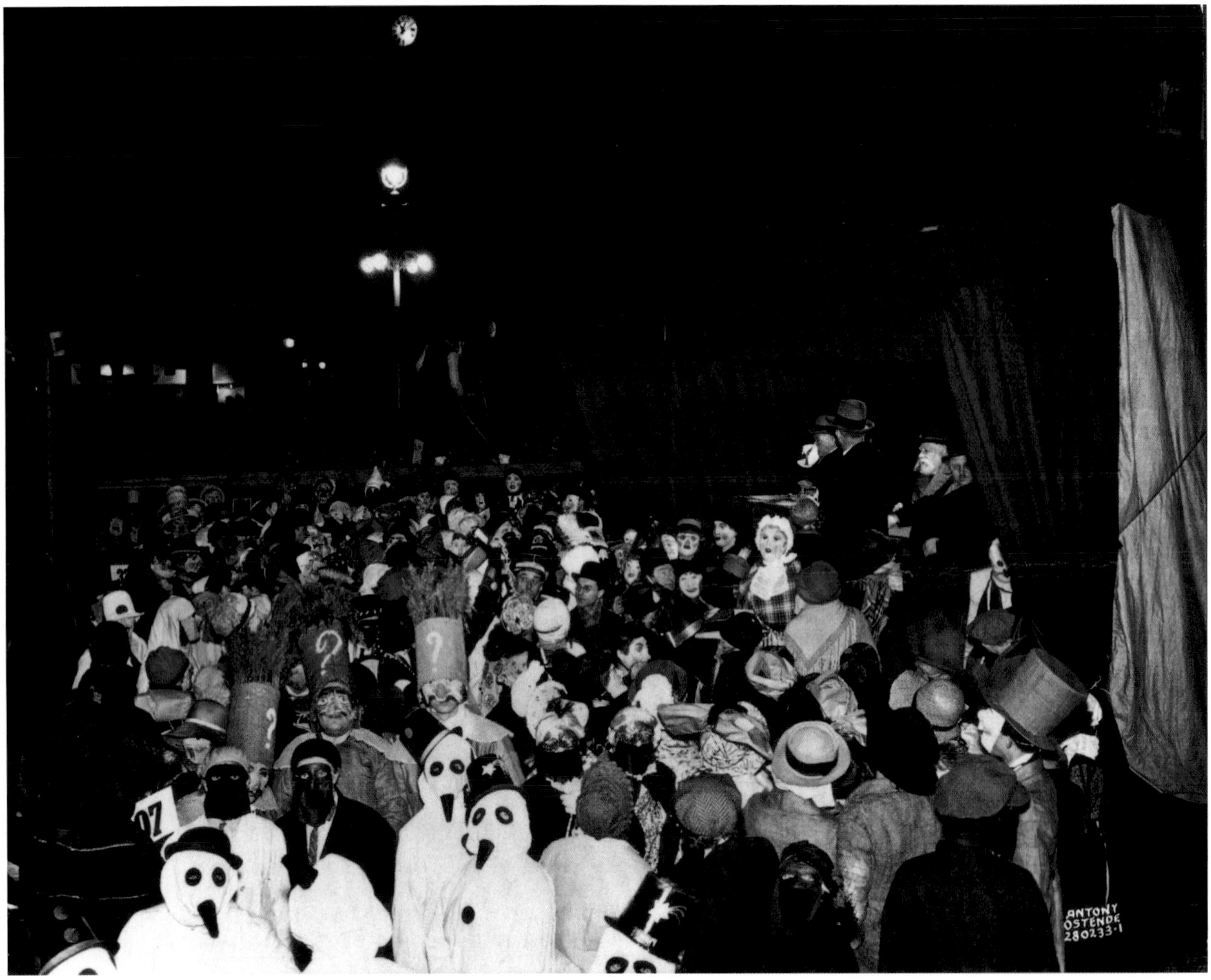

Crowd at Ostend Carnival; James Ensor seated on the stage at top right. Ostend, 1933. Photograph by Maurice Antony

1920
A retrospective exhibition is held in honor of Ensor's sixtieth birthday at Galerie Georges Giroux in Brussels. Ensor sells six works to the Musées royaux des Beaux-Arts de Belgique in Brussels, including two drawings from the Aureoles series. His ballet *La Gamme d'amour,* conducted by Léon Delcroix, is staged at the Galerie Georges Giroux and is well received by the public.

1921
The first edition of Ensor's *Écrits de James Ensor* is published. A monograph on Ensor is also published, written by journalist and critic Paul Colin. At the urging of Franck, the Koninklijk Museum voor Schone Kunsten in Antwerp acquires seven major paintings by Ensor, financed by members of Kunst van Heden.

1922
A monograph on Ensor, written by poet Grégoire Le Roy, is published. A complete set of the artist's graphic collection is acquired by the Musée Plantin Moretus in Antwerp.

1923
Elected corresponding member of the Académie Royale des Beaux-Arts in Brussels; becomes a full member in 1925.

1924
The art journal *La Flandre littéraire* publishes a special issue devoted to Ensor. The ballet *La Gamme d'amour* is staged by the Flemish Opera in Antwerp under the title *Poppenliefe*, or *Romance of the Marionettes.*

1926
Ensor's work is presented at the Fifteenth International Venice Biennale as part of the Belgian Pavilion.

1927
Ensor's work is exhibited in Germany for the first time at the Kestner-Gesellschaft in Hannover; this exhibition also travels

to the Galerie Paul Cassirer in Berlin and Galerie Neue Kunst Fides in Dresden. *La Gamme d'amour* is performed at the Théâtre royal in Liège.

1928
Exhibitions of Ensor's work are held at the Städtische Kunsthalle in Mannheim and the Leipziger Kunstverein in Leipzig.

1929
On April 24 King Albert I bestows the title of Baron on Ensor. The largest exhibition of Ensor's work to date is held at the Palais des beaux-arts in Brussels, where *Christ's Entry into Brussels in 1889* is exhibited publicly for the first time. Paul Fierens, a Belgian curator, publishes a monograph on Ensor, and a special issue of *Cahiers de Belgique* devoted to Ensor's work is published. Russian artist Vasily Kandinsky visits Ensor in Ostend.

1930
A monument to Ensor, sculpted by Edmond de Valériola, is erected near the Ostend Kursaal. German artist Erich Heckel visits Ensor and paints his portrait, now in the collection of the Wallraf-Richartz-Museum & Fondation Corboud in Cologne. *La Gamme d'amour* is revived at the Théâtre royal in Liège on December 2, and again on January 8, 1931.

1931
Jean Teugels's book *Variations sur James Ensor* is published.

1932
A major retrospective of the artist's work is held at the Musée national du jeu de paume in Paris. *La Gamme d'amour* is performed for charity at the Théâtre royal in Ostend on December 17.

1933
Meets Albert Einstein at the restaurant Au coeur volant in De Haan-an-Zee, near Ostend. That same evening the French Minister of Culture, Anatole de Monzie, awards Ensor the medal of the French Légion d'Honneur at a ceremony at the Ostend Casino.

1934
Ensor is declared "Prince of Painters" at a celebration in Brussels, organized by the painter Jean Vervisch.

1935
A second catalogue raisonné of Ensor's prints, edited by Ensor's friend Albert Croquez, is published. The City of Ostend organizes a celebration to commemorate Ensor's seventy-fifth birthday.

1936
An exhibition of Ensor's work is held at the Leicester Galleries in London. This is Ensor's first one-man exhibition in England.

1937
An exhibition of Ensor's work is held at the Galerie de l'Elysée in Paris.

1939
A major exhibition, including nearly three hundred works, is organized by the *Gazette des beaux-arts* in Paris. Ensor's engravings are exhibited at the Graphische Sammlung Albertina in Vienna. World War II breaks out; Ensor remains in Ostend until the war's end.

1940
Ostend is bombed on May 27–28, and three paintings, including *Sick Tramp Trying to Warm Himself* (*Le Pouilleux indisposé se chauffant*, 1882; p. 84, fig. 2) and *The Haunted Furniture* (*Le Vieux Meuble*, 1885/c. 1890), and a series of etchings owned by the Museum voor Schone Kunsten are destroyed in a fire. The Museum of Modern Art acquires *Tribulations of Saint Anthony* (*Terribles Tribulations de Saint-Antoine*, 1887; plate 37); this is the first acquisition by an American institution of a painting by Ensor.

1942
In December a false announcement of Ensor's death is made in Belgian newspapers and abroad.

1944
A one-man exhibition is held at the Buchholz Gallery in New York.

1945
The Galerie Georges Giroux in Brussels organizes a second exhibition of Ensor's work, *Hommage à James Ensor*. Ensor becomes president of the organization La Jeune Peinture belge. Ensor's sister dies on December 27 at the age of eighty-four.

1946
A retrospective exhibition is organized by the National Gallery in London.

1948
L'Association les amis de James Ensor is founded in Ostend. Paul Haesaerts directs a film on Ensor titled *Masques et visages de James Ensor*. The writer J. P. Hodin visits Ensor in Ostend.

1949
Following a three-week illness, Ensor dies on November 19 at the age of eighty-nine at the Sacré-Coeur hospital in Ostend. He is buried on November 23 at the Notre-Dame-des-Dunes cemetery in Mariakerke near Ostend.

1951
The Museum of Modern Art organizes the first retrospective in the United States of Ensor's work and publishes the first volume on Ensor in English. The show travels to the Institute of Contemporary Art in Boston, the Cleveland Museum of Art, and the City Art Museum in St. Louis.

SELECTED BIBLIOGRAPHY

Compiled by Blair Hartzell

Writings by the Artist

James Ensor: Lettres. Edited by Xavier Tricot. Archives du futur. Brussels: Éditions Labor, 1999.

Lettres à Emma Lambotte, 1904–1914. Edited by Danielle Derrey-Capon. Preface by Philippe Robert-Jones. Brussels: Centre international pour l'Étude du XIXe siècle and La Renaissance du Livre, 1999.

"Les Lettres de James Ensor à Octave Maus." Edited by Francine-Claire Legrand. *Bulletin des Musées royaux des Beaux-Arts de Belgique* 15, nos. 1–2 (1966): 17–54.

Mes Écrits ou les suffisances matamoresques. Edited by Hugo Martin. Rev. and enl. 6th ed. Brussels: Éditions Labor, 1999.

Monographs

Alechinsky, Pierre, et al. *Ensor.* Brussels: Musées royaux des Beaux-Arts de Belgique; Tournai: La Renaissance du livre, 1999. (English edition, 1999.)

Avermaete, Roger. *James Ensor.* Monographies de l'art belge 1, no. 4. Antwerp: De Sikkel; Brussels: Éditions du Cercle d'Art, 1947. (English edition, 1951.)

Becks-Malorny, Ulrike. *James Ensor, 1860–1949: Die Masken, der Tod und das Meer.* Cologne: Taschen, 1999. Reprint, 2005. (English editions, 1999 and 2000.)

Berman, Patricia G. *James Ensor: Christ's Entry into Brussels in 1889.* Los Angeles: J. Paul Getty Museum, 2002.

Brown, Carol, ed. *James Ensor, 1860–1949: Theatre of Masks.* London: Barbican Art Gallery and Lund Humphries, 1997.

Colin, Paul. *James Ensor.* Translated by Hans Jacob. Potsdam: Gustav Kiepenheuer, 1921.

———. *James Ensor.* Junge Kunst 59. Berlin: Klinkhardt & Biermann, 1931.

Cornette, Arthur J. H. *L'Œuvre de James Ensor.* Paris: Musée national du jeu de paume and Gauthier-Villars & Cie, 1932.

Croquez, Albert. *L'Œuvre gravé de James Ensor. Catalogue raisonné établi par Albert Croquez, son ami, et orné d'un portrait d'après la toile de Jules Joëts.* Paris: Maurice Le Garrec, 1935. Reprint, Geneva: P. Cailler, 1947.

Croquez, Robert. *Ensor en son temps . . .* Preface by Franz Hellens. Ostend: Éditions Erel, 1970.

Cuypers, Firmin. *James Ensor: L'Homme & l'œuvre.* Artistes contemporains 2. Paris: Les Écrivains Reunis, 1925.

———. *Aspects & propos de James Ensor.* Bruges: A. G. Stainforth, 1946.

Damase, Jacques. *L'Œuvre gravé de James Ensor.* Geneva: Motte, 1967.

Delevoy, Robert L., and Pierre Alechinsky. *Ensor.* Antwerp: Fonds Mercator, 1981.

De Maeyer, Marcel. *James Ensor.* I Maestri del colore 169. Milan: Fratelli Fabbri, 1966.

De Maeyer, Marcel, and Walther Vanbeselaere. *James Ensor.* Basel: Kunsthalle Basel, 1963.

Demolder, Eugène. *James Ensor.* Brussels: Paul Lacomblez, 1892.

Desmeth, Paul. *James Ensor.* Artistes de Belgique. Brussels: L. J. Kryn, 1926.

De Zegher, Catherine, ed. *Between Street and Mirror: The Drawings of James Ensor.* New York: The Drawing Center; Minneapolis: University of Minnesota Press, 2001.

Dörner, Alexandre, Herbert von Garvens-Garvensburg, and Wilhelm Fraenger. *James Ensor: Festschrift zur ersten deutschen Ensor-Ausstellung.* Hannover: Kestner-Gesellschaft, 1927.

Draguet, Michel. *James Ensor ou la fantasmagorie.* Paris: Gallimard, 1999.

Edebau, Frank P. *James Ensor: Gemälde, Zeichnungen un Grafik aus den Sammlungen des Kunstmuseums Ostende.* Bensberg, Germany: Museum der Stadt Bensberg, 1968.

Edebau, Frank P., and Maurizio Calvesi. *Ensor: Dipinti, Disegni, Incisioni.* Milan: Electa, 1981.

Eggum, Arne, and Sissel Biørnstad. *James Ensor.* Oslo: Munch-Museet and Oslo Kommunes Kunstsamlinger, 1982.

Elesh, James N. *James Ensor: The Complete Graphic Work.* The Illustrated Bartsch 141. 2 vols. Edited by Walter L. Strauss. New York: Abaris, 1982.

Ensor dans les collections privées. Brussels: Galerie Isy Branchot, 1965.

Farmer, John David *Ensor.* Preface by Frank P. Edebau. New York: George Braziller, 1976.

Fels, Florent. *James Ensor.* Collection Peintres d'hier et d'aujourd'hui 8. Geneva: Pierre Cailler, 1947.

Fierens, Paul. *James Ensor.* Collection "les artistes nouveaux." Paris: G. Crès & Cie, 1929.

———. *Les Dessins d'Ensor.* Brussels: Éditions Apollo, 1944.

Florizoone, Patrick. *James Ensor: Les Bains à Ostende.* Brussels: Snoek-Ducaju & Zoon and Pandora, 1996.

Fosca, François. *James Ensor.* Brussels: Éditions du Palais des Beaux-Arts, 1929.

France, Hubert de. *James Ensor: Proeve van gecommentariëerde bibliografie/Essai de bibliographie commentée.* Biblografica belgica 53. Brussels: Commission belge de bibliographie, 1960.

Franz, Erich, et al. *James Ensor (1860–1949): Visionär der Moderne. Gemälde, Zeichnungen und das drucksgraphische Werk aus der Sammlung Gerard Loobuyck.* Albstadt, Germany: Galerie Albstadt, 1999.

Garvens-Garvensburg, Herbert von. *James Ensor: Maler, Radierer, Komponist.* Hannover: Ludwig Ey, 1913.

George, Waldemar. *Exposition James Ensor.* Art contemporain d'Anvers. Paris: Galerie Barbazanges-Hodebert, 1926.

Geyer, Marie-Jeanne, Dieter Koepplin, and Nadine Lehni. *James Ensor: Œuvre gravé. Collection Mira Jacob/Das Drucksgraphische werk. Sammlung Mira Jacob.* Strasbourg: Éditions Musées de la Ville de Strasbourg; Basel: Kunstmuseum Basel, 1995.

Giménez, Carmen, and Francisco Calvo Serraller. *James Ensor.* Madrid and Bilbao: Banco Bilbao Vizcaya, 1996.

Guralnik, Nehama, ed. *James Ensor: 1860–1949.* Translated by Tirza Posner. Tel Aviv: Tel Aviv Museum, 1981.

Haesaerts, Paul. *James Ensor.* Preface by Jean Cassou. Brussels: Éditions et ateliers d'Art Graphique Elsevier, 1957. Rev. ed., Brussels: Meddens, 1973. (English edition, 1957. Reprint, 1959).

Hammacher-Van den Brande, Renilde. *Ensor: 1860–1949.* Rotterdam: Museum Boymans-van Beuningen, 1961.

Hellens, Franz. *James Ensor.* Nieuwe kunst 6. Amsterdam: Van Munster, 1925.

Heusinger von Waldegg, Joachim. *James Ensor: Legende vom Ich.* Cologne: DuMont, 1991.

Heymans, Vincent. *Ensor et les médecins: Un Diagnostic.* Edited by Catheline Périer-D'Ieteren. Annales d'Histoire de l'art et d'Archéologie de l'Université Libre de Bruxelles. Cahier d'Études 5. Brussels: Centre de Recherches et d'Études technologiques des Arts plastiques, 1997.

Hoozee, Robert. *Squelette regardant chinoiseries (1885).* Edited by Dominique Allard. Brussels: Fondation Roi Baudouin, 1995.

Hoozee, Robert, Sabine Bown-Taevernier, and Jan Frederik Heijbroek. *Ik James Ensor: Tekeningen en prenten.* Brussels: Ludion, 1987.

Hoozee, Robert, Lydia M. A. Schoonbaert, and Herwig Todts. *James Ensor 1860–1949: Schilderijen, tekeningen en grafiek, een selectie uit Belgisch en Nederlands bezit.* Utrecht: Centraal Museum Utrecht, 1993.

Hostyn, Norbert. *James Ensor: Leven en werk/Vie et œuvre/Life and Work/Leben und Werke.* Bruges: Stichting Kunstboek, 1996.

———. *Ensor: La Collection du Musée des Beaux-Arts d'Ostende.* Ghent and Amsterdam: Ludion, 1999.

Hostyn, Norbert, and Patrick Florizoone. *Art graphique d'Ensor en confrontation*. Ghent: Snoeck-Ducaju; Antwerp: Pandora, 1999.
James Ensor. Mannheim: Städtische Kunsthalle, 1928.
James Ensor: Meisterliche Handseichnungen, 1880 bis 1888. Zurich: M. Knoedler Zurich AG, 1983.
James Ensor. Prints and Drawings from the Collection of the Municipal Museum Ostende. Estampes et dessins de la collection du Musée Municipal d'Ostende. Ottawa: National Gallery of Canada, 1973.
James Ensor: Radierungen aus der Sammlung A. Taevernier, Brüssel und der Hamburger Kunsthalle. Hamburg: Hamburger Kunsthalle, 1969.
Janssens, Jacques. *James Ensor*. Paris: Flammarion, 1978. Reprint, 1990. (English edition, 1978. Reprint, 1986.)
Kiefer, Theodor. *J. Ensor*. Recklinghausen, Germany: Aurel Bongers, 1976.
Langer, Heiderose, and Siegfried Salzmann. *James Ensor: Radierungen*. Bremen: Kunsthalle Bremen, 1992.
Lebeer, Louis. *James Ensor: Acquafortiste*. Monographies de l'art belge 5. Antwerp: De Sikkel, 1952.
Legrand, Francine-Claire, and Catherine Fache. *Ensor, la mort et le charme: Un autre Ensor*. Antwerp: Fonds Mercator, 1993.
Legrand, Francine-Claire, and Gisèle Ollinger-Zinque. *Ensor, cet inconnu*. Brussels: La Renaissance du Livre, 1971. Reprint, 1990. Rev. and enl. ed., 1999. Edited by Danielle Derrey-Capon.
Le Roy, Grégoire. *James Ensor*. Brussels and Paris: G. Van Oest & Cie, 1922.
Lesko, Diane. *James Ensor: The Creative Years*. Princeton: Princeton University Press, 1985.
McGough, Stephen C. "James Ensor's *The Entry of Christ into Brussels in 1889*." PhD diss., Stanford University, 1981. Outstanding Dissertations in the Fine Arts. New York and London: Garland Publishing, 1985.
Min, Eric. *James Ensor: Een biografie*. Amsterdam: Meulenhoff, 2008.
Ollinger-Zinque, Gisèle. *Ensor par lui-même*. Brussels: Laconti, 1976. (English edition, 1976.)
Papanikolas, Theresa, and Kevin Salatino. *Doctrinal Nourishment: Art and Anarchism in the Time of James Ensor*. Los Angeles: Los Angeles County Museum of Art, 2009.
Pfeiffer, Ingrid, and Max Hollein, eds. *James Ensor*. Frankfurt: Schirn Kunsthalle Frankfurt; Ostfildern-Ruit, Germany: Hatje Cantz, 2005. (English edition, 2005.)
Piron, Herman T. *Ensor: Een psychoanalytische studie*. Antwerp: De Nederlandsche Boekhandel, 1968.
Ridder, André de. *James Ensor*. Maîtres de l'art moderne 31. Paris: Éditions Rieder, 1930.
San Nicholas, Juan, and Robert Rosenblum. *James Ensor: Grabador (1860–1949)*. Madrid: Fundación MAPFRE, 2007.
Schneede, Uwe M., Günter Metken, and Walther Vanbeselaere. *Ensor: Ein Maler aus dem späten 19.Jahrhundert*. Stuttgart: Württembergischer Kunstverein, 1972.
Schoonbaert, Lydia M. A., et al. *James Ensor: Belgium um 1900*. Munich: Kunsthalle der Hypo-Kulturstiftung and Hirmer, 1989.
Schoonbaert, Lydia M. A., et al. *James Ensor*. Paris: Musée du Petit Palais, 1990.
Schwob, Lucien. *James Ensor*. Brussels: Cahiers du Journal des Poètes, 1936.
Stevo, Jean. *James Ensor*. Brussels: Éditions Germinal, 1947.
Szeemann, Harald, et al. *James Ensor*. Zurich: Kunsthaus Zurich, 1983.
Tannenbaum, Libby. *James Ensor*. Preface by Paul Fierens. New York: The Museum of Modern Art, 1951. Reprint, 1966.
Taevernier, Auguste. *Le Drame Ensorien: Les Auréoles du Christ ou les sensibilités de la lumière*. Ghent: Erasmus, 1976.
———. *James Ensor: Catalogue illustré de ses gravures, leur description critique et l'inventaire des plaques/Geillustreerde catalogus van zijn gravures, hun kritische beschrijving en inventaris van de platen/ Illustrated Catalogue of His Engravings, Their Critical Description and Inventory of the Plates*. Ghent: Erasmus, 1973. Reprint, Ghent: Snoeck-Ducaju & Zoon; Antwerp: Pandora, 1999.
Teugels, Jean. *Variations sur James Ensor*. Ostend: Éditions l'Acquarium, 1931.
Todts, Herwig. *James Ensor: De noche cartografiaba mis sueños. Obras en las colecciones del Koninklijk Museum voor Schone Kunsten de Amberes (KMSKA) y del Museum voor Schone Kunsten de Ostende (MSKO)*. Salamanca: Caja Duero; Sevilla: Caja San Fernando; Antwerp: Koninklijk Museum voor Schone Kunsten, 2004.
———. *James Ensor: Paintings and Drawings from the Collection of the Royal Museum of Fine Arts in Antwerp*. Antwerp: Koninklijk Museum voor Schone Kunsten and BAI, 2008.
Tricot, Xavier. *Ensor dans les collections privées II*. Brussels: Galerie Isy Brachot, 1985.
———. *James Ensor: Catalogue raisonné des peintures*. 2 vols. Antwerp: Pandora and MIM, 1992. Rev. ed. forthcoming. (English edition, 1992.)
———. *Ensoriana*. Ostend: L'Hareng saur, 1985. Reprint, Antwerp: Pandora, 1995.
Tricot, Xavier, et al. *Bonjour, monsieur Ensor*. Ostend: L'Hareng saur, 1985.
Vanbeselaere, Walther. *Rétrospective James Ensor*. Antwerp: Musée Royal des Beaux-Arts: 1951.
———. *L'Entrée du Christ à Bruxelles*. Brussels: Éditions Weissenbruch, 1957.
Vanbeselaere, Walther, Jean Cassou, and Marcel Abraham. *James Ensor*. Paris: Musée National d'Art Moderne and Presses artistiques, 1954.
Van Gindertael, Roger. *Ensor*. Milan: Alfiere & Lacroix, 1975. (English edition, 1975.)
Van Puyvelde, Leo. *L'Ardente peinture d'Ensor*. Paris: Gazette des Beaux-Arts et Beaux-Arts, 1939.
———. *The Works of James Ensor*. London: Arts Council of Great Britain, 1946.
Verhaeren, Émile. *James Ensor*. Collection des artistes belges contemporains. Brussels: G. Van Oest & Cie, 1908. Rev. eds. Brussels: Jacques Antoine, 1980, and Paris: Éditions du Sandre and Éditions L'Harmattan, 2006.
Vester, Karl-Egon, et al. *James Ensor*. Hamburg: Kunstverein in Hamburg, 1986.
West, Paul. *James Ensor & Paul West*. Secret Museums 5. Paris: Flohic Éditions, 1991.

Works Including the Artist

Adhémar, Hélène. *L'Art flamand d'Ensor à Permeke*. Paris: Musée de l'Orangerie, 1970.
Barr, Alfred H., Jr., ed. *Masters of Modern Art*. New York: The Museum of Modern Art, 1955.
Block, Jane. "Les XX and Belgian Avant-Gardism, 1868–1894." PhD diss., University of Michigan, 1980.
Canning, Susan M. "A History and Critical Review of the Salons of *Les Vingt*, 1884–1893." PhD diss., Pennsylvania State University, 1980.
Catoir, Barbara, Erwin Mitsch, and Alice Strobl. *Gustav Klimt, Egon Schiele, James Ensor, Alfred Kubin: Künstler der Jahrhundertwende/Artists at the Turn of the Century*. Edited by Irène Kutter. Zurich: Knoedler, 1983.
Cortés, José Miguel G. *Visionarios: James Ensor, Max Klinger, Odilon Redon, Félicien Rops*. València: Generalitat Valenciana, Consorci de Museus de la Comunitat Valenciana, and Museu de Belles Arts de València, 1998.
Delteil, Loys. *Henri Leys, Henri de Braekeleer, James Ensor*. Le peintre-graveur illustré (XIXe et XXe siècle) 19. Paris: Chez l'auteur, 1925. Reprint, New York: Da Capo Press, 1969.

Edebau, Frank P., Arne Eggum, and Martin Urban. *James Ensor, Edvard Munch, Emil Nolde*. Regina, Saskatchewan: Norman Mackenzie Art Gallery, 1980.

Fuchs, Rudi, and Jan Hoet. *Flemish and Dutch Painting: From Van Gogh, Ensor, Magritte and Mondrian to Contemporary Artists*. New York: Rizzoli, 1997.

Gerstein, Marc S., and Eric Zafran. *Mask and Eye: The Graphic Work of James Ensor and Odilon Redon*. Waltham, Mass.: Brandeis University, 1967.

Goddard, Stephen H., ed. *Les XX and the Belgian Avant-Garde: Prints, Drawings, and Books, c. 1890*. Lawrence, Kans.: Spencer Museum of Art, University of Kansas, 1992.

Haesaerts, Luc, and Paul Haesaerts. *Flandre, Essai sur l'art flamand depuis 1880. Impressionisme*. Paris: Éditions des chroniques du jour, 1931.

Heusinger von Waldegg, Joachim, Herwig Todts, and Norbert Hostyn. *James Ensor: Schrecken ohne ende*. Wuppertal: Von der Heydt Museum, 2008.

Hirsh, Sharon L. *Symbolism and Modern Urban Society*. Cambridge and New York: Cambridge University Press, 2004.

Jonsson, Stefan. *Tre revolutioner: En kort historia om folkert 1789, 1889, 1989*. Stockholm: Norstedts, 2005. (English edition, 2008.)

Langui, Emile. *Gloires de la peinture moderne. Hommage à James Ensor: Braque, Chagall, De Chirico, Dalì, Ernst, Matisse, Picasso, Klee*. Brussels: Éditions de la Connaissance, 1949.

Legrand, Francine-Claire. *Le Groupe des XX et son temps*. Brussels: Musées royaux des Beaux-Arts de Belgique; Otterlo: Rijksmuseum Kröller-Müller, 1962.

———. *Le Symbolisme en Belgique*. Brussels: Laconti, 1971. (English edition, 1972.)

Lemonnier, Camille. *L'École belge de peinture, 1830–1905*. Brussels: G. Van Oest & Cie, 1906.

Maus, Madeleine Octave. *Trente années de lutte pour l'art: 1884–1914*. Brussels: Librarie l'oiseau bleu, 1926.

Ogura, Tadao. *Ensor/Magritte*. Tokyo: Shueisha, 1974.

Ollinger-Zinque, Gisèle, et al. *Les XX, La Libre esthétique: Honderd jaar later/Cent ans après*. Brussels: Musées royaux des Beaux-Arts de Belgique, 1993.

Pingeot, Anne, and Robert Hoozee, eds. *Paris-Bruxelles, Bruxelles-Paris: Réalisme, impressionisme, symbolisme, art nouveau*. Antwerp: Fonds Mercator; Paris: Réunion des musées nationaux, 1997.

Robert-Jones, Philippe. *Du Réalisme au surréalisme: La Peinture en Belgique de Joseph Stevens à Paul Delvaux*. Brussels: Laconti, 1969.

Robert-Jones, Philippe, et al. *Belgian Art: 1880–1914*. New York: Brooklyn Museum of Art, 1980.

Schampers, Karel, et al. *Ensor, Hodler, Kruyder, Munch: Wegbereiders van het modernisme/Pioneers of Modernism*. Edited by Talitha Schoon and Karel Schampers. Rotterdam: Museum Boymans-van Beuningen, 1988.

Stevens, MaryAnne, and Robert Hoozee, eds. *Impressionism to Symbolism: The Belgian Avant-Garde 1880–1900*. London: Royal Academy of Arts; Ghent: Ludion N.V., 1994.

Vanbeselaere, Walther, Denys Sutton, and Lydia M. A. Schoonbaert. *Ensor to Permeke: Nine Flemish Painters, 1880–1950*. London: Royal Academy of Arts, 1971.

Van den Bussche, Willy, and Ludo Beheydt. *Ensor et les avant-gardes à la mer*. Tournai: Renaissance du livre, 2006. (English edition, 2006.)

Van den Bussche, Willy, et al. *D'Ensor à Delvaux: Ensor, Spilliaert, Permeke, Magritte, Delvaux*. Edited by Van den Bussche. Ostend: Provinciaal Museum voor Moderne Kunst, 1996. (English edition, 1996.)

Les XX, Bruxelles: Catalogue des dix expositions annuelles. Paris: Centre International pour l'Étude de XIXe Siècle, 1981.

Articles and Journals

Note: Significant early writing on James Ensor was published in the journals *L'Art moderne* (1881–1914) and *La Jeune Belgique* (1881–1897).

L'Art Belge (December 1965). Special issue devoted to James Ensor. With contributions by Marcel De Maeyer, Marcel Fryns, Paul Haesaerts, Félix Labisse, Jean-Pierre Paulus, Gérald Schurr, and Jean Stevo.

Les Arts plastiques, no. 1 (January–February 1950). Special issue devoted to Ensor. With contributions by Jean Cassou, Paul Fierens, Paul Haesaerts, René Huyghe, Louis Lebeer, and Jean Stevo.

Avermaete, Roger. "James Ensor: Der Graphiker." *Der Cicerone* 20, no. 2 (November 1928): 723–28.

Barr, Alfred. "Ensor's *St. Anthony* and Other Recent Acquisitions." *Bulletin of The Museum of Modern Art* 9, no. 2 (November 1941): 4–5.

Benjamin, Walter. "James Ensor wird 70 Jahre." In Rolf Tiedemann and Hermann Schweppenhäuser, eds. *Gesammelte Schriften* 4, part 1. Edited by Tillman Rexroth. Frankfurt: Suhrkamp Verlag, 1972: 565–67.

Bounameaux, Henry. "Ensor-Knopff: La Querelle d'une image." *Bulletin des Musées royaux des Beaux-Arts de Belgique* 41–42, nos. 1–4 (1992–1993): 127–47.

Cahiers de Belgique, no. 1 (January 1929). Special issue devoted to Ensor. With contributions by A.-H. Cornette, Paul Fierens, J-E. Sonderegger.

Canning, Susan M. "The Ordure of Anarchy: Scatological Signs of Self and Society in the Art of James Ensor." *Art Journal* 52, no. 3 (Autumn 1993): 47–53.

———. "La Foule et le boulevard: James Ensor and the street politic of everyday life." In Jane Block, ed., *Belgium: The Golden Decades, 1880–1914*. Belgian Francophone Library 3. Edited by Donald F. Friedman. New York: Peter Lang, 1997.

———. "In the Realm of the Social." *Art in America* 88, no. 2 (February 2000): 74–83, 141.

Dalmasso, Franca. "Disegni di Ensor d'après les maîtres." *Critica d'arte*, no. 131 (1959): 30–42.

De Maeyer, Lies. "Modernistiche aspecten van Ensors silhouettekeningen en aquarellen van 1880–82." *Museummagazine*, nos. 3–4 (1985): 48–61.

De Maeyer, Marcel. "De mystieke dood van een godgeleerde van James Ensor." *Jaarboek van het Koninklijk Museum voor Schone Kunsten Antwerpen* (1962–63): 131–58.

———. "De genese van masker-, travestie- en skeletmotieven in het oeuvre van James Ensor." *Bulletin des Musées royaux des Beaux-Arts de Belgique* 10 (1963): 69–88.

De Smedt, Raphaël. "Hellens et Ensor à travers *L'Art moderne* (1908–1914)." *Bulletin des Musées royaux des Beaux-Arts de Belgique* 42–44, nos. 1–4 (1994–95): 279–306.

De Smet. Frédéric. "Impressions d'atelier: James Ensor." *Gand Artistique* 4, no. 12 (December 1925): 249–68.

Eisenman, Stephen F. "Allegory and Anarchism in James Ensor's *Apparition: Vision Preceding Futurism*." *Record of The Museum of Princeton University*, no. 46 (1987): 2–17.

Fierens, Paul. "James Ensor." In Charles Bernard, et al., *Peintres belges contemporains*. Brussels: Éditions Lumière, 1946.

La Flandre littéraire 2, no. 6 (January 1924). Special issue devoted to Ensor. With contributions by Franz Ansel, Claude Bernières, Daan Boens, A. J. J. Deln, Georges Eekhoud, [Hippolyte] Fierens-Gevaert, Franz Hellens, Gaston Heux, Edmond Joly, Hubert Krains, Edmond Picard, Georges Ramaekers, and André

De Ridder, Henri Vandeputte, Georges Virrès, Marcel Wyseur.

Ford, Brinsley. "Obituary: Baron James Ensor." *Burlington Magazine for Connoisseurs* 82, no. 479 (February 1943): 50–51.

Haesaerts, Paul. "Quand James Ensor peignait *L'Entrée du Christ à Bruxelles.*" *L'Œil* 131 (November 1965): 28–32.

Haydn-Huntley, George. "Munch and Ensor." *Gazette des Beaux-Arts* 24 (December 1943): 363–74.

Hermans, Georges. "Un 'Cahier d'Ensor' d'Emma Lambotte." *Bulletin des Musées royaux des Beaux-Arts de Belgique* 20, nos. 1–4 (1971): 85–121.

Heusinger von Waldegg, Joachim. "James Ensor: *Selbstbildnis mit Staffelei* (1890). Ein Allegorie." *Wallraf-Richartz Jahrbuch* 50 (1989): 251–69.

Hodin, J. P. "Une Visite à James Ensor." *Les Arts plastiques*, nos. 7–8 (July–August 1949): 251–60.

Hubert, Renée Riese. "Verhaeren et James Ensor." *Cahiers de l'Association Internationale des Études Françaises*, no. 34 (May 1982): 179–92.

"James Ensor. Peintre et graveur." *La Plume*, no. 232 (December 15, 1898). Special issue devoted to Ensor. With contributions by Edgar Baes, Christian Beck, Louis Delattre, Jules Du Jardin, Max Elskamp, James Ensor, Arnold Goffin, Théo Hannon, Hubert Krains, Georges Lemmen, Camille Lemonnier, Maurice Maeterlinck, Camille Mauclair, Octave Maus, Constantin Meunier, Pol de Mont, Maurice des Ombiaux, Edmond Picard, Georges Rency, Blanche Rousseau, Octave Uzanne, Émile Verhaeren. Reprint, 1899.

Jonsson, Stefan. "Society Degree Zero: Christ, Communism, and the Madness of Crowds in the Art of James Ensor." *Representations* 75, no. 1 (Summer 2001): 1–32.

Kaplan, Julius. "The Religious Subjects of James Ensor, 1877–1900." *Revue belge d'archéologie et d'histoire de l'art* 35, nos. 3–4 (1966): 175–206.

Leonard, Mark, and Louise Lippincott. "James Ensor's *Christ's Entry into Brussels in 1889.* Technical Analysis, Restoration, and Reinterpretation." *Art Journal* 54, no. 2 (1995): 18–27.

Lesko, Diane. "Ensor in His Milieu." *Artforum* 15 (May 1977): 55–62.

———. "James Ensor and Symbolist Literature." *Art Journal* 45, no. 2 (1985): 99–104.

Mont, Pol de. "De schilder en etser James Ensor. Een bijdrage tot de geschiedenis der kunst van den laatsten tijd." *De Vlaamsche School* 8 (1895): 110–19.

Morel, Dominique. "James Ensor et *La Plume.* Histoire et fortune critique de la première exposition personnelle d'Ensor à Paris (1898–1899)." *Gazette des Beaux-Arts* 118, no. 1474 (November 1991): 205–12.

Morrisey, Leslie D. "James Ensor's Self-Portraits." *Arts Magazine* 54 (December 1979): 90–95.

Muls, Jozef. "James Ensor: Peintre de la mer." *Conférences de la Diffusion artistique des Musées royaux des Beaux-Arts*, March 9, 1941. In *Musées royaux des Beaux-Arts de Belgique: Conférences, 1940–1941.* Brussels: Publications du Patrimoine des Musées royaux des Beaux-Arts de Belgique, 1941: 3–14.

Myers, Marshall N. "James Ensor's *The Tribulations of Saint Anthony*: Permutations of the Excremental Vision." *Arts Magazine* 54 (December 1979): 84–89.

Ollinger-Zinque, Gisèle. "Les Auréoles du Christ, ou les sensibilités de la lumière de James Ensor." *Bulletin des Musées royaux des Beaux-Arts de Belgique* 17, nos. 3–4 (1968): 191–202.

Pallucchini, Rudolfo. "Ensor à la Biennale." *Les Arts Plastiques*, no. 3 (July–August 1951): 167–70.

Pica, Vittorio. "Trois artistes d'exception: Aubrey Beardsley, James Ensor, Edouard Münch." *Mercure de France* (August 15, 1905): 517–30.

Pradel, Marie-Noëlle. "Dessins de James Ensor." *La Revue du Louvre et des Musées de France* 14, no. 2 (1964): 97–102.

Ridder, André De. "James Ensor à Ostend." *Variétés* 2 (June 15, 1928): 59–67.

Schiff, Gert. "Ensor the Exorcist." In Mosche Barasch and Lucy F. Sandler, eds., *Art: The Ape of Nature. Studies in Honor of H. W. Janson.* New York: Harry N. Abrams, 1981: 719–37.

Schiff, Gert. "James Ensor: *Skeletons in the Studio*/James Ensor: *Squelettes à l'atelier.*" *Bulletin Annuel de la Galerie Nationale du Canada*, no. 4 (1982): 27–38.

Schoonbaert, Lydia M. A. "Addendum Beschrijvende Catalogus 1948. Een verzameling tekeningen van Ensor (deel I)." *Jaarboek van het Koninklijk Museum voor Schone Kunsten Antwerpen* (1968): 311–42.

———. "Addendum Beschrijvende Catalogus 1948. Een verzameling tekeningen van Ensor (deel II): De Hollandse Reis." *Jaarboek van het Koninklijk Museum voor Schone Kunsten Antwerpen* (1969): 265–84.

———. "Addendum Beschrijvende Catalogus 1948. Een verzameling tekeningen van Ensor (deel III): Schetsen naar leven model uit de periode 1879–1885." *Jaarboek van het Koninklijk Museum voor Schone Kunsten Antwerpen* (1970): 305–32.

———. "Addendum Beschrijvende Catalogus 1948. Een verzameling tekeningen van Ensor (deel IV): Schetsen naar natuur en getransformeerd door de verbeelding." *Jaarboek van het Koninklijk Museum voor Schone Kunsten Antwerpen* (1972): 285–311.

———. "Schilderend geraamte van James Ensor." *Jaarboek van het Koninklijk Museum voor Schone Kunsten Antwerpen* (1973): 321–37.

———. "*Gazette des Beaux-Arts* en *The Studio* als inspiratiebronnen voor James Ensor." *Jaarboek van het Koninklijk Museum voor Schone Kunsten Antwerpen* (1978): 205–21.

———. "James Ensor, Pioneer of Modern European Art." Translated by Alison Mouthaan-Gwillim. In *The Low Countries: Arts and Society in Flanders and the Netherlands. A Yearbook.* Edited by Jozef Deleu. Rekkem, Belgium: Stichting Ons Erfdeel, 1994–95: 156–67.

Tannenbaum, Libby. "James Ensor: Prophet of Modern Fantastic Art." *Magazine of Art* (November 1943): 244–49.

Tricot, Xavier. "Métaphores et metamorphoses de James Ensor." *Artstudio*, no. 18 (1990): 46–59.

———. "James Ensor, Prince des masques." In Alice Ertaud, ed., *Masques: De Carpeaux à Picasso.* Paris: Musée d'Orsay and Éditions Hazan, 2008: 162–67.

Van Puyvelde, Leo. "A Tribute to the Painter James Ensor." *Message: Belgian Review*, no. 15 (January 1943): 45–47.

LENDERS TO THE EXHIBITION

Albright-Knox Art Gallery, Buffalo
The Art Institute of Chicago
Bibliothèque royale de Belgique, Brussels
Columbus Museum of Art, Ohio
Dexia Collection, Brussels
Collection Thomas and Lore Firman
The Flemish Community
Fondation Challenges, The Netherlands
Fondation Socindec
Gallery Ronny Van de Velde, Antwerp
The J. Paul Getty Museum, Los Angeles
Groeningemuseum, Bruges
Kimbell Art Museum, Fort Worth
Koning Boudewijnstichting, Brussels
Koninklijk Museum voor Schone Kunsten, Antwerp
Kunstmuseum aan zee, Ostend
Menard Art Museum, Komaki City
The Metropolitan Museum of Art, New York
Musée d'Art moderne et d'Art contemporain de la Ville de Liège
Musée d'Orsay, Paris
Musées royaux des Beaux-Arts de Belgique, Brussels
museum kunst palast, Düsseldorf
The Museum of Modern Art, New York
Museum voor Schone Kunsten, Ghent
National Gallery of Canada, Ottawa
Philadelphia Museum of Art
Staatsgalerie Stuttgart
Université libre de Bruxelles
University of California, Berkeley Art Museum and Pacific Film Archive
Wallraf-Richartz-Museum & Fondation Corboud, Cologne

Anonymous lenders

PHOTOGRAPH CREDITS

The publishers have made every effort to trace the copyright holders and photographers. In those instances where rights holders could not be located, the Museum requests that any information concerning such rights holders be forwarded, so that they may be contacted for future editions.

We thank those who wish to remain anonymous and the following:

Albright-Knox Art Gallery, Buffalo: 133; Jennifer Anderson © The Art Institute of Chicago: 143 top; © Maurice Antony. Courtesy Collection Ronny Van de Velde, Antwerp: 83, 200; Photography © The Art Institute of Chicago: 19, 21 right, 54, 136 top, 190; Les Arts décoratifs, Paris/Jean Tholance: 94 right; Courtesy BAI: 15; Bibliothèque royale de Belgique, Brussels. Cabinet des estampes: 37, 145; Benjamin Blackwell © Regents of the University of California: 188; © Bridgeman Art Library: 124; © Bridgeman-Giraudon/Art Resource, NY: 115 middle; Courtesy Christie's Inc.: 186; Columbus Museum of Art, Ohio: 156; Niels Donckers: 60; Erwin Donvil: 86 bottom; Vincent Everarts, Brussels: cover, 51–53, 74 top, 82, 95 right, 132, 142 bottom, 143 bottom, 153 bottom, 162, 166, 171, 173, 175, 180; © The J. Paul Getty Museum, Los Angeles: 29 top, 36, 71 bottom; Courtesy Fondation Pierre Gianadda, Martigny: 176; Grafisch Bureau Lefevre, Brussels: 61–63, 65, 98 top, 152 top; Thomas Griesel, Department of Imaging Services, The Museum of Modern Art, New York: 134, 146; © IRPA-KIK, Brussels: 38 top, 39 left; Courtesy Koninklijk Museum voor Schone Kunsten, Antwerp: 25, 31, 115 left; © Kunstmuseum aan zee, Ostend: 57, 84, 150–51, 159, 185; © Kunstmuseum aan zee, Ostend, Collection Town of Ostend: 38 bottom; © Kunstmuseum aan zee, Ostend/Lauros/Giraudon/Bridgeman Art Library: 3, 64; © Kunstmuseum aan zee Archives, Ostend: 24 bottom, 196–98; © Kunstmuseum aan zee Archives, Ostend. Fonds Xavier Tricot: 24 top, 39 right; Robert Laprelle © Kimbell Art Museum: 11, 12, 147; © Erich Lessing/Art Resource, NY. 68, 115 right, 174; Robert Lorenzson © Private collection: 78; Courtesy Lukas – Art in Flanders: 45, 55, 59, 67, 69, 71 top, 72, 76, 81, 135, 138–39 top, 140, 144, 149, 152 bottom, 157, 160, 167–69, 181; Hugo Maertens, Bruges: 47, 73, 79, 103 top; Peter Maes, Ghent: 20; Menard Art Museum, Komaki City: 183; © The Metropolitan Museum of Art/Art Resource, NY: 187; The Pierpont Morgan Library, New York: 105 bottom; Musée d'Art moderne et d'Art contemporain de la Ville de Liège: 58, 70; Musées royaux des Beaux-Arts de Belgique, Brussels. Archives de l'art contemporain, Fonds Octave Maus, Gift of Albert Vander Lindin: 17 bottom; Museum Folkwang, Essen: 107; museum kunst palast, Düsseldorf: 77, 87; © National Gallery of Canada: 184; © Philadelphia Museum of Art/Art Resource, NY: 189; © Private collection/The Bridgeman Art Library: 177; Rheinisches Bildarchiv, Cologne: 66; © Réunion des Musées Nationaux/Erich Lessing/Art Resource, NY: 56, 153 top; © Scala/Art Resource, NY: 21 left, 23, 94 left; © Luc Schrobiltgen, Brussels: 1, 165; Speltdoorn et Fils, Brussels: 17 top, 48–49, 75 top, 103 bottom, 154, 163; © Staatsgalerie Stuttgart: 93, 142 top; © Tate, London/Art Resource, NY: 98 bottom, 110 bottom; Jordan Tinker © Private collection: 170; Courtesy Collection Ronny Van de Velde, Antwerp: 136 bottom; Piet Ysabié/Museum voor Schone Kunsten, Ghent. Courtesy Lukas – Art in Flanders: 29 bottom, 105 top

TRUSTEES OF THE MUSEUM OF MODERN ART

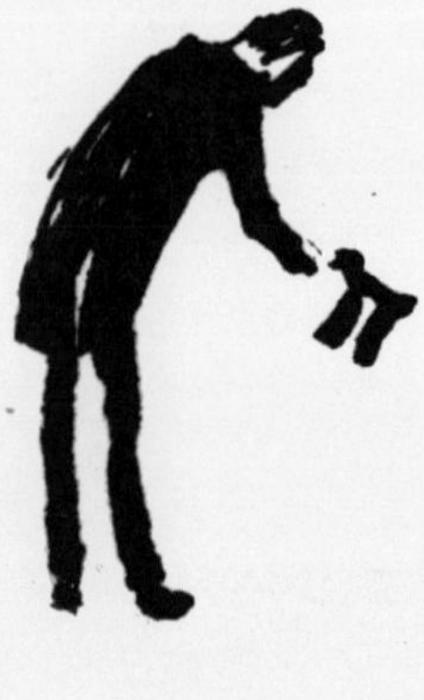